Belonging in America

NEW DIRECTIONS IN ANTHROPOLOGICAL WRITING

History, Poetics, Cultural Criticism

George E. Marcus, Rice University

James Clifford, University of California, Santa Cruz

Editors

Nationalism and the Politics of Culture in Quebec
Richard Handler

Belonging in America: Reading Between the Lines
Constance Perin

Belonging in America

READING BETWEEN THE LINES

Constance Perin

THE UNIVERSITY OF WISCONSIN PRESS

Published 1988

The University of Wisconsin Press
114 North Murray Street
Madison, Wisconsin 53715

The University of Wisconsin Press, Ltd.
1 Gower Street
London WC1E 6HA, England

First printing

Printed in the United States of America

For LC CIP information see the colophon

ISBN 0-299-11580-1 cloth

Human society is composed of symbolic processes, in the sense that what we are to ourselves, what others are to us, what we are to them and they to themselves, consist outwardly of words and acts which inwardly are beliefs to which we attach values. In other words, the social relations and entire social organization of any human society consist of evaluated beliefs and their expression in human conduct.

W. Lloyd Warner
American Life: Dream and Reality (1953)

Contents

Belonging in America

Introduction

MORE THAN MEETS THE EYE

Too early one morning several years ago barking cut through my sleep. From my fifth-story bedroom window I could see in the garden of the house next door the same pair of cocker spaniels who had been serving as my second alarm clock—but at about half-past seven, not just after six. Their usual routine didn't even include barking. About five minutes after being let out the back door, they'd announce they were ready to come back in, speaking with throaty, polite yelps. I'd lived comfortably on this schedule for about a year, and now, after these six o'clock alarms on a second, then a third, morning (I kept waiting for someone else to complain), I was bewildered and thoroughly put out. On the fourth day, I decided I had to do something.

Never having met these neighbors, I didn't know their names and couldn't telephone. Sitting down at my desk to write them a note, the right words wouldn't come; I tore up draft after draft. How in the world to tell perfect strangers, yet neighbors, that they were annoying me? I agonized over whether I was being too forward, or a patsy for their lack of consideration. I worried over putting them on the defensive and making them mad. Still another day passed, and again the dogs woke me too early and barked too long. I finally put down just four ideas: that I was a dog-lover, that I admired the way they had trained theirs, that I hadn't been bothered before this, and that surely it was some temporary aberration. I wrote on some stationery with my name on it, and yet, still shy about the whole thing, I dropped the note into their mail slot without ringing the bell.

The next morning I answered my phone to hear, "This is Susan Morris, your next-door neighbor. I'm terribly sorry you've had to live with that ruckus—my husband and I just got back from a trip. My daughter and son-in-law were staying here to take care of the dogs—but letting them out much earlier than we do, and then going back to sleep! I hadn't told them what our routine was." I was hugely relieved at such a civilized response, and said so. I was about to say, "Thanks very much for calling," when Mrs. Morris said: "That's not all. I want very much to meet you—I want to meet anybody who could send me such a note and sign their name. I feel that I'm ready to like you!" I was amazed: "You mean to say that you've had anonymous complaints about your dogs?" "Oh, yes. They're the usual kind." As much difficulty as I'd had fetching up the social skills to deal diplomatically with so simple (and common) a situation, it never occurred to me not to sign my name, even though I avoided a face-to-face conversation.

Brooding about the meanings of her experience and my own, as anthropologists will, I began to feel that there might be more to them than met the eye. The whole idea of *neighbor* became a first preoccupation. If we choose to acknowledge neighbors, we can't be sure anything good will come of it, and if we ignore them nothing bad will necessarily happen— nothing like the scoldings of friends and relatives. Of all the relationships we have, those with neighbors probably have the least clear lines around them. Those ambiguities became the starting place of this study of American culture: American ways of defining the many lines of life and what may lie between them. I'm speaking of such lines as those we draw between business and pleasure, home and work, relatives and friends, between the things we do for love and those we do for money, between what is private and public, between good and evil . . . and, as well, those between family and community, between the genders, between the species, between adults and children, between the races, between body and spirit, even between city and suburb.

Whether definite or dotted, faint or unmistakable, however drawn or however welcome, every line is in the service of giving shape to the many ambiguities of our common life. Chafe as we may at some and try as we will to redraw them, the ideas they represent tend to be stable. The chief reason for their existence and persistence is that we wouldn't know how to act without our ideas about individualism and independence, honor and dishonor, reputation and respectability, choice and duty, cooperation and competition, spontaneity and control, trust and suspicion, shame and pride . . . .

So do we play upon ambiguities, yet ambiguities also play upon us. In personal life, we're apt to talk them out; in work life, we map them out; but in social life, we're more likely to act them out, mutely coping with uncertainties and confusions, contradictions and ironies that inevitably escape our nets of meaning. Not always allusions whose layers of connotation can lead to the pleasures of discovery, ambiguities can bring on painful, disappointing encounters with social paradoxes and unreliable understandings. For when lines do not hold and people are confused about what their experiences mean, their most socially divisive, destructive, and estranging impulses can be revealed.

Listening for meanings with which we interpret and act in our daily worlds of neighbors, friends, and relatives, of men, women, children, and dogs, each of these five essays is a variation upon that single theme: what

Americans make of their encounters with ambiguities, and what those encounters then make of Americans' hopes for a clearer sense of community and a higher quality of justice. In charting both the ambiguities and the meanings, we may better understand, so to change, the reasons why belonging in America is more problematic for some than for others.

I began by listening to suburbanites all around the country talk about their neighboring experiences. Wanting to hear "American ideas," I listened to men and women living in what is generally regarded as the "mainstream," those who have at least reached the suburban, single-family-detached episode of the American Dream. The "American middle class": not knowing what it is any more precisely than anyone else does, I've relied on this indigenous ideal of suburban residence and homeownership, which immediately implies another defining characteristic, namely, white race. The populations of most suburbs are white; suburban zoning and real estate practices are likely either to discriminate against nonwhites or to "steer" each race into separate enclaves; the cultural sources of those residential patterns are the subjects of my last book (Perin 1977). I took this widespread pattern of segregation and of prejudice to be one among many important facts about the mainstream which dominates the drawing of so many American lines.

I sought out suburbs not obviously rich or poor, where the greatest range of people by occupation, education, and income might be likeliest. I taped interviews with white Americans who own single-family-detached houses in the commuting suburbs of Minneapolis, San Francisco, Houston, and Washington, D.C. Of course they spoke of previous experiences elsewhere—I heard about Philadelphia in Minneapolis, Chicago in San Francisco, Palo Alto in Houston. Every interview was graciously given; neither the persons nor the specific suburb are identified. We discussed the ways they think about neighbors and what they do when things somehow go wrong between them. When neighbors are noisy or their children get into mischief, when dogs on the block knock over garbage cans or mess up the garden, I asked them, what do you do? I also listened to building inspectors and dog officers, policemen and police chiefs, professional managers of apartments and condominiums, ministers and social workers, members of the League of Women Voters and of New Neighbors. I've watched the daily press ("Neighbors Help Out in Blizzard"), monitored television, listened to tales told by my friends and to those of perfect strangers. When answering anybody's questions about what I've been writing over the last several years, I've heard story after story after story.

These discussions with about 100 handpicked people obviously were never intended to be a representative sample: they were meant as yeast for raising still more questions in my mind about the ways in which Americans interpret many aspects of their lives. I've also drawn on newspaper reports of single events, popularized social science, testimony at congressional hearings, not for reliable facts or principles, but as texts of this culture to be puzzled over for what they say yet leave unsaid. The estimable research of scholars in many fields has also been essential to the understandings I've arrived at. To help me see between the lines by which I also live, before setting out for the field I tried to defamiliarize myself by visiting countries having high residential densities, where relations with neighbors were likely to be salient. I spent several weeks in Holland, the United Kingdom, and Japan, hearing about their concepts and practices from the most expert informants I could find, namely, colleagues in anthropology, sociology, law—English-speakers all. I wasn't trying to develop an ethnography of their neighbor relationships, but only to listen for issues that I might not have thought to consider, as well as for sheer differences in their lines and concepts. In turn, their experiences in, observations of, and questions about American concepts and practices were equally valuable in disorienting me. These travels were whetstones for sharpening my observations at home, and I make no cross-cultural comparisons on the basis of them; they were methodological, not substantive, forays.

In this limited ethnography of ambiguities and meanings I have two aims: to have illuminated general human processes involved in constituting cultures and to point to some American cultural particularities. Concerned mainly with identifying ambiguities and meanings, I haven't also suggested how they might vary by class, ethnicity, race, religion, and region. Ignoring these differences says only that this work is but a beginning of another way of studying cultures. The very notion of culture has conjured coherence, clarity, and configuration: culture seen as a tapestry of legible, predictable patterns—a design for living. But we know now that those seamless connotations do only partial justice to cultures. From their incoherencies, confusions, contradictions, enigmas, paradoxes, and conflicts, and the meanings behind them, social orders both endure and change.

Some meanings are more audible than others: some we speak of in whispers, some hardly at all. What we take entirely for granted we are likely to speak least about: a culture's silences are the most familiar to its members, in this and every culture. Only by putting words to those meanings that go without saying do they stand a chance of being explicitly considered and reconsidered. What is left unsaid remains undiscussible and nonnegotiable; thus does culture coerce. Putting words to them allows us to hear their meanings more clearly, to recognize the ambiguities they cannot contain and sometimes create, and to observe what we do with our discomfort.

These five essays move from speaking of the more to the less acknowledged, from more readily negotiable experiences to those that are less so, and from matters specifically American to those more generally human. The earlier essays discuss more familiar experiences and insights; those pleasures of recognition may cushion later discomforts at hearing about matters Americans might prefer remain undiscussed. The first two essays consider themes Americans tend to speak of only *sotto voce*, as it were: the frictional undersides of everyday relationships with neighbors that may make for less of a sense of community than some might like. "The Invisible Neighborhood" lays out some of the conflicting paths by which we pick our way through the incongruities of individualism and interdependence, community and family, and between the single-family ideal and the realities of housing prices, divorce, a mobile population, and suburban isolation. The second essay, "Properties of Community," speaks of ways that homeownership, the real estate market, and a sense of community can intersect one another and juxtapose personal and economic relationships with national and local understandings of reputation and respectability. From their encounters with these ambiguities, men, women, and children come to see differing meanings in community.

The third essay sits on a middle ground between meanings we do and do not acknowledge. "Perfect Dogs" takes up the peculiar and astonishing powers of American dogs to blur species lines to become our "best friends" and "members of the family." Dogs can also erase property lines, and members of the family on the loose can become the bane of neighborhood gardeners and joggers. Unleashed dogs are also vulnerable to injury, straying, and death. In trying to understand the apparent ambivalence of many dog-lovers whose pets roam, I found another way of speaking of the trust that makes society possible.

The last two essays approach matters about which this and many other cultures are more likely to be mute. Whatever a society regards as taboo is likely to be disquieting and, in that, all the more absolute and nonnegotiable; I expect that to be true of these essays. "Imperfect People" examines social prejudices of various kinds as arising partly from how we understand *difference* per se and partly from ideas about what it means to be a human, yet animal, being. Why are many unmistakably human beings treated culturally as though they belong to another species and put into the least favorable places, socially, economically, politically?

The final essay, "The Constitution of Men and Women," suggests why women continue to be susceptible to being the second sex. It speaks of Western civilization's most deeply held beliefs about a universal way that this species draws the line between itself and every other: cleanliness training. That training relies on moral concepts of shame, disgust, and control, and it affects every person's capacity for self-esteem and expectations of social respect. In trying to be members of this species in good standing, human strategies take on the appearance of male superiority and female subordination, and jeopardize fundamental justice for both sexes.

In the conclusion, "Silence as *The Other*," I draw out several implications of having considered a closer relationship between human biology and culture and of having articulated some of Americans' least ventilated presuppositions and perceptions. In all, I am speaking of disappointments with an often thin sense of community and a diluted quality of justice. The better to realize our practical hopes and our constitutional ideals, we can at least try to decipher both the ambiguities and the meanings standing in the way. Americans have silently drawn these many lines; we can discuss how to redraw them.

DIGGING FOR MEANINGS

Three tools of my anthropological trade have been indispensable in searching out these silences: doubt, attention to symbols, and the inseparability of human biology from behavior. Doubt is the crowbar with which cultural anthropology unboxes received and unexamined notions—here, both popular and professional definitions of community and the people who populate it. To see community not only as a local system of family, political party, and social club, but to acknowledge it as also being constituted by ideas about such intangible properties as trust, honor, and reputation; and to recast our ways of thinking about men, women, and children to consider instead the ideas and beliefs through which their social places and rewards come to differ—these are the aims of this doubt.

Second, questing for American meanings includes the obligation to follow their symbols and signs wherever they point. Men, women, children, and dogs are literally themselves, to be sure, but each also represents beliefs about the stages of life, for example, or about domestic versus political roles. To relate symbols to their referents, I speak to a wide range of topics—but even so, that may not suffice to clarify what are irreducibly complex human experiences and behaviors. Any single sign is likely to be the consequence of intricate chains of presupposition, belief, history, and myth. For all that they address, these essays trace out only a few of these links.

The third tool of my trade is license to acknowledge the social significance of human biology alongside every other influence on behavior. I kept wondering about my lack of spontaneity in that experience with my neighbors' barking dogs. Why couldn't I have rung their bell on the very first morning or dashed off a note without giving it a single second thought? I realized that I felt caught up in a situation with no clear lines around it: I had no certain map of meanings for dealing with them. For me, the situation was socially ambiguous, and as I studied what natural scientists have learned about human responses to ambiguity, I discovered that they appear to be entwined with anxiety and fear, feelings that can result in paralysis, avoidance, and attack. Those findings certainly matched my behaviors up to a point: I delayed, couldn't write, and I didn't ring my neighbors' bell.

"Intolerance for ambiguity" is not merely a personal trait; it has the social sources and aggrandizing consequences that these essays try to document. When shared systems of meanings become unreliable, how to act becomes uncertain. With those meanings, we define our social expectations. Whatever is believed to dismantle meaning and thereby disable action evokes both curiosity and fear; whatever calls certainty into question comes under the headings of novelty, incongruity, confusion, sheer difference, and discrepancy. On the one hand, humans socialize curiosity and arousal as learning and development and, on the other, these essays suggest, humans socialize fear responses of freezing, flight, and fighting as social discrimination, stigmatization, and withdrawal. As I discuss in more detail shortly, fear and anxiety are neurophysiologically autonomic responses which I propose to be as biologically significant in ordering human affairs as are sex and subsistence. How fear and anxiety are socially transformed depends no less than sex and subsistence do on particular belief systems and particular ecological and historical contexts.

As provisional as the understandings of the neurosciences and behavioral biology are today, they suggest significant subtleties that are generally overlooked in accounts of social alienation and social hostilities. Throughout these essays, I call on these subtleties to shed light on puzzling aspects of common social practices and patterns. As background for my interpretations, I provide in the following section a sketch of natural scientists' understandings of human experiences of ambiguity, anxiety, and fear and how I see these understandings as being helpful to cultural analysis. None of these theories is radically new, but it is fair to say, I think, that they have not been widely incorporated into a literature that tends to rely on models of intellectual rather than affective processes.

Why so explicit a move toward modern biology from a cultural anthropologist? The answer is not a detour but a short story that weaves together some earlier and more recent strands of my thinking about the constitution of social order. In *Everything in Its Place: Social Order and Land Use in America*, published at the end of 1977, I introduced the possibility that the study of culture in its own right could add to our understandings of patterns of metropolitan development. The ethnography documented the prevalence of prejudice toward those who are seen to be interstitial or oblique to valued social statuses as defined by American ideology and norms. I found that Americans see renters, blacks, children, the elderly, people with low incomes, together with the signs of them in housing and geographical location, as being culturally unsettling. I suggested that, like the peoples of many ancient and exotic societies, Americans attribute dangerous social powers to whatever and whomever are seen as being marginal to or in transition between clearly defined social statuses.

How cultural anthropologists approach the concepts of marginality and transition has not only been a central preoccupation within the discipline, but their understandings have been influential outside it, in psychology, political science, sociology, for example (M. S. Davis [1983] 1985; Jones et al. 1984; Merelman 1984). Discourse about marginality and transition forms an important domain in both classical and modern cultural anthropology (more so perhaps than in any other discipline); attention must be paid to rites of passage, trickster folktales, clown performances, myths, and the cyclical positions offered by a sociological system. Tales and myths about fabulous and confounding gods and tricksters reveal mysterious powers attributed to those socially "in between." Partly human, partly animal, these mythical creatures are "enemies of boundaries." People who are actually in social limbo evoke awe and fear of what others believe to be their polluting and contaminating powers, especially evident in transitional phases when people are crossing "thresholds" and thereby are neither here nor there (van Gennep [1908] 1960). During the middle phase, initiates have been stripped of their former status, and in this "liminal" (Latin *limen*, or threshold) state, they have not yet moved across the next line to become incorporated into a new social category. Fearsome powers are also widely attributed to people with unclear or marginal social status, especially strangers, foreigners, and those crossing the line between life and death.

The motif of borders and boundaries in myths and cosmologies echoes that of ritual thresholds. The ancient Egyptians' god Seth is a messenger and omen of evil and death and "venerated in borderlands everywhere" (te Velde 1967: 118). Seth is the "god of confusion" who reverses all ordinary expectations, disturbs the peace, deserts his friends, and crosses lines of every kind. Hermes too: thief, trickster, and culture hero of the Greeks, he is also the "god of roads" and an ambassador who protects people from strangers. Hermes operates strictly between the lines, playing stealthily and roguishly with customs and law; in many cultures ritual clowns and tricksters personify anarchy obscenely, scatologically, humorously, and, sometimes, terrifyingly (Babcock 1975; Radin [1956] 1972).

In the American cases of transition and limbo, I said: "My point is not that actually being outside of or marginal to particular categories matters, for that will always be. Nor will the 'achieving society' give up its abundance of rationalized steps and hurdles; some people will not 'qualify' as members of valued categories. What does matter is the sub rosa institutionalization of contamination beliefs and opprobrious trickster stereotypes. . . . Whether the hurdles and criteria of qualification are defined fairly is not the issue here. Rather, the fact that there is this social bent to clarify ambiguous statuses by social beliefs about their polluting powers needs to be recognized. . . . Renters and women, blacks and browns, the divorced and the single, children and the elderly and all that stands for them, in cities, buildings, and spaces, convey their constituted meaning of being neither here nor there, neither one thing nor another. We invent confusion even as we do order. Interstices are as much created and charged with significance as they are simply there. Nothing prevents us from putting a higher value on them" (Perin 1977: 124, 127).

Although my analysis was put in terms of indigenous ideologies which posit such people as being anomalous vis-à-vis American ideals of success, homeownership, and a scripted life course, as I worked with the materials for this book and began to consider the nature of responses to ambiguity per se, I saw that my earlier "explanation" of the "dangers and powers" attributed to them remained just as descriptive as that of the prevailing liminal discourse. *Why* does marginality have those emotional consequences? And it remained just as addicted to the social science version of the pathetic fallacy; that is, I too was attributing human powers to abstract, intellectual constructions.

> [T]here are other dangers to be reckoned with, which persons may set off knowingly or unknowingly, which are not part of the psyche and which are not to be bought or learned by initiation and training. These are pollution powers which inhere in the structure of ideas itself and which punish a symbolic breaking of that which should be joined or joining of that which should be separate. It follows from this that pollution is a type of danger which is not likely to occur except where the lines of structure, cosmic or social, are clearly defined. . . . This is as near as I can get to defining a particular class of dangers which are not powers vested in humans, but which can be released by human action. The power which presents a danger for careless humans is very evidently a power inhering in the structure of ideas, a power by which the structure is expected to protect itself. (Douglas [1966] 1970: 136)

My collusion in functionalist explanations also kept gnawing: "Once having created both negative and positive meanings, what does society do with them? The low cultural rating bequeathed to renters, minors, women, blacks, and central cities sharpens the definitive achievements of their opposites and makes more crisp the attainments of the categories owner, adult, male, white, and suburb, sweetening the struggle to achieve in so categorizing a world" (Perin 1977: 125). That ironic tone only masked my feelings that stigmatizations are unredeemable social and personal tragedies for many Americans. Denying large groups of people their right to self- and social respect is arrogating the power to deny others their right to belong. The scientific study of the cultures of industrial societies does only half its work by documenting such facts; it should be discovering why they exist as well (N. J. Davis 1978: 363–364; Rawls 1971).

For all the kinds of evidence that pioneers of liminality discourse have made more central and for all their detailed attention to the myriad practices associated with transition and its ambiguities, their explanations of these phenomena tend to be more cognitivist, structural, and rationalist than affective, despite the fact that anxiety about and fear of various kinds of "dangers" are the chief subjects of the discourse:

> We can only approach primitive mentality through introspection and understanding of our own mentality. . . . To solve the puzzle of sacred contagion we can start with more familiar ideas about secular contagion and defilement. In English-speaking cultures, the key word is the ancient, primitive, and still current "dirt." Lord Chesterfield defined dirt as matter out of place. This implies only two conditions, a set of ordered relations and a contravention of that order. Thus the idea of dirt implies a structure of ideas. For us dirt is a kind of compendium category for all events which blur, smudge, contradict, or otherwise confuse accepted classifications. The underlying feeling is that a system of values which is habitually expressed in a given arrangement of things has been violated. . . . Cultural intolerance of ambiguity [in preliterate societies] is expressed by avoidance, by discrimination, and by pressure to conform. (Douglas 1968: 338, 339)

The liminal attributions people make and their beliefs about and behavior toward "defilement" are obviously emotional. The discourse instead makes them into intellectual constructions acting as "mediators," perhaps "to 'recover' energy and affect within the context of a structuralist perspective" (Rosaldo 1984: 151). Models of human affect are not even incorporated into some of the discourse's insights about emotional content; models of perception, knowledge acquisition, logic, and cognitive dissonance are relied on instead (Douglas 1968: 338). For example, ". . . it is not always an unpleasant experience to confront ambiguity. Obviously it is more tolerable in some areas than in others. There is a whole gradient on which laughter, revulsion and shock belong at different points and intensities. The experience can be stimulating. The richness of poetry depends on the use of ambiguity, as Empson has shown" (Douglas [1966] 1970: 50; see also Douglas 1968: 339). Or affects are condensed in "social roles" that are "structurally inferior or 'marginal'" because of "the symbols that cluster around them and the beliefs that attach to them, such as 'the powers of the weak,' or, in other words, the permanently or transiently sacred attributes of low status or position" (V. Turner 1969: 110).

Liminal discourse historically has depended on a static, wholistic, and hierarchical image of social structure and of social classifications—for example, "from the . . . viewpoint of those concerned with the maintenance of 'structure,' all sustained manifestations of [liminality] must appear as dangerous and anarchical, and have to be hedged around with prescriptions, prohibitions, and conditions" (ibid.: 109). The assertion that "intolerance" and the feeling of "danger" "must appear" does not constitute explanation. Or affects are handled tautologically—"by definition," based on inexplicit reference to set-theoretical principles of inclusion and exclusion: an "innate sacred-taboo quality of all boundaries which derives from their ambiguity" (E. Leach 1976: 71). "The more sharply we define our boundaries, the more conscious we become of the dirt that has ambiguously got onto the wrong side of the frontier. Boundaries become dirty by definition and we devote a great deal of effort to keeping them clean, just so that we can preserve confidence in our category system" (ibid.: 61). "Whenever we make category distinctions within a unified field, either spatial or temporal, it is the boundaries that matter; we concentrate our attention on the differences not the similarities, and this makes us feel that the markers of such boundaries are of special value, 'sacred,' 'taboo' " (ibid.: 35). Once having named categories, we only perceive them as being separate; naming them suppresses "our recognition of the non-things which fill the interstices [and] then of course what is suppressed becomes especially interesting" and as well a "focus . . . of anxiety. Whatever is taboo is sacred, valuable, important, powerful, dangerous, untouchable, filthy, unmentionable" (E. Leach [1964] 1972: 49).

Liminal discourse has been using "overload" notions of communication theory in parallel with nominalism and theories of repression: ambiguity is socially reduced by relabelling to conform with existing categories; it is physically controlled by killing "deformities"; it is avoided altogether; it can be "labelled dangerous"; or it can be made use of in its own right, as in poetry (Douglas [1966] 1970: 52–53). The ultimate explanation is functional, cognitivist, and structural; for example:

> a rule of avoiding anomalous things affirms and strengthens the definitions to which they do not conform. . . . Attributing danger is one way of putting a subject above dispute. It also helps to enforce conformity. . . . In general [reflecting on our main classifications and on experiences which do not exactly fit them] confirms our confidence in the main classifications. (Ibid.: 51–53; see also V. Turner 1968: 581)

A seasoned literature on the political, economic, and institutional sources of war, nationalism, racism, genocide, ethnocentrism, prejudice, and xenophobia also privileges a cognitive approach that relies on logic, gestalt principles of perceptual organization, and communications theory; this discourse does not account for the affective etiology of prejudice and stereotyping (e.g., Allport 1958; Klineberg 1968). One authoritative theory of prejudice declares, for example, that its "distortions" and "misattributions" result from logically constructed classes and names for them, such that prejudice results from "errors and biases of thought and perception" (Pettigrew 1982: 5–13). Such analyses are, moreover, likely to declare that the "intrinsic" or objective characteristics of each group's beliefs and customs, genes and history, resources, solidarity, and powers are the relevant factors; less common are analyses based on a more general symbolic process through which the significance of any one group in the meaning systems of any other may affect the kind and degree of social response and interaction (LeVine and Campbell 1972; Herzfeld 1980b; Tajfel 1981).

I found others also asking about the adequacy of liminal discourse to account for the topics of its domain. Psychological experiments have found that the precision attributed to logical processes is much overstated: categories are more likely to be continuous than separate and clear cut (Rosch 1977, 1978). Reexamining native taxonomies previously said to account for the designation of "anomalous" creatures, one anthropologist suggests that "rather than falling between taxa they may be separate ones in their own right; rather than being negatively 'anomalous' they may be positively *singular*. . . . We must be careful not to invent anomalies where they do not exist. . . . Whereas the inbuilt, rigorous logic of ethnographic method easily gives rise to anomalies, the informal logics of folk systems permit its avoidance" (Ellen 1979: 14). Another anthropologist takes explicit issue with the discourse's account of the relationship between ambiguity and pollution in an ethnography that revealed how pollution beliefs follow from the ways that ideals figure in everyday life, "rather than from classificatory ambiguity" (Galaty 1979: 813). A linguist and philosopher suggest convincingly that people tend to understand one kind of experience in the terms of another, that metaphors more so than "bounded" categories (themselves doubtful, on the linguistic evidence of "fuzzy sets" and "hedges") are a basis for behavior: any one metaphor is a "reverberation down through the network of entailments that awakens and connects our memories of our past . . . experiences and serves as a possible guide for future ones" (Lakoff and Johnson 1980: 140).

In reanalyzing about 175 trickster tales he had collected from the Kaguru (East Africa), T. O. Beidelman proposes that they depict figures that "are not truly marginal," and in explaining why, he sets liminal discourse in a new direction: "Such figures are not odd in that they cannot be fitted into Kaguru categories, but are odd in that they represent recognized characteristics, feelings, motives and roles that cannot all be met by the same person or in one situation. In this, then, they are far from being liminal, for they exemplify key dilemmas involved in combining Kaguru belief with successful social action, something at the heart of social life. . . . Anomalies serve didactically to stimulate Kaguru moral imagination so as to understand existential dilemmas which involve choice in conduct and ends, rather than categorical puzzles [as assumed in liminal discourse]. . . . [T]o consider dilemmas is to consider affectual, moral commitment. Nothing less would drive Kaguru to embrace the embodiments of their confusions and conflicts in stories, in ritual, and in the etiquette of their every day life. . . . In so doing, Kaguru speculate about the nature of their morality and experience, and strike a connection between their vision of the ideal and their experience of the 'real.' . . . Morality, with its constraints and affectual implications, is more basic to what symbols are and do than is epistemology" (Beidelman 1980: 32–34). Conduct, affect, and choice entered liminal discourse.

Although danger, dilemma, and malevolence are its chief subjects, the emotions of fear and anxiety are ethnographic facts that the discourse's structural, sociological, and cognitive vocabularies had been bracketing away. The discourse's analytic terms remain the indigeneous terms— "dirt," "pollution," "filth," "sacred," "taboo," "unmentionable," "untouchable," "danger," "power"—thereby naturalizing rather than questioning the reasons for their emotional force. "Uncleanness or dirt is that which must not be included if a [cognitive] pattern is to be maintained. To recognize this is the first step towards insight into pollution" (Douglas [1966] 1970: 53). In other words, liminal discourse had been folding the problem into the solution: why are such negative and extreme conceptions implicated in states and events of social transition and cognitive ambiguity? Why these feelings and not others?

I set about reading the specialist literature on fear and anxiety. By 1982 I'd steeped myself in works produced by animal ethologists, developmental and cognitive psychologists, and neurophysiologists, beginning with Donald O. Hebb's classic, "On the Nature of Fear" (1946), and ending with Jeffrey A. Gray's two synthetic works (1971, 1982), in which, based on experimental evidence, he suggests neuropsychological models of human fear and anxiety. Then and more recently, I've found some but scant support within cultural studies for introducing more explicitly biological concerns: "There exists an obvious need for thick and sharp ethnographies focused on various aspects of social behavior . . . in particular, those behaviors dealing with social styles and those which reflect general visceral activities and functions," so suggests an *Annual Review of Anthropology* article, "Culture, Behavior, and the Nervous System" (Fabrega 1977: 429). Clifford Geertz allows in his 1983 Distinguished Lecture to the American Anthropological Association, "Anti Anti-Relativism," that although little good is likely to come of "sociobiology," "neuroscience" seems to be "on the verge of extraordinary achievements" (Geertz 1984: 268).

Looking neither to determine nor to reduce but to synthesize some well-accepted understandings of neuropsychology and the constitution of cultures, I aired my concerns at the 1982 meetings of the Northeastern Anthropological Association and the American Anthropological Association with a paper, "Thinking in Categories, Acting on Meanings: Reinterpreting Liminality." Rather than seeing liminality in terms of taxonomic classification, perception, and thinking processes, influenced by Peirce's "logic of relatives" I saw it in terms of semantic systems and social practices.

> "Where ordinary logic talks of classes the logic of relatives talks of systems. A system is a set of objects comprising all that stand to one another in a group of connected relations. Induction according to ordinary logic rises from the contemplation of a sample of a class to that of the whole class; but according to the logic of relatives it rises from the contemplation of a fragment of a system to the envisagement of the complete system." (Peirce in Milton Singer 1978: 210)

I proposed that emphasizing affective and social processes leads to "shifting from a taxonomic to a systematic perspective—not the categories of set theory, but grounded systems of difference; not classificatory logic and 'mediating' concepts, but the constructing of matrices of meaning and choosing; not order and disorder, but human processes of invention, making metaphor, and transformation through which humans provide concepts for what is, in their absence, defined as ambiguous and anomalous. This analysis also asks us to consider linking the poetics of meaning to a positivism not of linguistic models but of affect as a neurophysiological resource that cultures manage each in its own way" (Perin 1982: 6).

Natural and psychological scientists intimate the plausibility of this possible synthesis—that unclear meanings can be as much involved in precipitating human curiosity, anxiety, and fear as are novel, unexpected, and inconsistent events and experiences—but they do not pursue it themselves (Mandler 1975: 26; V. Hamilton 1983: 118). Few studies of the relationship between semantic processing and anxiety have been made outside of contrived laboratory experiments (Brehm and Cohen 1962; Festinger 1957), and even fewer studies have observed this relationship ethologically or psychologically in human adults (Charlesworth 1974: 264). The "assumption that mature adults are afraid only of real danger, plausible though it may seem, is profoundly mistaken" (Bowlby 1973: 152), but we lack contextual observations of adults that parallel in quality those of fear in primates and children. Yet, for an anthropology of knowledge, the few "efforts [there have been] to specify actual neurological or physiological mechanisms . . . make it clear that anthropology must forge some serious links with the neurobiological sciences if it is to get anywhere" (Crick 1982: 296).

My concerns are not with either evolutionary or developmental processes. Those are the specialties of sociobiology, behavioral biology, and biological anthropology. My concerns are with the sources, dynamics, and manifestations of particular affects in social thought and practices. Human behavior does not "reduce" to these processes by any means, but it surely represents them. The rudimentary sketch I draw next of natural scientists' tentative models is intended only to share the background of understanding from which I've viewed responses to ambiguity in various social practices. Needless to say, these models and others contesting them are guiding experiments at levels of detail well beyond this discussion. My readings remain interpretive; the modern neurophysiology of fear and anxiety is but a lens for reading commonplace cultural evidence.

KEEPING THE LINES STRAIGHT

The scientific story of curiosity and of fear and anxiety is the same story, and it begins with the comfort that clear lines give us. Consensus about what things mean is a social expression of the biological drive to equilibrium, the feeling that "God's in his heaven—all's right with the world." With such comfort we hope to begin and end every day, but in between, we hope for activities that move us, make us curious, and are pleasurably stimulating. We like to see different friends, sample cuisines, wear new clothes, see the latest movies. But humans put definite limits on the magnitude of change and novelty they will experience. Beyond some threshold, different in every culture, different even for close relatives, instead of finding simple difference stimulating and pleasurable, humans can find it making them afraid and anxious. The difference that evokes pain becomes fearsome; the difference that brings pleasure becomes delightful.

Fear and anxiety in mammals are manifested neurophysiologically in autonomic behaviors of freezing, flight, and, when unable to flee, fighting. Each is a sign of experiences that are enough above that threshold to be felt as pain. To whatever it perceives as being "too" different, the brain responds as it does to stimuli of pain, frustration, and fear (states now thought to be functionally and physiologically equivalent) (Gray 1971: 141; 1982: 290). In turn, mammals' chief responses to frustration and pain are immobility and avoidance (Hebb 1946: 270–271; Brehm and Cohen 1962: 224–225).

What pushes this species beyond equilibrium is decidedly different from what pushes every other. Humans' concern with physical survival has also to be concern for preserving and enhancing the ways they make sense of their experiences, the meanings through which they live. In responding to what they believe threatens those meanings or denies them expected rewards, people, I suggest, turn "freezing" into stereotyping, "flight" into avoidance, withdrawal, and social distancing of many kinds, and "fight" into socially depreciating, denigrating, and disrespectful conduct as well as into overtly social and physical aggression. Just as a culture shares the meanings defining homeostasis so does it share, and institutionalize, many such versions of distress.

That is, discrepancies are identified with the pain they provoke; the pain is displaced on them. So does displeasure take on a life of its own; whatever distresses becomes a sign of that distress, just as whatever pleases is credited with being delightful and inspiring. The "dirt," "pollution," and "dangers" of liminal discourse are displacements of pain. People assail the messengers bringing the news that meanings are under siege. But unlike overt hostility toward law breakers, the reasons for hostility toward culture breakers are likely to be outside of awareness, because the meanings at risk are likely to go without saying. Distancing, dishonoring, and disparaging depend less on facts than on meanings being called into question.

In Jeffrey Gray's models, the brain's septo-hippocampal system compares actual with expected stimuli; it is a system that appears to be present "in all contemporary mammalian species and perhaps even in all vertebrates since birds and fish respond to anti-anxiety drugs in much the same way as do rats and monkeys" (Gray 1982: 48). This system lies within the brain's limbic system, which probably controls feeling states and their expression. At one level, the septo-hippocampal system distinguishes between "novel" and "familiar" stimuli, and at a second level, its function is to deal with more complex comparisons, or to "troubleshoot." This same system also brings to a halt behavior that is "maladaptive either because it leads to punishment, or because it no longer leads to a reward" (Gray 1971: 160; 1982: 14). In humans, more phylogenetically recent structures may also play a part, especially those having to do with language (located in the temporal and frontal cortext) (Gray 1982: 49, 418).

Studies of fear put a subtle twist on the folk axiom that "we fear the unknown": not the new and the unknown, but what is *already known* controls the onset of fear and anxiety. For example, infants show "stranger fear" not toward what is totally strange, but toward what is partly so—"the unfamiliar combination of familiar things." A "distorted voice coming from a familiar face, a mask over the face of a familiar person speaking with a normal voice" arouses infants' distress compared with the "unusual voice or the mask alone." Chimpanzees go into "paroxysms of terror" when they see a familiar attendant wearing another's lab coat and when they view an anesthetized chimpanzee, a skull, and a clay model of a chimpanzee head (Hebb 1955: 252, 244). This model of the central nervous system suggests that chimpanzees experience these differences or ambiguities as severe interruptions of their schemata of lab attendants and of fellow chimpanzees.

Equilibrium is the brain's ideal state (some scientists call it a drive as basic as hunger, sex, thirst), and above a certain threshold it seems to be inherently limited in its capacity to assimilate into what is already known, events, information, and experiences seen as novel or otherwise unexpected—that which we call threatening. The brain's strategy is to keep clear and certain what is already clear and certain. But when contrasts only gently prod equilibrium, curiosity is aroused and people get much pleasure from their explorations (Hebb 1949: 231). To clarify paradoxes and inconsistencies, people seek more information or look for information that will change their expectations so that the surprising no longer can surprise or threaten. Or people may dampen down novelties by finding the familiar in them (Berlyne 1960: 169). Empathy is another way: we seek ourselves in unfamiliar others.

My reading of modern neurophysiology suggests that biologically we are constituted to learn and not to learn, to assimilate new experience and to resist doing so, simultaneously. Educational practices institutionalize these biological limitations, knowingly or not, in gradually layering new information into what is already known; educational institutions are perhaps our premier social forms for dealing with the human resistance and attraction to new concepts and information. But to protect ourselves from the unpleasure of "too much" ambiguity and discrepancy in everyday life, we are on our own.

The number of interpretive and conduct systems ("belief systems," "schemata," "world views," "mind sets," "tapes") the brain keeps in working memory seems to be limited, and so a simple variety of experiences, events, and ideas can put equilibrium at constant risk. Learning reduces whatever we perceive to be unexpected, ambiguous, and inconsistent, of course, yet fear of novelty diminishes for another reason as humans mature: people gain the ability to read cues of *potentially* unfamiliar, frustrating, and disrupting experiences, the better to avoid them in the first place (Hebb 1949: 256). That same avoidance is expressed in people who have a high degree of "intolerance for ambiguity"; people who are narrow-minded or provincial live within few and intensely entailed interpretive systems, all the more susceptible to fear because a threat to one is a threat to all. Like everybody else, they "freeze" into familiar meanings to avoid the pain and frustration of whatever seems too discrepant from the social rewards and sanctions they count on.

"Culture shock" is no exaggeration of the neurophysiological response.

When customary expectations are interrupted or frustrated, the metaphor is correct: that pain may be as great as, if not greater than, the pain of mild punishments. To experience culture shock is to be without appropriate constructions of events and experiences; it is to lose the ability to shape expectations of what will follow—to lose the ability to act, that is. When cultural knowledge is confused and we are in the dark about what to infer, we can be immobilized, and by reason of that helplessness, distressed and afraid. People then tend to become more aware of their previously automatic behaviors, so that cultural confusion may not only limit the ability to act, but may elaborate into even more limitation (Mandler 1983: 100–101). Travel can be narrowing, that is, by making us exceptionally aware of meanings we have taken for granted but which are now useless guides to conduct.

Laughter is a first cousin to shudders of distress: both are products of the same semantic and visceral processes. Of the many kinds of laughter there are—"the laughter of relief from anxiety, the laughter of agreement, the laughter of sudden comprehension (the famous 'a-ha-experience,' perhaps really a 'ha-ha-experience'?), the laughter of triumph, the laughter of embarrassment, and the laughter of scorn"—in all of them is "some factor that is associated with threat, discomfort, uncertainty, surprise or, in a word, arousal and some factor that signifies safety, readjustment, clarification, or release. . . . All types of verbal wit or humorous anecdote seem to incorporate a divergence from the expected, a change in something familiar which leaves enough resemblance to the familiar for some of its responses to be evoked and yet contains some feature that frustrates these responses and thus provokes conflict, uncertainty, and surprise" (Berlyne 1960: 258–260; see also Hebb 1949: 258). The nuances of wit juxtapose the familiar and unfamiliar, the expected and the surprising; laughter sometimes dissolves into tears of pain.

Equilibrium corresponds to human "identity," then, if we consider identity to be the familiar meanings and conduct that we tend to lock into for the comforts they guarantee. These allow us to know, without having to think twice, what sanctions and rewards are part and parcel of relationships that matter most to our well-being. Otherwise, we may expect rewards but get punishments instead. Only among "our own kind," as we put it, do we so readily understand what acting one way or another signals, with both the least chance for misinterpretation and misstep and the most opportunity for spontaneity, recognition, and esteem. Not only are the ideas and ideals governing conduct salient in this life, but, for most of the world's peoples, they govern the quality of a next life as well.

The subjects taken up in liminal discourse—the myths, tales, and rituals documented from other times and places—I see as being evidence of the constancy of our species' biological constitution and its parallel capacity for constructing local meanings in thousands of ways. Throughout these essays, I reread rites, myths, tales, and exotic practices as being at once an indigenous poetics and a descriptive ethology of human experiences of discrepancy. I see them as being metastatements recording the human inability to deal with more than a few meaning systems at a time, our susceptibility both to curiosity and to culture shock. For example, the pervasive motifs of boundaries, crossroads, and messengers speak to the difficulty of entertaining "the unfamiliar combination of familiar things": only gods, not limited by a human brain, can take pleasure in meeting "foreigners" at crossroads of customs. Along with everything else these imaginative forms are and do, they are human products reflecting and commenting on our species' biological experiences of keeping meanings intact in order to be able to act.

A major trope of liminal discourse is its opposition between "order and disorder." "Order" is not a single entity in experience, I suggest, but a continuum embracing "disorder." Order, seen now as a semantic and neurophysiological issue, is merely a resting place, a home base, not the place we want to stay at forever, for only by living somewhat above equilibrium do we experience learning, laughter, delight, refreshment, aesthetic pleasure, enthusiasm, thrills . . . . When we are pulled "too far" away from the anchors of equilibrium, then there is that pain of helplessness and all that humans do when they experience it, including calling it chaos and disorder.

The meanings people bestow determine what they will fear. That is the dilemma of our species as makers of meanings. Meanings are essential guides to conduct, and the ability to act and react in predictable ways is essential to life. That people seek and are rewarded by ideas, people, and events that are novel, unfamiliar, surprising, inchoate, and complex is undoubted; that there are limitations on a tolerable level is just as clear. How any event or experience falls along this continuum is above all a cultural question, a question of its meaning. That meaning determines its perceived degree of discrepancy; that perception governs the appearance of pleasure and of fear, anxiety, paralysis, retreat, and attack. Whatever distresses is, one way or another, to be avoided. Whatever gives comfort is, one way or another, to go without saying, to be taken entirely for granted.

To survive, human beings fear and avoid whatever they believe calls into question the meanings they live by—different ideas, incompatible or discrepant ideologies and cosmologies, and the familiar yet unfamiliar events and experiences that we sum up as "change." The fear is not fear of such challenges for their content alone but for their import: they are signs that embedded meanings could become unreliable guides to conduct, our own and others'. How people create, hold onto, and act on meanings is a key to social order, ours and every other. We may think in categories, but we act on meanings. When spines of meaning slip a disc, our ability to act is impaired; in itself helplessness can make people distressed, fearful, and anxious. For fear is (or is born of) the inability to act and to predict the consequences of acting; anxiety is a conflict between possible ways of acting. "Helplessness and disorganization *are* anxiety" (Mandler 1975: 199).

Keeping meanings intact is self-preservative, yet it is all too often other-destructive. Maintaining the equilibrium that is "identity" motivates endogamy and sets the limits of exogamy; the comfort of membership is a major issue, if not the major issue, of any social group. Read as signs of "too much" unfamiliarity, "others" often suffer the consequences of our drive to equilibrium. Maintaining the comforts of belonging is often purchased at others' expense with the currency of invidious beliefs that those living by other lights are innately inferior or degraded or degenerate and should be so treated. At the least humans take refuge in prejudice, at the worst we allow holocausts, and in between, we can foment social strife, wholesale injustice, and lives of pain.

REPRISE

These understandings leave no room for complacent functionalisms. Our own age of reason has yet to acknowledge then to transform the ways people respond to confusions of meanings. A palette of fear and anxiety still colors social responses to questions that ambiguities never cease to raise about the clarities we must have.

Even when we think we have caught it all, much "reality" remains inchoate, for no matter how fine the mesh of meanings, our lines can do only so much (Fernandez 1974, 1979). Life *is* a continual playing upon ambiguities, and "mainstream" American ideals, standards, and norms are our ways of trying to give them shape. There is no perfect way to do that, maybe even no other way. But we need not compound that existential fact by misunderstanding or not understanding why we act as we do. Drawing lines has consequences. These essays ask whether these are the meanings and the consequences we want.

By the same token, Americans whose behavior is discrepant from shared norms can indeed be dangerous signs of another kind. Some give us realistic reasons for fear. We'd be foolhardy not to do all we can to avoid neighbors or strangers with illegal handguns, people high on drugs, drunk drivers, thieves, cheaters. But social deviants and cultural discrepancies are not the same. In a nation founded on the principle of dissent, why should "meanings breakers" be treated even more hostilely than law breakers? We remain culturally helpless even while we may be legally powerful to stop some Americans from being alienated, disvalued, denigrated, and disparaged simply for being themselves.

We regulate meaning systems affectively, cognitively, and experientially with a threshold of arousal, a predicate of curiosity, a law of avoidance, a rule of distance, a principle of immobility, an axiom of aggression, a postulate of projection. Biologically, we are constituted to explore and expand our store of meanings and, simultaneously, to resist doing so. Familiar meaning systems are lodes of conservative energies, mined to provide the visceral comforts of equilibrium. They can be contested successfully, from within or without, only gradually, only when changes are more attention- than fear-arousing, more certain to be rewarding than not. Meaning systems are nongenetic yet biologically sustained mechanisms through which sociocultural systems both persist and change.

In its several senses, then, "constitution" bridges the semantic, biological, and social dimensions these essays explore: the constitution of meaning—the ideas by which we construe our world to make it more intelligible, less uncertain; the human constitution—our species' biological dispositions; and our American Constitution—its principles enabling the negotiation and renegotiation of meanings we live by.

How people wrestle personally with their feelings of belonging and alienation novelists, poets, and playwrights can better tell. "A book must be the ax for the frozen sea within us," Kafka put it. The frozen seas around us concern me. These essays search out cultural icebergs sinking our hopes, freezing us out. If we can sound out their meanings and trace the shape of their symbols, they may no longer block belonging and thriving in America.

Note on Typography

To help see between the lines, in the essays that follow I've introduced two typographic conventions into the text. Small capital letters are a sign that the word represents a constellation of implicit ideas which I am trying to trace out explicitly—for example, NEIGHBOR, WOMEN, MEN, CHILDREN. *Words with an initial capital letter represent those implicit ideas—concepts so familiar and necessary that they are likely to pass us by: American agreements about the meanings of Love and Money, Public and Private, Trust and Suspicion, for example. Capitalizing them is a reminder that parsing these concepts is no small endeavor. In both cases, once the point is made, the conventions are suspended.*

THE INVISIBLE
NEIGHBORHOOD

*Among the most familiar lines Americans draw are those
between their personal and public lives, between their own families
and everybody else's, between their house and their neighbors'. And
among the most important lines, for when the borders between these
dimensions of life are breached politically or personally, the outcries are
loud and clear. These conventions are so unproblematic that our cultural
landscape reproduces them exactly: the very iconography of American
suburbs—their predictable configurations of single-family houses, fences,
hedges, and lawns—signals some of the ways people control their experiences of anything and anybody "too" different from themselves and too
much of a departure from the concepts supplying the meanings they
live by.*

*Yet life as lived within these various walls can present a more blurred
picture. Americans seem to know, without being able to say why perhaps, that blood and legal ties may have little to do with the cultural
realities of family; that the priority of civic law over family rules is
juridically one thing and culturally another; that the ideal of community
hospitality is tarnished by the isolating experiences newcomers can have;
that civic virtue is publicly extolled while private loyalties are culturally
suspect.*

*This essay begins this book's illustrations of many of the ways we
play on such ambiguities and how they play upon us. Like the others
that follow, this essay drafts a thesaurus of American ambiguities and
meanings. In editing these entries, bringing to bear what usually stays
between the lines, we begin to shape rather than merely receive culture.*

Stepping outside the doorway of home, leaving those nearest and dearest
to us, we hope to feel we belong in the world beyond. On the other side
of that line, our first potential connection beyond the intimates of that
interior life is with neighbors—the men, women, children, and dogs on
our street and around the corner. Between the potentialities and realities
of that connection much about belonging in America is revealed. That is
because our relations with neighbors are not what they seem. An invisible

neighborhood runs beneath the one we live in, designed by the ways we see the differences between FAMILY and COMMUNITY: American concepts of Private and Public, Home and Work, Privacy and Interdependence, Choice and Duty, Trust and Suspicion, Friendship and Kinship . . . .

Standing at the crossroads of family and community are NEIGHBORS, and with ideas about Privacy, the master key to the residential environment, we turn off their ambiguous charge. Of all the relationships we have, those with neighbors are likely to be the most ambiguous; they can be many things, and nothing. Outside our closest circle of KIN and the FRIENDS we share our houses with, only neighbors might see us offstage in our bathrobes taking in the paper, wearing our shabbiest clothes to paint the trim. But letting them past the front door and deeper into that circle? The quintessential American way of thinking about neighbors, spoken by a woman in suburban Minneapolis: "People who are sort of there when you need 'em—that's the best kind of neighbors. And friendly, but they do respect your privacy. 'Love thy neighbor'—but don't pull down the fence."

How Americans act toward their neighbors varies greatly—it depends on the situations of our lives and the part neighbors might play in them: the *meanings* of neighbors change. Defined in the dictionary only as "someone nearby," neighbor takes its other associations and connotations from its context. Farmers live in uninterruptedly good relationships with those nearest by, in a network of mutual aid; they will readily acknowledge, that is, that they had better. A woman who grew up in farming country in California, now watching the subdivisions coming in, says: "In the country, you can fight with anybody you want to—but not your neighbor. You never know when you're going to need them or when they're going to need you."

Villagers and dwellers in small towns may endow their neighbors with meanings braided from so many other associations that NEIGHBOR is just one of the strands. Neighbors are likely also to be kin (if not now, perhaps in future); employers and employees live down the street or around the corner from one another; so do teachers and pupils, lenders and debtors, shopkeepers and customers. In smaller, more or less self-contained settlements neighbors are signs along paths of memory and expectation. The same might be true for people in some neighborhoods of big cities, especially those still serving as enclaves, villages, or ghettoes.

These days our neighbors add little starch to the fabric of our social lives, it is said, especially because we can so easily wheel around our allegiances and interests, satisfying our need for belonging beyond the borders of any neighborhood. "Community" can be found everywhere, not just on the suburban or city street where you live. True enough: Americans have a penchant for groups of all kinds—our families first of all, and churches and synagogues, political, work, and hobby groups, schools, associations, and clubs. Even so, the hope persists for a sense of community along our block and in the neighborhood, but if it seems to be weaker than many would like, it may be because the social contract with neighbors is peppered with confusing clauses. Those articles of our tacit constitution introduce more ambiguity into that relationship than any other we are likely to have as men, women, children, and the people owned by dogs.

To find the meaning of neighbor at any given time, via the same process by which we get to all our meanings, we position it among every other relationship. "My neighbor is more an acquaintance than a friend." "My neighbor is a better friend than any relative." We define each relationship through its contrast with all others: each takes on its texture and shape from its felt differences from and similarities to every other. A system is at work, our ideas about any one relationship hinged to those about every other. "He's my cousin, but I wouldn't call him a friend." RELATIVES, FRIENDS, LOVERS, ACQUAINTANCES, ENEMIES, STRANGERS—the meaning of each allows us to outline our expectations of each other's actions and to behave accordingly.

Relationships with neighbors always include some other relationship. Because each person next door or around the corner may be friend, relative, acquaintance, enemy, and stranger, neighbor doesn't tell the whole story. Because we don't settle once and for all throughout our lives the difference between neighbors and each other kind of relationship, neighbor carries no predictable meaning. We decide in each instance how we will act, running through all possible choices. We may think in the categories shaped by typologies and taxonomies, but we act on and live by meanings. This system of ideas hinging our personal relationships is a moral system, then, because it guides our choice of actions.

The ideas go without saying, of course: they are the core concepts of our society. In our American system of personal relationships, these silent concepts are Intimacy, Trust, Obligation, Choice, Reciprocity, Love, among others, and all their shadings of intensity in our feelings and the weightings we give them in practice. We receive each one embedded in its invisible social history, and throughout our lives use it to give coherent shape to all our experiences. Nothing in our individual and common life fails to draw on these core concepts. The smallest gestures are signs of them—as shaking right hands is a sign of Trust and holding left and right hands a sign of Intimacy.

The natural ambiguity of neighbor arises from the variety of concepts its meanings can draw on. Some are compatible, others not. When they reinforce each other, we can experience a clear sense of community. When they contradict one another, they can confuse our choices and impair our ability to act. In fostering helplessness, these contradictions leave us vulnerable to social anxieties. Spatially, neighbor is, by definition, Near, a concept connoting others, especially Coming First and Degree of Influence. Concerning events, the nearer in time, the more Influential, we believe; concerning people, we think that Nearest is Dearest. But experiencing our relationship with a neighbor as STRANGER or ACQUAINTANCE contradicts those notions of Near, First, and Influential: the neighbor as stranger employs the wholly contradictory concepts of Far and Distant.

When Nearest is not Dearest, it is especially confusing. The spatially close neighbor who remains acquaintance or stranger upends those concepts. The Commandment to "Love your neighbor" furthers the confusion —Love, but not the Sexual Love reserved for spouse, according to that same Law. For Close and Love come paired with the meanings of Blood and Intimacy; these endow RELATIVES with the deepest intensity and heaviest weight of all American personal relations (D. M. Schneider 1980). When neighbors are friends, we fine tune our idea of Close in our actions toward them, always holding out some of that same moral space of Intimacy and Love for each relative by blood and marriage. What each one of them means, in turn, is modulated by religious, ethnic, and personal emphases on the kind and degree of Obligation, Reciprocity, Trust with which we act toward children, grandparents, aunts, second cousins, fathers-in-law, and ex-wives.

Consider how this system of personal relationships accommodates the stranger, set apart from all others with the concept of Distance, yet confusing by being in our midst—Close, yet also New to us. "Making room" for strangers is making moral space for them and choosing among various concepts in acting toward them. With Trust, we would transform them into . . . friend? or lover? relative? Will the stranger crowd *us* in the moral space we occupy with relatives and friends? Generally speaking (universally speaking, it would seem) until we choose how we will act—with what shadings of Trust, Reciprocity, Intimacy—strangers will be feared, avoided, and often as not, in societies the world over, cheated or labelled witch (Bourdieu [1972] 1977: 228–229; Levine 1979: 30; Sahlins 1965). Xenophobes deal with strangers as the instant equivalent of ENEMY, acting on the ideas of Attack and Destroy.

The stranger is the universal crosser of lines, from far to near, unfamiliar to familiar; the stranger is whomever we cannot place within our accustomed order, that fenced-in semantic field where each member becomes endowed with meaning. To assimilate the stranger into that field of personal relationships, its topography may have to shift and we may lose our bearings. Making a new friend of the stranger may change the way we think, both about the concept of friendship and about the friends we already have. For it is not stranger per se that is unsettling, *but the necessity it signals of realigning* what is already in that field: the possibility that the concepts organizing a settled system will have to apply in untried ways, leaving us unsure how to act and what to expect from others. The stranger, as person, event, perception, or idea, unsettles meanings we live by.

Neighbors, those nearby, familiar strangers, fenced out entirely or brought in annually, stagger under a profusion of crossed lines. Most people take the same path in preserving their equilibrium: Americans are likely to flee these ambiguities by not knowing their neighbors at all.

DRAWING FAMILY LINES

Fences, hedges, yards, and gates carve out the snug boundaries of each blood FAMILY, unique in lineage and history, lore and insider meanings. At home, in the bosom of familiar meanings, we are at our freest, out of public view, spontaneous and unguarded, tending to one another's upsets and replenishing each other's equilibrium for ambiguities and hurdles beyond the hearth. Strangers are kept out, and newcomers are taken in only after careful deliberation. Even the parking space out front is appropriated as family land, as neighbors' visitors soon find out. They may talk over their back fences and track the children and dogs who find a way over and under them, but Americans seldom let their property lines lose their edges. In those parts of the country where property bounds aren't customarily marked, they can readily be imagined—each family has a good idea just where its neighbors' lines meet theirs.

Everywhere that fences and walls, lawns and yards matter so does Privacy. Through this concept more than any other perhaps we reveal our preoccupations with the social ambiguities of the civic interdependencies we also cannot live without. Every family finds its way down the path we construct between Individualism and Interdependence. Taking responsibility for one's own family and at the same time discharging the obligations of citizenship is a struggle, never easy, never resolved once and for all by any of us perhaps. In insisting on its privacy, every family rests from that conflict.

Because Americans think privacy is in shortest supply there, fences and lawns matter a great deal in suburbs. "Do you think that people have the most personal privacy in rural areas, small towns, large cities, or the suburbs of large cities?" was one question in a Louis Harris survey of attitudes toward privacy (Louis Harris and Associates and Westin 1980: 18). The responses are broken down by the region of the respondents'

Most privacy in:	Region of the USA			
	East	Midwest	South	West
		(percent)		
Rural areas	34	42	41	29
Small towns	9	9	16	20
Large cities	32	30	26	31
Suburbs of large cities	15	10	10	8
Not sure	10	9	7	12

residence. Americans think that they have the least privacy in suburbs and small towns, the most in both rural areas and big cities.

Privacy also anticipates potential interruptions beyond a pleasurable threshold, and the more the house itself represents this same insulation from the unclear demands of neighbors, the better we like it. Owning a single-family-detached house provides the very most privacy, something like 80 percent of American families believe. Indeed, of the kinds of housing Americans prefer, "there is *no* second most popular choice" to owning a single-family-detached house, although, of course, these beliefs and preferences have to yield to pocketbook realities (Dillman, Tremblay, Dillman 1979: 14, 16). Even among those 65 or older, rather than give up the costs and cares of a house, about 45 percent still prefer it, compared with between about 24 and 30 percent whose first or second preference would be to rent a duplex or an apartment. Even those without a spouse at those ages agree.

Still, no one wants total privacy all the time. Little else in social life keeps us dodging so ambivalently between our understandings of Independence and Interdependence, Individuality and Community, as do relationships with neighbors. Good neighbors leave you alone *and* they watch out for you. A preoccupation for a woman in Minneapolis is "trying to keep my distance" in the neighborhood—but she welcomes the nosiness too. "There are certain people who know whenever you drive up and down the street, for instance. People think, 'Well, I wonder where she is going.' They sort of remind me of my next-door neighbor at my parents' house in a small town in Wisconsin. It comes out later on—'I saw you, as I was sitting having breakfast. I see you going by every day, and bla, bla, bla. . . .' If you've been on vacation, they'll say, 'I haven't seen you driving up the street this week,' which is OK, I suppose, in a way, because they do watch out for your house—and for you. And if something happened they would probably come and check on you, too. So it depends on what you are in the mood for." Divorced and living with her young son in the same house as when she was married, she doesn't want people "noticing what I am doing all the time, if I'm doing something that people won't approve of. I tend to be more liberal than a lot of the people here."

The chief symbol of privacy and guarantor of each family's claim to it is an unblemished lawn—free from weeds, dandelions, dog feces, or planted tires. And from children at play. The house front too is to be freshly painted, without peeling or blisters, but it is the lawn that carries most of the burden, "not a blade of grass out of place." An "immaculate" lawn, I often heard, is the ultimate objective, for it seems to belong more to the neighbors than to each household, "a kind of compulsory public housekeeping . . . a tax imposed by neighborhood consciousness" (Riesman 1957: 390). A Minneapolis woman puts it: "I guess when you get down to the basics, you darn well better keep your grass cut and your front yard looking halfway presentable." What happens if you don't? "I think someone might make a comment, like 'Do you want to borrow my lawnmower?' And I'm sure the neighbors would talk—'What in the world is going on over there? They must be sick, there must be a problem.'"

Private matters stay out of the yard, sometimes: "One thing I've never seen in this neighborhood is a fight between a husband and wife. I've never heard any husband and wife screaming at each other, which I'm sure they must do—whereas in the other neighborhood, occasionally there was one couple that would have a really good fight—once a month." In the backyard? "No, in the front—throwing his clothes out of the door and everything. You're asking me some hard questions here!"

Nor is the lawn meant for children to use, in the experience of a California woman: "My husband is a gardener, and people will call up and ask him to put in a clover lawn. He sees they have three kids, and tells them, 'Why don't you get this park blend so kids can play on it?' 'No, I want the clover.' So their kids are playing out on the street. I just can't understand why someone would plant a nice lawn that your kids can't play on."

In a Virginia suburb with a good many condominiums, "doing something like putting a tire in the yard and painting it white would cause a disturbance in the neighborhood." Why would it trouble people? "The tire wouldn't have a damn thing to do with that. It would have to do with an investment of ego. 'I'm not an Okie. I don't have tires in my front yard. I have nice boxwood.' It's a matter of prestige and if my friends drive in here and they see that tire, they say, 'Oh, you've moved back to the Bronx.' I speculate that's what makes them uncomfortable. I know that we had one neighbor who was very untidy—let the grass grow and had a gymnastics mat out in the yard and various other pieces of junk. People would turn their heads when they walked by. I think that was more related to 'That's a punch at my ego, at *my* nice house.'"

One of the few lines we can make concrete are property lines, yet fences are as much owned by their neighbors as by each family, and jointly financing them can become a "hassle," says a California building inspector who has seen several: "Getting surveyed for a fence—that's when neighbors don't get along. We always try to impress on both neighbors that what they ought to do is pool their money, get a surveyor, get that property line defined, and then build their fence together, as a unit. A cooperative venture. It lowers the cost for both of them. But when they find out what the cost of the survey is, they don't cooperate, and sometimes they get into a hassle." Interdependence mixed with Individualism is a recipe for social ambiguity and its brew of bad feeling.

Fences are believed to resolve hassles, too, according to a building inspector in suburban Minneapolis: "Occasionally a fence has gone up because of a dispute. They hire a surveyor for $400–500 just to locate the property line. One pair of neighbors ended up with an expensive surveyor because they weren't speaking. It was going to separate them, it was the Berlin Wall. They didn't get along because of a problem with their kids. They wanted to put up the highest fence they were allowed—a six-foot fence, the most private. So it's just like a wall. That's what they wanted. It was redwood, and they did their whole backyard. They probably spent $2500."

"We've recently gone to court on fences," another inspector reports. "One was ugly and both were improperly located." Were they in the category of a "spite fence"? Had there been a disagreement? "Oh hell yes! We sure do know about spite fences—that goes on every day. They'll even try putting up a small fence of chicken wire—anything to irritate their neighbor, and then you get into a scrap about it. Then the one will call us, then the other one will call us, and it's just back and forth. And you're right in the middle as the great arbitrator."

After a quarter of a century, one "spite fence" was coming down in a Boston suburb. An eight-foot-high stockade fence had been put in about 1957, five years before Hingham's zoning law forbade them. One of the principals, "an upper middle class Yankee gentleman," recounted its history to a newspaper reporter. There had been a path between the hedge in his garden that "was kept well worn by the flow of dogs and children back and forth. Even the women of the two houses used the path to visit during the day, and the man now recalled that he and his neighbor had met on occasion in one another's back yard for a drink. The dispute started simply enough, according to the man: The neighbor's dog would come over and defecate on his lawn and nothing would be done about complaints. 'It seems pretty silly now, doesn't it,' the man asked, 'that two families wouldn't talk to each other for 25 years because of a dog. . . .'

"There were other grievances, to be sure. The man said his neighbor's lawn at the border had been a couple of feet higher in grade than his own, and that one late winter day of exceptionally heavy melting, the neighbor made troughs to channel the water out of his own driveway and into a hollow on the man's lawn where it killed three young apple trees.

"Then, said the man, his neighbor had had the gall to suggest that he cut down the remaining mature apple trees and bring in fill so that the two lots could be joined in one continuous sweep. The man could think of no grievances on his neighbor's side. Shortly after this incident, the fence went up and except for driving by each other's houses, the families never saw each other again. . . . There were times along the way, he confided, after his neighbor's wife had died of stomach cancer followed by his own wife's death from a heart attack, when he was nearly moved simply to go over and visit. But after so much time, where do you start? What do you say? . . . Whatever, the man never went to visit his neighbor" (Chamberlain 1981: 29).

Some people have tried it both ways, with and without fences: "I like to live with walls around our yard. We've lived for years with rock walls, and we like the idea of having that separation. We've lived mostly on army posts and one thing we don't like is that lack of privacy. The fact that everybody owns the yard in common, everybody runs across it, all the kids run across it. We liked it when we could move and get a place that was separate, our own, that we could fix."

Common use and common ownership violate the ideal of Private Property, but when there are children, some like the lines to be blurred. "I lived in a new development in southern California without any fences between the houses, and as it grew, people wanted to put in walls. I'm not interested in walls. I just thought it was neat to be out of an apartment and in a house and with people. I wanted us to get together—there was a big area in the middle just right for a swimming pool we could all share. Everybody had kids. Oh, no. We had to have fences. Not only fences but cement block walls. And so I said, 'Well, I'm just not interested.' The people next door asked whether we were going to pay half—we had a huge lot—and I said, 'No.' They said, 'All right, we'll put it up and we'll put it six inches into our side of the line, and if you touch it, we'll sue you.' So we said, 'Oh, put in the wall, we'll pay for half of it.' What are you going to do?

"Nobody paid any attention to anybody anymore. The kids were all playing in the street, and here we were—this was an upper-income area—we'd moved out of an apartment so the kids would have a place to play and they're all playing in the street because you landscape your backyard and nobody can play in it."

A man still getting used to living in California doesn't quite believe the reasons his neighbors give for wanting to put up a fence: "One thing that concerned us when we got out here in California from Maryland was that most people have fences. Back East you don't necessarily see fences. An Easterner comes out and says, 'Hey, what's this fence business? Are they physically trying to separate us?' You do get that idea about it. Both neighbors came over and asked if we'd pay half for the fence, and the answer was 'no' only because we don't believe in fences. Six-foot fences, everybody has them. They say they don't want the children or dogs to leave. But that's unreal—all the children play right out on the road here." Like many of the lines we draw, the symbol matters more than any "reality."

Physical boundaries of fences and lawns are only one way of maintaining family privacy and its protections. A moat of rules also works on its behalf: Americans cultivate "this-family" law, each FAMILY constituting its very own customs and norms, unique meanings and codes for conduct through which fault is found, blame assessed, and punishment meted out. And conduct that yields praise and reward. "In *this* family, we . . ." is a phrase of pride used to set it apart from every other. Family talk: the intimate names and nicknames, the single word or gesture evoking shared memories and lore, and treasured mementoes and tales of the family's founders (origin myths are likely to include one famous, or near-famous, relative). By its unique history and traditions, each family maintains its own core of meanings and, through them, its integrity.

So inviolable is that core of meanings that the influence of national or local community culture takes second place. A study of codes for conduct in five societies, the United States among them, finds that families' cultures are stronger than is the wider culture—"sharing *inside* the family is higher than sharing among [those] who belong to different families in the same society," suggesting "that by no means all of what is involved in sharing culture is brought into the family from the society at large" (Swartz 1982: 318–319). Are those other systems of meaning seen as discrepancies from those that are comfortable, predictable, and entirely under the family's control? Letting in another culture's meanings and the conduct they promote is what we know as "assimilation," but it is simultaneously accompanied by that "resistance" we acknowledge less. "Intergenerational conflict" is a variant of the resistance: when adolescents find attractive alternatives and options beyond the family threshold, they call into question their family's culture, and, made anxious by such novelties, parents label them "corrupting" or worse, urging their children, to whom these are more stimulating than threatening, to keep their distance.

Americans respect every other family's law as they want their own to be. Friendship defers to kinship. Children's carpooling, for example:

one custom is that without specific permission, no matter how disruptive another's child, the driving parent has no right to threaten or even to warn. If the driver should do so, explanations are in order, but they may not always hold together what had been a friendship between parents. A couple in a Washington, D.C., suburb had recently moved from a townhouse "cluster" to a single-family house in the same town. I asked them, If I were coming to live here, what "unwritten rules" might you write down for me? The man's answer revealed a different set of customs: "Don't let your children get too wild. In the cluster, there was a lot of pressure on children from *all* the parents who would tell any one of them when to head in, so they weren't just going free all the time. But that was peculiar just to that block in the cluster. Another two blocks over there were a lot of difficulties with children when people other than their parents *wouldn't* tell them, 'Hey, don't make so much noise. Don't ride your skateboard in front of my dining room when I'm having dinner.' Our block would tell them that because there were a lot of people in the block who had been there from the beginning, and we all handled our kids the same way. So the 'rules,' as you put it, in that block were very different from the one 100 feet away. People had a terrible time there. I used to ask them, 'Well, why don't you tell the children to be quiet?' Well, they didn't know they could. They didn't know the rules in their block."

"They didn't know they could" tell other people's children what the rules were—or perhaps they didn't think they ought to. Even children will sit on their right to obey only family law. A California woman told me: "In this neighborhood there have been times when parents don't respond to problems with the children. A little boy down the block had a *pointed* bamboo stick. I was watching my neighbor's little boy, he's about three years old. He was out on the sidewalk running a toy car up and down. I was standing at the window watching, and this other little boy had the stick held like a javelin and was going to stab him with it. I went outside and said, 'You put that stick down.' He looked at me and said, 'You can't tell me what to do.' And I said, 'Oh, can't I? Give me that stick.' So I took it away from him and put it in my garage. 'I'm going to tell my mother on you,' he said. 'Go ahead and tell.'"

The rules of each "house" are to be obeyed by outsiders. "When kids are in my yard and they don't behave, I send them home," a woman in a Minneapolis suburb told me. "I'd never spank them—just tell them they're out of line." Family law is "the one place where I draw the line," even with "very close friends," a California woman told me. "I will tell my kids they have to do this or that and they'll mention it to a close friend. Then she'll say something against what I've told them, and they think they don't have to obey me. But my friend has learned that that's one place where I draw the line. What I tell them and what my husband tells them, that's absolute, that's it."

Privacy also includes secrecy, for few families are without secrets deserving to be kept. Secrets certainly about money, and about character: the idiosyncracies and bad habits of relatives near and far, or the last binge, or the games, sexual or bridge, of spouses and friends. A woman heading a church-sponsored counseling service told me that whenever teenagers in that suburb get into one or another kind of difficulty—from drinking, drugs, or sex—the "family walls," as she put it, go up, but not so much to protect a troubled member as to defend against outsiders' knowing. From neighbors people hide away sorrows and troubles, maintaining public face above all; Close, and for that, rarely Intimate.

Because Americans respect what goes on in each family as so strictly a private matter, little is known about family moral order, according to the authors of the first nationwide study of the incidence of violence in the family. The rule of family privacy is so strong "that it prevents the victims from seeking outside help" (Gelles and Straus 1979: 36). One finding which "opened the eyes of many people who previously had thought that family violence was uncommon as well as deviant" is that "one in four men and one in six women approved of a husband slapping a wife under certain conditions" (ibid.: 17). The "rate of severe violence in homes where the father is a blue collar worker is 16%, while the rate in homes where the father is a white collar worker is 11%. Although this is a substantial and significant difference, it is smaller than the difference typically found in examinations of official reports of child abuse" (ibid.: 30). "With the exception of the police and the military, the family is perhaps the most violent social group, and the home the most violent social setting, in our society. A person is more likely to be hit or killed in his or her home by another family member than anywhere else or by anyone else. Nearly one out of every four murder victims in the United States is a family member" (ibid.: 15). Nor does social class appear to be related to the use of physical force at home. In another study that collected anonymous reports from college students, 16 percent of them reported that, in their last year of high school, one or both parents had used physical violence. In working- and lower-class families, physical force may seem to be prevalent only because police, social workers, or researchers are more likely to get inside of them (Aldous 1977: 115).

This stress on family privacy and the autonomy from wider norms it affords is possibly a "modern development" occurring only within this century. Earlier, outsiders were likely to have been an audience in a family's life, observing how its members fulfilled their duties and exercised their rights with one another. As a form of surveillance, their presence may have brought family behavior into more conformity with public norms, more so than now, that is. In colonial America (following the European tradition), children who were "put out" to live with other families for their education or an apprenticeship to a trade became the outsiders in others' families. So too with servants who were widespread among families in all economic groups for long periods of our history (B. Laslett 1973: 486). Taking in lodgers and boarders has not been common practice in this century, even among lower-income families. In 1903, for example, about 22 percent of working-class families had some income from boarders and lodgers in the previous years, but by 1930 only about 11 percent of families had lodgers; in 1940 the figure was 9 percent, and by 1960 it was down to 3 (ibid.: 485).

Servants are the only outsiders who don't violate the norms governing the composition of the ideal American family.

PROFANING THE FAMILY

The "single family" ideal was last declared the national norm in 1974 when the United States Supreme Court held that single-family-detached houses may be occupied by no more than two unrelated individuals. Zoning laws intend single-family houses to be occupied only by those who are members of a "f-a-m-i-l-y," as one justice put it, no matter how large that family, whether composed of "two or twenty" relatives. The decision was the Court's response to a suit brought by several unrelated people who challenged a Long Island town's zoning ordinance forbidding such groups to live in single-family-detached houses (*Village of Belle Terre* v. *Boraas* 1975). During the oral argument before the Supreme Court, there was this exchange between the justices and Lawrence Sager, lawyer for the group (the Court's transcripts of oral arguments do not identify justices by name):

> *Question:* And you say that the Village, in this case at least, has no constitutional power to define the family . . . the way they did?
> *Mr. Sager:* I think that's right.
> *Question:* And could not confine it to, what I think what sociologists now call a nuclear family. Is that it?
> *Mr. Sager:* I think that's right.
> *Mr. Sager:* The familial bond which satisfies this [ordinance's] test can be a good deal more remote than the nuclear family. It can be, for example, a remote cousin, uncle, grandfather.
> *Question:* Well, tribal. They can't define it in tribal terms.
> *Mr. Sager:* Tribal terms may be more accurate, Your Honor.
> *Question:* Well, your clients do not form a family do they?
> *Question:* By your definition, they do, don't they?
> *Mr. Sager:* They do not—I think we'd have to ask whose definition was being drawn on, Your Honor. By sociologists' definition, I'm not sure; by the Village of Belle Terre's, certainly not. By mine, they certainly formed a single housekeeping unit. As a practical matter, their dinner was—

Question: My question was: Is it family—f-a-m-i-l-y?
Mr. Sager: They are not what I would call a family, Your Honor.
(U.S. Supreme Court 1974: 30)

Dissenting from the majority opinion, Justice Thurgood Marshall said of the ordinance:

> It permits any number of persons related by blood or marriage, be it two or twenty, to live in a single household, but it limits to two the number of unrelated persons bound by professional, love, friendship, religious or political affiliation or mere economics who can occupy a single home. Belle Terre imposes on those who deviate from the community norm in their choice of living companions significantly greater restrictions than are applied to residential groups who are related by blood or marriage, and compose the established order within the community. The village has, in effect, acted to fence out those individuals whose choice of lifestyle differs from that of its current residents. . . . There is not a shred of evidence in the record indicating that if Belle Terre permitted a limited number of unrelated persons to live together, the residential, familial character of the community would be fundamentally affected. (416 U.S. 16, 17, 20)

Not a FAMILY and blessed on that account in the Court's eyes, then, a GROUP living together is mundane, even though the effects it has may be no different from those produced by a family: either way, 20 people living together will make for much traffic, noise, and general commotion, but only that of a group is to be considered an earthly nuisance! So is it punished for having erased the line around FAMILY.

Isn't this preoccupation with a "single-family-detached" norm a postindustrial development? Isn't it an American tradition for more than one generation or married sisters and brothers to live together as an "extended family"? Doesn't the absence of even a single grandparent in the nuclear family violate a long-standing American ideal? No, the record shows: in 1875 only about 8 percent of households were composed of three or more generations, and in 1960, only 5 percent were (Pryor 1972: 589). Never a major pattern even earlier, the multigenerational household can properly be called a minor family form. That the "small family" tradition hasn't much changed nearly 100 years later is evidence of the consistent American norm that each family should live on its own.

Nor is this small-family form new to Americans with European roots. The individual family household prevailed as the dominant pattern in preindustrial England and Europe, and some of our misconceptions appear to have arisen from sociologists who had assumed otherwise, before the facts were in, as a "matter of ideology . . . nurtured by a wish to be able to believe in a doctrine of familial history" only now being investigated empirically (P. Laslett [1972] 1974: 73). None of this is to say, of course, that Americans have to live with their kin in order for their love and interest in one another to prosper. Relatives extend themselves emotionally even if they don't extend their family boundaries, perhaps even more freely and amiably with protective distance. All evidence today points to Americans' maintaining high levels of contact with relatives living near and far. "Ma Bell" and her new offspring keep families in touch over long distances, and over short distances they do it themselves.

"Much of the 'community solidarity' of Middletown is really kinship solidarity," a 1980 study of Muncie finds, following up the Lynds' earlier findings: "When there are relatives living in town, especially close ones— parents, brothers and sisters, or grown children—they are seen, talked to, and visited more frequently than are friends or neighbors. When Middletown people need assistance or advice, they are apt to turn to their relatives, if there are any available, and usually there are" (Caplow et al. 1982: 200). Their parents also live in Middletown, 43 percent of adults report, and for another 18 percent they live within 50 miles. Of their grown children, 54 percent also live within the city and 14 percent within 50 miles. Still living in Indiana are 74 percent of parents, 59 percent of brothers and sisters, 75 percent of their grown children, and 54 percent of other relatives (ibid.: 379).

In a study of Americans' personal relationships, the only one of its kind in recent years, about 1250 Americans provided the names of those they have an active personal relationship with—19,417 names in all of people who provide them various kinds of emotional support, social companionship, and practical help such as giving advice, listening to personal worries, helping out with painting and plumbing jobs, having each other over for dinner and going to the movies, sharing leisure interests, and taking care of their house if they go away. For each name, the people in this sample characterized the kind of relationship it is (neighbor, relative, co-worker, friend, acquaintance), which of them they feel especially close to, how far away they live, whether they are alike in ethnicity, religion, occupation, and the extent to which they provide support, companionship, and practical help (C. Fischer 1982).

Of these 19,417 personal relationships, 42 percent are with kin, both closely related and less so. People with the least amount of education average 8.2 kin, but those with the most education average 6.8, despite including a wider range of categories in their networks. The most-educated group include in their networks many more co-workers (0.7 named by the least educated, 2.8 by the most), as well as many more people who are "just friends" (2.5 compared with 6.8) (ibid.: 41). That is, the most occupationally mobile and, presumably, least traditional people name as many kin as friends (6.8). Furthermore, middle-income people name more kin than those with either low or high incomes (ibid.: 81). All told, this is surprising evidence perhaps that the largest group in our population, contrary to widespread belief, doesn't use its economic mobility or its worldliness to run from its roots. But at the same time the evidence is testimony to the strength of a kinship ideal that turns other forms of family into culture breakers who are to be avoided and disvalued socially—and legally.

That contradiction between reality and a "Platonic essence" of family continued to plague social science until recently, insisting "upon the reality of a universal form of the family" and treating "real families in the world" as only "imperfect shadows" (Skolnick 1979: 299–300). FAMILY remains the constitutive, elementary unit of every social order, construed as it is through singular yet variegated concepts. Americans believe it to be set apart from every other social unit by their concept of the Sacred: the "family is a sacred institution and the fundamental institution of our society. . . . [T]he monogamous family is the outcome of evolution from lower forms of life and is the final, divinely ordained form" (Lynd and Lynd 1937: 410). Its "immaculate lawn" is sacred ground, and that sanctity envelops its neighborhood, as a matter of constitutional guarantee in the Belle Terre decision: residential areas are rightly regarded as a "sanctuary" providing the "blessings of quiet seclusion" (416 U.S. 9).

Family also depends on husbands and fathers for its legitimacy, and mothers and children have their place derivatively. While women and children are wiring their neighborhood networks, their husbands and fathers are held to the ethos of the yeoman, sturdy and independent, ready to pick up and go when industrial opportunity knocks. Beginning with the Homestead Act and cresting with the Sun Belt shift, America has offered its bounties to those free to go after them. A man's family is supposed to be socially self-sufficient, a machine-part of industrial order, geared to accompany him in their pursuit. So it comes to be that women's and children's ties along the block with neighbors and their braidings into the community can be more than brakes on mobility. These can turn into signs of men's failure in a work system mined with the risks of failure: immobile families can mean a man misses a chance at the next rung up, just as shattering as a demotion.

WIDOWS and DIVORCEES are cultural discrepancies from the ideal family norm. They experience both stigma and hostility. Profaning the sacred quality of family, widows and divorcees bear a stigma not put on widowers or divorced men: the absence of a man breaches the norm of family, for its definition insists on the presence of a man, as marked by the U.S. Census category "female-headed household." The widow is stranded between being married and unmarried, and for perpetually upsetting social equilibrium, she is thrice feared. She stands not only as deviant from the ideal, but as fateful warning and dangerous siren. "It could happen to us," happy couples can see. "The widow is stigmatized and she has to fight against society's automatic tendency to consider her taboo because her husband is dead," Lynn Caine writes of her own experiences. "The progression from wife to widow and back to woman is a hard one. It is impossible for some widows and they sink into that lonely ghetto of widowhood until they, too, die" (1974: 143).

The breach calls for sanctions, and the first one is isolation (Lopata 1973: 193, 272). The widow is "ostracized by our couple-oriented society," as it keeps its distance from whatever is dissonant to the sacred family form. Feeling like "an untouchable," the widow also feels "empty and incomplete because, like most women, she gained her identity through marriage. And when her husband dies, there she was. A widow. Empty. Without her husband to validate her existence. Without an identity of her own. . . . Being a widow is like living in a country where nobody speaks your language. A country that considers you an untouchable" (Caine 1974: 120).

Widows forced out of local society yearn to belong again. The president of a Houston homeowner's association recounts the complaints he has to deal with from residents: "What I'm getting is an excuse to interact with another human being. They're lonely people. Oh, loneliness is a very substantial problem in our neighborhood. In many cases, these are widows." The lines around MARRIAGE and FAMILY force them onto the sidelines, oblique and incongruous.

Another punishment is the pass. "Neither shall you covet your neighbor's wife," nor, the Ninth Commandment should be amended to include, your neighbor's ex-spouse or widow. "I knew one woman," a woman in Houston told me, "who encouraged another to get out of an intolerable marriage—and then had nothing to do with her out of fear of her own husband's interest in her! People in a neighborhood pull away from divorced women. They fear that divorce will reflect on them. They fear that the problem would come into their house. Even children will turn the problem off—when the divorced woman called her friend, the children wouldn't give her the message." Fears are transformed into polluted, contagious people, to be fled from.

A divorced woman in Minneapolis told me that among her neighbors "the stereotypes are that if you're a divorced woman, you're having different people coming and going. They just assume you're loose. When my son and I came back from a weekend with a male friend of mine who my neighbors had seen a lot here, they asked my son if he was an uncle. They just wanted to hear my son say he wasn't our relative. It would be worse elsewhere, because I know the people here and they know I know a lot about them and they know a lot about me. If they didn't, everything could easily get blown out of proportion. That's why I'm glad I had already lived in this neighborhood before getting divorced." Yet, she went on, "since I've been separated I've had a couple of experiences of neighbor men coming here and thinking that they were the great answer to my situation. I just played it real cold and got them out of here. They think, 'Oh, she is such a poor thing, she must need me,' or whatever it is. They like to feel important. The one has persisted three or four times, whenever I see him. If his wife goes upstairs for something he would get real obsessed with his masculinity." Does he come over here? "No, it is right at their house, when I am over there. I don't put myself in that situation if I see she is going to be leaving us. I get busy doing something else."

Divorce rates confirm that marriages are as likely to be tenuous as strong, and temptation alone may be enough to break a threadbare bond. Some of neighbors' social distancing may be one way of resisting it. Women may go especially slow in welcoming newcomers, or in making neighborhood friends at all, to limit their own temptations as well as their husbands'. Discussing differences in couples' social lives, one woman observed to me, "Men don't stray from their yards"—perhaps as the simplest of all ways not to stray maritally.

The prototypical family represented by the inviolable couple keeps the unmarried well beyond its social pale, more so in suburbs perhaps than in cities. Husbandless or wifeless people, lacking legal ties to another person, stand outside any sanctioned relationship, except to their natal families, which are likely to be in another neighborhood or a different city. Men who are widowers, divorced, or bachelors carry their gender's cultural significance with them like a shell insulating them from the social punishments visited upon single women. Their welcome at dinner parties signals the difference. Precisely when single women may eat with married people who are entertaining is carefully circumscribed: almost never at dinner. Now married, a once-divorced woman recollected that even her closest married friend during her separation and after her divorce often invited her only for lunch. "When I started dating my present husband, my friend asked immediately, 'How soon can I have you down for dinner?' Now I should say that she had never given me the slightest feeling that she didn't want me to be around her husband when I was on my own. But there is something about the social dinner in the home. She just wouldn't invite me without a partner."

The guest list for meals is itself a cultural product of ideas about Sex and Time of Day; just as the "extra man" is a dinner staple, the extra woman is an anomaly, partly because the "social dinner in the home" combines Home and Work as an extension of the man's occupation. But perhaps also because hostesses may be protecting themselves and married guests from a siren's call.

CONVERTING FRIENDS TO FAMILY

Yet only when sitting for its portrait does the American family raising children illustrate the long-standing ideal form of an American "nuclear," "independent," and "intact" family. Leaving aside the increasing population of single-parent households, the snapshots of everyday life, even for wife-husband households, reveal quite another image in three common situations: when they have young children, when they have any children at all living at home, and when they settle into newly developing areas—and as the baby-boom population crests in founding its own families, it will have little choice but to settle in the new suburbs edging the old. In these circumstances, the everyday routines of wife-husband families give lie to the American ideal of the "single-family" detached from and personally independent of all others. In each of these situations FRIENDSHIP among NEIGHBORS crosses the line into KINSHIP—more so, however, for women and children than for men. Withal, however, Americans also believe that indelible lines separate NEIGHBOR, FRIEND, and RELATIVE and that they ought to stay that way.

Each family should not be personally interdependent with any other, according to the weight Americans place on Individualism, keeping clear residentially, now as in earlier times, even of its own branches. Families should express concern for their relatives, offer financial aid, and participate in each other's life ceremonies, but even relatives should not live with one another or pool their resources—so state the prevalent norms. Americans' overwhelming preference, historically and currently, for the single-family-detached house is as much a sign of individualism as of privacy.

When FRIENDSHIP seeks equal footing with KINSHIP it stumbles into a thicket of amorphous forms fashioned from the concepts through which we know and experience neighbors, relatives, and friends. Wholly made from relationships with neighbors who had been strangers, who then became friends who feel like relatives, these "extended" forms of "family" or "household" are ambiguous all around. They confound friendship by using the same metaphors in experiencing it as apply to kinship, yet these forms are incongruous with the concepts of Blood and Law ruling our recognition of kin: we are supposed to have our relatives only through birth, marriage, and adoption. Even when we have them by marriage, the ambiguities can remain, as ubiquitous tensions toward in-laws attest.

The "joking relationship" with mothers-in-law (or jokes about them) is one common expression of anxiety.

"You know everybody on the block and for blocks around when you have young children," so agrees a group of Minneapolis women. Without them, neighboring is minimal; with them, another form of "family" comes into being. About 75 percent of women having three or more children are intensively involved with their neighbors compared with about 20 percent of women without children, according to a study of the neighboring activities of about 600 women in 12 Chicago suburbs and city neighborhoods. Suburban women who have children and also work outside the home still are in touch with neighbors—about 75 percent of those with one child, 80 percent of those with two, and about 85 percent of those with three (Lopata 1971: 283).

"Women without children are withdrawn and miserable because they're out of social life," observes a woman in Houston. "It's not a real community without children. When we were new here, it was one of my children who first knocked on a neighbor's door and led the way for the family." A study in an Ohio subdivision reports that "if you have young children it is next to impossible to keep apart" from neighbors, and when you do not, you "live a life quite separate" from them; people without children made fewer friends (Bracey 1964: 125).

"Neighboring" waxes and wanes throughout the life cycle, even as we are never without neighbors nor cease to be neighbors ourselves. Neighboring is not a lifelong activity, and it doesn't come naturally. Neighboring is almost wholly contingent on offspring in American society, and it frequently lasts only one long moment of the life cycle. Belonging in most suburban neighborhoods depends on having children: "It's not a real community without children." Simply because his children have grown up and moved away, a minister in a Minneapolis suburb lacks "anything in common now" with his neighbors: "Out where I live now, on a lake, there are all kinds of homes around us. When we first lived there it seemed like it was 100 miles away from everyone else. But now we are like ships that pass in the night. On Sundays, for instance, you sit out in the back yard, and there isn't a soul around. They are off to cabins. And during the week they're at work. You don't get to know them. Once in a while somebody will come around—we have a residents' association—and you don't even know the guy who just called on you to give money for keeping the weeds down on the lake. It's kind of sad, or maybe it's because I am getting older, but I used to know my neighbors around here. I think what enters into the picture a lot about this community-feeling business is that my kids have grown up and they have left the nest. My wife and I ramble around in our house alone, and we don't have anything in common now with all these other people. We used to when they had their kids. That's part of the ball game."

"Fourteen years ago we had really close relationships with our neighbors," recounts a man in Minneapolis. "I think it has more to do with your age than where you live. The kids were the same age, and we were more concerned with staying home and raising kids. That just lends more time to socializing with your neighbors and being friends. We did nothing more than move two miles to the east, and the whole situation changed. Our kids were older, and we became more involved with church and school activities. Some of our neighbors were older. It changed completely how we looked at our neighbors. We were very friendly, but we weren't as close as we were with our old neighbors." Another man adds: "I have a lot of friends dropping in from church, both friends and neighbors. But now more friends from church. I have more to do with people down the block whose kids play with mine than with people on either side in their 50s and 60s whose kids are all gone."

Although the life cycle seems to take precedence over income, education, ethnicity, region, and race, there are other patterns. For example, women living in "ethnic neighborhoods" are likely to regard as stranger any neighbor not also belonging to her nationality and religious group, no matter the ages of her children. Nor are families with low incomes likely to convert neighbors into friends when they feel they cannot reciprocate in the exchanges of food and help that do so much to define friendship. They certainly won't if they feel, as poor people can, that neighbors, no differently from the rest of the world, will victimize and exploit them (Lopata 1971: 260–261).

Not only after but before the child-raising stage, Neighborliness has so little meaning (which is to say that it enters into so few choices) that the neighborhood is neutral if not negative social space. Households without children find them nuisances and are not beyond saying so. "We do not need to socialize any more," an older couple explains with relief, but as they were raising their children, noise and mischief were borne mutually. No longer need their conduct be predicated on the Reciprocity on which community depends; noise and pranks become only irritations. A single man has become "a big bad bear," faced with the antics and teasing of 28 children on the block, says one of the mothers in a San Francisco suburb: "One big irritation is that we have a single man living across the street, in his early 30s who's lived here about three years. In the last year, he's become very annoying to all of us because he doesn't have children. Children are children to a degree. My children have always been taught to respect other people's property. But I don't think that doing a somersault on a lawn is any reason to get all huffed up and puffed up. I don't know whether he needs to get married or he needs to move. It's just that simple." What did he do to the child who turned the somersault? "Just mouths off—a lot of threats. We know him well enough to let it go. All the kids have gotten together—they pulled a plug, and turned off the main switch in his electric line. When he moved in he was friendly and sweet and everybody's good buddy. And then he just kind of made an about-face. The kids have gotten to the point where they either ignore him or they mouth back at him. There's one day where he's all sweetness and honey and the next day he's like a big bad bear. There's evidently something bothering him, but still there are 28 children on this block who have their rights."

Children's need for other children can even keep grandparents connected with neighbors way past their time—or inclination. "My husband won't speak to this messy neighbor, but when our granddaughter visits in the summer, his six children are the only ones she has to play with. So I keep up a friendly enough relationship, despite."

When you have "small children," one woman in Minneapolis told me, "mothers stay home all day and hope to God someone will come over and see them." "Pediatricians around here began to find that women were bringing in perfectly healthy babies with trumped-up complaints, and soon discovered that they just wanted the social contact. These women were especially stuck in their houses, and didn't just *feel* isolated and removed, but actually were," reports a man who works for his Virginia suburb's weekly newspaper.

Neighboring waxes when mothers and children have little choice but to be each other's constant companions. Their isolation and confinement to children's chatter are as little "naturally" satisfying to women as they are to men, and they work free of feeling thwarted as whole human beings by belonging to an alliance of like-situated women and children for the stimulation, empathy, and recognition only they can offer. The mother-to-mother relationship is so treasured that mothers will openly put aside "this-family" law: "Our children's fights are not ours." Another mother puts it, "When kids are involved, it's best to let them figure it out and not get involved."

The dailiness of her exchanges with "convenient" neighbors blossomed into "close friends," and one Californian finds the distinction impossible to maintain. While I was there, her son was playing with a boy on the block whose mother had had surgery that week, and she was taking her turn having him stay over. "I'm sure that in any friendship you'd exchange favors. It's just that neighbors are convenient for more of your everyday needs, like borrowing things or watching children if you have a doctor's appointment, rather than leaving them across town with friends. So I guess we *use* neighbors more than we do friends, actually. But a lot of my neighbors have become my close friends. There are four of us within this block that have become very close." Fellow homemakers constituted about 30 percent of all the people full-time homemakers named in C. Fischer's study of personal networks. Compared with the proportion of work friends of "highly educated professionals," for example, homemakers reveal "considerably more immersion in a homemaking 'world'" (C. Fischer 1982: 223). "Women with children at home had fewer friends and associates, engaged in fewer social activities, had less reliable social support, and had more localized networks than did otherwise similar women without children. . . . And, as other research has shown, children take a psychological toll too. Mothers reported feeling more harassed and generally felt worse than did other respondents" (ibid.: 253).

Nor do children flourish without playmates. One mother feels that her son's early years without playmates "really changed his life." The family, now in a modest subdivision in California, had lived in "semicountry" in Illinois for several years: "We had a couple of acres, just lawn and woods—it wasn't planted or anything. We thought, what a great place to bring up a child—except for one thing. It wasn't that it was so far out, but it was undeveloped and there weren't any other children around. Our neighbors weren't close, and I just agonized for my youngest boy. It really changed his life. I really feel that it will be a long time before there's compensation for what he missed in the beginning." He was shy of children his own age, preferring those much younger, she told me. Both mother and child were overweight and she commented spontaneously how, in their mutual isolation and boredom, they had taken to the consolations of food.

Just about as soon as children no longer require a caregiver's constant attention, their natal family boundaries expand to take in playmates of neighboring households or those found at their neighborhood school. "I never see my kids from morning to night in this neighborhood—they have so many other kids to play with." I asked a man in California, Where would you prefer to live? "Upcountry, but my kids need the neighborhood relationships. They're teenagers and it's very beneficial for them." A Houston woman agrees, speaking for her husband too: "We don't depend on the neighborhood but my children do. They play outside along the block."

These children's alliances are a second way in which the idea of FAMILY surreptitiously expands to include nonrelatives. Changing and shifting as they may, these alliances take on a life of their own, to their families' relief and distress, camping out at each other's houses, grazing through pantries and refrigerators. By virtue of following the rules of each house, they are "adopted" into it. "My children know the rules of this house, and if their friends don't abide by them, I just say you can't have them here," says a man in California.

Teenagers rehearse their coming departure from their families by investing most of their energies outside it. Their deepest cares are bound up with friends. Studies also show what parents keep finding out—that peer influence often outweighs theirs. Even so, parents feed and indulge whichever of their teenagers' friends they disapprove of least, knowing how much of a difference they make to the family's life as a whole. These alliances of adolescence distort the ideal of family markedly, carving out another cultural iceberg: familial stresses can be misperceived as interpersonal when they may instead be reflecting incongruities between the galaxy of Blood, Law, and the Sacred, from which family takes its meanings, and the constellation of Choice and Loyalty, which sustains friends.

Pioneers sharing the experiences of settling into newly developed areas is a third way that families become mutually involved as they never did before or will after. They work on joint projects, borrow and lend equipment, and share their skills, time, and personal resources. After a time, these temporary work groups dissolve and people fade back into the familial self-sufficiency that is the American standard. Weathering a pioneer phase on any frontier nourishes a unique solidarity, and as a growing population continues to suburbanize the metropolitan hinterlands, belonging to a "kindred of cooperation" (Mayer 1966) is an experience many more Americans will have.

"All young families had moved into this tract even before the city had approved the street, and they all became very, very close," a woman in California remembers. "The children and the mothers and eventually the husbands. We've more or less depended on each other for transportation to shopping centers, and if a mother was ill, we'd gang up on her and go in and clean her house. A birth or someone had a hysterectomy, we all went to her house and cleaned up. We helped each other build fences and put brick walkways in and had barbecues, and all the women were running around in the morning trading babysitting and all. But about two years ago people began selling the homes, moving to other areas. Some we've kept in close contact with. The ones we haven't, surprisingly, are the ones who stayed right here in town. But the new people who've moved in are all working in the daytime, the women aren't home, there's just nobody there, and so we don't have much of a close relationship anymore."

Reporting the most neighbors in their active, personal networks in C. Fischer's study were people who lived in new and fast-growing neighborhoods. One was "a relatively new development of modest single-family homes, inhabited by young families, and situated in one of the most distant communities" located in a "rapidly growing resort and retirement area of the Sierras." The other, "a quiet, family neighborhood with somewhat more spacious and slightly older single family homes" was located "near the downtown of an explosively growing city an hour from San Francisco" (C. Fischer 1982: 99).

Having enjoyed the "communal neighborhood" phase, one man in California was nevertheless without regrets when it came to an end: "I'm not an interdependent person within the neighborhood. I don't live in what you'd call an interlocking type of neighborhood. It started out that way. The first summer after I moved in, everybody at night was out in front sitting around talking. You had a certain degree of communal neighborhood—you help me, I'll help you type of thing. I'd say that lasted two years. We used to have block parties, and I don't know of anything along that line in the last five years. . . . I was raised on a farm, and my experience there was of a *real* interdependency, more so than the basic suburban neighborhood where there's really not much need. If I really have to have something, if I need trash hauled, I'll go hire it hauled. I don't rely on somebody else."

Sharing hardship builds one of the most enduring "experiential gestalts," and it commonly results in solidarities that are describable only as KINSHIP (R. T. Smith, 1978). "When my husband was in the navy and we lived in navy housing, even though people kept coming in and going out, I think I formed some of my most lasting and fast and best friendships in that period. Because when we were there we were all in the same boat, we all had little kids, we were there in this particular group of housing because our husbands were all pretty much the same rank, so we all made the same amount of money, and everybody knew what everybody else made. We all had the same amount we could spend on entertainment. And my husband would go out to sea and maybe the husband of the gal next door would be home, and so if I needed anything to be fixed, he'd come over and fix it for me, and vice versa. So much in common right down the line, the way you part your hair and shine your shoes."

These three common experiences feel like kinship because they too draw on the absence of Choice: neighbors offer none. Like blood relatives and the in-laws who come with a spouse, neighbors are a given in these situations, while friends are selected. Only the neighborhood is a matter of choice. Neighborhood "character" and "reputation" (the cultural package that real estate agents sell) are the only index we have to the individual characters and reputations of the people living there. We take who we find.

As we do in our families: "You can't choose your relatives, but you can choose your friends." "If they weren't your relatives, they probably wouldn't be your friends." Being unwilled and involuntary, relationships with blood relatives and in-laws are set apart from all others—together with unique obligations and rights that go without saying. In these three situations—having very young children, having any school-age children at home, and settling into a newly developing area—neighbors offer prospective relationships just as involuntary, just as mutually obligating, and just as taken for granted.

"I have two very, very close friends right here in my neighborhood," a woman in Minneapolis told me. "I consider them just like family, and we exchange things all the time. Borrowing back and forth. I don't even think of them as gifts anymore. If I made something extra, I'll bring it over. One of them is a wonderful cook and she'll do the same. So I don't think of them as favors or gifts. It's just something that we do."

Under these circumstances the residential domain follows the same contours as that of kinship, drawing on the same concepts and their signs— Blood, Law, and Love (D. M. Schneider 1980). From the neighborhood, a territory in the natural world, flow social connections as unchosen as those supplied by Blood and Marriage. Vows taken in the neighborhood social contract are as binding: "Love they neighbor." "Keep up with the mowing and painting." "Take in the trash cans." "Don't park here."

Sharing territory confers consubstantiality; that is, in sharing common ground, people believe themselves to share common substance, analogous to Blood. "The substance of which people are made is . . . closely identified with the substance of which . . . place is made" (D. M. Schneider, 1979: 165). Our common conversational opener, "What's your hometown?" expresses that belief in these powers of homeground—or motherland or fatherland, province or district, even a part of town—to substantiate a social bond. Like the genes of our bloodline, that territory, we believe, remains an indelible and telling part of our being. Finding themselves to be from the same hometown, Americans feel nothing less than what they call a bond of kinship.

They may not last, these daily criss-crossings, as long as the ties of blood or even marriage. Children leave home, couples move away, the women lose touch. Yet, like blood ties, they do endure biologically: in *memory* "imperishable," these experiences create vaults of irreplaceable feelings of pleasure, gratitude, loyalty, love. "I think I formed some of my most lasting and fast and best friendships in that period," says that woman about her time as a navy wife. As most of us can say of school and college peers, military mates, and high school buddies.

Yet, despite these three common experiences of neighbor as a friend who feels as close as a relative (if not more so), American norms insist that those are entirely different kinds of relationships that ought to stay that way. Friendship takes a weak second place to the highest value put on involvement with relatives and an exclusive intimacy with spouses. Sociologists label women's and children's friendships as "secondary," describing them as "socializing," or merely "support," in accordance with the norm that the only relationships really mattering are the "primary relationships" of family.

Americans also believe that you can't count on friends the way you count on "real" relatives. To Americans, friendship has an "interstitial quality" (D. M. Schneider 1980: 53). Unlike a relative, "a friend is dropped if the friend fails to maintain desirable standards of loyalty, or solidarity, or fidelity. Performance in a friend is everything, for there is nothing else. A good friend is one who executes the tasks of loyalty with skill and courage and dispatch. A good friend is there in time of need and does not bumble the job. And a good friend is dropped for failing to meet the proper standards of performance. . . . Friends are relatives who can be ditched if necessary, and relatives are friends who are with you through thick and thin whether you like it or not and whether they do their job properly or not. You can really count on your relatives" (ibid.: 54). Friends are, all told, ambiguous relatives.

Nearby strangers, however, "come through better" than can distant kin. "Especially because we don't have relatives around here, my neighborhood offers my children and myself the kind of security that having relatives around offers other people. Without them, you need somebody else that cares about you, I mean *genuinely* cares about you and what happens to your life. Our neighborhood comes through better than relatives," says a woman in Minneapolis. As it did in the time of Hesiod, eighth century B.C.:

> He who findeth a good neighbor findeth a precious thing.
> When on your home falls unforeseen distress,
> Half-clothed come neighbors, kinsmen stay [at home] to dress.
> (*Works and Days*, lines 340–346)

PENALIZING NEWCOMERS

Keeping the lines straight around FAMILY and COMMUNITY helps us maintain equilibrium in the face of life's unceasing incongruities and discrepancies. Yet both have little choice but to deal with real strangers: communities see the arrival of NEWCOMERS, families decide to realign themselves by taking in FRIENDS and IN-LAWS and by producing the next generation. Social succession is never without frictions, and community habits and family customs deal with their disruptions to the status quo, each in its way.

In this mobile society, newcomers are numerous. For their welcome and a sense of belonging in a new community, they depend willy-nilly on old-timers. Cold-shouldered more often than not, the newcomer, who is STRANGER and OUTSIDER as well, experiences the social forces that novelty, discrepancy, and ambiguity set in motion. In being seen as signs of social disequilibrium, the personal comforts of belonging can elude newcomers for a long time. No matter what newcomers may do as individuals, they are likely to be afflicted by the social pain built into old-timers' strategies for resisting a realignment of familiar meanings. OLD-TIMERS may freeze NEWCOMERS out, deny their presence, keep them at a distance, or fight against their interests.

Throughout America's settlement, each newly arrived ethnic and racial group has had to look to OLD-TIMERS for its first step up the ladder but, more than likely, instead met stone walls keeping them out. The NEWCOMER category alone sets off its own social alarms. "We all get along just fine—all our ethnic groups, French, Irish, Italian, Yankee—and Newcomer," says a resident of a New England town experiencing high rates of growth.

Real differences from old-timers also keep newcomers outsiders. Seniority is a social asset partly because important resources—money, skill, power—accumulate only over time. That old-timers are reluctant to share these goes without saying. But that does not seem to tell the whole story: even where old-timers and newcomers are social equals sharing the same standards, beliefs, sensibilities, and manners, the distinction is maintained and the old-timer cadre dominates (Elias and Scotson 1965: 104, 149, 179).

Newcomers take their exclusions personally, stunned by the social potency of the hostilities their novelty arouses. So problematic is this category that we have no nationally consistent or locally reliable set of customs for greeting and including newcomers. To the contrary: their prolonged quarantine and extended initiation rites are penalties for being new. During "the first two years of residence half of the newcomers don't get much beyond membership in church, unions, or PTA though some plunged into fund raising. But there is a sharp increase in participation in the two to five years after arrival" (Packard [1972] 1974: 250). In between, my interviews found, is a sharp increase in disappointment, bewilderment, bitterness, and genuine social hardship.

More humane norms are in order, says one commentator: "Though an immediate neighbor's role may be less than that of a friend, he should be a person who welcomes you to a community, who sees that you have a chance to meet a variety of the neighbors who might interest you, and who has a special understanding with you that you will help each other in emergencies" (ibid.: 145). Such arrangements are not widespread, however, for "neighbors have become undependable at helping newcomers integrate into the new community," and in their stead, about 4000 "newcomer clubs" across the country have come to specialize in what neighbors don't provide. "Newcomer clubbing becomes a way of life and a world of its own, usually quite apart from the world of the people who consider the town their home town" (ibid.: 151).

A brochure of advice put out by United Van Lines is hardheaded: "'The days of neighbors welcoming new families are almost gone. You will have to make the first move in most cases'" (ibid.: 147). An informal survey of customs for welcoming newcomers asked, "'In your neighborhood is there any common practice for welcoming new neighbors?'" In one town labelled "'transient,'" 90 percent said, "'No,'" but in another called "'stable,'" 64 percent also said "'No'" (ibid.: 206–207).

Newcomers get together in clubs because old-timers don't make a first, or second, move. A Philadelphian transplanted to Minneapolis faced that fact: "I knew from living back East in that community that you had to go and call on someone if you're the newcomer. People may not come to you. They may, but they may not. And I know that's even more true now that I've done it myself. *You're* the one who has to ask people in, and *you're* the one who has to ask people to go places." Is that because they don't really *need* you? I asked. "Yes, you have to show them that they need a new acquaintance. Otherwise they already have enough friends."

Should the new person in a neighborhood be the one to knock on doors? I asked a woman in Minneapolis. "No. You pay a penalty for moving into an established neighborhood, and you just have to wait. Children are a big key. Children aren't afraid to get things going." With a deep sigh, another Minneapolis woman recollects: "We've lived here five years, and it took a long time before I felt comfortable in the neighborhood. People just don't come rushing forward. I would have felt a little awkward introducing myself. I think it's better if the old-timers who've come here first take the initiative." The social dominance of old-timers is a fact of life to her.

A couple in a Virginia suburb discuss the relations between newcomers and old-timers:

Woman: "Newcomers have a difficult time becoming part of things. The old-timers are generally saturated with friends and people they know and don't have enough energy for them."

Man: "You met them in the spring. An April day like today, everybody would go out and take a walk. If you move in in November you probably wouldn't meet any of your neighbors until now."

Woman: "Old-timers don't go out of their way, unless they have something very much in common like a child of the same age, the same profession. But just because people happen to move in—no."

The change in women's days also has its effect: with many more women working outside their homes, the daily neighbor just isn't around. A woman in California points out that neighborhood "unfriendliness" could be a result of that: "Newcomers especially from out of state have a more difficult time—I feel for these people, I really do. They complain about unfriendliness in their neighborhoods. That's the hardest for me to understand, because when we were young we found a great comradeship with our neighbors. We were all in the same financial strait. Now that's lacking because so many women are working full time."

The unfriendliness isn't everywhere, of course. The nice gestures don't need to be explained: "My wife brings any newcomers a pan of rolls. She's done that since we've been there, six years. When she sees they're done unloading the truck she brings over a pot of coffee and a pan of rolls and says, 'Welcome to the neighborhood.' "

The New Neighbors' League is a national organization with local chapters devoted to dealing wholly with the obstacles to belonging that old-timers put before newcomers. From the presidency down to each committee chair, any one person holds the job not longer than about six months. Through this quick turnover of each position, the league symbolizes its members' hopes that the old-timer world at large will be as flexible about and generous with its social assets. A woman in Houston calls New Neighbors a "lifesaver, a godsend, or any of those other terms, for me and countless women."

In warding off the dangers they attribute to newcomers, old-timers are perhaps passing along their own experiences of quarantine. A man in Virginia tells of living for several years in a suburb near Boston: "I stood every working day on the train platform at the same time each day, and it was three years before anyone spoke to me. In those same years, my wife kept waiting for her name to come to the top of the waiting lists for volunteer jobs in the community. All the jobs were taken—even volunteering at the local hospital—and only deaths or a job change would get her to the top of the list." They were happiest upon leaving.

Utterly desperate, a woman newly moved to Minneapolis finally turned to the New Neighbors' League. She had children, she lived in a completely settled residential area, and yet: "We felt isolated moving out here from Pennsylvania, and we expected that joining a church would be helpful, but it wasn't. That was the one place where we joined immediately—maybe too fast. That was a real learning experience. My oldest boy was in his third year of confirmation classes, and we had to find a church right away. So we took the closest one, and it didn't work. We still belong to it, but we found out very quickly, after attending every single function that they had, that they were extremely, well 'cliquey' is really not quite the word—but anyway. You'd see people there, and they'd say 'Hello,' and that would be the last you'd see them til the following Sunday, and they'd say 'Hello' again. We'd go, the six of us, to functions—a potluck supper—and we took up a whole table. Only if someone had an extra kid would they come and join your table. It was really very difficult, especially upsetting because at that time we had nothing else.

"Finally, my husband said that he was going to speak to the minister, to see what he'd suggest because I was really upset. The minister said the same thing happened to him! That he was here about six years before he felt that he was a member of the congregation rather than just the minister. He said he knew it was difficult, but once you're accepted, it's great. But you don't always have six years."

When newcomers want to do things the American way and they seek advice from a typical etiquette manual, they'll find full cognizance of the antipathies, apathy, and suspicions old-timers are likely to entertain toward them. *Vogue's Book of Etiquette and Good Manners* lists "Four Don'ts":

> Out of a sincere desire to become part of the community, a well-intentioned newcomer can sometimes alienate the established residents. Here are suggestions for avoiding some fairly common pitfalls. . . . *Don't join groups indiscriminately*, whether you are interested in them or not. The local historical society, for instance, is unlikely to mean anything to you at first, and joining it will not turn you into a ready-made, established resident. . . . *Don't thrust yourself at once into local politics.* However active you may have been in your former community, you should bear in mind that you do not yet know the particular tenor and problems of this one. It is better to remain in the background, listen, and learn before showing any inclination to become involved, even if asked to participate. . . . *Don't make immediate, large contributions* to local institutions or causes, such as the public library or the town beautification program. You cannot care about these things as the residents do, and they know it. Such donations look like an attempt to buy one's way into the community. If asked, it is best to give a modest amount. . . . *Don't give a big cocktail party* for everyone in your area whether you have met them or not, or before you have been called on. Some people believe this a practical way to make friends. On the contrary, it violates the custom that residents take the initiative. (*Vogue* 1969: 581–582)

After following *Vogue's* advice and keeping the lowest of profiles, newcomers can work their way into things by taking on the unappealing jobs in community organizations, notably that of raising money: a contemporary form of hazing. Unpopular groups will be especially glad of them; any organization already short of members will "instantly appreciate" them. The Virginia couple discuss newcomers and their condominium homeowner association:

Woman: "Most clusters have about twice-yearly cluster parties, where you get together, everybody bringing some food. About one-third of the people show up, and that number only after making a real effort of calling up and sending out flyers."

Man: "You're lucky to get 30 percent of the people to come to any group meeting."

Woman: "If newcomers take an active part, it's instantly appreciated. They're not going to be newcomers very long."

In having been first-come and first-served by fate, accident, or design, old-timers in a community not only lay claim to having more rights to its resources. They keep tight control over social succession, worrying how newcomers will realign local social order. Fending off newcomers takes many forms—the "environmental protection" movement and its "no-growth" companion are recent collective tactics. Estimating their public costs is an initiation rite spawning a research industry, especially in suburbs: what newcomers may bring in tax revenues, the public services they require may use up, and when municipal income and outgo are not in balance old-timers see themselves as paying newcomers' costs, a belief that does not consistently or automatically correspond to the fiscal facts (Ellman 1976). Nevertheless, the belief persists widely that newcomers cost more in public services than do old-timers, and proposed developments not showing a tax "profit" are likely to be rejected by local planning and zoning boards. As much to the point may be the fact that "growth" adds to the supply of housing available, thereby lowering the resale prices of the housing already there and occupied by old-timers keeping close track of its market value.

America's settlement history is convincing evidence that NEWCOMER dominates any other considerations: the same ethnic groups had very different receptions in the various regions depending on which groups preceded them and which came after. That is, their ethnicity (language, food preferences, social customs, and religion) played less a part in their welcome than their position in the sequence of arrival and the place they were allowed to take in the systems of meaning of those already there. The two understandably have become confused, given the fact that for 350 years this country's growth has been seeded by one-time newcomers from overseas. For example, immigrants who were Irish, Jewish, and Japanese had far from uniform experiences. In the West, the Irish "met far less resistance than they did in New England, where the social system had congealed long before their arrival. . . . In San Francisco Jews acquired an especially favorable status from their large share in molding the basic institutions of the city. On the other hand, they have endured a particularly bad situation in Minneapolis where they had arrived late in the city's development. The same relationship applied to the Japanese in two adjacent California towns in the early twentieth century. In one the Japanese settled first and were accepted in the civic life of the American society that grew up around them; in the other they came later and met bitter persecution as their numbers grew" (Higham 1963: 113).

Regional and local histories of welcome are likely to be unique anthropologies of local knowledge; how local schemata of meanings were constituted determined how new arrivals were regarded, whether as guests, visitors or tourists, temporary residents, permanent settlers, or intruders. New arrivals are also favorite topics of gossip, perhaps another expression of the anxiety they arouse in being Near but still Outside, a sign that the receiving group is gradually realigning itself to give them realistic shape: gossip as a rite of purification administered by old-timers to acclimate themselves gradually to changed circumstances.

Definitively belonging within a system of meaning is socially critical, even in temporary situations. For example, shipboard cliques made up wholly of simultaneous newcomers form so early in the voyage that anyone wanting to join in even a day later is likely to pay the penalty of having little or no say in the group's arrangements, forced to fall in with the favored spot for deck chairs and meal sittings (Wood 1934: 47). It is the speed with which cliques form in an inchoate setting that is remarkable; the haste suggests how crucial to social survival shared meanings are.

People in transit are, by definition, neither exactly here nor there, and in societies the world over, calling established meanings into question, they bear the brunt of social hostilities in remarkably similar ways. Today's patterns for dealing with strangers and newcomers are mirror images of those the poetics of discrepancy expresses in rites of passage. In the first act of these social performances, special rituals separate people from their starting place; in the second act, they enter limbo; and the third incorporates them into their social destination. "[C]hanges of condition do not occur without disturbing the life of society and the individual, and it is the function of rites of passage to reduce their harmful effects," so wrote Arnold van Gennep ([1908] 1960: 13), anthropologist and folklorist, in his classic study of hundreds of rites of birth, initiation, marriage, death, and travel, among others, in many societies. Through these rites "a person leaves one world behind him and enters a new one" (ibid.: 19). "For groups, as well as for individuals, life itself means to separate and to be reunited, to change form and condition, to die and to be reborn. It is to act and to cease, to wait and rest, and then to begin acting again, but in a different way" (ibid.: 189).

These performances act out the biological processes involved in maintaining meaning and "reducing the harmful effects" of novelty. The rites play out the neurophysiological processes of immobility, startle, and gradual accommodation. These rites themselves introduce an overload of novelty, as it were, to the ordinary routines of daily life, and to defuse their charge, these performances are socially compartmentalized, stylized, unchanging, frozen. A familiar form cushions the impacts of unfamiliar events. Too much discrepancy and the arousal ends in paralysis: the solemn occasions of ritual and the special times for telling myths and folktales are themselves figurative metastatements of the paralysis.

Limbo is marked by the "pivoting of the sacred": "A man at home, in his tribe, lives in the secular realm; he moves into the realm of the sacred when he goes on a journey and finds himself a foreigner near a camp of strangers," just as a pregnant woman "also becomes sacred to all other women of the tribe except her close relatives; and these other women constitute in relation to her a profane world. . . . Thus the 'magic circles' pivot, shifting as a person moves from one place in society to another. The categories and concepts which embody them operate in such a way that whoever passes through the various positions of a lifetime one day sees the sacred where before he has seen the profane, or vice versa" (ibid.: 12–13). These ritual passages occur in graduated steps, protecting both the central character, the cast, and, most of all perhaps, the audience from the pain of sudden changes to the status quo.

"For a great many peoples a stranger is sacred, endowed with magico-religious powers, and supernaturally benevolent or malevolent" (ibid.: 26). Why this should be so has been one long-standing mystery a biological perspective on meaning might clear up, by proposing that these are powers of human neurophysiology and not, as liminal discourse has assumed, that they "inhere in the structure of ideas." The "sacred" quality represents the awe and anxieties the group experiences in this disequilibration of its meanings. The fears are displaced on the person in passage: limbo is that time, I suggest, where meaning has least force and where, as a consequence, fear has the most. "The novices are outside society, and society has no power over them, especially since they are actually sacred and holy, and therefore untouchable and dangerous, just as gods would be. . . . During the novitiate, the young people can steal and pillage at will or feed and adorn themselves at the expense of the community" (Douglas [1966] 1970: 114). From all that is meaningful, those in limbo are utterly discrepant.

Rites of passage, the wild eccentricities of tricksters and clowns, and fabulous gods of confusion and boundaries are often interpreted as having the function of keeping people toeing moral lines. Pollution beliefs are said to keep people from breaking taboos, for example, or tricksters "act out" for culture-abiding citizens their forbidden impulses to trample the rules. Whatever the social functions may or may not be, these are more fundamentally a poetics of discrepancy, each expressing human responses to novelty and to the ambiguities of change that exceed a threshold.

Nowhere is this poetics more evident than in the universality of rites of the first time. That "only the *first time* counts is truly universal and . . . everywhere expressed to some extent through special rites . . . of founding and of inauguration (of a house, temple, village, or town). . . . For a stranger there are also rites on the occasion of his first entry; then he is free to go out again and to re-enter. . . . The first haircut, the first tooth, the first solid food, the first step, the first menses—all are occasions for ceremonies. . . . [O]nce the new domain or situation has been entered, the repetition of the first act has a decreasing importance. Furthermore, psychologically, the second act no longer presents anything new; it marks the beginning of habituation" (van Gennep [1908] 1960: 175–178). That rites of the first time should have been found universally necessary is evidence, I suggest, of the human ambivalence toward novelty and difference.

Some Japanese villagers associate strangers who appear among them with animal spirit possession, attributing to them "mystical and evil qualities," which, like the widespread association of strangers with the evil eye and witchcraft, are believed to cause "mental derangement" (Yoshida 1981: 95). Yet in villages of northeastern Japan where strangers are not allowed to settle at all unless they establish fictive kinship relations with a prominent family, that negative association is rarely if ever made (ibid.: 88). That is, the local social order assimilates newcomers in its own preexisting terms, a version of stereotyping that extinguishes their novelty and the fears it evokes. Where this strategy is not part of the local social repertoire, however, newcomers retain their force as discrepancies and interruptions, and they arouse fear responses, which are displaced on them. That witchcraft, the evil eye, and animal spirits "derange" what is regarded as mental equilibrium speaks to human limitations in assimilating differing meaning systems. Messengers need not bring bad news.

"In this remote corner of Virginia, as in most American communities," writes Russell Baker from Kilmarnock, "the established folks have a pejorative term for the infestation of strangers in the county. A recent arrival is referred to as a 'come here,' to distinguish him from the long-term resident, who is a 'from here'" (1981). In the town of Bedford, Massachusetts, established in 1630, high-tech industries are bringing a much-needed fiscal infusion, but even so old-timers call newcomers "blow ins." Information is also a resource old-timers part with reluctantly. In and around Boston where I live, street signs are frequently missing and posted directions confusing. Newcomers understand the message: if you don't already know your way around, you don't belong here.

REPRISE

Our own acted commentaries on this endless challenge to make and keep meanings intact are telling this same story. Subtle or harsh, the denigration and rejection accorded to newcomers to neighborhood, community, institution, or club can be powerful sources of alienation. Cliques at church and six-year initiation rites can push families to flee into themselves, especially when these cultural rebuffs are taken personally. But also "newcomers" in American society are blacks and browns, already long-standing citizens of course, but newcomers to the white insiders who already enjoy civil rights. That newness seems to be keeping disparagement and prejudice on tap toward them. A reason, in these recent decades, that blacks and other minorities haven't been experiencing significant gains occupationally and socially may be that this culture's "magic circles" are placing them in limbo.

Women's and children's interdependence with neighbors and school-mates paradoxically puts them betwixt and between in the American scheme of things, and some of that cultural pall hovering over women and children once they move beyond the confines of their proper place at home and neighborhood may be fall-out from these daily threshold crossings for companionship and cookies. Their fate is to be culturally considered neither fully human nor fully social beings, anomalies by comparison to the "single-family" ideal. But if their lives are to have a depth and tex-ture they cannot do without, they have no choice but to be straddlers and go-betweens, fuzzying the lines between community and family, neigh-bor and friend, friend and relative. Not just neighbors, nor just friends, yet certainly not relatives, we would insist, there is no term for their intimate and altogether essential relationships, no concept with which to place them exactly. They are cultural discrepancies who pay a price for the juxtaposition they make of our ideas about kinship and friendship.

Nor is any wider significance of kitchen kindreds and children's flotil-las acknowledged. These forms of social solidarity and belonging women furnish themselves, beholden to no dispenser of social recognition. Love, Reciprocity, and Cooperation are concepts by which we define the domain of HOME, relationships that are considered to be "merely" Domestic and wholly Private. By contrast, our ideas of Citizenship emphasize belonging in the community as a public matter: sitting on boards and committees, running for and holding office, joining in the PTA, volunteering with the Red Cross, working on local political issues—a public arena legitimated by the formalities of charters and Robert's Rules of Order. Cultural out-laws, then: straddling the concepts through which we constitute kinship and friendship, women's and children's kindreds and alliances are allowed only half a life in society, like all so-called anomalies. Nobody wants to be set beyond the pale of belonging—especially not if they are already WOMEN and CHILDREN, and especially if women are husbandless, poor, and not white.

Considering HOME to be totally "private" and "domestic" has also been used to keep women from entering the public sphere. Only since 1975 has it been unconstitutional to exempt women from jury duty, a practice earlier justified on the grounds that " 'the great majority [of women] constitute the heart of the home, where they are busily engaged in the twenty-four hour a day task of producing and rearing children, providing a home for the entire family, and performing the daily household work, all of which demands their full energies' " (Okin 1979: 263). That is the opinion of a federal district court upholding, as the Supreme Court had previously, the right of states to legislate the exemption of women from jury duty, despite the Sixth Amendment, which requires juries to be composed of a cross-section of the community.

In breaking out of the single-family mold women and children appear anomalous to men, whose intimate and domestic energies are more likely to be confined within their family. To men's dismay, family lines are broken, jeopardizing its integrity as a corporate unit bearing their name; the meanings of family are different for them. It's not just that women's and children's intimacies and involvements may dissipate those they are supposed to reserve for their own families, nor that their behavior is eccentric to the ideal family form. In acting on Interdependence rather than Individuality, they stress Cooperation over the Competition that pervades men's occupational lives. Their wives and children may live through bridges, but middle-class men seem to rely on moats to insulate WORK from HOME, BUSINESS from PLEASURE, MONEY from LOVE, for reasons the next essay explores.

Mothers' and children's friendships up and down the block and around the corner are prime, cherished signs of a strong sense of residential community. When mothers take turns greeting children after school and children rotate sleep-overs, they epitomize the difference between belonging and not belonging to a neighborhood: trust is strong enough to support bridges between households. It had better be: it is simply not possible to live as an American mother or grow up as an American child without transcending family boundaries day in and day out. Until the children leave home, permeable family lines are a necessity, especially during the earliest years of child-raising. The district schools have their part to play, as do preschool centers in churches and private homes. The single-family-in-its-neighborhood and in-its-school-district raises American children. Families dissatisfied with these outside resources experience themselves as incomplete, somehow deficient.

"We moved here for the children" breaks down the line between NEIGHBORHOOD and FAMILY; it pulls the neighborhood right into the midst of FAMILY, where Americans are convinced it belongs. The neighborhood, with its playmates, schoolmates, and their parents, is another MEMBER OF THE FAMILY or as essential to the constitution of a household as the kitchen stove, however we want to put it. Nourishing neighbors and schools are so important that parents, married and single, take on the burden of long commuting journeys, even expensive moves, once finding the "right neighborhood" for women's companionship and for the schooling and peers it provides their children.

Especially during the child-raising years, ideas about neighborhood are culturally all of a piece with kinship, and they too make use of the principle of endogamy; families are fussy about who lives in their vicinity and might edge into their circle. Once having moved into a neighborhood for the "character and reputation" it is advertised as having, if neighbors don't provide women and children with satisfying alliances, families will seriously consider moving. By investing in the social insurance of "homogeneity," Americans believe they are lowering the risk of incurring those financial and emotional costs. Homogeneity yields the comforts of equilibrium, and in our cultural shorthand, income level alone has come to substitute in solidarity for religion, ethnicity, language, race. Income indexes the "market neutrality" we ingenuously (or desperately) believe will bring the American concept of Equality to life.

Properties of Community

Searching for deeper meaning in their private lives, Americans may also be trying to create coherence among the different compartments that industrialization manufactures for job, for family, and for special communities of interest. To feel all of a piece, living as a whole human being in a fault-free world of work-home-community, is to live in a world where economic, familial, personal, and civic experiences all together make sense. And when they don't, to be able to say why, for the experience of coherence includes insight into why it is missing.

Rather than speaking of community through the more familiar framework of ways that individuals form into groups and groups structure community, this essay instead searches out American ideas about trust and honor, conflict and cooperation, love and money, home and work . . . to see how they do and don't contribute to that coherence. In some of Americans' most commonplace experiences of local life these ideas can contradict and confuse one another. When Americans seek credit, mortgages, a job and a better job, their personal reputations are created and judged locally, but are critical nationally. In protecting their major investment, in the way that both national and local real estate markets would have them believe they should, homeowners' interests more often than not work against both democratic ideals and the practical hopes of minorities and of younger and older people, perhaps the same ages as their own children and parents, to share in a suburban quality of life. In giving second place to personal relationships with neighbors and first place to economic interests, homeowners may be putting limits around the local fund of social trust.

On their own in negotiating such ambiguities and paradoxes, many members of a buffeted middle class can become hard pressed to act on their fundamental social decency or, put otherwise, can find it increasingly difficult to limit the harms they do one another and those less fortunate.

The territory of home gets into our blood, somehow, and our address comes to be as much a part of our being as anything else about us. More than identity is at stake these days, however, as safety of property and person casts the meaning of neighbor in new light. The search for a clearer sense of residential community can be sparked by fear as it may never have been lit by love. But once drawing the wagons around the fire, it may be nearly out, smothered under the ambiguities of our neighbor relationships. Especially throwing Americans off social balance is the role of real estate in American life: NEIGHBORS are also TRADERS, and no matter how critical property lines are, they turn out to be imaginary when it comes to "property values." Melting away, despite fences, hedges, and gates, property lines must yield to the bottom line drawn by mortgage lenders, property appraisers, and real estate agents: the resale value of each single house is at the monetary mercy of those around it.

In homeowners' calculus, the physical appearance of their block matters the most, and to keep their neighbors up to snuff, Americans are prone to complain about them to city officials. "We do take people to court, and that news gets around," says a building inspector. "They say this is a city of laws, not people. You have to maintain some sort of balance in the neighborhood. You protect property values along with it. As an example, the lady that complained on the fellow that I just told you about with the seven cars in his yard, the lady next door to *her* has her house up for sale. And that motivated part of the complaint, although they've complained lots in the past. The real estate agent told her that she would have to decrease what they could ask for her house by about $5000 just because of the neighbors. And that hurts." Her neighbor, says a woman in a Minneapolis suburb, doesn't live up to the block's standards: "I've been putting up with it, but if ever I go to sell my house, I'll report him. I'll get him cleaned up before I advertise it—no doubt about it."

Five men in Minneapolis nodded their agreement as another told me: "We do look for people moving into our neighborhood who have similar goals, similar values, who act somewhat like us, keep their property up to the same extent we do—so on and so forth. You find yourself saying, 'That guy doesn't belong here.' Either he doesn't keep his property up or he's too fastidious and he needs an even better place or whatever. Having common goals is very important. That's the first thing I look for. Like the next-door neighbor moving in, the first thing I watch for, is he going to mow as often as I do and is he going to keep up what is sort of the norm in the neighborhood or is he going to bring it down? Of course you can't afford to buy property and not keep it up—it's too great an investment. Real estate is so tight around here, the agents rush to any available property. I sure hope that keeps up!"

"The norm of the neighborhood": Americans seem more comfortable with keeping a firm line between Money and neighborly Love, for the trader relationship appears to prevail in this domain of multiple meanings. I asked that group of Minneapolis men, You're all friends through church but you've never lived as neighbors, is that right? "That's why we're still friends!" they chorussed. That also echoes a pattern found in C. Fischer's study of Americans' personal networks: homeowners are least likely to discuss personal matters with their neighbors, and they are "more likely to cite neighbors only with respect to neighborly activities, especially looking after the house" (C. Fischer 1982: 102). Moreover, those people mentioned "who would look after the house were definitely not likely to discuss work and tended not to be sources of loans" and other kinds of intimate support (ibid.: 385). About one-third of the neighbors named at all "were named in answer to only one specific question: who they would ask to care for their homes when away" (ibid.: 98). Of all people who looked after the house, these 1250 Americans named neighbors 47 percent of the time, friends 17 percent, and spouses, parents, children and co-workers about equally, between 5 and 7 percent of the time. For discussing personal matters and seeking advice, out of 19,417 people in their personal networks, neighbors were mentioned only 13 percent of the time, compared with 40 percent for friends, 41 percent for spouses, 23 for parents, 21 for co-workers (ibid.: 386).

That's not to say that civility doesn't prevail: about 92 percent of this sample reported that they chat out of doors with a neighbor. In the lowest density places, 69 percent have neighbors who drop in on them; about 61 percent in the densest areas do too. In semirural areas, 59 percent invite a neighbor in, compared with a surprising 62 percent in the heart of the city, and only 58 percent who do in suburbs. In the least dense areas, 36 percent borrow small items like sugar and nails from neighbors; between 45 and 49 percent do in small towns—and, surprisingly again, 42 percent do in the city (ibid.: 375).

However few of their most vitalizing personal relationships the neighborhood may furnish people with, it remains the lifeline of the real estate industry, banks and insurance companies, and, not least, American households: about 64 percent of them have put just about everything they have into buying a house. The maintenance and appreciation of a house's value, which is to say, its *resale* value, depends on how well everybody else on the block and in the neighborhood keeps up their lots and houses. So it is that with "homeownership" goes membership in a trading bloc of prospective homesellers, each household influencing every other's price in the housing resale market. Neighbors' mutual interests keep them at the very least aware of one another's mowing habits—and alert to the possibility of new neighbors who won't share their norms for property maintenance.

Or who they *believe* won't: most suburbanites believe that apartments and townhouses (even two-family houses) and the renters associated with them will bring down the resale prices of single-family housing. American beliefs that SUBURB and CITY are not to be confused with one another outline the patterns of the metropolitan mosaic. By the kinds of housing available will be known the kinds of people living there, and kept at bay are those who haven't attained the American ideal of homeownership. Suburbs keep out higher-density developments and their renters, by which cities are culturally defined, as part of their comfort-seeking strategy, but it is one that also keeps millions doubtful about belonging in America—blacks, browns, people with low incomes, the handicapped, nontraditional families, even elderly suburbanites themselves, and nowadays, young adults who once called suburbs home.

A mixture of housing costs and types interrupts the comforts of the homogeneous serenities of single-family suburbs. No matter that people living within look-alike housing are themselves likely to be as different from one another as they are similar, housing uniformity itself is a sign that everything is in its place. Whatever is unfamiliar is a sign of uncertainty, and to protect themselves from distress, groups of all kinds— neighborhood, ethnic, religious, or social—set themselves apart more emphatically (often by attributing to themselves more solidarity and homogeneity than they have). What their status quo already offers members in the way of rewards and opportunities may not necessarily be just or even sufficiently satisfying, but, for the purposes of getting on with living, what is already known is at least familiar and, in that alone, safer. Expecting the members of any group to upset its status quo is asking them to be the perpetrators of their own distress; from whence heroes and heroines.

Suburbs are the habitat of the single-family-detached house, as the history of automobiles, housing prices, population growth, and highways would have it. No matter where apartment houses are located, but especially when they are taller than the customary garden apartments, they are believed incongruous with the idea of FAMILY, from which suburbs' meaning is constituted. Even two-family houses, common in many American cities, aren't usually allowed in suburbs. Single-family houses with a self-contained unit for rent are nevertheless widespread in suburbs; but, in being dissonant with the ideal, they're also illegal in most places. Should citizens want to make them legal (allowing their own children or parents to live in suburbs at prices they can afford), the outcry at zoning hearings drowns out that possibility. Townhouses or row houses, historically found in cities, share "party" walls and blur the lines between households. They have been making a suburban appearance only in strictly limited areas where landscaping and road layouts create well-buffered, taut boundaries to separate them definitively from single-family-detached enclaves. And even when they are condominiums and not rented, their higher density in and of itself associates them with both cities and renters.

Americans believe that social homogeneity will more readily make for relationships founded on Trust, Affection, and Reciprocity. These also constitute our notion of COMMUNITY. But even more important to the continuity of community are our ways of construing Conflict, Dissent, Nonconformity, simple Disagreement (Perin 1986). Community depends for its strength and endurance on how people come to terms with one another's differences, living together as we must. But negotiating differences can make people so uncomfortable that they find ways to avoid doing so. This essay explores a number of subtle and varied ways in which Americans habitually retreat from social frictions and conceptual confusions.

Trust and Conflict are the real properties of community, so well known as to be unknown. They are not completely under local control, however. Belonging to one local community or another may be a matter of choice, but most Americans have no option other than to belong to a national economic "community" that is their sole source of credit, insurance, and jobs, but which depends, I was surprised to learn, on information supplied by these same neighbors. It's little wonder that, treading between both a personal and a market relationship with neighbors and then on top of that having their financial fates determined nationally, Americans living in single-family suburbs can find domestic tranquility and promoting the general welfare often to be beyond them.

TATTLING ON NEIGHBORS

"Neighbor," in Ambrose Bierce's *Enlarged Devil's Dictionary:* "One whom we are commanded to love as ourselves—and who does all he can to make us disobedient" (Bierce 1967: 203). In the literature known as community studies, that darker side of American neighbor relationships is, however, only occasionally documented (Gans 1967: 159). Speaking mostly to the sunnier moments, the few studies there are generally confirm what we know from experience. Friendly neighboring relationships are more plentiful when there are children; when neighbors are also kin; when people are long-term residents and elderly; when people feel they have something in common (age, income, religion, ethnicity); when women are home much of the time; when people see each other outdoors in warm and snowy weather; when residents are middle-class (working-class people spend more time with relatives than with either friends or neighbors);

when friends and relatives live so far away they have little choice (as in fast-growing areas, rural places, boomtowns, and other outposts). And when people aren't renters but homeowners.

"The kind of neighbors dictate to a certain extent how happy you are in that neighborhood. If you have people that you get along well with, that observe your property lines and things like this, that have kids that don't scrap with your kids all the time, then you're fortunate": domestic tranquility, defined by a man in a Minneapolis suburb. What goes wrong between neighbors? Noise, dogs, fences, garbage, crab grass, parking . . . any and all can work themselves into irritations, quarrels, even feuds. That these frictions sometimes carry more emotional resonance than might be seemly is one consequence of a confusion between Personal and Market relationships.

"People take a lot of pride in their community and their homes," a building inspector says. "And the minute someone doesn't take that same pride, whether he puts root killer in his lawn and has no weeds, while the guy next door has millions of dandelions and the seeds are blowing over onto his yard—it's a property value question. They want the standards kept very high because they're paying top taxes, and they want the highest possible property value they can get. That's their motivation." As for going over to the neighbor, I asked, and saying, "Look, those dandelion seeds are blowing . . ."—why is it that they don't do that? "Well, some don't have the guts, frankly." What kind of guts does it take? "It takes someone who is not afraid to go over and—confront. People don't like confrontations. They aren't aggressive in nature, the average person. So they will not confront. I resent that myself, too, because then they involve us and I know they have not tried to solve their own problem, and I'd much rather they solve their own problem. And when you talk to them you know they don't have the courage of their conviction to go over and confront the situation, to sit down like a gentleman and talk about it and, you know, arrive at some mutual understanding. And some of these neighborhood feuds—you know, they're people who've been friends for years. When they're done, they completely dissolve those friendships. It's a very sad thing to see. Very sad thing."

About neighborly transgressions Americans tend to fume and hold their tongues—to their neighbor, but not to city hall. They complain—*anonymously* to building inspectors, dog wardens, homeowner associations, and, sometimes, the police: they'd complain more often to the police if it weren't that they have to identify themselves. Local public officials generally regard it as their duty to take each complaint seriously and to investigate. The building inspectors and animal wardens I spoke to around the country used the same tag line about the neighborly frictions they get called in on: "I could write a book!" In a Minneapolis suburb, population 50,000 in 1977, "one man works full time on nuisance complaints—that's all he does eight hours a day. He makes thousands of visits a year to private homes." That means thousands of anonymous calls.

The anonymity in which homeowners cloak themselves and their lack of "courage" to confront I see partly as inhibitions born of the multiple meanings of neighbor: they are uncertain about how to behave. "We check out every call whether it's anonymous or not," says the building inspector in a Houston suburb. "Simple thing like 'A lady's got a compost pile next door to me and it's attracting rats. Will you come and talk to her?' Or they don't even say that—they won't say their 'neighbor,' but Mrs. So and So. But you know it's got to be a neighbor in that area even though you don't have their name. Our job is to get the people to comply and not necessarily resort to what you might call a drastic act of issuing citations. Now of course we do issue citations—that's generally the final part if they haven't cooperated with us. The problem is a PR job—to get people to comply and still have them like you. People will call to say 'A neighbor's tree is growing over my yard. Would you get him to cut it down?' We don't have that jurisdiction. *You* can ask him, I tell them, and they say, 'Well, you know he won't cut it unless you say something to him.' 'Just keep trying,' we say. Generally we just tell 'em that's a civil thing between you and your neighbor."

Requiring callers to identify themselves cuts down on complaints, a police officer in one Minneapolis suburb finds: "People possibly complain more frequently to the building department than to us because when they come to us, it calls for involvement on their part—they have to state the fact that they've made the complaint. Whereas with the building inspector, he can inspect it without necessarily having the name of the complainant." The police may find themselves not so much handling a complaint as being in the center of a fight: "If they say that the Jones kids next door are always bothering them, sure, we'll talk to the Jones kids and try to figure it out. But frequently we find that the Jones kids are retaliating for something these people have done. It isn't right, obviously, but it's understandable." Much that's "petty" is going on, says the police chief of a Minneapolis suburb: "There are a lot of things we get—many petty things that could be resolved between neighbors that never should come to the attention of the police department. It's absolutely ridiculous. Absolutely ridiculous."

Getting "turned in" makes people angry. Sometimes they will know who's responsible for it, but when they don't know, and often they won't have a clue, everyone up and down their block can become suspect. Already fragile enough, trust is at further risk. A building inspector in suburban Minneapolis told me: "When a neighbor complains and you inspect and tell that person to clean up, they know who complained. And they know it's from some other motivation. They know who it is. Generally it's the neighbor either one side or another after they've had bad feelings and words. So by the time we get there, they pretty well know. And the thing that they're angered about is not that they're being told that they're violating any ordinance. It's the fact that somebody turned them in. That's foremost in their minds."

It is "making a fuss" to discuss with a neighbor what irritates them, I often heard. Their irritation may not be wholly justifiable, they seem to be saying, or perhaps their inhibition signals a fear of retribution. One California woman is afraid of "reprisals": "It is inevitably unpleasant to disagree. Throughout the years we've had disagreements over kids. They'd come over and maybe break something, and vice versa. When our neighbor was complaining about other kids, things were stolen and mud was thrown on their door. If there were toughs living next door, I'd be afraid and wouldn't upset the applecart. I'd be afraid of them if my daughters were left alone at night. One of my daughters is afraid that if my husband yells at boys riding their motorcycles around here, she'll have reprisals at school."

That's a "common" fear, says one building inspector: "People generally want the city to handle the case without involving them. And this causes me problems because the court is always suspicious of government bringing a case in, one neighbor against another. I like to have the person complaining come in. *But they many times won't do it!* They say, 'We don't want to get involved. He may take it out on my kids or he may do something to me.' Oh, that's common. They want the city to take care of it. They like to use the city as the third person to make cases."

A California woman shouted to her neighbor's dog to get off her lawn—a message she wanted her neighbor only to overhear: "I don't like to handle differences face to face. I'm chicken. I'd rather make a comment loud enough to be heard rather than to say to that person, 'I do not like you.' Because I don't want an out and out fight, a wild disagreement and then going home with bad feelings. I'd rather let them know how I feel without saying it." A Minneapolis man says, "I'd rather not confront the person and create a bad feeling or maybe escalate a feeling which is already not too good. I suppose it's a question of how gutsy you are."

People may lack knowledge of how to go about "approaching their neighbor," another man thinks: "My last job was deputy post commander in the military. The phone used to ring all day long with one person complaining against the other. Usually, you've got one sorehead in the community and everybody seems to pick on him. Then he's the one that's complaining against all the neighbors around. I often wondered why the guys just don't *talk* to him. It would be so much better than sending the MP's!" What is it, I asked him, that makes us think we can't talk to each other?

"Part of it is just not knowing how to do it. A lot of people just don't know how to do it. A lot of people just don't know how to approach their neighbor. If they do it in anger, you know you're in for a problem, and if they wait and cool down, a lot of times they'll feel it wasn't that important. I guess we haven't been taught how to approach a neighbor, for one thing. We're in the church—and there again I think that's what gives us a common bond—you're given an idea of how to approach a member of your fellowship when you've got a difference, but to apply that same concept to your neighbor who might not share your beliefs, you're most times hesitant to do that. Theoretically, we should demonstrate to our neighbor what we are able to do in church. We probably don't work on it hard enough. Maybe we don't care enough." The common bond of belonging to the same church is clear, but the meanings connecting neighbor to neighbor juxtapose and blur, leaving us unsure of how to behave, unsure of whether the contact will be satisfying or distressing.

I asked this group of men who belonged to the same church to compare dealing with family frictions and dealing with neighborhood encounters. One man explained: "In a family you can create hard feelings today, but you'll have dinner together tonight and breakfast tomorrow and you get a chance to patch things up in a family. And with neighbors you can ruin that chance because we don't see our neighbors that often or that closely, and so maybe that's why you tend to overlook things too. In the family before you have these disagreements you usually precondition the family to a condition of love and concern for one another. Maybe if we had that same relationship with a neighbor, then we could afford to have these more frequent confrontations over even minor differences without a danger or a fear that it would disrupt the harmony in the neighborhood."

Neither anger nor complaints, but "learning to live with it" is another common axiom: "Our neighbor's dog pees on our lawn, but we'd rather continue to have coffee with them than mention it. We've learned to live with it. They put up with our several cars, and we've mentioned how appreciative we are of that." A couple with seven children in California takes a barking dog in stride on the assumption that their children might be equally annoying now and then: "We have dogs on either side of us, and when the master's gone the dog barks until he's back. That's just one side—the other side, the dog is a magnificent animal. I wouldn't go over and complain because I have seven children and things might have annoyed them. I can put up with it—if it happened day in and day out, I might. They're nice people, and I like them, so we just put up with it."

One neighborhood friction was handled gracefully, a Minneapolis woman reports, only because the relationship of friend prevailed over that of neighbor: "I have a friend in my neighborhood who came over one day and said, 'I want you to know I've called the dog catcher. I'm sick of the dogs in this neighborhood.' They hated animals and tolerated ours because we were friends. She was active in garden clubs and her lawn was immaculate. There wasn't a blade of grass that didn't belong there. She said it wasn't just our dog but other dogs. That she'd just had it, that it has nothing to do with us personally. She just wanted us to know she'd called the police and the dog catcher. She was angry. But before she left my house she said she was having a party the week from the following Saturday, and would we be able to come? And we're very good friends. We go to each other's daughters' showers and weddings and see each other every month. She used the law enforcement to get rid of something bothering her." I asked if it had been effective. "Oh yes, we all watched our dogs a little bit more because we had a very active dog catcher at the time. It was another case where she wasn't angry at us personally. She was still our friend. She was open and honest. I suppose I'd been negligent too. Everyone had a dog except this one family. The dogs chose their lawn to do their damage, and that's wrong." ("Negligent" dog owners get the next essay to themselves.)

Small frictions go undiscussed "because we seem to be very careful to be removed from each other," says another suburban woman. "I tell you we are too isolated from each other around here even to make jokes about the small things that cause tension. We really are. We talk to each other in the yard. We don't ever get very intimate or very close. And maybe that's some of the reason you don't say something about a barking dog or the weeds or even joke about them."

Complaining works the other way around as well: complaints about property sometimes mask personal troubles, building inspectors find. "The first thing I learned to do is always check the yard of the person who's making the complaint. Many times their situation is worse than the one that they're reporting. So they've had a fight at the coffee party, and they haven't gotten on, and so she turns her neighbor in. 'I'm going to turn you in to the health department.' She calls in here, and so we go out there. Sometimes we find that their situation is worse than the neighbor's! Then sometimes there isn't any basis for a complaint at all—they're just harassing that person."

Or their reciprocal agreement to ignore one another's "disobediences" breaks down. The inspector in another Minneapolis suburb tells a similar story: "Some people call as soon as they see someone in their neighborhood breaking the law and others will put up with it for months. It seems that the ones which put up with it for a long time and then call—what stimulates it is something other than what the real problem is. Usually it's the result of a battle between the kids, or something else. To get even, they complain about these people having garbage in their yard for a long time. The people complained about, they'll say, 'But I've had the cars here for nine months and nobody ever said anything.' Okay, so why all of a sudden do they complain? Usually it's because their kids tore through their yard or they got into a fight, or they fought on a school bus. Something is causing them to get back."

After 40 years of living next door, an anonymous complaint in California masked something deeper: "You'd be surprised the number of times people try to use the city. They immediately point out what they think is a code violation of one type or another, yet they're not experts in what's in the code. One case we had where people were living adjoining each other for as much as 40 and 50 years. One lady complained that her neighbor's water drained onto her flower bed. And yet upon investigation we found her flower bed was two feet higher than the neighbor's property. She brought this up because her neighbor built a patio with a roof that obscured part of the view from a window where the lady ate her breakfast. Now she no longer had a view of the trees in the distance. So she complained about something else. The roof was perfectly legal."

Another building inspector refuses to get drawn in: "After you receive two or three phone calls, you pick up some background on a complaint. Then you're able to sift the chaff from the wheat and say, 'Here's the facts of life now. I'm not going to get into it because you're mad at your neighbor. Here's what you've got to do. You do this and then you're done with me. I don't want to be involved with your neighborhood scrap.' Or you learn that people don't want to talk to their neighbor. They don't want to get involved. They're not fighting with them, but they just don't want to have anything to do with them. They'll call up and say, 'So and so next door, they don't put the covers on their garbage cans and they don't cut their yard.'"

A Houston building inspector finds that sometimes complaints can merely be an excuse: "We take all complaints on the assumption that they're legitimate. One neighbor complained about dog droppings in her yard and an atrocious odor. We went over there—and found nothing. The differences there weren't over dogs. Something else was going on to upset those neighbors with each other."

Complainers should try to handle things themselves, one building department inspector suggests: "Very often when you go out, they want to know who made the complaint about them. That's the first thing they ask. Sometimes when I get a complaint, I ask if they can communicate directly with the neighbor. Most of the time, they say they can't. If they say they can, I suggest to them, 'If you have that good a relationship, why don't you talk to him? Maybe your problem isn't as big as you make it.' And usually, they'll resolve it themselves."

Sometimes people do try to handle things themselves, but get nowhere. A woman in suburban Minneapolis recounts "an episode right here": "I tried to get the mailboxes consolidated—they're strung out all over the place on this side of the street—but it was too expensive. I have a rock garden that I made after three years of weeding. It's on a right-of-way for sidewalks and mailboxes, but it's ours to maintain. A new house was going in just across from it, and after the woman and I had agreed that she'd put her mailbox at the edge of my garden, I came home one day to find it right smack in the middle of it. She just said, 'This is the most convenient place for it, and that's where it's going to be.' I said that my husband would be home that weekend, and that he'd be glad to move it for her. She said that she'd *paid* to have it put there and it was not going to be moved. It's still there. That was their first day living here. Other things have happened since, and other people in the neighborhood have gotten to know them. They will do what they want to do, period, regardless of what anyone else wants. That's the way they are. I even went to the city about it because I was really disturbed. They said they can't get involved, that they just have to hope that when things like this crop up that people have sense enough to do things amicably so there isn't a neighborhood dispute about it."

Anonymous complaints and the "unfriendliness" in a neighborhood are distancing devices, ways of taking flight from the contradictions of being both trader and neighbor. In drawing the line between their Personal and Property relationships, suburban neighbors may be financially adept, but, as a consequence, socially clumsy. The anonymous call to city hall is the move of an astute trader, not a loving neighbor.

This difference between personal and property relations may help to explain why, as is so often observed, renters "never get to know their neighbors." Renters are likely to consider neighbors as being prospects for *only* a personal relationship. Urbanites, more likely to be renters than owners, list fewer neighbors in their personal networks, but more of those listed are also their friends: urbanites (for whom neighbors compose only 13 percent of their total networks) label 80 percent of neighbors as friends, compared with about 68 percent of neighbors who are also friends of people living in less dense areas. Urbanites are more likely to invite neighbors in than are people in small towns! "The more urban the community, the closer respondents reported feeling toward listed neighbors. And the more urban, the greater the range and intimacy of activities respondents shared with those neighbors" (C. Fischer 1982: 377, 101). Even though urbanites name fewer neighbors in their networks than they do kin, co-workers, and friends, and fewer neighbors than do suburbanites and small-towners, they have more intimate relationships with those whom they do include than do homeowners.

Why might that be so? Not in a relationship involving financial issues, its personal quality is unambiguous, and renters can be clear-eyed about what to expect from each other. For them, discussing the weather in the elevator is for openers that could lead from one thing to another; for suburbanites, talking "crab grass" in the yard can remain the entire encounter. Without that layering of property and personal relationships, renters can allow Nearest to come closer to Dearest. Yet facing so large an array of possible relationships, renters and urbanites may then use privacy to be selective and to withdraw protectively.

In making the anonymous call to city hall, homeowners seem to be saying that while they maintain an Impersonal relationship with neighbors, they believe themselves to have a Personal one with government. Taking their complaint to government legitimizes it; were it made over the back fence, their complaint might carry more insult than weight. Perhaps the anonymous complaint is analogous to the secret ballot through which we not only authorize and delegate our personal representation in this democracy. The secret ballot, a repudiation of monarchy, allows no tyrant's reprisal, no king's retribution. Is the anonymous complaint conceived as a parallel right, to protect against neighbors' witchery?

In any case, Americans seem to have and act on a conception of a personal, primary, and direct relationship to government (the state is the one out of 50 they live in). "We check out every call," that local public official said, and we want to get people to comply, he added, in a way that assures they will continue to *like* us. Government reciprocates, in suburbs at any rate.

KEEPING THE CONDOMINIUM'S PEACE

Condominium ownership clearly exposes those hidden financial clauses of neighbors' social contracts. Being so explicitly legal and financial, this relationship clears up some of the estranging confusions between Love and Money—the Love and Reciprocity which HOME signifies alongside the competitive Money tied up in it. Condominium ownership makes no secret of the trader relationship, but even so, when tranquility gives way to troubled waters, how Americans construe Disagreeing Agreeably seems to sabotage their capacity to do so.

Having no choice but to collaborate with one another in managing their common property, condominium residents overtly blend the personal and property bases of their relationship into a legal relationship. "When you meet somebody that you haven't met before at the pool," a condominium resident observes, "chances are you'll see them again, so you can't—I don't think you'd want to—turn a cold shoulder to anyone. You never know when you'd want to talk to them in the future about something to do with the condo, or when you'll be on a committee with them." Some people find it "more friendly than in a single family home development . . . because we see each other more often at the pool, and we see each other a lot at board meetings, and we've had some problems that we've all had to work out together. I think there's a feeling of togetherness" (Tulin 1978: 192). Feelings of goodwill notwithstanding, condo owners act on the market-driven reciprocity expressly built into their relationship from the start.

Condominium owners also rely on third parties to negotiate their differences—their association board officials. About half of condominium residents are willing to discuss directly with their immediate neighbors any frictions such as noise leaking between party walls or over the patio fence, while the other half would take the grievance to the board. But if the annoyance were constant—the stereo always pitched too loud, the children never quiet on Sunday mornings—most would head for the board. Getting back at each other is also not uncommon—taking neighbors to task with anonymous complaints or spitefully picking up on their slightest infraction of the rules (ibid.).

Living in a condominium herself, a Houston woman is also employed as a professional advisor to the boards of about 60 homeowner associations. She finds that people use their board the same way individual owners use local government: "Every time something's stolen from a mailbox, they call the association and want them to prosecute, but they will not testify. Now you cannot get through to them that that's a federal violation—and for them to go stick their own neck on the line. They assume that the association will prosecute everything.

"Every now and then, somebody will call and say that the people next door aren't married and living together—and they've got kids. They want the association to do something—that's the first question—to get them out. There's nothing it can do. The biggest complaint will come from pets, all the way around. That's common everywhere, in any kind of subdivision. 'How do I keep somebody else's pet off my lawn?' (We've got one fantastic neighbor who walks his dog with a bucket and a shovel. And he's got a huge dog.) People call to complain about cats scratching the paint on their cars. We tell them we can't do anything about it—go back and solve it yourself. People need to realize there are things they need to take care of legally on their own. You know, like for mail theft you go to the federal authorities. And for any type of breaking and entering or theft or damage you go to the sheriff or the police—the association just cannot do anything. For example, we get a number of child-abuse or child-neglect complaints—you know, what can the association do? The homeowners really get upset when we tell them to call the Child Welfare Department. But the biggest thing is that most condominium owners will not take the responsibility for what they say. They want to be anonymous. In the case of mail theft, they said they knew who was doing it. 'Go to the police,' we'd say. 'No, I'm afraid of their father.'"

The president of the association of a large single-family subdivision in Houston says: "I'm like the mayor of a small town, being president of our civic club. My phone begins ringing on a Saturday morning at 6:30. The most incredible variety of inconsequential problems as well as more substantive ones. Little old ladies who get up early and stay up late, whose cat was impregnated by a neighbor's cat or attacked by a dog or there's somebody suspicious in the neighborhood. Or there's violence and vandalism, and they call me along with the cops. There are three phone calls that are usually made—one is to the police department, one is to the civic association's security patrol service, and the third is to me—because there is somehow this conventional wisdom that the president of the civic club can and should be mindful of what goes on regardless of the day or the hour."

Common ownership, predicated on Cooperation and Sharing, is incongruent with American ideals of Individuality and Independence: condo owners are legally tied and unable to flee distresses or conflicts. Fighting may be their response. Even as condominium ownership may free former owners of single-family-detached houses from burdensome chores and may liberate would-be renters from a one-sided landlord-tenant relationship, it tethers them to a time-consuming, often conflictual process of reaching agreements with neighbors and co-owners. The bottom line of that consensus is financial, more often than not. Conflicts can also arise over all kinds of matters former apartment dwellers or single-family homeowners were accustomed to taking for granted. For example, where utilities aren't individually metered, as can happen in clustered developments, owners can get into fair-sized snits over the way other people who run their air conditioners day and night use more electricity yet pay the same for it.

Going to court has become one of the standard facts of condominium life—suits arising between individual owners and their board or association (and, as well, between associations and condo developers who are being called to legal account for construction defects). Moreover, the condo rule-book is thicker and many more possibilities for infraction exist, for not only do residents have to abide by their association's by-laws but by local codes and ordinances governing building, health, and zoning as well. So "cooperation" can include scrutinizing and controlling individuals' choices of front-yard shrubs, trees, flowers, or vegetables, choice of house colors, or even the hobby of feeding birds. Conflicts also come up over open spaces that are actually owned in common, but the owners of the units adjacent to them come to feel proprietary toward them because they keep them free of debris and weeds.

The usual array of neighbor complaints about each other's pets and children can also include complaints about renters. Condos are widely used as a speculative investment, and while owners wait to take their profit, they may rent them out. Absentee landlordism becomes a major issue: tenants rightly expect them to worry about property upkeep and maintenance, but these half-hearted landlords may not. The other owners living around these units blame the resident renters, however, not the owners— and daily neighborly discord prevails. Moreover, renters, falling so far short of the norm and ideology of homeownership, are special targets of hostility (a subject I take up soon).

One long-time homeowner-association board member in suburban Washington, D.C., told me that, finally, it had become the agreed custom that when he and any residents happened upon each other—out walking the dog, in the yard, at the post office—no homeowner-association issues would be discussed. He had his fill during every other waking moment and, all too often, when he expected to be asleep. The Houston woman who is a specialist in getting homeowner associations organized and keeping them running, told me: "Our directors—none of them paid— are serving 15 to 18 hours a week, after working a 40-hour a week job. And unless the spouses halfway understand what's going on, they get sick and tired of having Thanksgiving dinner interrupted or a vacation interrupted or their sleep interrupted. And it really gets bad when the wives are cussed out. That's the biggest thing. The wives do not like to be cussed out on the phone, and a lot of homeowners will do that. They get tired of those types of phone calls, and they tell their husbands to get out of association work." Men seem to be the directors, I observed. "Yes, I'm not quite sure why. I guess we've had about six women directors in the 60 associations I know about."

Volunteer "burn out" from dealing with residents' confusions between private and public, independence and cooperation is commonplace: once concluding their term on an association board, some residents can never again be persuaded to take on any other job even though they continue to live there. "Where I live there's 518 units, and at any given point in time over the past four years, there's been a maximum of 10 families working in the association. You take five of those as director and maybe five somewhere on the side, and yet the other 500 homeowners expect everything to be taken care of by them." Why is there such a low rate of participation? I asked. "In older condo communities, they've been told that it's 'maintenance-free' living, and so they expect that. For any association to work you've either got to pay with money to get a full-time management company or maintenance man, or you've got to pay with homeowners' time. Second, I don't think above 2 or 3 percent of the population understand what a homeowner association is—and realtors' sales pitches aren't helping that problem out any. And then other than that I think it's just more or less the American way of life. It's 'Do what I want to do when I want to do it.'

"In committees, the turnover is almost continual. If you can get a committee chairman to last six months, you've really done well. Board directors—either they get out in three or four months or they'll stick around for a year or two. In several associations around here, I've only heard of three that lasted their full three-year term—that's probably out of about 60 or 70 directors in all. A lot of it's due to the transient nature of society—you know, they're transferred, they move, they leave the subdivision for a different city or a better subdivision. But a lot of it is they just flat get annoyed with being expected to do everything by themselves. Once they've served on the board, they will seldom do committee work.

"It's not a matter of getting out and doing something less hectic. It's a matter of getting out, 100 percent. And in most cases you don't even ever see them vote again. They just vanish. Won't give their proxy to anybody. I can almost count on the fact that we're going to get nothing out of them, which is sad. Because they, better than anybody else, understand the problems that are going on. If you could get them back in, not necessarily even as a committee chairman, but just as a person on a committee, at least you would have something to fall back on."

Nor has the contemporary commune movement been free from the fallout of similar ambiguities. Combining HOME and WORK from the start and valuing Sharing and Interdependence over and above Independence and Individuality, communes also turn out to be more temporary than lasting. Social wariness and third-party mediation are also present. But communes provide one unique lesson. Twin Oaks in Virginia was inspired by B. F. Skinner's 1948 novel, *Walden Two*. At the end of 1971 the community consisted of about 45 people—36 members and about 10 visitors at any given time. For so small a group, "a surprising amount of communication is formal and impersonal instead of face-to-face." The commune radio broadcasts its own news, written opinion surveys keep members aware of each other's ideas, and the bulletin boards are well-used for notes. Meals and work can be scheduled individually and members can arrange to stay clear of each other's paths for days. "The whole group meets together rarely. At one time, complaints about other people were taken to a third person known as the generalized bastard, so that direct confrontation was avoided" (Kanter 1972: 27).

That "generalized bastard" is one of several peace-keeping devices American communes use. "Confession and self-criticism are practices common to many utopian communities; the individual continually measures himself against the standards of the perfect society. . . . In case the individual is not always aware of his lapse from ideal standards, many communities practice mutual criticism, a group encounter in which the group scrutinizes carefully the behavior of each person . . ." (ibid.: 37). At one of Synanon's eight California communes "mutual criticism is the central activity of the community. It occurs in a continuous twenty-four-a-day stream called the perpetual stew, which has a constant influx of people who enter for varying stretches, perhaps ten hours, perhaps thirty." As a symbol of striving for perfection, the "stew" also includes lectures, language lessons, talks by outside experts, or announcements (ibid.: 37–39).

Even "the most anarchistic commune theorists" eschew ambiguity: they emphasize the "importance of clear expectations and group agreements" (ibid.: 54). "Intentional" and voluntary, these communities attempt to keep the layers of meaning straight, but in the "unintentional" communities of residential America unclear expectations and inexplicit yet coercive rules govern. A "generalized bastard" out in the open is one thing; using local officials to sneak up on neighbors is another.

A genuine dilemma becomes apparent, however: in seeing themselves as social or moral equals, as Americans believe they are, one rule of thumb is not to take any sort of superior attitude, and criticizing another's behavior certainly carries that connotation. Directly complaining to a neighbor can readily be seen as telling them what to do. When a personal show of superiority is culturally forbidden, substituting the impersonal, yet legitimate, authority of local government and homeowner boards makes much sense.

American convictions about avoiding a fuss and not settling one face to face do, however, have a social cost. They ostensibly keep the local peace, but the person who's been "turned in" is likely to remain permanently suspicious of neighbors once the anger boils off; long-time friendships come to grief. Using a third party only when *both* neighbors ask for help would be one way out. Why don't building inspectors and homeowner board members stipulate that they will respond only to such requests and leave it squarely up to residents to deal with anything else? One inspector has come to insist on a mediation role, participating only if he is brought in by both parties. Why aren't regular dates for block or neighborhood inspections of property housekeeping announced? Perhaps because local government is doing its part in maintaining the fiction that neighborly Love has nothing to do with the Money tied up in the house.

BEARING FALSE WITNESS

Neighborhoods are the penultimate nesting box of ourselves as social beings: our family house within a neighborhood, that inside a city within a state joined in this Union, one of many nations among nations. Coming home, we close the door to face only ourselves in the hall mirror and our intimates in the living room. Once leaving home and their loyalty, trust, and affection, we have no choice but to come under the spell of the community's "notion of honor," the sole source of our reputation, the resource upon which our belonging among friends, at work, and to memory depends. Only in a community can reputation come into being: "whenever men collect together as a distinct community, the notion of honor instantly grows up among them; that is to say, a system of opinions peculiar to themselves as to what is blamable or commendable; and these peculiar rules always originate in the special habits and special interests of the community" (Tocqueville [1840] 1945: 247).

As I searched out the many ideas by which we understand "neighbor," I came upon the startling fact that the federal government condones the use of NEIGHBORS as INFORMERS in credit, insurance, and employment investigations. Americans' local reputation among neighbors, as determined by their community's "peculiar" system of opinions, is of intense concern nationally. Neighbors can provide information essential to the American rites of passage we know as "getting a credit rating," and, most particularly, "getting a mortgage" and the insurance usually required along with it, as well as moving up to a new job—despite the fact that neighbors may play a peripheral role in one another's daily rounds for all kinds of good reasons and know little about one another. We don't have the right to know the names of those neighbors or the friends giving their opinions and observations to investigating companies. Nor do banks or insurance companies have to spell out either the methods by which they obtain the information or the standards they use in judging consumers' "character and reputation" (Federal Trade Commission 1979: 30). We can't correct such reports before they're filed and circulated—only afterwards.

Until a favorable credit, insurance, or job investigation report is on file, these rites of social passage can reach a dead end. What national credit and insurance companies regard as "blamable or commendable" none of us can avoid. Their "peculiar rules" and "system of opinion" are the ultimate arbiters of a "notion of honor" that brings us houses, insurance, credit, promotions, and jobs. They claim to judge our reputations, and then impose sanctions more powerful than any: not heaven or hell after life, but the wherewithal to exist in this one.

"'Little Brother' is the hard-to-reach private organization that determines whether you are a good retail credit risk," observes William Safire, writing on the dangers of unwarranted information gathering. "Deadbeats do not deserve credit, but a great many honest livebeats have found themselves denied the right to live life on the installment plan because of computer foul-ups or the indelibly recorded judgments of vindictive neighbors" (Safire 1974). For Little Brother doesn't work alone. He relies on his twin—the neighbor who is, under federal law, a legitimate source of personal information determining the reputation we enjoy or suffer with would-be creditors, insurers, and employers. That reputation is likely to be the precipitate of neighbors' opinions, anonymously given and indelibly recorded.

> Do you have a charge account? A home mortgage? Life insurance? Have you ever made a personal loan or applied for an important job? If the answer to any of these questions is "yes," it is almost a certainty that somewhere there is a "file" on you which shows how you pay your bills, whether you have ever been sued, arrested, or have filed for bankruptcy. Some of these files include your neighbors' and friends' views of your character, general reputation or mode of living.

That paragraph introduces the Federal Trade Commission's Consumer Bulletin Number 7, "Know Your Rights under the Fair Credit Reporting Act" (n.d.). Consumers' rights remain limited, however, for they may never know the names of the neighbors or friends passing on information about them: their anonymity continues to be protected.

What information do credit investigations seek from neighbors? Here are just a few of the more than 100 questions neighbors can be asked, excerpted from nationally standardized interview forms submitted in evidence at congressional hearings.

> What would you estimate his net worth?
> How was worth acquired? (Inherited, from business, investments, etc.)
> What income has he from other sources? (Stocks, rentals, inheritance)
> Any indication he is not increasing his worth and income?
> Do you learn he is pressed financially?
> Is he now, or was he in the past, considered a fast, careless, or reckless driver?
> Do you know of any traffic arrests, charges, or convictions?
> Is there anything unhealthy about his appearance?
> Is he unusually nervous, or any indication of business strain?
> Does he smoke cigarettes?
> Does applicant drink daily or almost daily?

Is there any criticism of environment or living conditions?

Is there any criticism of applicant's character, morals or associates?

How is dwelling maintained? Above average for area, Average for area, Below average for area, No apparent maintenance

How is yard and premises? Neat and uncluttered, Little or no care, Unsightly or badly cluttered

How is housekeeping? Neat and clean, Cluttered, Dirty or unsanitary
(U.S. Congress, House 1970: 270–303; see also U.S. Congress, Senate 1975: 296–363).

Who are the fieldworkers who ask those questions of our neighbors? Part-time students, off-duty policemen, housewives, and retired people, usually poorly paid and often overworked. Bonuses have been a common incentive for them to develop the "adverse" and derogatory information that makes the insurance companies and banks feel they're getting value for their money (Whiteside 1975; Federal Trade Commission 1980: 2–4). The FTC has issued orders in recent years that this practice is illegal.

If there is a theory of social order behind casting NEIGHBORS as IN-FORMERS, it has to be inferred, for nowhere is it explicitly stated. Perhaps it relies on presuppositions about the relationship between personal order and social order: That neighbors in our Puritan tradition are rightfully the personal guardians of community norms and standards. That public opinion is a powerful and positive force. That to keep a large, diverse population on even keel, many forms of social control are needed, and economic incentives for being temperate, clean, sober, industrious, stable, and thrifty are unusually effective. That because citizens do not have an automatic right to credit, insurance, or jobs, they should be prepared to give up some of their privacy in return for those opportunities.

Americans' views of the relationship between personal and social order, however, are definitely different from these assumptions. Overwhelmingly, they regard many of those questions quoted above as being improper, even as they recognize the logic of others. The majority of Americans feel that information appropriate for insurance underwriting decisions consists of a person's sex, drinking habits, type of employment, health and medical history. Americans are not convinced that there is a relationship between any other matters and risk. To ask job applicants directly or to ask their neighbors, friends, and associates what "kinds of friends" they have, 87 percent of the public regards as improper, and asking about the "type of neighborhood" in which the applicant lives, 84 percent find improper, as do 77 percent regard questions about the applicant's spouse, 74 percent about membership in political and community organizations, and 62 percent about records of arrest without conviction (Louis Harris and Associates and Westin 1980: 507). Life, medical, and health insurance companies should not have the right to ask for information on the applicant's lifestyle, say 77 percent of Americans, or, say 71 percent, about the applicant's moral character (ibid.: 522). Heterosexual relations between unmarried adults is a matter of private choice that should be left to the individual and not regulated or forbidden by law, 79 percent of the public believes; 70 percent feel that way about homosexual relations in private between consenting adults; 59 percent about abortions, and 55 percent about using marijuana (ibid.: 493). The authors of this study, made under the auspices of the Sentry Insurance Company, conclude that "the insurance industry must do a better job of communicating the reasons why information is collected if they are to avoid more rigorous controls" (ibid.: 521). To do that, it will have to furnish convincing evidence of a correlation among reputation, character, and risk levels.

Neighbors who are also friends who know a great deal about one another are nevertheless unlikely to know many financial details. When people meet for the first time and are getting to know one another, I asked a woman in a Minneapolis suburb, do you think that there is any sort of "code" question for income? "I can't think of any code question that I'm ever asked, or if I ask people. And I guess I do wonder about incomes—I think incomes are very interesting. It's not because I'm nosy, but I always had the feeling that in this neighborhood, for instance, if you took 10 or 20 families and you took everybody's income and gave them the same number of children more or less, and you gave them all the same income per year, say, $25,000, I bet you half of them would be in debt and crawling, wondering how they're going to make the next payment. Another bunch would have a certain amount in savings—they wouldn't be spending as much on material things as the people in debt are. Some of them would be out spending a lot of money on entertainment, others would be spending money on painting or art. But they would live such divergent lives, it would be unbelievable. Looking at their homes, you'd think some were making money hand over fist, and looking at their furnishings and the way they lived, that others weren't hardly making anything.

"I think personal finances are one of the most hidden things in the world. I think people talk about sex before they talk about money. You get couples together or women together, and they'll admit to all kinds of sex and the most intimate things before they'll talk about what their incomes are, and how they spent it or whether they're in debt or how much money they actually make per year. I think it's one of the things we were always brought up on, that your finances are personal. Been handed down from generation to generation.

"Among my three closest friends I don't know what each of their personal finances are. I don't know what kind of taxes they pay. I know what their houses are worth, but I don't know what their husbands make or what one of them is getting in alimony. I don't know how much they're in debt. I don't think they are, I think they're both rather frugal like I am. But I don't know. And I know a lot of intimate things about them. We all say to each other, 'Oh, I can't afford this or that this month.' I know one friend entertains a lot. I know that their sons are in hockey and that type of thing and that's very expensive. Some days I'll have a pair of baggy and patched pants on—I wear them for housework—but you know, you look at me some days, you wouldn't know whether I was affluent or not. So I don't think you can really tell by clothes either."

To a group of five Minneapolis women I put the question, With whom do you generally talk about money outside of your immediate families? "Money problems, or how much you make? Nobody ever tells you how much they make. That's an intimate thing. People don't talk about their income or how much in debt they are." Only when people are visibly spending money, is it discussed, says a woman in Minneapolis: "Neighbors might talk about money only when they see someone getting a lot of new things that are obviously expensive. Because just to live on this street everyone has to have a certain amount of money because of the price of the house. Everyone here is pretty much equal." That one of the largest investigation companies "used two neighbors as sources for estimating [his] yearly salary . . . surprised" Robert Ellis Smith, a lawyer and the publisher of the monthly *Privacy Journal*: "I suggest that they are the worst possible sources for sensitive information of that sort" (R. E. Smith 1979: 72).

"You shall not bear false witness against your neighbor," one of only Ten Commandments. Once upon a time when he was a member of the U.S. House of Representatives, Edward I. Koch of New York City found himself rejected for a life insurance policy, and pressing the company for the reason, an agent finally told him off-the-record that a neighbor had told an investigator that Koch had leukemia. Still far from sick, Koch demanded that they reexamine his file. Ultimately the company agreed that the neighbor had maliciously provided false information. Partly spurred by this experience with a neighbor-informer, Koch co-sponsored with Barry Goldwater, Jr., the Privacy Act of 1974.

Not an isolated case, according to the Federal Trade Commission: "We have found that consumers complain most frequently about reports which contained allegedly inaccurate and highly inflammatory information. Of particular concern is the characterization of their habits or life-styles by neighborhood sources not in a position to have relevant facts" (Goldfarb 1979: 159). Yet, the U.S. Privacy Protection Study Commission concluded, "While credit bureaus may profitably exploit the speed and efficiency of modern information-processing technology, it is hard to see how the computer can replace the inspection bureau field worker who specializes in interviewing neighbors and associates" (1977: 320). Although the law requires corroboration of such subjective information by two sources, credit-reporting companies can put on the record uncorroborated and unconfirmed information simply by identifying it as such. Moreover, the Fair Credit Reporting Act permits credit-investigating companies to disclaim responsibility for the accuracy of what they report; yet the same files pass from creditor to would-be creditor, from one part of the country to another.

A single credit-investigating company, The Credit Bureau, Inc., reported to a Senate committee that it makes "approximately 300,000 disclosures annually" to citizens, but it "does not maintain statistical information or studies showing the number of reports that contain errors" (U.S. Congress, Senate 1980b: 776, 779). Equifax reported to the same Senate committee that every day their 3300 "field representatives interview in person and by telephone over 150,000 people" to fill consumers' credit dossiers, making "over 10.6 million reports per year" (ibid.: 759). In 1979 it "averaged over 1,500 disclosure interviews per month with people who came into our offices or called us on the phone"—those relatively few Americans who take the time to find out what has been said about them (ibid.: 741, 742).

The U.S. Department of Commerce justifies its policy of protecting the anonymity of neighbors at their request on the grounds that "sources would not cooperate if their identity might be revealed later to the consumer" (ibid.: 74–75). That protection the American Civil Liberties Union has attacked eloquently, without effect on subsequent legislation. Yet even the ACLU hasn't raised the issue of using neighbors as informers at all.

> To permit a source of information which may ruin a career or bring financial disaster to a family to remain beyond the possibility of discovery for such redress as the defamation, privacy, or other aspect of the tort law may afford is to invite the vicious, the jealous, the irresponsible, and the vindictive safely to assassinate their enemies and seek sanctuary in a statute, the purpose of which they have subverted. . . . What anonymity of sources guarantees is irresponsibility of informants. The jealous neighbor, the spiteful ex-wife, the disgruntled competitor, the crackpot local gossip can freely and irresponsibly vent their grievances, secure that they can damage without risk to themselves. That is not the way a sound credit system gets reliable information. If the informant is not willing to be identified, the presumption should be indulged that the information is unreliable. We are the product of a centuries old system involving confrontation and adversarial testing. An informant who elects to give derogatory information but declines challenge, dispute, or confrontation is electing a course contrary to our basic principles, and information from such a source is tainted (ibid.: 1152–1153).

To the contrary, the Federal Trade Commission finds neighbors valuable as informants precisely for their reliability. "Indeed, basic common sense would suggest that, in certain instances, neighbors and other acquaintances are capable of being reliable sources for information about a person's health or criminal record" (Federal Trade Commission 1980: 26–27).

Both the Bill of Rights and the Fourteenth Amendment prohibit only federal and state interference with the constitutionally protected right of privacy (McLaughlin and Vaupel 1975: 806). But the Debt Collection Act of 1982 would seem to have made federal "invasion" of financial privacy more overt: private credit-investigating firms have access to the files of parents and children who still owe for college loans, and those of heads of firms who have borrowed from such government agencies as the Small Business Administration. The General Services Administration in 1984 established "direct electronic links between about 100 Federal agencies and seven major credit reporting companies that keep records on more than 100 million individuals and companies" to get credit information before the government grants loans (Burnham 1984). These private companies sell their information to employers, banks, and insurance companies.

The questionable quality of information that private firms develop in their investigations is no deterrent to their being widely employed. Federal agencies—the Justice Department, the Civil Service Commission on behalf of the AEC, NASA, the Peace Corps, FHA, and the VA among others—have customarily used private credit-investigating companies to investigate prospective employees, and such information is routinely exchanged among local police departments, state welfare agencies, and credit bureaus (McLaughlin and Vaupel 1975: 808–812). The Office of Personnel Management, as a "stopgap measure" for catching up on a backlog, has recently augmented its own staff of investigators by contracting with private firms, but found that, compared with about 5 percent of unsatisfactory investigations of its staff, "38 percent of the background checks conducted by private investigators were unsatisfactory and had been returned for more work" (Tolchin 1986).

"Character and reputation" are the main concerns of credit, insurance, and job investigations, but the "relevance and propriety" of the range of subjects they delve into remain unsubstantiated with actuarial proof. Here is Senator William Proxmire trying to learn about these correlations from a witness for the insurance industry at hearings on Fair Credit Reporting legislation:

> *Mr. Webster:* As far as sexual morality is concerned . . . we are concerned with people who depart from the normal practices of the society in which we are underwriting insurance.
> *Senator Proxmire:* Why are you concerned? Do you have any mortality tables regarding this?

Mr. Webster: No, but any underwriter given the chance can probably go back through his files and see some of the cases that have resulted in early claims because of some moral hazard.

Senator Proxmire: This is just conjecture.

Mr. Webster: It is not conjecture. I have seen several cases in my experience.

Senator Proxmire: If it is not conjecture, why don't you have mortality tables?

Mr. Webster: Mortality tables are of value only if you have a very large number exposed to the risk. But in any insurance situation there are also special hazards which, of course, bear on the risk.

Senator Proxmire: You mean we don't have a large number of people who engage in immoral practices at one time or another?

Mr. Webster: I am not judging on morality, Mr. Chairman.

Senator Proxmire: You certainly are. That is why this question is asked.
. . .

Mr. Webster: The industry is judging on the hazards which immorality might bring about, not the actual fact of immorality. We are not sitting in moral judgment at all. We insure people I am sure—

Senator Proxmire: I am sure you are sitting in moral judgment—because your judgment of their moral behavior determines whether or not you will give them insurance.

Mr. Webster: It is not the immoral behavior, it is the risk that will be run by an individual in certain circumstances. Is there a hazard or is there not?

Senator Proxmire: But you have no statistical basis for judging that risk. You have no tables you said, you just have a feeling about it.

(U.S. Congress, Senate 1969: 291)

The actuarial logic of it all continues to escape Senator Proxmire:

Senator Proxmire: . . . Question 6 asks the inspector to classify the applicant's yard into three categories: one, "neat and uncluttered"; two, "little or no care"; three, "unsightly or badly cluttered." What in the world does this have to do with mortality? Is a man a poor life insurance risk because he doesn't have a neatly mown lawn? It could be the other way around.

Mr. Webster: Yes, it could.

Senator Proxmire: If he is mowing that lawn too vigorously, that might be the end of him. . . . When I get back home tonight I am going to have to straighten up my yard. I didn't realize that was a relevant element in insurance. (Ibid.: 293)

Credible correlations between personal characteristics and risk levels in credit, insurance, or employment simply do not exist.

To a large extent, the relevance-propriety issue in insurance stems from some insurers' belief that they should insure only those of "high moral character," and should shun those whose mode of living differs from what society considers normal. In a society as diverse as ours, however, determining what "society considers normal" is no easy task, and relying on the independent judgment of underwriters to make this determination has led to considerable difficulties. . . . Insurers have historically enjoyed considerable latitude in determining what information is and is not necessary to a given decision about an individual. Underwriting is far from an exact science. Moreover, industry spokesmen argue that the cost of collecting information is a powerful enough incentive to collect only relevant information. Yet others claim that insurance institutions collect a great deal of information whose relevance is questionable. Indeed, the industry has been criticized for *not* taking advantage of its actuarial and computer expertise to refine its relevance criteria. (U.S. Privacy Protection Commission 1977: 322; this commission was appointed by the president and was composed of members of Congress, representatives of the insurance and banking industries, credit investigating companies, and citizens.)

Take the offensive toward investigations soliciting information from neighbors—that's the advice of a lawyer specializing in privacy problems: "When you are told that an investigation . . . will be conducted [notification is required by law], alert your neighbors, even the ones you do not know well. Tell them not to co-operate if you wish; it will not hurt you. Tell your insurance company that you do not think these 'investigations' are very reliable, and provide alternative means to verify your reputation. . . . Anticipate problems. . . . If you have a disgruntled neighbor, or if you are 'cohabiting,' or if your neighbors have seen you intoxicated or behind in your bills or both, tell the insurance company and explain. . . . Tell the insurer that you're a good risk anyway and offer evidence. . . . Watch what you say if an investigator asks you for information about a neighbor. Ask for identification, check with your neighbor first. Don't pretend to be an expert on your neighbor's finances, health, drinking, or smoking. Don't worry about hurting your neighbor if you simply say you don't feel that such interviews are proper or fair. Don't leave the impression ever that there is adverse information that you can't or won't talk about" (R. E. Smith 1980: 64).

Neighbors by all accounts get little inside information about one another, yet, paradoxically, these American "credit" investigating companies and the industries buying their services ask to hear what neighbors don't really know. Perhaps even more insidious is that, despite all that has been said about unreliable credit investigations and threats to constitutional rights, no word has been uttered about any wider implications of using neighbors at all as sources of personal information. Nor, for that matter, has using friends been questioned either. Are the personal questions asked of neighbors those to which they know the answers if they're not also friends? Being asked to "inform" introduces doubt into neighbor and friend relationships alike. The leverage to do anonymous harm to friends' and neighbors' opportunities for credit and jobs not only multiplies the meanings of these relationships, but it can obliterate the very trust on which community depends.

PROTECTING HIS GOOD NAME?

Men often remain outside of the "notion of honor" growing up in their residential community, it would seem, removing themselves from its "system of opinions . . . as to what is blamable or commendable," in Tocqueville's phrase. That men have far less to do with neighbors than do women or children is a pattern widely observed but little explained. Although 89 percent of Americans "do not feel that their neighbors know too much about their personal lives" (Louis Harris and Associates and Westin 1980), what men and women consider to be "knowing too much" seems to differ. " 'What I talk about [with my neighbors] and what my wife talks about are two different things,' " said one man in a study of the neighboring patterns of middle-class men, all having middle-management jobs, all but five with children (Useem, Useem, and Gibson [1960] 1974: 158). Of these 75 men, only four "had neighbors whom they also counted as friends. . . . The rest mention that their wives count some neighbor women as friends, but that they do not" (ibid.: 171). Once the men are home from work, "women who visit in each other's homes during the day do not visit each other." One man commented, " 'I occasionally see the neighbor lady running out the back door when I walk down the street' " (ibid.: 158). Even though marriage itself leads people to have more social ties around home, fathers do not have as strong a local network as do mothers; moreover, "married men reported fewer confidants than did never-married men" (C. Fischer 1982: 253).

Trust and Depth constitute the lines we draw to distinguish friends from acquaintances, and women and men appear to differ considerably in friendship's place in their experiences. Speaking of differences between strangers, acquaintances, and friends, a woman in Houston says: "A stranger is someone you know very little about. An acquaintance you know more about their comings and goings and activities. And a friend you share feelings with and more of your inner self. You have to develop a trust with that person and feel comfortable to take the risk of sharing, and that is what takes time, to get to that point. With an acquaintance we would talk about more superficial things. A friend would be deeper, sharing their feelings." After marriage, men tend to limit their friendships. A study of the relationship between stage of life and number of friends of younger and middle-aged men found that while about 91 percent had friends before marriage, 76 percent did after. Those who do maintain their friendships as they move toward middle age see fewer of their friends regularly, see them in couples-oriented activities, are less likely to discuss "difficult personal problems with them." The care they express for one another is "not often expressed directly, but more often in acts of mutual help or sacrifice" (Farrell and Rosenberg 1981: 194–198). In general, however, men "gratify intimacy needs inside the family. Old friends get separated as they seek out jobs and homes. Within the marriage maintenance of old friendships often creates strains. A man's wife may become jealous of the time spent away from home. Or the man himself may become jealous of his wife's attractiveness or attraction to his friends. Finally, the demands and expectations of husband and father roles lead men to feel that they have less time available to spend with old friends or acquire new ones. . . . Friendship groups are, by middle age, dominated by issues of status, acquisition, and mutual use, surely corruptions of what we normally regard as intimacy. Mass society theorists may have overstated their case, but our culture does appear to encourage a gradual de-personalization of self and an impoverishment of relationships outside the family" (ibid.: 202).

The possibility that neighbors' espionage may matter in crucial decisions about employment, credit, and insurance may be one source of the different ways women and men draw the lines between their private and neighborhood lives. Their work and their financial status are critical to the meanings of husband and father. For middle-class men, "occupational life and family relationships are sacred; they are within the zone considered private and are not open for conversation with neighbors"; men's conversation centers around "sports, weather, lawns, cars, house improvements." And crab grass, the topic mentioned most of all, they discuss standing up in their yards, in semipublic space. "Confidences are not exchanged" about occupational life. The axiom is that "what the man does at work is 'his own business' which should be respected as being private." Great care is taken that "a man's off-work activities do not reverberate into the occupational sphere of his life. . . . This 'taboo' applies to the women as well as to the men. Women are expected to not carry tales about their husband's occupational role beyond the confines of the home," and most especially "to be avoided is living next door to—that is, having as a close neighbor—a person with whom one is associated closely in an occupational role" (Useem, Useem, and Gibson [1960] 1974: 170).

Men's occupational experiences may put their distinctive marks on the lines they draw; they find in family life the equilibrium that work and career stresses can upset daily. Moreover, occupational life—in corporations and small businesses, professions and trades—in compliance with the

American Creed, maximizes Self-Interest and Individuality, in contrast to the Interdependence essential for women and children. Men's privatization may be a tactic for avoiding that conceptual conflict.

During my discussion with six men in Minneapolis, all members of the same church and living in different parts of the metropolitan area, one asked the others: "I'm curious about you guys—do you find that your wives seem to be better acquainted with the neighbors? Helen seems to know the neighbors *all* around the place, and I can't even remember the guy behind me hardly." A chorus of "Oh, yes." Another man: "I'm constantly asking Peggy who the couple is behind us, and she knows all of 'em and she too goes and meets 'em when they first move in. I'm at work and don't see 'em. I've been away on a trip, and I'll come home and say who are those people, and she'll say they've been there two weeks. I just don't see them."

Speaking for herself and her husband, a Houston woman says: "We don't depend on the neighborhood, but my children do. They play outside along the block. My husband certainly doesn't depend on the neighbors at all—none, zero. But that's the trend of the neighborhood. The whole neighborhood is like that."

Men are not likely to "take the initiative" socially: "We have a neighborhood card club—the women have a club and then there's a couples' club," says a Minneapolis woman. "And through that, most of the men have become better acquainted. They've struck up friendships and found they have similar interests. But the men didn't take the initiative, it was the women. I think we lived here about two years before my husband knew very many people in the neighborhood. And for me, it was probably about half a year."

"Men hold back," says a woman in a California suburb. "There are about three couples in this neighborhood that we're friends with, after about three-and-a-half years of living here. My husband would call one man a friend, and I would call the three women friends. Two of the three women were friends almost from the time we met, we had a lot in common. The first time we sat down for coffee, we got to know each other very well. I didn't rub noses, shall we say, with the third woman until months after we moved in. My husband knows one man well. But men, I don't think, give like women do, as far as becoming intimate goes. They hold back. They don't seek out thoughts or feelings. My husband's very comfortable with this one man and that's about it."

A woman living in Minneapolis experienced that same difference between women and men: "We had a problem with one of our boys—he didn't graduate and had to stay an extra year. I'm not one to keep things to myself—I've got to find someone to talk to. Now my husband is just the opposite. If we have a problem with any of the kids, he doesn't feel that anybody in this world should ever know about it. And he never talks to anybody about it. But I just can't be that way. Maybe men are different. I don't suppose that they have much opportunity to go around and talk either."

"A neighbor and I coached Little League and we coached soccer together, but we never went beyond that," says a man in California. Men hang back and "don't stray from their yards at all," according to a California woman: "That's how you meet other people—through your children. Hunting them up or chasing them over to their playmates. They're the ones that are the least inhibited, and they're the ones that make the friends the quickest. And it's the men in the neighborhood that make friendships the very last. And oftentimes they don't stray from their yard at all. It's the woman's initiative to have people over for dinner, or to get to know them."

Men aren't around home as much as women are likely to be, that is true. As increasing numbers of women are employed outside the house, they aren't having as much to do with neighbors either. Yet when both men and women spoke to me about the difference in their friendships, they themselves didn't claim that only men's work schedules kept them out of things around the neighborhood. Nor did the men describe themselves as "shy" or the women speak of their husbands as "unsociable." Although occupation and personality surely play a part for both sexes, they don't seem to tell the whole story.

For all their concern with "preserving privacy," Americans in fact experience few neighborly intrusions, a sociologist reports:

> My greatest surprise as an Englishman [studying an Ohio suburb] came from the limitations which so many Americans put to the desirable activities of a good neighbour, and the stress laid on preserving privacy. And remember, the word "privacy" was not mentioned by the interviewer; nor was any phrase suggesting privacy. The question put was, "What do you understand by a 'good neighbour'" or, "How would you describe a 'good neighbour'?" . . . Is this fear of the invasion of privacy justified? What do householders want to keep private? In both [England and America] they seem to want to be able to exchange conversation with their neighbours at all times, and to extend or receive helpful family services in times of emergency. In both countries they fear "noseyness" from neighbours by which, presumably, they mean that the neighbours might discover, by accident if not by design, information about the family way of life which they would not especially like communicated to others. . . . Whilst the fear of prying neighbours was

constantly referred to, [few American] families admitted that they suffered
from this nuisance. This suggests that the fear was either based on slender foundations or that neutralizing measures had proved effective. (Bracey
1964: 79, 84–86)

That 89 percent of Americans feel that neighbors don't know "too
much" about their personal lives attests to the success of privacy strategies
(Louis Harris and Associates and Westin 1980). But this fear of "prying
neighbors" may not have such a "slender foundation" if they can be pressed
into local service as national informers. Men may not need to fear that their
wives will tell financial or job secrets to neighbors, but they could well fear
that the neighbors will make it their business anyhow. Americans getting
behind in their credit payments can find themselves reading a collection
threat like this:

> "This is to advise you . . . that an investigation may be made whereby
> information may be obtained through personal interviews with neighbors,
> friends, or others with whom you are acquainted. Such an investigation
> may be found necessary by us to aid in our efforts to collect the outstanding
> balance on your account. You have the right to make a written request
> within a reasonable period of time for a complete and accurate disclosure of
> additional information concerning the nature and scope of this investigation.
> Why make it difficult? Pay now or call us for suitable terms." (U.S. Privacy
> Protection Study Commission 1977: 52)

Even if neighbors giving these "personal interviews" should not be cooperative, field investigators are instructed in bringing them around. Their
training manual tells them to "proceed from the impersonal to the personal. People do not readily talk to strangers about the personal reputation
and morals of their friends and acquaintances. However, after first talking
about impersonal areas (identity, employment, and health), they have less
hesitancy to cover more personal matters." To get to these, interviewers
are supposed to ask open-ended questions, such as " 'How is he regarded?'
instead of, 'Is he well regarded?'; or 'How much does he drink?', not 'Does
he drink?' " (ibid.: 324).

In trying to relate "character traits" and personal habits to credit worthiness, credit and employment investigations scant the factors that research finds most strongly correlate with the responsible discharge of
debt obligations: unemployment and illness are the main sources of debtor
default. Only 4 percent of defaulters can be classified as deadbeats, people
"who walk away from their obligations," but the debt collection industry
uses this pejorative term in justifying "its harsh debt collection practices
on the grounds that debtors in default are disreputable people who have
deliberately walked away from their obligations. . . . [It uses] midnight

telephone calls, threatening letters and hounding of the debtor, his employer, relatives and friends" (Caplovitz 1977: 238–239). The "stable" person has a good character, it is believed. What of the economy's "stability" and its capacity to provide employment? If employers' "stability" were the criterion, the credit system would have to work differently. The "character and reputation" of employers and their economic and business advisers—the choices they make as entrepreneurs and savants—are obviously fundamental.

If the employment, promotion, and loose privacy protection practices of many companies on the Fortune 500 list are any indication, men's local reputations can follow them, and the jobs they need, all over the country. About half (48 percent) of these companies use investigative firms to collect or verify personnel information, but about a third of them don't review these firms' operating policies and practices (Linowes 1980: 195). Pinkerton's, Inc., specializes in employment investigations, and the firm's own witnesses told the Privacy Protection Study Commission that "in a neighborhood check, they examine 'primarily reputation and character.' 'We would even describe a house,' said one witness, 'whether it is well maintained, the grass is cut, depending upon the type of position.' Although they said they would not ask specific questions about sexual activities or preference, Pinkerton witnesses also said they would specifically inquire about current and past drug use and alcohol consumption" (U.S. Privacy Protection Study Commission 1977: 332).

"There's no law against hiring me," is the headline of an advertisement by Equifax Services appearing in *Personnel Journal* in June 1982.

> Why hire me? Because I work for Equifax and can help you meet EEOC and legal hiring requirements. Plus give you the specific information you need to make a sound decision. My method? An Equifax Pre-Employment Report. The fair way to protect the privacy of your applicant. While you protect your company from possible future losses. Hire me, and you actually hire the entire Equifax field force. That's right. 3,600 people located throughout the U.S. and Canada. Ready to find the facts you need. This includes data on job experience and performance, honesty, reputation, attitude, eligibility for rehire, absenteeism, health, and abuse of alcohol or drugs, if any. (84)

An employment report can be transmitted in a long chain of disclosures that may affect job options and promotions. Even "Welcome Wagon" companies may sell data on new families—occupations, religion, and purchasing habits (Westin 1968: 160).

Women and men seem to differ in challenging the investigative practices that keep them from participating in marketplaces for jobs, credit, and insurance—so former senator Paul Tsongas observed while sitting as chairman of the Subcommittee on Consumer Affairs. Commenting on the testimony of a woman who won damages as the victim of a false investigative report, he said, "It's always a woman who decides to fight back. I don't know what's wrong with men. They kind of take these things in stride" (U.S. Congress, Senate 1980b: 218). Not in stride, I suggest, men are more likely to "take these things" frozen by fear. Women have less to lose because they participate less to begin with in these markets. Are women basing their challenges on being kept out and men mounting none for fear of finding themselves kicked out?

Constitutionally protected by anonymity to make use of what they know or think they know, neighbors may make a national issue of local reputations. The consumer credit dossier combines with personal and local judgments the objective criteria needed by national economic markets, an incongruity that rubs Americans the wrong way, as their attitudes toward appropriate credit inquiries reveal, but not only as invasions of their privacy: does this confusion immobilize trust and pen men in their yards?

Reputation is working capital; it is possibly the prime symbolic product and resource of economic and political order (Bourdieu [1972] 1977). But are "reputation and character" the true subjects of these investigations? They seem to confuse honor with respectability. Pinkerton agents may stop at the lawn, but reputation can be assessed only by getting behind a social front. Respectability is the public face that character wears while meeting norms for cleanliness, manners, housekeeping, dress, sobriety (P. J. Wilson 1973). Respectability can mask character: newspaper reports of suburbanites indicted for crimes often report that their neighbors, hugely surprised, had thought them to be "entirely respectable, just what you'd expect of a good neighbor."

Reputation, on the other hand, condenses public knowledge of the ways people choose to act—with relatives and friends, strangers and employees, tenants and clients, students and colleagues. It strikes the balance of our strengths and weaknesses as we fine-tune our responses to life's exigencies. The norms of each kind of community we belong to—familial, occupational, religious, associational—weight our responses, and men—more so than women, it seems—try to keep these compartmentalized.

Even two current incomes may not be enough to pay for all the things mainstream Americans have decided they need, not to mention those they can't do without—doctors and dentists, sports and dogs, vacations and piano lessons, gardens and furnishings, tuition and cars. Credit rides in tandem with work, and being able to get a line on it is as important an asset as any skill or money in the bank. Gossip can jeopardize credit, the next mortgage, family insurance, and a better job—men expect themselves to be able to look forward to all of these. In 1971 Congress passed the first law giving consumers credit rights, the Fair Credit Reporting Act. Opening hearings in the House, Congresswoman Leonor Sullivan said that she prefers to call it the "Good Name Protection Act": "One's reputation remains today, as it has always been, the most precious thing we own" (U.S. Congress, House 1970: 1).

RENTING THE DREAM

The newest newcomers to American suburbs are those least likely to be homeowners. RENTERS. The single-family-detached houses filling suburbs' great expanses signify OWNERS. RENTERS, associated with apartments, row houses, and two-or-more-family houses, have been, by and large, confined to cities, mainly because suburbanites so actively have excluded them.

"The suburbs are as simple as ABC," says a man outside of Washington, D.C. "Adultery, Barbecues, and Children. In another version of those ABC's, the C stands for Crabgrass—that is, your *neighbor's* crabgrass that gets across your property line and infects your lawn. I don't know much about the adultery or the crabgrass, but barbecues and children for sure. And that's why we like it out here."

"Out here" in implicit contrast to "in there"—downtown, the city, the central city. Suburb and city are each precipitates of American meanings, crystallizing American hopes and fears about families—children, women, and men. They also capture American thoughts about the kinds of places promising the most satisfying sense of community: Uniform or Varied, Small-town or Cosmopolitan, Friendly or Anonymous, Spread-out or Concentrated. The children and the barbecues: nurturing offspring and sharing suppers are what families are all about, and suburbia is all about families. And about being among "our own kind," more uncertain in cities where the population appears to be more varied. Unlike suburbs, cities are believed to be about "never knowing the people down the hall," and about stunting children's growth. Cities are believed to be an environment where the social trust children rely on is at a premium and where children also find the outdoors hedged about by all sorts of obstacles: maybe an elevator ride and a long walk between the apartment's front door and the playground, or a hazardous bike route to a friend's house, and certainly, it is supposed, dangers from perverts and thieves on the bus or in the subway on the way to a movie. In suburbs, that line between indoors and out fades, and the larger fund of trust there—the essential nutrient for gardens of children—accounts for Americans' honest albeit stock response "We moved here for the children."

The facts are that within just about every city there are residential neighborhoods with single-family houses that are little different in layout or population from those associated with suburbs. The higher population density in cities is not uniform, but likely to be concentrated in a few close-in neighborhoods. Then, too, suburbs are coming increasingly to share many features in which cities are supposed to specialize—jobs, first of all. Suburbanites also see city dwellers coming out to their concerts and plays, restaurants and jazz clubs. But also coming to reside in suburbs are crime, poor people, disappointing schools, run-down neighborhoods, and renters.

The house as symbol of the single-family ideal loses none of its power, despite both high divorce rates and high housing prices. These social and economic realities create a demand that could be partly met by converting single-family-detached houses into two or more units. But the meanings overwhelm those realities: opposition to conversion is vociferous, even though advocates respond by guaranteeing that in outward appearance the converted houses will not hint at the number of dwelling units within. In some New Jersey towns, for example, whole subdivisions of single-family-detached houses illegally maintain a separate unit for rent located in what had been the garage; were these facts to be acknowledged by amending zoning and building codes, the symbol would be extinguished.

> "A homeowner is something very special. We enjoy working on our homes, and we take pride in them. When a homeowner starts renting out part of his home, it changes things. He starts looking on his home as a rental unit. We see them taking less pride in their homes. . . . This is down zoning, which lessens property values. . . . Once they allow this, they can move on to high rises and, who knows, I could wake up with a factory next door. Apartments are a sign of deterioration. It takes the sparkle out of the American Dream just knowing that there are apartments on the block."
> (Geist 1981)

So said a Connecticut woman watching as her neighbors constructed rental units in their single-family houses.

Until recently, Americans have dreamed themselves to be on a ladder whose steps lead them through a wholly natural, temporal, and evolutionary progression: first a city-dweller, then a suburbanite; first a RENTER, then an OWNER. To keep renter and owner each in its proper place, time must be harmonious with space: being spatially out of place is the same as being out of step chronologically. Renters are a sign of *temporal* discrepancy in this recurring American dream, evoking suburban opprobrium.

In developers' proposals for higher-density housing shouted down at zoning hearings across the land, anxiety-producing renters are characterized in the mythical idiom of tricksters and clowns. Renters, Americans believe, are by nature morally deficient, unstable, and dangerous (Perin 1977: 116, 118–119). People who rent are a different and lesser species, morally unqualified by that final rung of getting a mortgage, and for that, stigmatized. They will infect others with contagious disrepute: "They will lower our property values" is owners' hue and cry following on any proposal to include renters on the block, in the neighborhood, or even anywhere within the suburb. Between the lines of every argument made against allowing apartments near single-family residential areas (even apartments for the elderly), that motif reappears.

Families might call apartments home, but they have been built to earn a profit for their owners: they may not be Profitable *and* Residential in American symbolic order, for Love and Money are forbidden to live side by side. To acknowledge how tightly the NEIGHBORS we are supposed to Love are entwined with Money cuts right across our cultural grain. Single-family areas are "zones where family values, youth values and the blessings of quiet seclusion, and clean air make the area a sanctuary for people," the U.S. Supreme Court's decision in *Village of Belle Terre* v. *Boraas* (419 U.S. 9) declared. To this "sanctuary" for the "sacred institution" of FAMILY, which is "divinely ordained," the profane idea of Profit is anathema, and forbidden.

The taboo is constitutionally enforced. Zoning's constitutionality was established in 1926 when the U.S. Supreme Court classified the apartment house as a business or trade properly excluded from *residential* districts (*Village of Euclid* v. *Ambler*). The apartment house is "a mere parasite, constructed in order to take advantage of the open spaces and attractive surroundings created by the residential character of the district," said the Court. To this day, the zones allowing apartments are likely to be located at the periphery, along arterials, highways, and, alongside Seth and Hermes, at busy crossroads. An ambiguous land use combining family love and developers' profit, apartments' proper place is in borderlands, preferably in territorially "gray areas" already socially betwixt and between, in keeping with renters' trickster motif. Designed to serve as traffic and land-use buffers on behalf of single-family residential zones, apartments are often intentionally built in unquestionably undesirable areas.

These attributions also shape renters' sense of themselves. The owner of a very large apartment complex at the Maryland edge of Washington, D.C., told me that she had had to convince her white-collar, middle- and upper-income tenants that, despite being renters, they could exercise political clout and demand municipal attention to the traffic and garbage collection problems they were having. They didn't at first understand as a matter of course that the taxes embedded in their rent entitled them to just as much say as homeowners have; they ended up electing "their own" member of the local city council. Nevertheless, the IRS continues to deny renters the same national citizenship rights as owners: renters may not deduct from their income taxes either the interest or taxes paid through their rent.

Housing is an index of occupational identity, and to live among renters as their meanings have been constituted could tarnish reputation and social esteem, more for men than for women, perhaps. Their separate house on its own lot is an emblem of honor in the occupational meanings men live through, but women may feel that association second-hand. Men don't express the same doubts about suburban living as women do, even as both agree suburbs are best for the children. Discussions with 30 couples, half urban, half suburban, one study reported, found that almost half the men wanted to live in suburbs more than their wives did, while only about four of the women were more positive than their husbands. Among these upper-middle-class couples there is a conflict over "the attachment of many wives to the cultural and social opportunities of the city and the desire of many husbands for the relaxation and status of a suburban home" (Saegert 1980: S104).

However blurred as the lines may have become between city and suburb, the differences between them remain powerful symbols, more evocative than reflective of current—and future—realities. The comforts promised by the American Dream have been giving way to the disconcerting surprises of interest rates, the baby boom and its baby boom, land costs, and divorce rates. Outcries of pain, of frustration, and of disappointed expectations are heard in zoning hearings throughout the land, as people cling to a dream being revealed as myth.

REPRISE

Giver of our sacred text on fences, Robert Frost knew how much more there is to them than meets the eye. Yet Americans consistently mishear "Mending Wall," deaf to Frost's irony and bite, for not in the least approving the rubric "Good fences make good neighbors," the poem calls it wholly into question. Americans fall upon it, however, as the golden rule of domestic life: a chain-link line of clarity.

Reminding his neighbor of their "outdoor game" each spring, the poet wonders as they "set the wall between us once again" what mysterious forces bring it down:

> Something there is that doesn't love a wall,
> That sends the frozen-ground-swell under it,

> And spills the upper boulders in the sun;
> And makes gaps even two can pass abreast.
> . . . The gaps I mean,
> No one has seen them made or heard them made. . . .

He muses about the reasons for walls at all:

> There where it is we do not need the wall:
> He is all pine and I am apple orchard.
> My apple trees will never get across
> And eat the cones under his pines, I tell him.
> He only says, "Good fences make good neighbors."

Still, only solid stones satisfy his neighbor's understanding of their relationship. For the poet, walls come last, if ever: he has to decide first "What I was walling in or walling out," and know "to whom I was like to give offense. . . ."

After weighing whether to try to jolly his neighbor out of his blind acceptance of "his father's saying," Frost turns from mischief to malice.

> Spring is the mischief in me, and I wonder
> If I could put a notion in his head:
> "*Why* do they make good neighbors? Isn't it
> Where there are cows? But here there are no cows. . . .
> Something there is that doesn't love a wall,
> That wants it down." I could say "Elves" to him,
> But it's not elves exactly, and I'd rather
> He said it for himself. I see him there
> Bringing a stone grasped firmly by the top
> In each hand, like an old-stone savage armed.
> He moves in darkness as it seems to me,
> Not of woods only and the shade of trees.
> He will not go behind his father's saying,
> And he likes having thought of it so well
> He says again, "Good fences make good neighbors."

Placing his neighbor beyond the pale of civilization, Frost sees him as a savage of the Dark Ages. When the light of reason takes us "behind" received wisdom, when we acknowledge the arbitrariness of our convictions, only then are we civilized, Frost is saying. Until then, fences are like answers to unasked questions.

The misinterpretation speaks to another American dilemma. Fences in good repair keep privacy intact; they also permit the concealments that Americans' dedication to the ideal of Moral Equality requires. Fences, lawns, and walls help us keep to ourselves information that could impair social trust between equals: Envy has been a neighborly issue since the beginning of moral time, and so has its twin, Shame. "You shall not desire your neighbor's house, his field, or anything that is your neighbor's," the Tenth Commandment, put last for special emphasis perhaps.

A sophisticated symbolic system animates this ideal, surpassing the facts of material and political inequalities. Income-homogeneous neighborhoods do their part. Look-alike housing, even its banal design, stands as a sign of a shared will not to heighten envy or foster shame. Blue jeans on everyone, janitors and executives talking over the game scores, Julia Child at McDonald's are some of the small democracies of mass society. Gossip magazines bring jet-setters down to the same earthly concerns everybody else has, a forced landing inside a national system of opinion. "Even where it was fairly obvious that the people living round about were different," observes Bracey, the British sociologist who studied Ohio suburbs, "attempts were made, repeatedly, to see the same qualities in the neighbours as they themselves possessed" (1964: 2). Middle-management men who remain in the same neighborhood while moving up in rank and salary try "not to let it show or let it interfere" (Useem, Useem, and Gibson [1960] 1974: 172).

The social shame that wealth can inflict and the social envy privilege can provoke leave Americans vulnerable, despite. The strongest domestic tranquilizer is the persisting American belief that there are only two classes, middle class and working class, which makes it possible to deny the existence of the really poor and the really rich and the doubt each casts on the American creed "All men are created equal. . . ." Fences wall in the American Dream and wall out its nightmares of reality.

Another reality is the increasing possibility of "home occupations," which also create a volatile zoning issue. Home occupations are often allowed in residential areas only after a public hearing, and their prospect can stir up almost as much neighborly rancor as dogs can. An architect carries on a successful practice within his house; to forestall his neighbors' envy—and complaints to city hall—he invites them to use his swimming pool, anytime. Zoning laws not only keep home from being profaned by work and love tainted by money, they also damp down financial jealousies. A building inspector in suburban Minneapolis speaks of the jealousies and the nuisances of "dance schools": "A lady starts out with 5 children—and I've seen this at least 10 times—she starts out with 5, and two years later she's got 15, three years later she's got 25 to 50 to 100. She puts an addition onto her house, she owns two Cadillacs, she's making more than her husband. There's 100 cars a day going through the neighborhood. Two things happen. Jealousy overtakes the neighborhood because they see her making money. And the other thing is that she's really creating a nuisance in the neighborhood. That's a lot of automobile traffic going there. So then that comes up under the zoning ordinance, and sooner or later they terminate her use permit."

"And to whom I was like to give offense . . ." Walls around single-family suburbs and pleasant city neighborhoods give great offense to the millions kept from wearing the badge of belonging in America. The same hidden clause excluding renters extends to others also believed to "lower property values." With their chief source of economic security under threat, Americans in their fear thus avoid and disparage blacks, browns, people with low incomes, the handicapped, nontraditional families, the elderly—people who are likely to be in the same categories of age, marital status, and income as some of their closest relatives. These contradictions set the groutings of the metropolitan mosaic, and chipping away at exclusionary housing patterns has proved to be nearly impossible: suburban systems of meaning frozen in place.

Renters have also of course signified people likely to be lower-income; yet even though a far greater number of lower-income Americans are white, the main preoccupation is walling out blacks and browns in order to maintain the status quo. Some people are renters because they are financially unable to get a mortgage, and today many who would have been able to own just a few years ago are being forced into this despised cadre. Or some are high-income renters who aren't attracted by the income tax incentives of ownership. Even some middle-income renters may be finding a better return in other kinds of investments. No matter these fine points: owners and renters are two systems of meaning powerfully shaping metropolitan space. Suburbanites have not wholly constituted them, however; many national economic events have taken charge of their fabrication. Federal insurance for mortgage lending was a key, first to the banks' recovery in the early 1930s, and then to unlocking the suppressed vitality of the construction industry. Once their risk was protected, banks began the profitable enterprise of converting a nation of depraved renters into a holy alliance of homeowners. Still other economic events may ultimately reshape these meanings when they prove instead to work against the market's interest. When single-family houses go begging for buyers, the market begins to take pride in renters, and when interest rates make single-family-house mortgages less attractive, the housing stock for rent is likely to increase, but, I daresay, only in places where there is already a fair-sized rental market. Homeowners who have become accustomed to the presence of renters are unlikely to see an additional population of them as being novel and unusual.

But the walls can offend suburbanites' sense of fair play. "Just to live on this street everyone has to have a certain amount of money because of the price of the house. Everyone here is pretty much equal." The price of housing puts everyone on an "equal" footing, no matter their race or anything else about them: "Obviously if you're going to buy a house you've got to have a certain amount of income to be able to maintain it," says a woman in Minneapolis. "I've always felt that anybody who could afford to live in a house in this neighborhood deserved to be here. I don't care what color they are or what their background was or how they speak, whatever the case may be. There's no other criteria for moving in here because there's a mixture of age here, a mixture of work backgrounds, there's elderly retired, there are people who aren't terribly intelligent or well spoken. There are two men living two doors away, there are divorced people, and there is a mixture of ways we bring up our children. I think you just simply have to be able to afford to move into the houses here."

Income and "caliber" go hand in hand for a Californian transplanted from Illinois: "When we lived in Skokie 9 or 10 years ago there was one black family, and at that time it was just unheard of. I always said, 'It wouldn't bother me.' If they could afford the type of home to be next door to me then they're the caliber of people that I would want in the area. I couldn't care less if they're white, yellow, black, red, or purple. And I've always felt this way. Color of skin doesn't mean anything. I worked with two black girls—they were shampoo girls in the beauty shop. One could sleep in my home, my house was hers. The other one I wouldn't turn my back on. And I don't feel that because there is one person who can ruin it for all that they should be categorized. So it wouldn't bother me if I had blacks living next door to me, that doesn't bother me at all, as long as they're not trash."

These are sincere convictions, I feel, that others should enjoy their same chance at living out the American Dream. At the same time, being concerned with keeping up the market value of their house, most people correctly assess their best economic self-interest: the property market sees only danger in those not conforming to the ideal mainstream. Not in charge of the criteria being used in judging market value, suburbanites' biggest investment forces them to go along and keep the hurdles high. Financial and domestic domains may be locally experienced, but they are nationally determined. Our culture is in charge—here, with compartmentalizing conceptions with which it finds a place for everything and puts everything in its place. The nearly blank record of compliance with the Civil Rights Act of 1968 demonstrates how culturally helpless to realign social order we remain, even as we may be legally powerful. The walls will come tumbling down ever so slowly, held up as they are by this infrastructure of symbols and myths.

Those unwritten books on neighborly discord in the files of suburban officials speak volumes about the ironies of these exclusive practices. They bear witness to a scarcity of social trust not the making of criminals or a preying underclass. The vital signs of trust and community are weak where we should expect them to be strongest, among Americans upon whom favor has smiled least ambiguously, whose reasons for distrust are fewest—it would seem.

Perfect Dogs

That familiar, special something between person and
pet dog has long inspired a comic, serious, and philosophical literature. For many awed writers—James Thurber, Virginia Woolf, Konrad
Lorenz, Robert Louis Stevenson, E. B. White, Charlie Schulz—and
their readers, dogs have much to tell to and about humankind. But the
social side of that relationship has been left largely unremarked: what
does the bond between people and dogs have to do with our collective
life?

To friendly social encounters between dog walkers and those attracted to their poodles or mutts must be added others that are less so, I
found. Once embarked on hearing Americans talk about their neighborly
relationships, I had no choice but to take account of their complaints
about antisocial dogs and the neighbors they own. Dogs sometimes transform neighbors from strangers into friends, as in my case, but often
enough, it seems, into adversaries if not enemies. Complaints about barking, trespassing, nipping, and attacking dogs all have a common source:
dogs off the leash away from home ground.

The most puzzling fact is that their loving owners are also putting
themselves and their families at risk: when unleashed dogs become lost,
strayed, maimed, or killed, their owners grieve. To understand the
ambiguous quality of this love and to suggest why the ambivalent population of dog owners is so large, this essay explores the very wordlessness
of the dog-human bond and finds in it not a surrogate for a child but
symbols both of mother and of the hard-won trust that makes society
possible.

The line between ourselves and other species dissolves when it comes to
dogs. "Man's best friend," we say of them. Then, dogs settle down at the
hearth without our giving second thought to this most silent incongruity,
the FAMILY DOG. But away from that hearth, like no other MEMBER OF THE
FAMILY, dogs can make special trouble up and down the block—threatening
and biting children, joggers, and bicyclists, barking loudly and too long,
and messing up gardens, driveways, sidewalks.

To the "ABC's" of the standard suburban package add D for dogs and the disorientations and distrust their doings can introduce to a clear sense of community. Don't misunderstand me, I'm a long-standing dog-lover (well before I came to see the point of cats) with irreplaceable memories of Boots, Torger, Happy, Rex, Schnapps. But these issues are inescapable: in the first five minutes of listening to suburbanites discuss neighbors, it became clear that dogs are the most worrisome population of the invisible neighborhood. "Dogs, like children, can be the glue or the solvent of the neighborhood," one man puts it. Says another: "Dogs seem to be a big problem in the suburbs. I think probably worse than kids really. Because you can control the toilet habits of the kids."

The trouble is doubled because dog owners, surpassing all understanding, are likely to be more defensive about their pets' mischief than about their children's. They brook no criticism of them. Their dogs are perfect. In my interviews, again and again I heard that people with bothersome dogs will deny their neighbors' complaints with far greater vigor than they would defend their children's misbehaviors, which is puzzling, considering that dogs have always been supposed to be "like children" to their owners. "My dog would never . . . bark for hours, dig or defecate on that lawn, tip over that garbage can, nip a jogger, bite a child. . . ." The denials are so predictable that animal control officers will investigate neighbors' complaints first hand and for days on end, the better to arm themselves with the facts.

I've observed many a defensive posture in dog owners. The words say that their dogs are perfect, but their body language, as they shift about, clear their throats, avoid my eyes, and pick up their chins, belies their assertions. Deny they do; dog owners and nonowners differ considerably in their perceptions of the problems that dogs cause: while 38 percent of former owners and 46 percent of people who have never owned a dog consider animal waste deposits a problem, only 22 percent of present owners do. Although 18 percent of nonowners acknowledge that dogs' attacking or frightening children is a common problem, only 9 percent of the owners do. About 55 percent of owners see no problem with dogs running loose, compared with 36 percent of former owners and 28 percent of those who have never owned one (Wilbur 1976: 32). The closer a loose dog is to the territory it calls home, the more aggressive it is likely to be—more so than a stray, that is (Borchelt et al. 1983: 66).

Dog-lovers have bad dogs and the public its problems with them mostly because owners let them run off the leash away from their own property, with all that follows a roaming dog. When dogs bark too long, too early, or too late, when they relieve themselves anywhere at all without respect for pedestrians, property lines, public health, or nurtured gardens, when they threaten joggers, bicyclists, and dogs smaller than themselves, when they chew carefully tied garbage bags and strew the weekly cans, when they scare older people who may be unsteady on foot, when they make a ruckus over mating, and when they bite, bad dogs are more than nuisances: they deplete the fund of social trust.

The leash is the sole solution, joining dog and owner as they walk away from their property. But many suburban owners will not use one habitually, and despite an increasing number of local leash laws, compliance is still largely voluntary. When discussing whether or not to pass them, communities all over America come face to face with how they think about Conflict: their biggest challenge seems to be to conduct democratic debate without resort to duelling. A majority of dog owners are opponents; humane society officials believe that the 55 percent who see nothing wrong with dogs running loose is a low estimate—more like 65–75 percent of all owners do. Most important of all, when loose dogs become lost, strayed, maimed, or dead dogs, their families, who love them beyond telling, can be plunged into anguish and grief. "Collie Lost, Looks Like Lassie . . . ," a note pinned to a lamp post in my neighborhood reads—pathetic, and perverse. For unleashed dogs, if they haven't already been picked off in traffic or attacked by larger dogs, are likely to leave home for good and become part of the stray population, sometimes forming into intimidating and predatory packs.

Humane societies, animal control specialists, and veterinarians all concern themselves with, in their terms, "irresponsible owners." These specialists see them as being lazy, careless, and inconsiderate of others, as well as unkind to their pets, exposing them to risk of life and limb. Most public policy recommendations ultimately depend solely on irresponsible owners' becoming responsible, but without pinning down what constitutes the difference between these two breeds of owners. Obvious differences between irresponsible and responsible owners are elusive; close observers tend to agree that both are drawn from the same populations; they live in poor and posh neighborhoods, on farms, on large suburban lots, and in city apartments; they belong to the same social clubs, churches, and political parties. Not knowing what else to do, policy recommendations keep suggesting the same nostrums that haven't worked in the past or they suggest solutions borrowed from other cultures but hardly applicable to the American case. Iceland, for example, once found that its dog population was disease-ridden and imposed very high taxes to discourage ownership altogether. Dogs are barred from Chinese cities, hardly a feat in a hungry, centralized society that includes them in its food system. In Prague, the dog license is free upon presentation of a certificate from an obedience school; otherwise, it costs $85. In the United States, the politician endorsing any such proposals already would have decided to retire.

The most puzzling questions of all: Why are dog lovers negligent and irresponsible in such large numbers? Why are their behaviors so obviously ambivalent? Those questions pushed me to ask: Why do dogs break through the species partition to become our relatives and friends? Why does the dog-human bond exist at all in this culture? Why do we insist on creating so ambiguous a difference between us? Vis-à-vis most other species, we want to keep the lines of difference clear, yet we blur this one.

"Irresponsible" owners' behavior is not an aberration: it is one dimension of the dog-human bond itself. Love and Loss are, I am suggesting, the concepts erasing the line between our species. The bond between people and dogs is formed from remnants of the one we once had with our mothers as babes in arms receiving essential nurture. Next to birth itself, separating from that earliest symbiosis is the first major experience of the distress of disequilibration. The bond with dogs symbolically re-creates both the trust of that time *and* the pain of separation. The two sides of this experience are the sources of that ambivalence by which some dogs become nuisances to their neighbors and lost to their owners.

While British meanings of the bond seem to be similar, I can't speak for other European cultures. In Asian societies dogs have neither the symbolic nor the real roles Westerners assign them. They are food and pariahs, yet work alongside farmers, herders, and hunters. Except in Japan, they have no place at home; yet Japan also has had one of the largest populations of stray dogs in the world. In traditional Shintoism, dogs are symbols for evil spirits, and in folk beliefs, vehicles for sorcery—perhaps these associations or Japanese kinship concepts for placing "members of the family" contribute to their dogs' widespread abandonment.

Even though dogs have been humans' companions for some 12,000 years, as best we know, the psychological and social nature of the pet-human relationship has been explored only in the last decade or so (Anderson, Hart, and Hart 1984; Beck and Katcher 1983; Fogle 1981; Shell 1986). The presence of a dog appears to have some influence on the effectiveness of psychotherapy, on extending the lives of people who have had heart attacks, on both calming and stimulating elderly and isolated people. These claims, all tentative, haven't yet been demonstrated beyond question, but why any of these consequences should even be anticipated remains unknown.

I haven't looked into the bond with cats, partly because cats seem not to come between neighbors as often as dogs do (although there are exceptions I've heard about) and partly because dog ownership is more prevalent. At last estimate, just over 56 percent of American families having at least one child over six also have at least one dog, and about 36 percent keep a cat—in all, about 68 percent of households with young children have at least one dog or cat. In households with no children, 33 percent have a dog and 24 percent a cat. These data are from a market research study undertaken on behalf of the American Veterinary Medical Association in 1983 (Beck and Meyers 1984). Compared with pet-food industry sources, they represent somewhat higher estimates: 40.2 percent of all households own a dog (34 million households in 1983), 27.3 percent, cats (23 million households). The dog population as of 1983 is estimated to be about 50.2 million, cats 46.2 million; dollar sales of dog food in 1983 were about $3.6 billion, cat food, $1.8 billion (Pet Food Institute 1984).

There are also regional and locational differences in ownership, of course. (These data are only sporadically collected by reliable researchers.) Estimates of dog-owning households range from 43 percent in the Middle Atlantic states to 60 percent in both the West South Central (mainly Texas) and Mountain states. In Baltimore in 1983, for example, 40 percent of households owned one or more dogs, 23 percent cats (L. H. Ross 1985: 77). In California in the 1970s, 67 percent of all households owned one or more pets—dogs accounted for 59 percent, 35 percent had cats, and 5 percent owned neither dog nor cat but some other pet. By kind of settlement—a city, a county seat, an industrial center, and a rural area—pet ownership in general also varied: in California, people in rural areas were most likely to own pets—77 percent, compared with 60 percent of those living in a county seat and a city—but still, 66 percent of households in the industrial center kept them. Only 18 percent of households consisting of five people had no pets; about 65 percent of one-person households had none (Franti, Kraus, and Borhani 1974: 477). About 68 percent of families having a dog kept one, 21 percent owned two, and 11 percent kept three or more.

A recent increase in rates of cat ownership may have an upper limit, however: dislike for cats is about seven times as prevalent as dislike for dogs and liking for dogs nearly twice that for cats. Dogs are Americans' clear favorite among all animal species—horses come next, then swans, robins, butterflies, and ahead of cats, which rank twelfth in preference, they like eagles, elephants, owls, and turtles. In this national sample of 2455 Americans 18 years old and over, on a seven-point scale calibrated from strongly like to strongly dislike, about 27 percent strongly like cats and just over 4 percent strongly dislike them. By contrast, 50.3 percent strongly like dogs and 0.5 percent strongly dislike them. About the same percentages (39) just plain like both species, but 8.4 plain dislike cats compared with only 1.4 percent who plain dislike dogs. (Toward horses 38 percent feel strong liking and 50 percent simple liking; almost nobody dislikes horses, strongly or weakly.) (Kellert and Berry 1980: 148–149.)

Cats are also less amenable to domestication than are dogs: their species' characteristics keep the line between us more firmly in place. *The Penguin*

Book of Pets (1978) classifies cats as "wild animals," in fact. From the cat lovers I know, my guess is that, as absorbing and endearing as cats are, both species keep watching each other from their own side of the line that dogs track across without a moment's hesitation. That's one reason I hear cat lovers give, in fact, for their dislike of dogs—that they give up their apartness (the "independence" cats specialize in) so readily.

UNGLUING THE NEIGHBORHOOD

American icons of Love and Fidelity notwithstanding, roaming dogs can bring out the worst in otherwise affable people. "The only problem I've ever had with neighbors is over dogs, and the way I handled it was face-to-face," reports a man in suburban Minneapolis. " 'Here's the problem, what are you going to do about it?' They've been very cooperative, apologetic, I guess, because when I get to that point, I'm pretty steamed. When I'm standing in your driveway with a shovel and some stuff on it, and I dump it in front of your door and say, 'I don't want it on my doorstep again.' There are several people like me who do the same thing—go right to the people and say, 'Your dog left this, it belongs to you, it ain't mine, and I don't want to see it on my property.' So pretty soon when you have two or three people do it to you, you get the message."

What happens to the relationship after that? "There's a little more strain. We had a big German Shepherd and we got rid of him. It wasn't fair to the neighbors, and it wasn't fair to him. The neighbors meant more to us than the German Shepherd. He really was an animal that was loved and it was really tough to get rid of him. So I can empathize with them, and again, it's like insulting your child, you take it a little personal. And with a dog, pretty soon he's one of the family and you feel the same way. And so there's a little more of a strain. Some people can handle that, and some, you can tell—well, we've just wiped out that relationship. But what do you do? You win some and you lose some." In all, a widespread "strain" on the neighbor relationship.

When dogs are the problem, it's often long-standing and difficult to resolve. "I called the animal warden because we have an ordinance that your animals can't keep disturbing everybody all the time. You have to take care of them so that they don't bother your neighbors. One dog was always getting loose, going on everybody's property and leaving its excrement. Plus it was real noisy at night. The owners had a night-cleaning business so they weren't there, and I had a newborn baby and every night I couldn't sleep I was really disturbed. Everyone was irritated. We did try to tell the neighbor first, many times, but he wouldn't do anything about it. So then we complained to the city. They moved away finally, but they never did solve it. As long as they lived there they never did anything about it because I don't think they understood the problem. They weren't here to hear it. If *they* had been sleeping, I think they would have taken care of it."

Or would they? "You'd think that the barking would bother the owners too," I commented to the dog warden of a San Francisco suburb. "It doesn't though," he replied. "More often than not it doesn't bother them. They've learned to block it out. I see people here become uptight about their animals, just like their children. If they're barking, they just tune it out." One woman going out to work every day, sure that her dog didn't bark as neighbors complained, was concerned enough that, out of curiosity, she left a tape recorder going. Sure enough, she was able finally to admit, her dog barked all the livelong day.

Every barking dog complaint has to be substantiated because owners will deny it, claims a building inspector in a Houston suburb: "The barking dog isn't as cut and dried a thing as it might seem. We watch it for a week. If we're going to court, we have to prove it's excessive. We have to keep numbers. People's first reaction to a barking complaint is that they're not in violation. The same way on dog-droppings."

"We trained our dogs to leave our 40-foot lot alone and go over to the neighbors'," admits a man in Minneapolis. Not an uncommon practice, according to a woman in San Francisco: "The people across the street have a very nice lawn and their dog is not allowed to go on it. They send it out at all hours to do its thing on someone else's property. My husband says that someday he's going to take the dog and slit its throat and dump it into the garbage can and haul it off to the dump. He's been threatening to do that for about four years now." Have you complained to the city? I asked. Have you spoken directly to your neighbor? "No, but I've yelled at the dog to get off our lawn, 'Get out of here, you're destroying my bushes, quit going to the bathroom on 'em, go on to your own property'—loud enough so they could hear it." Dog leavings are not only an invasion of privacy, but a clear sign of disrespect for lawns and all that they signify.

Nor, as we have seen before, is it always really the dog that's getting up the neighbors' dander. "We've had barking dog complaints where we went out 30 to 40 times because a neighbor has, for some strange reason, got it in for another neighbor, and they will continue to call and call and call. We go up and down the block, knock on every door, and find out is there really a problem. A lot of times a neighbor will say, 'No, there's no dog barking around here,' when in essence there is—because they themselves don't want to get involved. We make it a habit not to drive up to the suspected house, but park down the street and wait to hear it if that's the one. We sit and wait and roll down the windows in order to see whether there is really a problem. Sometimes when you do that and everything is quiet, you learn there really isn't one." A feud over barking led neighbors in Colorado Springs "to bomb each other's mail boxes and allegedly shoot out each other's windows" (Darneal 1976: 196). One day each month is given over to dog cases in Middlesex District Court in Massachusetts; in Portland, Oregon, they need two days monthly, and sometimes half the neighborhood shows up, just about ready to take the law in its own hands (Fletcher 1981: 48). In Santa Barbara, California, the city attorney's office will provide professional mediation for dog-related disputes.

"Oh, yes, definitely there are feuds," the animal officer in suburban San Francisco told me. "We had one that was sort of funny because of everything that came out of it. First the complaint was about the neighbor's dog: 'Can't you do anything to get them to control their dog?' Then, we'd get a call about that neighbor, who had a cat: 'What can they do to keep their cat off my property?' We went so far as to tell them that you can actually put a cat on a leash and it will learn to walk on it. I've seen little children walking cats on a leash. Well, the lady put her cat on a leash to take it for a walk, and we get a humane call! Nothing inhumane about that at all. But—we were the go-between. We were the way to get back at the neighbor."

A young woman working in the city hall of one of the suburbs around Minneapolis chatted with me while I was waiting to see the building inspector. I'd been there before, and she knew of my interest in complaints brought by neighbors. A barking dog, she told me, had been disturbing the sleep of many of her neighbors for a couple of years, and they were distraught about what they might do about it. Amazed that it had gone on so long, I asked, Have they spoken to the owner? "Oh, yes, many times. So often, in fact, that he's installed an answering machine to take the calls while he was sleeping!"

TAKING RESPONSIBILITY

"Irresponsible" owners are likely to be those who, time after time, defeat the enactment of local leash laws, often initiated both by "responsible" owners and by nonowners. Veterinarians, public health officers, dog trainers and breeders, and animal ethologists are unanimous about the necessity for leash laws—and their observance—everywhere, except perhaps on farms where dogs are part of the workforce. In rural areas, however, free-roaming dogs can be a special menace; they may worry cattle or lather sheep (chasing them into a run so they become overheated and then die from exposure to lower air temperatures). In most states, worrying dogs may be killed on sight, and their owners are without recourse.

Romantic landscapes as soft-focus backdrop to handsome-dog-running-free are images advertisers use in selling dog food—images that humane societies, dog breeders, and veterinarians aim to convert to handsome-dog-beautiful-person, each at the end of a leash. The conviction that dogs should be allowed to run freely, that it's in their "nature," partly perpetuates these social problems. Nostalgia does its part too: in his home town on the prairie, one dog-lover told me, just seeing the dogs out for their stroll put him in mind of their owners and gave him a warm glow of belonging. He was young then, and his town had few automobiles, far fewer people, and even fewer dogs. Yet dogs can get ample exercise at the end of a leash, and some can even get enough hanging around the house all day. Backyard dog runs cost little and are easy to construct.

Wandering dogs have topped the list of the subjects that citizens complain about to their local council members, mayors, and officials, yet one survey found that "animal regulation was not among the twenty-seven major problems of primary concern to municipal officials." For these officials, the issue is politically hopeless, because "many municipal officials view animal regulation as a problem that will continue to plague communities no matter how much study, funding, or management is devoted to it. Animal regulation is among the most sensitive of community issues and the local government manager or elected official who attempts to mediate between pet owners and the non-pet owning public is almost certain to succeed in alienating both segments of the community" (Hodge 1976: 3). Municipal officials, always hesitant to take a firm position on animal control, "almost always [preface their] statements with how much they personally love dogs, as if encouraging responsible ownership is anything less than an expression of love. New York City's sign telling owners they must clean up after their animals is prefaced by the word 'please.' I have never seen any other posted directive so tentatively and politely worded" (Beck 1974a: 34).

Politicians know better than to take sides in local debates on leash laws. After a vituperous and tense debate in the Wellesley, Massachusetts, town meeting a few years ago, during the roll call vote, one by one, each local pol took a walk, exiting to their constituents' laughter. For the fifth time in two years a leash law went down to defeat. "This is the craziest issue I've ever witnessed in a town meeting," says one citizen. One woman switched from her earlier opposition only after her husband had been forced to retire his daily bicycling because neighborhood dogs chased and nipped him, threatening his flesh and his balance. The leash law, she says, was "the most emotional issue since fluoridation." The leader of the opposition had once been a colleague and collaborator in the League of Women Voters.

Politicians can also be surprised at a strong mandate from constituents demanding leash laws. Polling the citizens in his area, one Cambridge city councillor found that it was not crime or housing, as he reasonably expected, but dogs that topped their list of acute local issues. Even 45 percent of dog owners perceive as a major community problem the fact that dogs run loose—not theirs, but those of "irresponsible" owners—and 65 percent of people never owning a dog agree. If the proportion of irresponsible owners were smaller, they would appropriately be considered merely deviants or scofflaws. Their magnitude and the public problems and public costs attributable to them make them, however, a nontrivial, ubiquitous social force.

Not strays, but pets allowed to be out and around on their own, are the source of most public problems, and the two most serious threats to health are dog-bite and parasitic infections. Other public problems and costs traced to irresponsible owners are abandonment and the maintenance of shelters and euthanasia facilities. Most dog bites—superficial wounds, fatal injuries, and attacks on wildlife and livestock—are perpetrated by pets. During the time when dog rabies was a major problem, up to the early 1950s, about 75 percent of exposures were from pets, not strays (Beck 1974b: 58). Epidemiologists call dog-bite a "disease of childhood" (Feldmann and Carding 1973: 957). Of all people bitten, 75 percent are under 20, and 41 percent are children under 10: in St. Louis 1 out of every 50 children aged five through nine is bitten annually, and the biters are likely to be the dogs of neighbors, even in the same block; about 25 percent of all reported bites in St. Louis occurred on the dog owner's street (Robertson and Iverson 1979: 75).

But reported bites of children are about one-tenth the actual rate. A survey of 3238 students in rural and small-town schools in Pennsylvania found that 46 percent remembered being bitten in their lifetime and 15 percent being bitten within a single year. The reported bite rate for children aged five to nine is 2 percent, but 19.5 percent remembered bites occurring in one year. The remembered rate for boys in their lifetime is 53.4 percent, 39 percent for girls. Neighbors' dogs account for about 29 percent of these bites, the family's own dog, 14 percent, and strays or dogs of unknown ownership, about 16 percent. Going to the doctor after being bitten by a stray is more likely than after being bitten by a neighbor's dog (Jones and Beck 1984). The larger the dog, the more serious the injury, and in recent decades, the trend had been to ownership of larger breeds.

This letter to "Ann Landers" appeared in *The Boston Globe* on March 20, 1983:

> Two weeks ago we buried our 4-year-old daughter. She was our only
> child and we cannot have another. Our darling little girl was attacked and

killed by the neighbor's dog. There is a leash law in our town, but our neighbors, like many others, paid no attention to it. The dog had to be destroyed and, of course, so is our long-time friendship with the neighbors.

The insurance company will not pay their claim because they failed to honor the leash law. That dog should never have been off their property. They will have to handle the lawsuit on their own, which means they will lose their home. Meanwhile, they are furious with us, but their daughter is alive and ours is dead. We would consider the loss of our home trivial compared with the loss of our precious girl, but naturally they don't see it that way.

Please, Ann, tell people who own dogs to obey the leash laws before a neighbor loses a child and they lose their home. (B25)

Standing in the way of the leash habit is dog owners' tendency to deny their dogs' natural propensities. Three veterinarians acknowledge in their handbooks this widespread trait of owners:

> Remember this: Hundreds of thousands are bitten by dogs each year, and most of these bites are administered by dogs who, to quote their owners, "wouldn't *really* bite." (F. Miller 1972: 180)

> [D]ogs in the city should never—and I mean never—be allowed off the leash. For one thing it is against the law. Chiefly, however, dogs cannot be trusted. Unlike cats, they are impetuous and incautious animals. And their eyesight is poor. They will suddenly dash across a busy street after another dog or a cat or after some imaginary menace, paying no heed to, or not seeing, oncoming cars. Even old and sedate dogs who have never done such a thing in their lives will suddenly behave in this manner. I have seen the too-frequent and too-tragic results of allowing dogs to walk on the streets unleashed. If you value your dog, don't trust him off his leash for a minute. (Kinney 1966: 86)

> I assume that owners who let their dogs off the leash are pleased to have everyone observe how well trained Fido is and how obediently he heels and comes when called. But most people are not at all pleased to see how a nicely mannered dog will suddenly pick on a smaller dog, usually one that is restrained by a leash and thus cannot escape, and start a fight or bite savagely. Not only small dogs are the victims—children or unsuspecting adults who might unwittingly (and unwisely) pat the strange animal can end up with a painful bite as a reward. (Dolensek and Burn [1976] 1978: 213–214)

LOVING DOGS, AMBIVALENTLY

A remarkable ambivalence seems to be built into the dog-human bond. Linguistically we'd have to find many another idiom to say all the things this culture sums up as "dogs." Expressing the ambivalence perfectly is a gimmick once used on the television program "Sneak Previews." Just at the moment when two film critics, assessing the new movies, announce their choices for "Dogs of the Week," a lovably cute dog appeared and barked briefly.

A "dog" is, according to my *American Heritage Dictionary of the English Language*, "an uninteresting, unattractive, or unresponsive person," and in the way those critics employ it, "a hopelessly inferior product or creation." "Doggerel" does appear to be related to the Middle English *dogge*, but "dogma" has quite different origins. A "dog" is also a "contemptible, wretched fellow." Plural, it means "the feet." "To go to the dogs" means "to go to ruin." "To put on the dog" means "to make an ostentatious display of elegance, wealth, or culture; to feign refinement; to be a phony." As an adjective it means "inferior, undesirable, not genuine," as in "dog Latin." "A dog's life" is an unhappy slavish existence; and "a dog's death" is a miserable, shameful end. "A dog's place" is at the social bottom.

This "peculiar human ambivalence" that seems to be part of the bond itself, James Thurber long since acknowledged. "Aspersions and calumnies" have accompanied affection throughout the ages:

> Dog may be Man's best friend, but Man is often Dog's severest critic, in spite of his historic protestations of affection and admiration. He calls an unattractive girl a dog, he talks acidly of dogs in the manger, he describes a hard way of life as a dog's life, he observes, cloudily, that this misfortune or that shouldn't happen to a dog, as if most slings and arrows should, and he describes anybody he can't stand as a dirty dog. He notoriously takes the names of the female dog and her male offspring in vain, to denounce blackly members of his own race. In all this disdain and contempt there is a curious streak of envy, akin to what the psychiatrists know as sibling jealousy. Man is troubled by what might be called the Dog Wish, a strange and involved compulsion to be as happy and carefree as a dog, and I hope that some worthy psychiatrist will do a monograph on it one of these days. Even the Romans of two thousand years ago displayed the peculiar human ambivalence about the dog. There are evidences, in history and literature, of the Romans' fondness for the dog, and my invaluable Cassell's Latin Dictionary reveals proof of their hostility. Among the meanings of *canis* were these: a malicious, spiteful person; a parasite, a hanger-on. The worst throw in dice was also known to the Romans as a dog. Caesar may have been afraid he would throw a dog that day he crossed the Rubicon. (Thurber 1955: 205–206)

In the rural South, dogs are today, as they have been traditionally, workaday partners in hunting, tracking, and guarding, and companions as well. An "unconventional" man is one who owns no dog. Yet these people handle their dogs callously, even cruelly, and, just as often, owners boast of their unalloyed fidelity and their rare abilities in sniffing out quail, coons, and rabbits (Jordan 1975). James Agee and Walker Evans saw the same ambivalence 40 years ago, and reported it in their classic *Let Us Now Praise Famous Men*:

> The dogs are all mongrel ruralhounds. . . . [T]hey are almost alarmingly
> rickety. . . . [D]ogs are never kindly touched by adults, unless they are pup-
> pies; the children play with them in the usual mixed affection and torture.
> The Gudgers feed Rowdy rather irregularly from their plates, seldom with
> a floor plate of his own. . . . [D]ogs, if they blunder into the way or are
> slow in obeying an order, are kicked hard enough to crack their ribs, and, in
> that manner which has inspired man to call them, in competition only with
> his mother, his best friend, offer their immediate apologies; the sickness or
> suffering in sickness or death of any animal which has no function as food
> or power goes almost unnoticed, though not at all unkindly so. . . . (Agee
> and Evans [1941] 1960: 217)

On the negative side of this ledger of Love should also appear the high rates of owners' failure to license their dogs and the high rates of abandonment of once-owned dogs. Not even half of all owned dogs are licensed: once straying, those animals are unlikely to be returned. And dogs will stray, given a rabbit to chase, a bitch in heat, or a travelling companion. Unable to trace ownership, most pounds will offer a dog for adoption after 48 hours or, at most, after one week. Then they will kill strays or let research laboratories have them. Because only about one-third are ever adopted from pounds, chances are that an untraceable dog will die. By not putting their dog's home address on the public record or attaching it to the dog's collar or tattooing it on a hindquarter, owners deny their dog's social connections and leave him to the mercies of strangers. Owners also abandon them in person, humanely. About 20 percent of the total dog population is turned in annually to humane society or municipal shelters in New York, Baltimore, and St. Louis (Beck and Katcher 1983: 104).

No American newspaper misses so much as a day of advertisements run under the "Lost Pets" column. Notices on neighborhood trees and telephone poles for the return of beloved dogs are as much fixtures of our social landscape as mailboxes. About 1000 radio stations participate in a "Pet Patrol Radio Directory" set up by the American Humane Associa-tion to broadcast missing-pet notices—about 35,000 over the past several years. Of all former dog owners, 24 percent no longer have their pets be-cause they were killed in accidents (18 percent) or ran away (6 percent) (Wilbur 1976: 25). One reason people give for not getting another dog is that they could not bear the grief its death would bring; of former owners, 23 percent felt their loss too keenly (Beck and Katcher 1983: 103). Yet, aching as the loss is, millions of owners are nevertheless doing too little, somehow, to be sure of avoiding the experience.

A minister in suburban Minneapolis was telling me that one of his neighbors had complained about his dog's getting into her garbage cans. As he rambled on, the story turned from Love to some kind of unacknowledged Hate. "It ticked me off because the dog didn't do that much damage, and only did it once or twice." Why did it tick you off? I asked him. "I suppose I felt defensive, hurt, I guess. I love my dog—everybody in the neighborhood loves him. He wouldn't hurt a flea. It did bother my neighbor, and I can understand that because, well, I don't like it either when dogs come over in our yard and crap. But she was on the phone two or three times. That's four years ago now—and every time I go by that house, I get negative feelings still. Our dog finally got killed by a car."

One man had had a dog that bit "three or four" children: "Our dog stays in at night. It will go out to go to the bathroom, and usually it doesn't wander off the property. It deposits it very conveniently on our driveway and comes back into the house. But that isn't good management—that's luck, I would say. If that dog hit the street and decided to go six doors down, there's not much I'm going to do about it or to control it. Matter of fact, the last dog we had, he was sort of all over the neighborhood." Did neighbors call you? I asked him. "No, not really. Not up to the time he went on a biting streak and bit three or four kids and the pound picked him up and we just left him there. That's the end of that dog."

Is there a difference between dog owners whose pets do and don't make neighborhood trouble? The animal warden in a Minneapolis suburb sees the difference this way: "A lot of these people who let their dogs out roaming and barking I see as would-be dog lovers. I think the dog is providing something for them; the dog is taking the place of something for them. They probably do like the dog, but they don't really understand it. They don't understand the dog's place in society, as I would put it. Their appreciation and love for that dog is not quite the same as it is for what I call a 'professional dog-lover.' I think there is a vast difference between those two types of people. I don't know why it goes that way, but I see it all the time. Would-be dog lovers really don't know a dog's place. The dog has taken the wrong place for them. They're almost like people who don't control their kids. They don't know where their kids belong. They don't know themselves where they belong. They're doing the same thing, in my opinion, with the dog that they do with their kids if they have them. They just don't know their place. Back when we passed the leash law, I can remember the turmoil and the chaos at the city council meeting. You heard people screaming and hollering against it. But, there were also people from some of the kennels singing a completely different tune, that there's nothing wrong with leashing a dog, that in fact a dog should be leashed for its own good."

A dog warden in suburban San Francisco, population 32,000, bears that out: "The leash law is designed to protect the property owner so that people have free access of the sidewalks and the streets. The one it protects the most is the dog itself. We average maybe a dog every two or three months now being hit by a car on the street. Prior to the leash law we were picking up four and five dead dogs a week, sometimes more."

The most puzzling aspect of the behavior of dog lovers opposed to leashing is the harm to their dog they provoke and the grief that family members will feel at its injury or death. The physical relationship between owner and dog, each at one end of a leash, is the most effective way not only to reduce socially unwelcome behaviors, but to prolong the dog's health and life. But only if local leash laws are enforced to their limit could the leash habit be instilled in some 20 million or so families who let their dogs roam, and no city or town can financially afford the additional policing an all-out effort would require. Nor can they afford it emotionally: meter maids in New York City have refused to be deputized to enforce that city's canine waste law. "We have enough trouble dealing politely with irate overtime parkers. Please don't add the high-strung dog owner to our daily round."

There's nothing inevitable about bad or lost dogs. Everything the negligent dog owner doesn't do, responsible owners find to be entirely possible. Responsible owners train dogs of all breeds not to bark when left alone, indoors and out. They train them to come when called, to sit, to heel, to stay. They teach them to use newspapers for defecation and urination when the weather conspires against the daily outing. On a walk, they position their dogs to deposit their waste where it will least harm other people's lawns and trees, and they keep public paths and parks free of feces by picking them up and putting them in the trash. Dog feces can precipitate a disease cycle carried in dirt; dog parasites may infect children with whom they often share the same backyards, parks, and playgrounds. A daily production of 187 tons of feces and 380,000 quarts of urine has been estimated in Houston; about half of a sample of dog stools taken from a suburban, upper-middle-class residential area tested positively for parasites such as roundworms and hookworm; none of the neighborhood dogs were strays (Burns 1978: 28).

Responsible owners protect the dogs of their neighbors from the surprise attack any dog is capable of mounting. They protect their dogs from their own dashing and straying impulses—impulses which combine with their poor eyesight to put them at risk. And if their dog isn't on a leash, it's within calling distance, reliably obedient. They protect neighborhood children from being traumatized by a bite and older people from being jumped upon. Responsible owners keep track of garbage collection days and put themselves on special alert to their dogs' temptations. They tenderly surrender their dogs to a humane death when that time comes, if their pets are sick or can no longer be kept; they don't drop them off on a country road or in a different neighborhood, abandoning them to their own limited wits. Their dogs mate at human discretion and not their species', which is, as the statistics on unadopted puppies remind us, non-existent. In all, there is nothing inherent in dogs or in the people they own that makes them an inevitably antisocial team.

As reprehensible and irresponsible as negligent owners may be, they are nevertheless second to none in adoring their dogs. Only superlatives will do on the positive side of the ambivalence; there are no gradations: people love dogs. They're not just fond of them, they don't like them just a bit—people *love* dogs. *I* love dogs. So strong is the positive side of the bond that even the definition of research problems suffers from the bias: in the relatively short time that the dog-human bond has become a serious subject for research, the preponderance of studies has been conducted without control groups and without longitudinal research design. For example, cases of pet-facilitated therapy seemed to suggest that the bond might be related to well-being and recovery from illness, yet structured studies show transient improvements without long-term gains. Nor do we yet know whether the stimuli pets offer are much different for isolated and elderly people from those of visitors and video games, for example. Even "experimental studies of the therapeutic value of pets in which control groups were used . . . revealed [none of the] dramatic therapeutic results similar to those noted in isolated case reports" (Beck and Katcher 1984: 416; see also Beck and Katcher 1983: 163–164).

Topping the list of "dramatic" superlatives is MAN'S BEST FRIEND. The positive side of the dog's relationship to people is lavishly phrased: the defining canine trait is said to be Fidelity—utter devotion, everlasting—a virtue neither KIN nor FRIENDS of the same species can offer. Scientists, not mere sentimentalists, describe the dog's capacity for unconditional, indeed "immeasurable," adoration. Konrad Lorenz says: "The fidelity of a dog is a precious gift demanding no less binding moral responsibilities than the friendship of a human being. The bond with a true dog is as lasting as the ties of this earth can ever be. . . . The plain fact that my dog loves me more than I love him is undeniable and always fills me with a certain feeling of shame. The dog is ever ready to lay down his life for me. If a lion or a tiger threatened me, Ali, Bully, Tito, Stasi, and all the others would, without a moment's hesitation, have plunged into the hopeless fight to protect my life if only for a few seconds. And I? . . . Every dog that ever followed its master [gives] . . . an immeasurable sum of love and fidelity" (Lorenz 1954: 139, 198).

William James: " 'Marvellous as may be the power of my dog to understand my moods, deathless as is his affection and fidelity, his mental state is as unsolved a mystery to me as it was to my remotest ancestor'" (in Papashvily and Papashvily 1954: 35).

PARENTING PEOPLE

The bond of good feeling between people and dogs seems to be fashioned from abundance, indeed, superabundance—an *excess* of Love having no rightful place in human relationships. People can bestow supersaturated feelings on a dog: but not on other people. George Bernard Shaw, ever doubtful, put it that animals in general "bear more than their natural burden of human love." Ambrose Bierce's definition in his *Devil's Dictionary*: "Dog, *n.* A kind of additional or subsidiary Deity designed to catch the overflow and surplus of the world's worship" (Bierce 1958: 19). Profuse feelings, the more potent for being visceral: dogs enter mutely into our deepest selves. Konrad Lorenz had one dog that "reacted to any symptoms of illness, and expressed her anxiety not only when I had a headache or a chill but also when I was feeling downhearted. She would demonstrate her sympathy by a less cheerful gait than usual, and with subdued demeanour would keep strictly to heel, gazing up at me continually" (Lorenz 1954: 133).

Standing in the shadows of all those things that dogs and owners do with and for one another—receive and give ecstatic greetings, take their partings hard, nuzzle, stroke, and paw, take walks, listen to monologues, play games, please with obedience and bones, guard the house, and just be there when we come home, stirring up, as Thoreau put it, the dead air in a room—I find a wholly symbolic relationship. That line from Agee and Evans keeps coming back: people have been inspired to call dogs, in competition only with their mothers, their best friends. The supersaturated feelings resonate with only one other human experience: when else have we ever actually received unquestioning devotion, utter adoration, a total absence of judging, unspeakably overwhelming trust, unspoken understanding, and unbounded love? When we have been babes in arms. To find again a MEMBER OF THE FAMILY and BEST FRIEND constituted by total trust and complete devotion after our infancy, we have to enter a symbolic realm. There we find that metaphysical bond of bliss, but find as well our distress at its coming to an end.

"Virtually all pet-keeping can be seen . . . as a form of pseudo-parentalism, with the animals standing in for missing infants, either because the 'parents' are too young to have real children, or because for some reason they have had children but are now without them. These are the conditions in which pet-keeping is at its most intense" (Morris 1977: 265). That belief is widespread, and to all appearances dogs do seem to be treated as we treat children (and all those less able to fend for themselves in adult terms). Even though the analogy to child care seems apt, many dog devotees never infantilize their pets or the species. Thomas Mann, James Thurber, and Helen and George Papashvily, for example, write with affection and with great respect for their dogs' admirable traits, never having had recourse to an idiom of infancy or dependency; nor do "professional" dog-lovers— breeders, trainers, and many enthusiastic owners I've listened to. Thurber says he always thought a dog-lover was a dog in love with another dog.

Citizens favoring a leash law in the town of Wellesley scoffed that their opponents "rhapsodize" about their dogs. This overspill of feeling leads owners to idealize, to the point of denying their dogs' every misdeed. "Why punish all dogs for the misbehavior of a few?" opponents of leash laws plead. To which proponents rejoin, "But every owner thinks their dog is perfect." Do they think the same about their children? I asked. "Curiously, they're more permissive toward their dogs. For example, if a child were to dig up my garden, the mother would or father would offer to replant it." "Responsible" dog owners often comment, "They wouldn't let their two-year old child out alone—why a dog with as much judgment?"

The parental bond goes the other way, I suggest: symbolically, we are the children of our dogs, whose species' difference signifies the pain of ultimately yielding those earliest parental ties as we live out our concept of Growing Up. This bond with dogs is a sign of fundamental properties of human existence as our culture understands them, and this same symbol is a key to the ambivalence which irresponsible owners act upon.

How dogs keep up their end of the bond contributes to its strength in equal measure. It's their nature to seek a companion more than a parent. Moreover, their popularity also rests on their species' patterns of socialization, which preadapt them to humans' (Messent and Serpell 1981). From the beginning of canine life, dogs' socialization differs considerably from ours. Three or 4 weeks after birth, the mother's constant care-giving ceases and by 7–10 weeks, weaning the litter is completed (Scott and Fuller 1965: 101). By 5 weeks, puppies begin to show the pack behavior of adults (ibid.: 106). Competing with one another for food but not for maternal care, they develop among themselves "strong dominance relationships" (ibid.: 174– 175). Moreover, "strong relationships develop between litter mates in spite of the fact that one litter mate never feeds another but instead competes with him for food" (ibid.: 178).

A puppy taken early from its fellows (at about three weeks) "will form its paramount relationships with people and become an 'almost human' dog that pays little attention to its own kind" (ibid.: 111). Taken from the litter at a later time, its strong relationships will be with both people and dogs, and still later (after about 14 weeks), its strongest relations will be with dogs and its ties to people will be relatively weak. Humans' earliest bond is between adults and their young, and not, as the dog's are, with contemporaries. Dogs' relationships with people mirror, then, their relationships with litter mates. (These observations and conclusions are those of zoologists John Paul Scott and J. L. Fuller, who published in 1965 the results of 13 years of experiments in dog breeding and social behavior; although they found breed differences in some behaviors, their evidence leads to the general conclusions I rely on here.)

In the wild, dogs work as a cooperative hunting pack to stalk food for all. "A well-developed leader-follower relationship is not a characteristic part of either dog or wolf societies" (ibid.: 175). What is often seen anthropocentrically as the "submissiveness" of dogs below the "top dog" suggests to me their positions in a cooperative food-getting system: the same kind of dyadic and dependent relationship of human child to parent is not a feature of canine social relations. But the human *family* in having something of a "dominance hierarchy" and a cooperative ethos provides a parallel to the litter and to the work group. None of this is to say that dogs may not be trained, wittingly or not, to fawn over a master or mistress or to be taught to act dependently. But their natural predispositions and capacities are otherwise. Their cooperative nature expresses itself in their readiness for obedience training, one reason why well-trained dogs are happier themselves and give their owners more pleasure.

Nor are dogs constituted to be "utterly devoted" to any one of us, in plain fact. *We* have those interests, which we do not relinquish despite dogs' showing us that our concepts of Dependency and Fidelity aren't theirs when they readily take to a new family or wander away without so much as a tear. The "one-person dog" is our myth (an observation dog-haters often make). Dogs respond equally to different handlers, Scott and Fuller find. The belief that the person feeding the dog receives the greatest amount of the animal's loyalty doesn't stand up under test; feeding is not necessary to the development of a social tie; dogs are interested in the food but not in the person providing it (ibid.: 177). Even when people never feed them or when they act passively toward them or punish them for making friendly overtures, dogs will become closely attached. "A puppy does not automatically love you because you feed it" (ibid.: 177; also 144). Scott and Fuller conclude that "feeding itself is a minor part of the care-dependency relationship" (ibid.: 177).

Yet, in anthropomorphizing dogs, feeding them is taken as the chief sign of their dependency, as it is for children's dependency. The belief in feeding as a source of dependency may be a way some people give care they want to receive, not an unusual occurrence in human relationships, when care may have a "forced, overdetermined quality [that] is often directed at others who neither seek nor welcome the 'caring'" (Rynearson 1978: 551; Róheim [1943] 1971: 48–49). That dogs may receive "the overflow and surplus of the world's worship" and "bear more than their natural burden of human love" are both cynical and clear-sighted observations.

SEPARATING FROM SYMBIOSIS

Through the earliest years the mother-child bond has three dimensions which provide the tripod for our life-long psychic organization: her intimate responses to the child's every discomfort serving to restore equilibrium; the child's first experiences of autonomy and self-confidence; and the child's feelings of anxiety, loss, and anger at having to give up some of the first to experience the second. The attenuation of the symbiotic relationship marks the beginning of Growing Up, setting us on the way to becoming emotionally mature and capable of founding families of our own.

The breaking of the earliest bond is the second experience after birth that humans have of discrepancy and its distresses. In this phase of separating and individuating, as it is called, we experience the painful interruption of that earliest schema, the symbiosis with mother. Studies of foundlings during their first few months find that they don't experience serious distresses, but in "vivid contrast," when infants are abandoned or orphaned at 8–10 months old they respond "with a protracted behavioral depression resistant to the most assiduous substitute care. Some of them developed a condition . . . called 'marasmus,' a gradual, steady, life-threatening wasting away" (Konner 1982: 330). At that age, their brain's development may be critical in registering the discrepancy between mother and other caretakers (ibid.: 223; Kagan 1981: 60).

Symbiosis is the "infant's initial ecology," or "schema." Jerome Kagan suggests that removal "from this ecology provokes the first social emotion."

> [Separation] might then be regarded as a reaction to a change in something like a sensory adaptation level, and particular degrees of change may lead to distress. Considered in these terms, the mechanism involved may be very primitive and appear very early. This may account for what we found in Guatemala, where the infants in the villages are constantly on their mothers' backs. We could not do some of our experiments because of the distress involved in removing them. Presumably we were abruptly changing their adaptation level for postural, tactile, and olfactory sensations. This would not, however, be a cognitive mechanism, whereas the response to incongruity would be cognitive. . . . I . . . regard [this mechanism] as belonging to a different category, and I don't have a name for that. (Kagan 1974: 243–244)

Becoming a separate person, that is the American way. As both agony and joy and as the lifelong source of many existential issues, the metaphysics of this developmental process also help to account, I propose, for high rates of dog ownership, for the meaning of the dog-human relationship, and for the acted ambivalence of some dog lovers.

Adamantly against the Wellesley leash law, one woman spontaneously told me, in a whisper full of feeling, "Our dog is more important to my children during their teens than ever before. They each tell him secrets, and he's a guaranteed friend when things aren't going just right for them." Not until adolescence do children favor dogs over all other pets; such figures as there are consistently confirm this. In the 1890s the American psychologist G. Stanley Hall orchestrated investigations of children's reactions to all aspects of the universe—to plant and animal life, clouds, the sun, the moon, atmospheric conditions, light and darkness (Bucke 1903: 198). Analyzing 2804 papers written about pet animals by children aged 6–17, one of these studies found that 43 percent were written about dogs, 28 percent about cats, 6 percent about canaries, 5 percent about rabbits, and 5 percent about horses, with lesser mentions of a great variety of birds and beasts. Only as children became adolescent did they increasingly favor dogs over other pets:

	Dog			Cat	
	Boys	Girls		Boys	Girls
Age			(percent)		
7	33	6		6	33
8	41	3		16	41
9	44	36		19	39
10	42	37		22	35
11	53	45		24	36
12	51	42		15	31
13	50	44		19	28
14	57	40		9	32
15	54	46		12	27
16	53	48		0	19

Percentages have been rounded.
Source: Bucke 1903: 462.

In the early 1970s a study of the animal "loves and hates" of 80,000 British children also found the proportion of children who liked dogs best increasing with age, from 0.5 percent among 4-year-olds, showing a peak of about 7.5 percent at age 13 (Morris 1977: 262–263). And a 1980 study shows that among both American girls and boys, but more pronounced among boys, there is a marked rise in preference for dogs at the beginning of puberty and cresting in middle and late adolescence (Jones and Beck 1984: 361).

During adolescence the first wholesale recapitulation occurs of the original separation from those earliest experiences of comfort. The disappointments of infancy make a more conscious reappearance, demanding a new coming to terms with both love for and anger toward parents; as well we know, adolescents live out a period of marked narcissism and ambivalence, needing their parents and still dependent, yet at the same time absorbed with themselves, their newfound competencies, and the alliances in whom they are mirrored. In creating their separate selves, they become critical and contrary. Symbolically available in the family dog are memories of the earlier bond at the very time when adolescents see their natal ties actually coming to an end, as they move on toward adulthood and parenting.

The relationship with dogs restates the character and structure of the earliest phases of the child's bond with mother, as Anglo-American societies constitute it (e.g., Ainsworth 1977; Bowlby 1969, 1973, 1982; Hamburg 1963; Rosenblum 1971; Scott 1971; Schaffer 1971; this theoretical and research literature on the subject is predominantly American and British.) In rough outline, the relationship follows a predictable course after the "peak of symbiosis" during nursing. At four to five months the child recognizes the mother as distinctly another being. That "differentiation" phase leads into the "practicing period," when the child moves away, crawling and climbing, soon to discover the elation of walking alone, the drunken joy of the toddler. At the same time, the child wants to share everything with its mother, coming back to touch base and seeking "constant interaction" or "rapprochement" with the mother, and with father and other adults as well. Approaching 25 months, the toddler's exhilaration begins to wear off, and the child begins to realize that "the world is not his oyster; that he must cope with it more or less 'on his own,' very often as a relatively helpless, small and separate individual, unable to command relief or assistance merely by feeling the need for them, or giving voice to that need" (Mahler 1972: 337). And as the peak of symbiosis subsides, the mother also changes her attitude. "It is as if she now realizes that the infant no longer expects the condition in which there is an almost magical understanding of need. The mother seems to know that the infant has the new capacity of giving a signal so that she can be guided toward meeting the infant's needs" (Winnicott 1965: 50). From then on, mute understanding plays less and less a part in the relationship, and the child's bent toward autonomy and activity plays more and more a part (R. W. White 1963: 76–80).

Staying in close touch while moving away to take in the world as a separate, effective being remains "the mainspring of man's eternal struggle against both fusion and isolation. . . . One could regard the entire life cycle as constituting a more or less successful process of distancing from and introjection of the lost symbiotic mother, an eternal longing for the actual or fantasied 'ideal state of self,' with the latter standing for a symbiotic fusion with the 'all good' symbiotic mother, who was at one time part of the self in a blissful state of well-being" (Mahler 1972: 338).

The "lost symbiotic mother" cannot be found in fact, so it is sought in symbol. The symbolic side of the relationship between dogs and people condenses this *overall* structure of the earliest human relationship, I am proposing. The symbiosis carried in empathy and nurture flowing "magically" from mother to infant, the child's envelopment in mother's whole being, the idealization of and identification with a "perfect mother," the child's active signalling and the mother's quick responses, the eventual yet painful evolution of independent mobility and verbal demands, the child's conflict between staying close and going away, and the mother's reluctance to part as well—the unique tone of the totality of that earliest, singular time, with all its love and its distresses, reverberates in the quality of feeling in the dog-human bond. The resonances of that first relationship are impossible to duplicate with another person; the contemporaneous bond is with another species. Should that tone be sought with other people, it is likely to transform into a kind of hum, an undercurrent of expectation charging adult intimacies with static, perhaps their most prevalent source of unwanted interference. When intimacies are altogether avoided, the disappointments at the ending of symbiosis have been translated into distrust. In the relationship with a dog, the idea of Trust is constantly renewed.

Separation, anxiety, and loss also provoke anger, and that is far less well acknowledged. For the fear of going it alone is not the only feeling at issue: anger is the critical dimension of the acted ambivalence toward dogs and of grief and depression. In children and adults, separation and loss arouse both anxious and angry behaviors. "Each is directed toward the attachment figure: anxious attachment is to retain maximum accessibility. . . . [A]nger is both a reproach at what has happened and a deterrent against its happening again. Thus, love, anxiety, and anger, and sometimes hatred, come to be aroused by one and the same person" (Bowlby 1973: 253). Both despair and hope fuel the anger—the child's hope that shrieks of distress will bring the mother back, despair that the separation will be forever, hope that the mother will be discouraged from leaving, despair to reproach her (ibid.).

Once separation begins and the child is uncertain of a parent's emotional availability, the ambivalent combination of hostility and dependence surfaces. The other events going on in a child's life around that same time—mother's next pregnancy, the birth of a sibling, the beginning of the rewards and punishments of toilet training—all compound the uncertainties of separation and of being wholly the center, wholly loved. Infant temper tantrums and the negative spells of childhood express that fury; if the anger is denied and submerged as a "bad" part of the self, the adult may later struggle even harder with Intimacy, Trust, and Self-Esteem. In the first year babies are "[a]ngry, aggressive, and resistant" at the same time as they "seek physical contact . . . but at the very point at which they are picked up may push away and want to be put down, only immediately to want up again, and this sequence of responses is characteristically accompanied by crying, fussing, or tantrum behavior" (Ainsworth 1977: 57, 62). Scientists studying human-canine relationships tend to acknowledge owners' anger and ambivalence only when reporting individual cases of psychopathology where dogs are actors and victims in idiosyncratic psychological and interpersonal dramas (Rynearson 1978; Simon 1984; Voith 1981). (Flush bit Robert Browning.)

To be human in Anglo-American cultures is predicated on an Individualism first harvested in the distresses of the disruptions to a primitive biology of meaning literally essential to survival. The anxiety recurs throughout life, no matter how competent and effective people become: "separation anxiety" is likely to recur in every experience of personal and social loss—the deaths of relatives and friends, but also divorce, changes of job, of residence, even of definitions of ourselves (Marris 1975). These experiences also are another kind of evidence that interruptions of stable, shared meanings are distressing and stressful whenever they occur.

Loosening the bond is not, then, a once-and-for-all event. As people experience other relationships, the original counterpoint of pleasure and pain is replayed in different keys. In its minor mode, psychoanalysts speak of the end of our "merger with mother" as "the depressive position," for infants may turn the anger in upon themselves, a yeast for depression throughout life. Lorenz recounts that his dog went into a depression upon being left behind, but of his own at the parting he does not speak. One study of hospital admissions for physical ailments alone (not for psychiatric or surgical help) found "a remarkably high incidence of major interpersonal separation and loss accompanied by feelings of helplessness and hopelessness—occurring shortly before onset of the symptoms leading to hospitalization. A variety of medical disorders were involved, not just the ones usually regarded as psychosomatic disorders." Even when people discuss the mere possibility of losing affection and respect from those close to them (and in an experimental setting) they show symptoms of anxiety, anger, and depression.

> Thus, disruption of interindividual bonds may have profound consequences in carbohydrate, protein, fat, electrolyte, and water metabolism, and on crucial functions of the circulation. . . . Such disruption is felt as deeply

unpleasant, and an extraordinary variety of coping behavior patterns may be mobilized to restore acceptance, affection, and mutual respect. Perhaps [a] serious threat to a key relationship may be as much [an] emergency in psychophysiological terms as threat of attack by a predator. . . . Threat to these relationships is equivalent to an attack on life itself. (Hamburg 1963: 316)

The "security" we attribute to relationships may reside more fundamentally in the stability of the meanings they sustain. Without shared meanings, we experience helplessness and hopelessness, the twin immobilities of anxiety and the depression it can foster. The loss of shared meanings is both shock and "psychophysiological emergency" whenever it occurs in life, and avoiding that loss has high priority. Epidemiologists find that people embedded within social networks are better able to withstand life's stresses than those who are isolated; married men, for example, are likely to live longer than those who are single.

In adults who are experiencing separation, clinicians commonly find, there is "a turbulent combination" of "intense possessiveness, intense anxiety, and intense anger. Not infrequently vicious circles develop. An incident of separation or rejection arouses a person's hostility and leads to hostile thoughts and acts [which] increase . . . fear of being further rejected or even of losing [the] loved figure altogether" (Bowlby 1973: 254). So too is the anxiety of separating exaggerated in infancy, as is almost everything about the world as children know it: parents are all-powerful and perfect, or they are "demons." Throughout life, then, the same experiences that recall those earliest symbiotic pleasures are inevitably suffused with memories of angry feelings. Normal and expectable, that anger, but the axioms of our cultures enjoin us to master signs of it, the earlier the better.

Parents' ability to transform infantile anger, raw and unprocessed, into negative feelings appropriate to the person, place, and time tests them more perhaps than any other task of children's development. It depends on parents' ability to see the "terrible two's" and childhood outbursts of abuse of them, of others, as temporary and natural. The better they do, the better able children are to relinquish its intensity: the more that parents react to it, the more they may foster infantile fantasies of omnipotence, in effect confirming to children that all out of proportion to their size and strength, they can hurt deeply. Children may thus come to believe that any expression of these feelings will have the effects they fantasize and, with infantile logic, magnify. Seeing themselves as the total center of their parents' lives, infants expect that their demands, no matter how overwhelming, will be met, and if not, the disappointments are ever greater.

Resembling symbiosis and its ending are the actual experiences children are likely to have with family dogs. In buying a dog "for the children,"

as 46 percent of parents do, they often expect it to introduce their children
to the "miracle of life," meaning mating, pregnancy, and birth. Yet from
the outset, acquiring a puppy obligates parents to explain its separation
from its mother and litter mates: children's experiences begin with a separated dog, an orphan, which is likely to whimper and cry in its distress at
simply being removed from what is familiar (Scott 1971: 237). Then, when
a female dog is giving birth, chances are the children won't see her in the
dark, quiet, out-of-the-way spot she is likely to favor. Children are more
likely to be witness to the "miracle" of weaning, the first attenuation of the
mother-pup bond which begins at about seven weeks. And then, teaching
pups not to nurse, the mother will growl loudly and rush at them as if to
bite if they keep trying (Scott and Fuller 1965: 171). When parents get a
dog for their preadolescent children, then, it may well be for themselves
as adults who, watching their children live through those stages, may be
recollecting their own experiences of symbiosis and separation.

Like teddy bears and security blankets that children smother, dogs are
said to act as the same sort of talisman, reminders of mother's comfort
and the experience of being at one with her, when loving her is loving
ourselves. Stroking them and holding private monologues, people express
the metaphysical bond, in which reliability and trust are never at issue.
When talking to their dogs (which people do as though speaking to a person), a "stereotypical set of changes in facial expression and voice pattern
[appears]. The face becomes more relaxed with a generalized decrease in
muscle tension especially evident around the eyes and the brow. The smile
. . . is more relaxed with less tension at the corners of the mouth. When
speaking to the animal the lips are frequently open and slightly pursed.
The voice becomes much softer . . . higher in pitch, and the speech pattern is broken into a small series of words frequently phrased as a question
and concluded with a rising intonation . . . followed by silent periods in
which the person solicits eye contact and answering gestures from the animal. . . . Sometimes the answer . . . is supplied for the animal" (Beck
and Katcher 1983: 11–12). Speaking for both self and dog, the person and
pet are metaphysically one and the same, echoing the earlier merger with
mother, and forgetting for the moment its end.

TRUSTING

The equanimity of our psychic tripod—that balance among our feelings
of intimacy, autonomy, and anger—is at issue in every significant human
relationship. Love is woven from these strands. Each pulling at the other
provides its strength. When our hearts are broken that tension essential
to love has given way. For the loss of a beloved—a spouse dies, a friend
moves away—sinks us into grief not just because the ballast of the close-

ness is gone. The ache of loss is at one with anger at the deprivation. This balancing act is at the heart of loving. The way we juggle these contradictory feelings has much to do with living contentedly with ourselves and living tranquilly with relatives and friends and neighbors.

The widespread ambivalence toward pet dogs—their idealization and their exposure to dangers—hinges on the developmental and cultural concepts of Separating and Individuating. That original schema organizing life itself flows back and forth between mother and infant; it is then transformed by our concepts of Growing Up and Individualism, and yet persists throughout life as a transcendental idea about Love for which no human object is ever again possible. Giving "complete and total love," "utter devotion," "lifelong fidelity," the mute and ever-attentive dog, constant, and in perfect communication, stands as a sign of the memory of that magical once-in-a-lifetime bond.

Those blissful memories do not, however, motivate the whole of this singular symbol, for the species difference is crucial. The difference acknowledges the painful reality of the original separation and every person's ultimate apartness from mother and from one another. So significant is the species' difference that members of the family though they are, dogs in France, at any rate, do not customarily receive human first or last names, for "human christian [*sic*] names cannot be given to dogs without causing uneasiness or even mild offence. . . . On the contrary, we allot them a special series: 'Azor,' 'Medor,' 'Sultan,' 'Fido.' . . . Nearly all these are like stage names, forming a series parallel to the names people bear in ordinary life or, in other words, metaphorical names" (Lévi-Strauss 1963: 204–205). The human names that Americans increasingly are giving dogs are an ironic recognition of the fundamental difference.

With or without dogs or other pets, the experiences of separating are everyone's. The Judeo-Christian tradition especially keeps us in mind of them. In the "origin myth" of Judaism, his mother placed Moses, a three-month-old infant, in a wicker basket set among the reeds of the Nile, in hopes of saving his life. Seeing the pharaoh's daughter rescue him, Moses' sister Miriam convinced her to allow his own mother to nurse him. After weaning, she returned him to the pharoah's daughter; Moses grew up as an Egyptian of the highest caste, eventually leading the Jews out of Egypt. So legend has it, then: a forced separation from symbiosis, then reunion, and the "individuation" of an entire people. Religious art depicts Mary and Jesus time and again during "peak symbiosis": Jesus a babe in arms, still nursing, still merged. A sign of God's spirit born in every person, the Madonna and Child are an emblem more prevalent than depictions of Jesus alone, either as youngster or adult. At his death Mary is again present, and the separation that follows is widely believed to be only temporary.

Becoming adults, we know we have awakened from that first dream.

Not an icon of infantility, the bond with dogs is a sign of the perpetual recapitulation of this most fundamental, profoundly felt struggle: to come to terms with the inevitability of the uncertainty and loss experienced in the disruption of the original and life-giving system of meaning without losing Faith and Trust in others or in oneself. The bond with dogs is a sign of Fidelity to human continuity, biological and emotional; it keeps available meanings through which people sustain their capacity for Trust. These are meanings constituting society itself, meanings that help to make it possible.

Standing as symbol of bittersweet reconciliation to that "eternal struggle against both fusion and isolation," the dog-human bond is predicated on these developmental and cultural processes which all dog owners share in, responsible and negligent. That there are personality differences between pet owners and nonowners seems to be doubtful (Friedmann et al. 1984: 307). None of us is free from separating and individuating with or without keeping dogs. Each of us works out a characteristic style for keeping our tripod in balance; the loop of closeness, separation, and disappointment is a leitmotif in our lives the whole of their length. In behaving toward beloved dogs so contradictorily, as negligent owners do, they reveal just how hard it is to keep a balance. By default, they can only be hoping that their dogs will get lost or hurt or killed. Unmistakably, they take chances with their dogs, themselves, and their families. Their free-roaming dogs may at the least harass neighbors as an agent of diffuse anger; at the worst, they might bite children on the block and perhaps be condemned to die. Just as they are sure that their pets, perfect as they are, would do no such things, these owners might find it equally difficult to acknowledge that Love in general is a flawed compound; that mourning for Love lost, strayed, or stolen includes heartfelt anger as well.

Responsible dog owners, like everybody else, may struggle no less with this most general issue of living, but they don't happen to have made their dogs a vehicle for it. For the perplexities arising in a social order so highly valuing Individualism and so deeply denying the pain its many forms of estrangement take, there are many other vehicles to choose from (or that choose us)—an incapacity for trust and intimacy, depression, abuse of alcohol and drugs, life-threatening, stress-related diseases.

REPRISE

Despite the beliefs of upwards of 99 percent of American dog owners that their pets are members of the family, the U.S. Census Bureau has never included them in its household population count. Scanting culture is nothing new, but when the law pertaining to dogs also fails to register the meanings of the bond, it becomes part of the problems it intends to help resolve, especially abandonment and dog-bite.

Make no mistake: going to law over dogs preoccupies neighbors and friends, landlords and tenants, parents and children, husbands and wives, ranchers and farmers whose relationships have been somehow chewed over by dogs. Courts hear cases for damages for dogs killed or injured by various means—cars, trains, and trucks, by the mistakes of druggists in filling veterinarians' prescriptions, by neighbors' dogs, and by poison. Neighborhood groups sue kennels. Biters are held to account. Divorce settlements assign dog-visiting rights. "Dog is Adjudged a 'Child' in Custody Case on Coast. . . . After a year of bitter divorce proceedings, a judge has awarded a childless couple joint custody of their dog in accordance with California's child custody laws" (*The New York Times* 1983a). Children sue parents for possession of the family dog. "Woman Loses Custody Fight With Her Parents Over Dog. . . . A family dog is a piece of property, like a washing machine or a television set, a Superior Court judge has ruled in denying a 20-year-old woman's bid to wrest a dog from her parents" (*The New York Times* 1983b).

Where losers will not let the matter rest, cases reach appellate courts, to the point of having created a "Canine Jurisprudence," which Roscoe Pound, an early dean of the Harvard Law School, predicted in 1896. Citing some few cases that had then been decided in appellate courts, Pound suggests that "the duties of dogs may be classified under two heads, (1) to abstain from barking, (2) to abstain from biting. For it has been ruled that the tracking up of freshly painted door-steps by a dog is not actionable" (Pound 1896: 173).

> [I]t is somewhat strange in this age of textbooks, that no one has produced a "compendious treatise" upon the subject. . . . If possible, the word Jurisprudence should find a place in the title. We have Medical Jurisprudence, Dental Jurisprudence, and others of the sort, and I could never see why an author who thought it worth his while to write on the law pertaining to horses, or on the law applicable to farmers, should omit the opportunity of giving us Equine Jurisprudence and Rural Jurisprudence. . . . At any rate, our author must ponder well before he discards Canine Jurisprudence. (Ibid.: 172–173)

(Despite this arch tone, Pound doesn't point to the pun of his interest in this subject.)

American canine jurisprudence is a brier patch of contradictory notions seeded by the impossibilities of assigning dogs to one side or another of two lines: those between property and not-property and those dividing animals from furniture. These continuing ambiguities may be sanctioning unwittingly the very antisocial behaviors the law intends to discourage, particularly roaming and abandoned dogs, and, much related to them, the incidence and prevalence of dog-bite.

Total "possession" of a "property" that can leave home under its own steam is impossible, and so property in dogs has been held to be of an "imperfect or qualified nature."

> The ancient common-law rule that dogs were considered an inferior sort of property, which for certain purposes was entitled to less regard and protection than property in other animals, has been changed to a great extent, either by statute, or simply by the evolution of the law, so as to recognize a full and complete property in dogs. Dogs are now generally considered as domestic animals, as much the subject of property or ownership as horses, cattle, and sheep. They have been held to be things of value, to come within the meaning of the word "chattel," as used in statutes intended to cover every kind of personal property, to constitute "property" within the meaning of a statute requiring the driver of a motor vehicle to stop after an accident involving damage to property, and to constitute "property" within the meaning of the constitutional provision against taking property without due process of law. Dogs are so far recognized as property that a civil action will lie for their conversion [theft] or injury. Likewise, in many states, statutes have been enacted making dogs subject to taxation, which, according to some courts, have the effect of making them property in the fullest sense, although others negative this proposition on the theory that such statutes are mere police regulations. . . . In some respects, however, property in dogs is of an imperfect or qualified nature, and they may be subjected to peculiar and drastic police regulations by the state without depriving their owners of any constitutional right. (*American Jurisprudence* 1962: 252)

Dogs are and are not PROPERTY; just as dogs are and are not RELATIVES.

But differences between dogs as PROPERTY and as KIN and FRIEND go unrecognized legally. The law confers on them solely the status of CHATTEL, with the unintended effect of sanctioning their casual acquisition, minimal care, and abandonment. "Love is the only thing that money can't buy" is one American proverb canine jurisprudence insists upon in denying claims for damages for injured or killed dogs. Damaged feelings cannot be compensated:

> In view of the general recognition of property rights in dogs, there can no longer be any question that dogs may have value, and the statement sometimes made that dogs have no market value can be regarded as only relatively true, since, although it may be difficult in the majority of cases to ascertain such value, it can be done in some cases. It may, however, be conceded that dogs have no intrinsic value if by that is meant a value common to all dogs as such, independent of the particular breed or individual.

The value depends upon the facts and circumstances of the particular case. In accordance with these considerations, the basis of recovery in an action to recover damages for the injury or destruction of a dog may be either the market value, if it has any, or some special or pecuniary value to the owner that may be ascertained by reference to the usefulness or services of the dog. But injury to the owner's feelings for a dog is not an element of damages, and it is improper to include an allowance for its sentimental value to its owner. If the owner cannot prove that the dog had any value, the law will imply at least nominal damages. . . . If a dog is killed wantonly or maliciously, punitive or exemplary damages may be claimed and allowed. (*American Jurisprudence* 1962: 399)

Only when Love makes a beeline to Money are feelings salient: in one case, an owner whose dog was shot became so "nervous" and "frustrated" that he was "forced to miss time at work"; only when translated into income were his feelings compensable.

Lawyers constructing a dog-injury or -loss case are likely to consult a companion volume, *American Jurisprudence Proof of Facts Annotated*, which is a "carefully edited compilation of trial guide material in text and in question and answer form designed to assist lawyers in preparing for trial and examining witnesses." They find this scenario for establishing a dog's value:

> *Actual value.* The actual value of a specific dog to its owner is admissable evidence, and may include testimony as to the dog's peculiar traits, qualities, breed, pedigree, prizes won, and ability to render services. While the purchase price is also properly admitted, a particular offer to buy the dog from the present owner is sometimes excluded as incompetent to show value.
> Q. Based on the considerations which you have named, what is the value of Isabella to you?
> A. She is worth . . . . . dollars to me.
> *Sentimental value.* Sentimental value of a dog affords no measure of recovery. Among the excluded matters are loss of a dog's company and deprivation of the amusement and pleasure which it bestowed.
> Q. What part of this amount, if any, is based on sentimental value?
> A. None at all.
> (*American Jurisprudence Proof of Facts Annotated* 1959: 624)

"Pleasure," "curiosity," and "caprice" are other terms used to account for the keeping of dogs, and like "sentimental," "amusement," and "pleasure," they connote trivial pursuits, having nothing in common with the concepts of Love and Loyalty sustaining people's bonds with KIN or FRIENDS. Figures mentioned earlier take on new meaning: dogs originally costing less than $50 or received free account for 88 percent of the total given up to shelters; those costing over $100, about 6 percent. Those received free were given up after an average of 17 months, compared with 36 months for those costing over $100 (Arkow and Dow 1984: 351–352). The monetary investment appears to parallel the emotional investment, and in supporting this "easy come, easy go" attitude of some, canine jurisprudence may also be reinforcing irresponsible owners' habits. One analysis of about 1500 pet owners surrendering their pets to a shelter in California "found that 70 percent . . . had decided to 'trash' their pet 'essentially for reasons of convenience.' The pet had become too much of a bother, or it cost too much to feed, or they were moving out of the area. In the throwaway society, pets were treated by many as another disposable item" (Dumanoski 1982: 36).

Were the law to acknowledge the kinship quality of the dog-human relationship, that attitude would likely be questioned. The judge presiding over a childless couple's divorce awarded them joint custody of their dog in accordance with California's child custody laws, saying: " 'Is our hate so strong that we are going to use this little dog to drive a final rusty nail in the heart of the other person? . . . Do you realize that I can order this dog sold or put to sleep? . . . But how much hue and cry would come up if we did that? You will share the dog on a monthly basis. I don't think either one of you won. I'd be terribly embarrassed to bring this issue before the public' " (*The New York Times* 1983a). Yet there it is, out in the open, the relationship with a dog as culturally meaningful as with a relative, and legally recognized as such.

But in the other case, decided in superior court in Hartford, Connecticut, the judge seems to have taken his opinion from the pages of *American Jurisprudence*: " 'To imbue a dog with value beyond that which the law attaches to it, the status of a chattel, by reason of the care and devotion lavished upon it by some and the tender place it may occupy in an owner's heart would be a perilous determination having repercussions beyond the resolution of this single controversy.' " Yet it is unlikely that a television set or a washing machine could prompt the intensity of this dispute between parents and their child: "The decision ended months of family conflict, which included taking the dog away without authorization, court orders that were ignored and a family boycott of Terrie Nawrocki's wedding this year. . . . The silver-gray dog now belongs to Miss Nawrocki's parents." The judge's decision upset a court order to share custody—"alternating two-week periods"—which he found to be unacceptably " 'akin to orders more typically emanating from the Family Court' " (*The New York Times* 1983b).

Canine jurisprudence is in fact built out of cases entailing Property relationships and Personal relationships, but it deals with them all under the heading of CHATTEL. Dogs who work with farmers and ranchers and with police departments and security companies and dogs being raised for breeding and sale the law appropriately treats in utilitarian and economic terms. But when dogs living as companion animals in cities and suburbs are killed or maimed and treated as "property" of the same sort, the fact that they are "adopted" members of families goes unacknowledged. Their negligible dollar cost together with the "peculiar and drastic" police regulations applying to them may play into irresponsible owners' fundamental ambivalence.

Conceivably, property law could cover workers and livestock; the jurisprudence of *family law*, concerned as it is with contracts setting out the rights of family members and their duties to one another, could apply to dogs belonging at home. The rights of family members and their duties to their dog and their neighbors could come under its purview, and sanctions and penalties would apply as they do to other kinds of breach of contract. To "license" families for ownership reflects a similar notion: humane society specialists suggest that at the time of purchase, sellers should be required to have buyers sign a statement promising to provide protection and good care, along with an estimate of the annual dollar cost of doing so. Most dogs aren't purchased, however, so a more general umbrella may be needed.

As with many matters that norms govern, enacting laws may not be the right way to deal with them, although the "scoop" laws of recent years requiring owners to pick up and dispose of their dogs' droppings has met with a fair amount of compliance and has permitted aggrieved citizens to channel their irritations. (The New York City Canine Waste Law was honored in 1979 with an award for *architecture* from the City Club of New York for allowing pedestrians the new freedom of walking with their heads up.) A new consensus drawing the line between the ethical and unethical behaviors of dog owners might be more to the point. It would require the cooperation, however, of the dog-food and dog-care industries which haven't yet joined with the cadre of specialists doing daily battle with the ambivalences negligent owners play out on susceptible neighbors and the public. Some manufacturers publish informative pet-care pamphlets dealing specifically with neighborly relations; owners can write away for them, but it's likely that anyone motivated enough to do so is already a responsible owner. One manufacturer now sponsors a program, "Cats and Dogs," on public broadcasting in which a veterinarian discusses all aspects of their care. But advertising in the mass media specializes in trivia, reassuring owners, for example, that dog food smells all right and is easy to handle, when it might be using the time to teach no-biting and no-barking training techniques, promulgating the leash ethic, and reminding owners of their communitywide responsibilities for health and safety. Instead, most advertising fatuously plays up the individualistic and personal side of the dog-human relationship and ignores its repercussions on the fund of social trust.

A second way that the law misrecognizes the nature of the bond may account for the incidence of dog-bite. The law not only fails to acknowledge but actually provides for the tendency of owners' to deny their dogs' main imperfection, namely the constitutional predisposition to bite. The doctrine of *scienter* rules in fixing liability for dogs' "savage nature," meaning biting people, attacking or stalking other animals with intent to kill them for food, and maliciously attacking other dogs. But, and here is the rub, the doctrine leaves it to the owner to be aware of his or her dog's vicious and dangerous propensities without the dog's ever having actually bitten a person or attacked another dog:

> Generally speaking . . . the gravemen of the action to recover damages for injuries caused by a dog is the knowledge of the owner that the animal is vicious or has mischievous propensities. This does not mean, however, that such knowledge is limited to actual notice or to actual knowledge by the owner; knowing that the disposition of the animal was such that it would be likely to commit an injury similar to the one complained of is sufficient. . . . Knowledge of one attack by a dog is generally held sufficient to charge the owner with all its subsequent acts. There need be, however, no notice of injury actually committed, and therefore it is unnecessary to prove that a dog had ever before bitten anyone. In this respect, it is stated that the old doctrine that every dog is entitled to "one bite" is out of harmony with a modern humanitarian society. The owner or keeper of a dog must observe manifestations of danger from him to human beings from other traits than viciousness alone, short of actual injury to some person, and cannot neglect to keep him in restraint until he has effectually killed or injured at least one person. (*American Jurisprudence* 1962: 344–345)

Owners' tendency to idealize their dogs makes of *scienter* a cutting tool without an edge, and the myth of one free bite lives on (about 80 years ago, it had been the law in some states, now generally replaced with the rule of strict liability). But where a negligence defense is still allowed, "one free bite" is a common defense. Until a dog *has* actually bitten someone or attacked another dog, owners are unlikely to acknowledge, no matter the breed, that it has such a "disposition," if even then. By that time, the dog has had its "one free bite," which, if it occurs within the family, is likely to remain a well-kept secret. I have heard dog owners blame the victims, even a four-year-old. Nor will they acknowledge that pet dogs will attack wildlife or run deer to death.

Biting by the family dog and by those of neighborhood families is far from uncommon, yet denial takes the field: stray dogs are claimed as the major culprits. "To blame strays is *not* to blame pets or their owners. How convenient to assume that dog bite was the product of wild fury rather than the bad breeding or training of beloved pets or the irresponsibility of the owner!" (Beck and Katcher 1983: 229). Furthermore, the bite rate seems to be a reflection of the numbers of "loose pets on the streets; the bite rate on Staten Island, a New York borough with many private homes, is four times the number reported from the borough of Manhattan, with its many apartment houses" and their leashed occupants (ibid.: 243).

Again, a new consensus is needed. Pet dogs are potential biters, and bites are preventable. "[O]wners can stop allowing dogs to roam, children-dog interactions can be better supervised, and parents, children, and dog owners can become more aware of the natural tendency of their pets to bite." With very little training in animal ethology, people can learn to "recognize what situations may lead to bites and what cues a dog emits that signal a potential bite" (Jones and Beck 1984: 362–363).

The behaviors of irresponsible dog owners result in more than just messy sidewalks, midnight howling, and nipping at the neighbors. These we are likely to take as nitty-gritty signs of alienation, doing their part to cloud a clear sense of community. Ironically, these dog owners deplete the fund of social trust even as they may be renewing their personal capacity for it. The line that's needed here is called the leash.

IMPERFECT PEOPLE

As familiar as Americans are with the facts of social prejudice and as familiar as its consequences can be socially, economically, and
emotionally, discrimination is more likely to be discussed as a constitutional issue than acknowledged as another cultural iceberg threatening
the qualities of community. As dotted as many ethnic lines have become and as common as hyphens are in constructing overlapping social
identities, differences still stand out. We negotiate them to one degree
or another in every sphere—at work, in the neighborhood, in school, at
worship, in civic coalitions, at supermarket and mall—and doing so, we
gain our sense of community. Prejudice, by definition, is the refusal to
negotiate differences; its blind condemnations inflict social injustice and
foment distrust.

People are protecting their practical, material interests from threat—
so familiar explanations of ethnocentrism suggest. What their symbolic or
semantic interests might be is instead the subject of this cultural account
of Western understandings of difference itself. Differences of skin color,
physical condition, sex, or age are undeniable, but rather than regarding
those as "brute" facts of life, as Charles Taylor makes this distinction,
the challenge is to see them instead as representing "institutional" facts
which are grown in those fields of conventional understandings through
which each culture construes such differences. American culture appears
to see such differences, as does the West generally, in a way that surreptitiously questions the species' membership of disabled people, children,
nonwhites, the elderly, women (even as still other conventions bring dogs
into the human family).

"The play of differences," writes Helen Vendler in an appreciation of
Roland Barthes' work, "is for Barthes the definition of linguistic utopia:
where all is difference, nothing can be marked off as 'different' and therefore to be hated. . . . Liberation from 'the binary prison,' the prison of
male/female, majority/minority, right/wrong—is it possible? Can there
be what Barthes called the Neutral? . . . To anyone who does not fit into
the binary categories of ordinary social reference . . . the Neutral is the
only nonimprisoning hope" (Vendler 1986: 48). What should we make
of the silence behind that "therefore"—different, and for that reason to

*be hated? Discrepancy theory speaks to its biological side; here, I add
to it some wider cultural and historical dimensions that have made the
very concept of difference so often socially absolute, nonnegotiable, and
imprisoning.*

How to belong in America remains an open question for each generation.
There are always thresholds, hurdles, and lines to cross in finding our
proper place, and rightly so, we believe—qualifying for kindergarten and
college, jobs and promotions, credit and mortgages, love, honor, and salvation. Being HUMAN, each rite of social passage reminds us, is only the
beginning, but at least there is no doubt that we are.

Or is there? Paradoxes abound. Simply as human beings MEN and
ADULTS have more standing than do WOMEN and CHILDREN. Then, CHIL-
DREN are human, we surely know that, and dogs aren't, facts easy enough
to keep straight except when culture takes them over. At one time or
another, most people come to believe that CHILDREN not theirs are ANI-
MALS, or, more kindly, monsters, menaces, and, you know, well . . .
CHILDREN. Over the whole of residential America are posted "No Children" and "No Pets" signs, keeping out the two icons of Domesticity
itself. TEENAGERS too, a breed kept apart, the epitome of incongruity, neither formed nor unformed—one day acting Mature, the next, Infantile,
to throw ADULTS off balance. As human beings, handicapped, deformed,
and disfigured people are also not perfect specimens, as the saying goes;
they are the chief recipients of distress: the freezing and staring we translate into stereotyping and the stigma of being seen as "not quite human."
Many contemporary ideas of perfection at the epicenter of equilibrium
constitute as candidates for distress still others—those who aren't white,
not handsome or beautiful, young . . . .

Ideas about the differences between animals and humans draw on
Western civilization's interpretations of Evolution, the relation of Instinct
to Rationality, the contrasts between Intuition and Control, Foresight and
Impulse. . . . Their representations in metaphors and myths are ubiquitous
in daily life. In being mistaken for questions they raise about how firmly
we can draw that line between ourselves and animals, many human beings
are then mistaken for the anxiety they arouse. Their places in the social
order are the least favorable socially, legally, politically. Their denigration
reflects doubts about our own rights to belong; that is, IMPERFECT PEOPLE
keep us wondering about that definitive difference.

In the Great Chain of Being, humans are one mammal among the
many—about 15,000—species of mammals. We are different from others
yet not wholly so, and from that worrisome ambiguity, less-than-perfect

human beings are perceived as resembling ANIMALS the more and placed below "perfect" people in the social order. In the past, they were actually killed. As early as 450 B.C., historians recount, physical form was "a starting point for any discussion of man's place or worth in the universe." The customary law of Rome, the Laws of the Twelve Tables, regarded human form as "a prerequisite for human social or legal status; whoever failed to meet this requirement did so because of God's anger toward men and should be destroyed. . . . A father shall immediately put to death a son recently born, who is a monster, or has a form different from that of members of the human race" (Friedman 1981: 179). Whose anger? Chimpanzees will kill their abnormal members, as do some other species (Lawick-Goodall 1971: 223–224). Are these fearful discrepancies they cannot flee?

Americans seem so concerned about keeping intact the meanings by which they conceive themselves to be unlike other animals that they keep their distance even from factual knowledge about them. "Americans appeared to possess an extremely limited understanding of animals," concludes a study for the U.S. Fish and Wildlife Service based on a national sample of 3107 people over 18. They responded to a questionnaire testing their factual knowledge of animals. "For example, on four endangered species questions, no more than one-third of the public gave the correct answer—e.g., only 26% knew the manatee is not an insect, and 25% correctly answered the questions, 'timber wolves, bald eagles and coyotes are all endangered species of animals.' . . . Additionally, just 13% knew raptors are not small rodents and one-half of the national sample incorrectly answered the question, 'spiders have ten legs.' A better but still limited 54% knew veal does not come from lamb, and only 57% correctly answered the question, 'most insects have backbones'" (Kellert and Berry 1980: 7, 11).

Ideals, norms, and standards, indeed even statistical averages, translate and are translated into the equilibrium of our neurophysiology. However we can get it, we seek comfort. Then deviation from norms is a matter not of simple difference but of "wrong" difference: it captures the discomforts of discrepancy. For example, social standards can't always be met throughout the phases of life, so that one time or another we're likely to experience society's judgment as being "unworthy, incomplete and inferior." Those governing "physical comeliness . . . take the form of ideals and constitute standards against which almost everyone falls short at some stage. . . . For example, in an important sense there is only one complete unblushing male in America: a young, married, white, urban, northern, heterosexual Protestant father of college education, fully employed, of good complexion, weight and height and a recent record in sports. Every

American male tends to look out upon the world from this perspective, this constituting one sense in which one can speak of a common value system in America. Any male who fails to qualify in any of these ways is likely to view himself—during moments at least—as unworthy, incomplete and inferior. . . . The general identity-values of a society may be fully entrenched nowhere, and yet they can cast some kind of shadow on the encounters encountered [*sic*] everywhere in daily living" (Goffman 1963: 153). These shadows exemplify the metaphysics of ambiguity.

Every anomaly and "stranger" announce that they cannot be accounted for by concepts that organize a familiar field of meaning; instead the "accounting" is made in the terms of the distress their differences arouse. Among Japanese "visiting gods," or stranger-gods, often represented by stones at thresholds and crossroads, is Ebisu, who is also anomalous in every possible way: one-eyed, deaf, hunchbacked, left-handed, and sometimes hermaphroditic. When treated hospitably, he is believed to bring longevity, good luck, happiness. *Ebisu* means "a stranger, foreigner, or person from a remote place," and in modern Japan the term still "carries the connotation of deformity and abnormality; for example, *ebisu-buna* means a malformed crucian carp, . . . *ebisu-zen* means abnormally arranged dishes on the table" (Yoshida 1981: 94). Difference casts threatening shadows.

The received concepts by which differences are understood are arbitrary, not given in nature, and are only those we use or invent at any given time. Neither their necessity to meaning or our incapacity to live without meanings is in doubt. Taking these concepts as given, however—verily, natural—we constitute long-lived institutions from them. With the reinforcements of history and the uses of power, they can form into implacable icebergs blocking the way to a more just, more humane society. When people are also mentally retarded, emotionally confused, physically crippled, younger or older, homosexual, or nonwhite, such arbitrary concepts irrelevantly diminish their rights to well-being and justice. Culture, history, and biology coerce us into laying claim to what should be ours constitutionally, our essential humanity and right to belong.

MORALIZING DIFFERENCE

Differences seem rarely to be neutrally observed in everyday life. Take the hands. Many societies differentiate between them with explicit moral principles: the right stands for good and positive values, the left for evil and negative, the one sacred, the other profane. Each hand signifies the spatial inscription of a cosmology, with the body taking an assigned place within that scheme. The right hand is often a sign of east and south, sky and front, above and sun, warm and summer, light and white, inside and male—all associated with positive values, and the left with negatives (Needham 1973).

Aristotle pronounced that "right is naturally stronger and more honorable than left . . . that the differentiation between right and left is a mark of man's superiority to the animals, and of his greater perfection." We inherit Aristotle's beliefs in the Latin roots: "dexter," the right, meaning "skillful, auspicious, and favorable"; and "sinister," "left, on the left, hence evil, unlucky (in augury the left side being regarded as inauspicious)." Aristotle was probably parroting "extremely old, and no doubt widespread Greek beliefs . . . that right is essentially different from, and superior to, left, the one good, the other evil; or the one connected in some way with masculinity, the other with femininity; or the one thought to be honorable, the other not honorable" (Lloyd 1973: 178). Superiority, Good, Masculinity, and Honor came to entail one another and to constitute the ancient meaning systems that remain wellsprings of Western equilibrium. They use far more than the hands as signs.

We owe still more to Aristotle: because the mean, as he defined it in the *Ethics*, "is a point equally distant from either extreme. . . . [E]xcess and deficiency are a mark of vice, and observance of the mean a mark of virtue" (Friedman 1981: 112). "The Greeks and Romans imagined themselves to be at the center of the civilized world and believed that their way of life constituted a standard by which all things far from that center were judged. The farther from the center, the more extreme a thing was, and therefore the more a 'vice' it was" (ibid.: 35). Their way of life constituted not a comparative "standard," for it was the only one they knew, I suggest, but simply a system of meanings which was already familiar, known, or believed to which *anything* "too" dissimilar, novel, and discrepant would evoke the distresses translated as "vice" and its variants in denial, negativism, and disapproval. Indeed, Aristotle's "mean" captures the biological midpoint between the extremes of neurophysiological under- and overarousal, and his moralizing again signifies the experiences of fear and anxiety.

In studies of various cultures, what appear to be innocuous, even technical, concepts and terms readily evoke feelings ranging along a continuum of good-bad, strong-weak, active-passive (Osgood 1979: 69–94; Witkowski and Brown 1978). People respond with pleasant feelings to relatively small differences but with negative and distressing feelings to larger ones, according to laboratory experiments on judgments of taste, temperature, saturation of colors, and hue, among other strictly sensory stimuli (Katz 1981: 120). The reasons seem to have eluded psychologists, but this biology of meaning may be able to suggest one: familiar norms and concepts, or more likely, webs of associations to them, are somehow represented by semantic and perceptual stimuli to which people respond positively, and vice versa. Whatever stands out from what is normal and expectable, furthermore, people generally weight negatively.

The Greeks and Romans perceived human differences from perspectives that contrast with those of Hebrews and Christians: to Greeks and Romans difference was "physical and cultural," while for Hebrews and Christians, it is "moral and metaphysical." Hebrew thought tends "to dissolve physical into moral states in contrast to the Greek tendency to do the reverse. Greek anthropological theory tends to objectify, or physicalize, what we would call internal, spiritual, or psychological states. Hebrew thought consistently inclines toward the reduction of external attributes to . . . manifestations of a spiritual condition" (H. White 1972: 10–11).

That "propensity for moralizing or drawing spiritual instruction from all aspects of the natural world" occurs in both preliterate and literate societies. In his fascinating study, *The Monstrous Races in Medieval Art and Thought* (1981), John Block Friedman documents the responses of the medievalists to other cultures. Other peoples were simply different in their customs, diet, speech, clothes, weaponry, and social organization, but the earliest travellers' reports perceived them "as monstrous because they did not look like western Europeans or share their norms" (ibid.: 34). In these medieval texts, any real differences were magnified and some were wholly imagined. Forty-one fabulous beings, notable for their physical abnormalities, diet, and social customs, fill out Friedman's catalog, as they earlier had been Pliny's subjects. Some of these beings were described as having backward-turned feet, "a lower lip . . . that protrudes so far that it can serve as an umbrella against the sun," genitals of both sexes, mouthless faces and living by smell, faces on their chests with no heads and necks; one eye, dog heads, six fingers, six hands, horse's hooves instead of feet; some of the women were noted as being especially hairy, some as having conceived as early as age five. The diets: they ate exclusively fish, or meat, or meat and honey; some ate raw meat; they drank from human skulls and ate their parents when they grew old. Some of them had unusual social practices: women lived without men (the Amazons); some peoples did not practice "marriage"; others gave wives to any traveller coming among them (ibid.: 8–25).

The Roman noun *monstrum* translated the Greek *teras*, meaning "portent," which was used to describe unusual births; Herodotus, for example, told of a mare giving birth to a hare. "[E]ventually the word came by transference to be used adjectivally of unusual races of men," and, ultimately, to refer "to any people who deviated from Western cultural norms" (ibid.: 108, 109). *Monstrum* "suggested a weakness or disarrangement in the familiar order of existence" (ibid.: 119)—an appropriately neutral description that the dynamics of anxiety and fear have loaded and taken over as signs of human virtue and vice.

> *Monstra* involved for all Latin readers the showing forth of divine will. In the classical period they were usually seen as a disruption of the natural order, boding ill; in the Christian period they were a sign of God's power over nature and His use of it for didactic ends. In popular and pious literature monsters were, therefore, closely connected with Christian miracles and the marvelous. It was in this light that Saint Augustine regarded them when he spoke of how, at the Resurrection, God would violate the course of nature by restoring monstrous men to perfect form. . . . If the races were signs from God, the question then arose: What were they meant to signify? This problem lent itself particularly well to the exegetical techniques so familiar to us in bestiaries, spiritual encyclopedias, and other homiletic works of the later Middle Ages. It produced a number of moral interpretations of the races that made them figures for various virtues and vices. The end result was a heightened treatment of alien peoples in didactic literature, exaggerating their unusual qualities so as to bring out their "monstrousness" in both the older and the newer sense. (Ibid.: 109)

"Certain medieval bestiaries interpolated among their animals a section on the Plinian races, and moralized them much as they moralized the pelican or the unicorn. Collections of exempla drew *moralitates* from the races, making them into figures for unattractive human qualities and vices" (ibid.: 122). Yet, it is "clear from the author's treatment" in the Douce Bestiary, created in the thirteenth century, "that he has no theoretical presuppositions that would lead him to choose some for virtue and others for vices: they hold little interest for him beyond the homiletic" (ibid.: 126).

Judgment was pronounced also on peoples' locations upon the globe, and medievalists discussed climate in the very terms of physiological equilibrium. "A temperate clime . . . is most keyed to the balance of the humors in people and to the perfection of their moral and political faculties. . . . [T]he person over whom heat or cold holds sway will be crude, violent, and unaesthetic [so Pliny held]" (ibid.: 52).

In many maps of the period peoples simply different from the map makers were pushed out to the edges and labelled without further ado as "monstrous." Distancing from distress is far from being only figurative. The texts accompanying these maps report observers' "terror," "awe," "horror," and then attribute to these peripheral peoples "perversity," "danger," "degeneration," "corruption." A map dated A.D. 926 labels "Ethiopia" (variously Africa and India) as a region "where there are men of diverse appearance and monstrous, terrifying, and perverse races as far as the borders of Egypt," but the map stresses only "their remoteness" without depicting these peoples or explaining any more about them (ibid.: 48).

The maps came to be consulted no less than scholarly and histori- cal writings, becoming "a source of authority equal in weight" to writers who would also draw on Augustine and Isidore, Pliny and Solinus. "It must have been a combination of the descriptions of these races, their names, and their pictures in such maps that helped establish their reality for medieval people." Even when the numbers of observers increased— "merchants, crusaders, pilgrims, and missionaries"—the myths and les- sons drawn from these strange "Plinian peoples" did not lose their force. Friedman suggests why:

> Hearsay and fictions about unfamiliar places die hard, of course. But curi- ously the direct personal observation of the East did not result in a corre- sponding reduction in the legends of the monstrous races said to live there. We must take into account at least two reasons why this should be so. First, there appears to have been a psychological need for the Plinian peoples. Their appeal to medieval men was based on such factors as fantasy, escap- ism, delight in the exercise of the imagination, and—very important—fear of the unknown. If the monstrous races had not existed, it is likely that people would have created them. (Ibid.: 24)

The second reason Friedman proposes is that "many of the fabulous races did in fact exist"—for example, Pygmies, Watusi, and Ubangi—but hardly as affect-laden descriptions depicted them; "headless" peoples were, in fact, probably wearing shields or chest armor (ibid.: 25).

"Fear of the unknown" does not, as I've said, adequately character- ize the process: what is already meaningful controls both the response to novelty and how that response becomes socially patterned and institution- alized. At the least, the "monstrous races" depend for their existence on shared beliefs promulgated by or through Aristotle, the Old and New Tes- taments, and medieval theology. Each belief system upon the globe gener- ates its own specific and particular social transliterations of distress. Ours remains no exception.

> [T]he Judeo-Christian view, infused by Hellenistic Platonism, was based on the belief in the creation of a single perfect man from whom all others were descended. It allowed, accordingly, of very little physical or social diversity. In short, men who did not wear clothes, who ate snakes or each other, and who did not cultivate the soil or form cities were quite likely to be explained by a corruption of the human species through some crime or sin. . . . Since God created Adam to embody his idea of the perfect man, all of Adam's descendants should be images of him; that they were not—and that some were less like him than others—was often seen as the

consequence not only of the Fall, but also of alien strains entering a tribal line of descent, so that the resulting people were less than fully human. (Ibid.: 89)

Thus did the medieval "mind" explain "social differences as the result of degeneration or decadence," as do our own *moralitates* continue to consign imperfect beings to a cultural hell.

SOCIALIZING AND INSTITUTIONALIZING FEAR

From the workings of one nineteenth-century mind a clear picture emerges of the ways that raw fear and pain can become displaced from neurophysiological responses into personal convictions and social patterns. The self-recorded experience of Louis Agassiz (1807–1873) upon being for the first time in "prolonged contact" with black people is the documented case in point. After this experience, Agassiz abandoned the scientific evidence of a single human species and became a lifelong, active proponent of racism. Professor at Harvard, founder in 1859 of its Museum of Comparative Zoology, and its director until his death, Agassiz was a Swiss naturalist and specialist in fossil fishes; he arrived in America in 1846 as a "devout creationist" who believed all human beings to be of one species (Gould 1981: 43). In 1845 he wrote of " 'the superiority of the human genre and its greater independence in nature. Whereas the animals are distinct species in the different zoological provinces to which they appertain, man, despite the diversity of his races, constitutes one and the same species over all the surface of the globe' " (ibid.: 44). The next year, he replaced these conclusions with racist convictions.

Until 1846 when Agassiz first observed blacks waiting on him at his Philadelphia hotel, he believed in "the doctrine of human unity," "the confraternity of the human type." His observations precipitated an "immediate visceral judgment" leading him to "instantly" abandon "the Biblical orthodoxy of a single Adam" and to advocate the racist line that each of the human races is a single species, each one ordered by " 'the relative rank [and] the relative value of the characters peculiar to each' " (ibid.: 44, 46).

Agassiz's experience of a "pronounced visceral revulsion" is recounted in his own hand (ibid.: 44). It provides a specimen case of the process I have outlined: It illustrates primary, unlearned, and unconditioned responses to discrepancy and their socialized consequences. It documents the relationship of novelty to fear as well as the manifestations of fear as stereotyping (the human version of freezing), the expression of fear as stigmatizing (our way of taking flight or distancing), and the transformation of distress as disparagement and abuse (as social forms of attack). Agassiz's career illustrates moreover how such personal transformations can be socialized and institutionalized.

Agassiz described the details of his experience in a letter to his mother written in 1846, telling "truth before all." Stephen Jay Gould found this "unexpurgated" passage among the Agassiz letters at the Houghton Library at Harvard, and "translated it verbatim, for the first time so far as I know" in *The Mismeasure of Man*, published in 1981 (45):

> "It was in Philadelphia that I first found myself in prolonged contact with negroes; all the domestics in my hotel were men of color. I can scarcely express to you the painful impression that I received, especially since the feeling that they inspired in me is contrary to all our ideas about the con-fraternity of the human type [*genre*] and the unique origin of our species. But truth before all. Nevertheless, I experienced pity at the sight of this degraded and degenerate race, and their lot inspired compassion in me in thinking that they are really men. Nonetheless, it is impossible for me to repress the feeling that they are not of the same blood as us. In seeing their black faces with their thick lips and grimacing teeth, the wool on their head, their bent knees, their elongated hands, their large curved nails, and especially the livid color of the palm of their hands, I could not take my eyes off their face [*sic*] in order to tell them to stay far away. When they advanced that hideous hand towards my plate in order to serve me, I wished I were able to depart in order to eat a piece of bread elsewhere, rather than dine with such service. What unhappiness for the white race—to have tied their existence so closely with that of negroes in certain countries! God preserve us from such a contact!" (Ibid.: 45)

Agassiz's testament of his experience follows the biological and social path I postulate. His experience begins from the embedded system of concepts with which he encountered novelty, those concepts through which, to a Swiss Christian and natural scientist, humans are "really men." *Discrepancy:* "'I first found myself in prolonged contact with negroes. . . . [T]heir lot inspired compassion in me in thinking that they are really men. . . . [I]t is impossible for me to repress the feeling that they are not of the same blood as us . . . especially [in seeing] the livid color of the palm of their hands. . . .'" *Pain:* "'I can scarcely express to you the painful impression . . .'" *Freezing:* "'I could not take my eyes off their face in order to tell them to stay far away.'" *Flight:* "'I wished I were able to depart. . . .'" *Avoidance,* as *Stigmatizing* and *Distancing:* "'degraded and degenerate . . . What unhappiness for the white race—to have tied their existence so closely with that of negroes. . . . God preserve us from such a contact!'" *Socialization:* "His conversion," Gould reports, "followed an immediate visceral judgment and some persistent persuasion by friends. His later support rested on nothing deeper in the realm of biological knowledge" (ibid.: 44).

Next, the penultimate steps, *Denigration* and *Stereotyping*. Writing in 1863, Agassiz said: "'Social equality I deem at all times impracticable [he supported legal equality]. It is a natural impossibility flowing from the very character of the negro race' . . . for blacks are 'indolent, playful, sensuous, imitative, subservient, good natured, versatile, unsteady in their purpose, devoted, affectionate, in everything unlike other races, they may but be compared to children, grown in the stature of adults while retaining a childlike mind. . . . No man has a right to what he is unfit to use. . . . Let us beware of granting too much to the negro race in the beginning, lest it become necessary to recall violently some of the privileges which they may use to our detriment and their own injury. . . .'" (ibid.: 48). He also rated Indians and Mongolians: "'The indominable, courageous, proud Indian—in how very different a light he stands by the side of the submissive, obsequious, imitative negro, or by the side of the tricky, cunning, and cowardly Mongolian! . . .'" (ibid.: 46). Agassiz's "'painful impression'" and what Gould calls his "immediate visceral judgment" seem not to be mere metaphors, then, but accounts of Agassiz's physiological response of distress to these signs dissonant with his convictions.

By whatever meanings Agassiz apprehended the white race, black people were a sign of discrepancy from them. From his biography and from his racist assertions, perhaps two concepts can be plausibly reconstructed. Hierarchy is one pivotal idea for this Swiss Christian and "devout creationist who lived long enough to become the only major scientific opponent of evolution" (Gould 1981: 43). An ordered human world is a ranked world, Lowest to Highest in all respects, physically and morally. "'There are upon earth different races of men, inhabiting different parts of its surface, which have different physical characters; and this fact . . . presses upon us the obligation to settle the relative rank among these races, the relative value of the characters peculiar to each'" (Agassiz, quoted in Gould 1981: 46).

Color differences have been from earliest recorded history "easily interchanged with moral polarities, and the blackness of immorality contrasted with the whiteness of salvation. The black Ethiopian was associated with sin and with the diabolical by homiletic writers . . . who explained that they were burned black not by the sun but by vices and sin. . . . [In] one very popular school text in the Middle Ages, the innocuous word 'Ethyopum' is interpreted allegorically: 'Ethiopians, that is sinners. Indeed, sinners can rightly be compared to Ethiopians, who are black men presenting a terrifying appearance to those beholding them'" (Friedman

1981: 65). For Agassiz, then, black people may have been a sign of sinners, the lowest rank of all.

Salvation is the second important concept for Agassiz. The edge position assigned to these "perverse races" in medieval maps is a fundament of the cosmologies these maps inscribe, and the spatial and temporal "remoteness" of these races is a sign of the justice of their exile:

> Some texts proposed that God had exiled the races because He saw that they were dangerous to humanity. Consequently their physical and social abnormalities were not at all evidence of the plenitude of the Creation and the "playfulness" of the Creator, but rather of God's protective care of His children, and of His power to pass on His curse from generation to generation. Writers [in the Middle Ages] who held such views regarded the races with awe and horror as theological warnings. (Ibid.: 90)

Did his proximity to these many signs of Sin threaten Agassiz's place among the Elect? Hierarchy in the service of Salvation may have governed his view, as an orthodox Christian, of who can be judged to be "really men."

The fact that Agassiz was "an extreme splitter in his taxonomic practice" may be more evidence of his preoccupation with Hierarchy. "Taxonomists tend to fall into two camps—'lumpers,' who concentrate on similarities and amalgamate groups with small differences into single species, and 'splitters,' who focus on minute distinctions and establish species on the smallest peculiarities of design. Agassiz was a splitter among splitters. He once named three genera of fossil fishes from isolated teeth that a later paleontologist found in the variable dentition of single individual. He named invalid species of freshwater fish by the hundreds, basing them upon peculiar individuals within single, variable species" (Gould 1981: 44).

Equally important as Agassiz's theology and classificatory turn of mind was his social position, which enabled him to bring about the ultimate step of this process, *Institutionalization:* "Agassiz was a charmer; he was lionized in social and intellectual circles from Boston to Charlestown. He spoke for science with boundless enthusiasm and raised money with equal zeal to support his buildings, collections, and publications. No man did more to establish and enhance the prestige of American biology during the nineteenth century" (ibid.: 43). Moving in circles of wealth and power, identified with America's then most prestigious institution, and an eminent authority, Agassiz was thus able to become "the leading spokesman for polygeny in America" (ibid.: 43). Although, finally, Agassiz's "students rebelled" and his "supporters defected," he "remained a hero to the public" (ibid.: 50). Without this forum for articulating and elaborating to laypeople his " 'painful impression,' " the history and tenacity of American racism among elites might have been quite different (e.g., Solomon 1956).

That Agassiz changed a long-standing intellectual position after his hotel experience is remarkable testimony to the superior force of an elementary neurophysiological response. Although Agassiz may have had intellectual predispositions toward the racist position—Gould mentions Agassiz's fears about miscegenation and a theory of the spatial distribution of the races—until his experience in his Philadelphia hotel, Agassiz had placed more weight on the logic of contrary evidence.

ABUSING THE HANDICAPPED

Children born prematurely, mentally retarded, with low birth-weight, or with congenital defects are more likely than normal children to suffer abuse at their parents' hands. In 45 percent of a group of only mildly retarded children, histories of "extensive physical abuse or neglect" were found (Zigler [1976] 1979: 183). Why this should be so is not known with any certainty; researchers suggest only that these parents may experience stress and anxiety at higher levels than parents of normal children. Frustration over their slower learning, perhaps, would be natural, but its harsh expression may have to do with retarded children's being doubly discrepant: not only are these children imperfect specimens of the species, but CHILDREN are considered to be IMPERFECT ADULTS as well.

The morale of parents of handicapped children may also be broken by the ice floe of stigma to which the family as a whole is likely to be consigned. "By definition, of course, we believe the person with a stigma is not quite human," Erving Goffman observes. "On this assumption we exercise varieties of discrimination, through which we effectively, if often unthinkingly, reduce his life chances. We construct a stigma theory, an ideology to explain his inferiority and account for the danger he represents. . . . We tend to impute a wide range of imperfections on the basis of the original one and at the same time to impute some desirable but undesired attributes, often of a supernatural cast, such as 'sixth sense,' or 'understanding' " (Goffman 1963: 15–16).

"The true Freak," writes Leslie Fiedler, "stirs both supernatural terror and natural sympathy, since, unlike the fabulous monsters, he is one of us, the human child of human parents, however altered by forces we do not quite understand into something mythic and mysterious, as no mere cripple ever is. Passing either on the street, we may be simultaneously tempted to avert our eyes and to stare; but in the latter case we feel no threat to those desperately maintained boundaries on which any definition of sanity ultimately depends. Only the true Freak challenges the conventional boundaries between male and female, sexed and sexless, animal and human, large and small, self and other, and consequently between reality and illusion, experience and fantasy, fact and myth" (Fiedler 1978: 24). Not the categories as we name them, however, but the *ideas* shaping lines between categories—Instinct, Rationality, Intuition, Control, Foresight . . . are the real subjects of discourse about the differences between humans and other animals. They remain submerged and unsaid.

Cripples have been long believed to be the work of the Devil, as have illnesses to be punishment for moral transgressions, beliefs still having subscribers (Sontag 1978). Discomfort displaces. A study of people's willingness "to enter into relationships of various degrees of intimacy with persons having different types of chronic illness and disability" found that of "22 target groups, every one was rejected to some extent, with the following being unacceptable even as next door neighbors: cerebral palsy sufferers, epileptics, paraplegics, dwarfs, hunchbacks. Sufferers from only a few relatively minor illnesses were acceptable as a relative (other than spouse) through marriage" (Katz 1981: 17–18). So pervasive is the ideal of Perfection that handicapped people use it themselves in comparing the severity of their disabilities, but not only in assessing their relative degrees of functional capacity. Their ranking becomes a matter of self-respect as well. Culture coerces.

Bringing into a suburban neighborhood a group house for the mentally retarded is "about as inconspicuous as bringing in a 747 with the wheels up." To move mentally retarded people from total institutions into supervised group homes in residential neighborhoods in New Jersey it has been found necessary to delay notifying neighbors until the purchase of the home is final. A nonprofit institution, "Our House, Inc.," which helps to implement this program, sets up "carefully orchestrated informational meetings with video-tape presentations, audiences full of sympathizers and plenty of complimentary coffee." The houses remain entirely residential in character, without fences or fire escapes, and in this case, six children, aged 10–16, were the prospective residents. " 'We take great pains to make our houses and our clients fit in. We buy their clothes at local shops— jeans for the women so that they aren't wearing the polyester stretch pants that they wore in the institution.' " Neighbor's objections are always the same: "It will decrease their property values; the street is too busy, and the children will be hurt; it is too far from the stores for the children to travel; another house would be better-suited, it is too far from the fire department." Neighbors who speak more openly of their own interests say: " 'This will destroy the character of the neighborhood. . . . It may be good for the retarded people, but they should not put it in a nice neighborhood like this. . . . We have our life's savings tied up in our home, and we rely on zoning to protect our investment'" (Geist 1982b).

Some neighbors support the home. "'Something like this makes people ask themselves questions about themselves that they would rather go through life not asking, let alone have to answer.'" But one neighbor opposing it suggests that "the degree of compassion among neighbors for the mentally retarded children seemed to be on a sliding scale that depended on the proximity of their property to the home. . . . 'I know how badly we look to outsiders for opposing this. But people should ask themselves, being truly honest, how they would feel if such a facility opened next door to them'" (ibid.).

In Massachusetts, stealthy tactics are no longer allowed. Although confrontations often will force out a halfway house, more often "it is grudgingly allowed to remain, always shunned, and its residents never accepted or given the kind of neighborly support that they need so much. . . . Invariably, it is the unannounced, dead-of-night appearance of the residents assigned to the house which triggers the concerns and fears. Many human service providers argue that these concerns and fears simmer so close to the surface that it is only by stealth that a group residence can be introduced into a neighborhood. To come in publicly, they argue, even attempting to involve the community in the planning for the program, is to invite organized opposition: court challenges, legislative petitions, even the cancelling of the real estate deal" (*The Boston Globe* 1981).

For "perfect" people, imperfect people who are "less than human" elicit a kind of culture shock; "normal" people become unsure that mortal systems of meaning and conduct will suffice in dealing with them. Normal people are paralyzed, they stare helplessly, and are unable to act. Their helplessness leads to outright avoidance or to their awkward "fear of saying or doing the wrong thing." "Too often the disabled are presumed to be unhappy and are pitied, avoided, treated as children, spoken for as if they are not there and not 'seen' as whole persons beyond the disability. . . . The personal discomfort of the able-bodied often stands in the way of their establishing rewarding human relationships with the disabled. Fear of saying or doing the wrong thing, a desire not to be reminded of the fragility of the body and a lack of experience contribute to painfully awkward social relationships or downright avoidance of the disabled" (Brody 1981b).

These inappropriate behaviors suggest that normal people are distancing themselves from discrepancy by freezing the disabled in a familiar system of meaning and conduct—the one reserved for CHILDREN—in order to continue to act at all. Disabled people are treated like CHILDREN because CHILDREN are IMPERFECT ADULTS: the same concepts constitute their meanings—Dependent, Uncontrolled, Unpredictable, and Immature. The focus on children by the "Jerry Lewis Muscular Dystrophy Association Telethon with its pity approach to fund-raising" is objectionable, writes Evan J. Kemp, Jr., executive director of the Disability Rights Center and himself disabled with a neuromuscular disease.

> The very human desire for cures for these diseases can never justify a television show that reinforces a stigma against disabled people. . . . With its emphasis on "poster children" and "Jerry's kids," the telethon focuses primarily on children. The innocence of children makes them ideal for use in a pity appeal. But by celebrating disabled children and ignoring disabled adults, it seems to proclaim that the only socially acceptable status for disabled people is their early childhood. . . . The telethon emphasizes the desperate helplessness of the most severely disabled. In doing so, it reinforces the public's tendency to equate handicap with total hopelessness. When a telethon makes disabling conditions seem overwhelmingly destructive, it intensifies the awkward embarrassment that the able-bodied feel around disabled people. By arousing the public's fear of the handicap itself, the telethon makes viewers more afraid of handicapped people. Playing to pity may raise money, but it also raises walls of fear between the public and us. . . . [B]arriers to employment, transportation, housing and recreation can be more devastating and wasteful of our lives than the diseases from which we suffer. (Kemp 1981).

One negative evokes another, just as one positive does another, for people tend to see things of like quality as belonging together and as causally related, according to one theory of cognitive balance (Katz 1981: 119). For example, physically attractive people are believed also to be kind, vivacious, poised; physical attractiveness, studies show, is a reliable predictor of how people will be otherwise evaluated (Berscheid and Graziano 1979). One physical disability likewise evokes the presumption of another: shouting at a blind person, for instance. "Normal" people tend to "talk down to a physically handicapped person as if he were mentally retarded and sometimes even as if he were deaf or blind, and they tend to be surprised at discovering that the disabled person may be quite intelligent and competent" (Katz 1981: 20). Searching for "cognitive balance," the brain constructs a congruence having nothing to do with the "sender" of the stimulus (attractive; disabled) and everything to do with the "receiver's" search for equilibrium.

When frightened by the concepts IMPERFECT PEOPLE signify in Western discourse—Degeneration of the Species, God's Curse, Alien Strain . . .— "normal" people can also attack. The families of children with disabilities, studies have shown, "are often subjected to stares, embarrassed silences, rude comments and disrespectful questions. . . . [M]any of the parents interviewed reported 'stunning moments when strangers would say something very hurtful, such as "How can you bring a child like that out in public?"'" (Collins 1986). Among "all types of visible disabilities, facial disfigurements seemed to provoke the greatest amount of anxiety and aversion in children and adults, [and people] marked with facial anomalies provoke stronger aversion than do blind people, even though blindness is the most feared disability and . . . considered to be most severe" (Katz 1981: 20). The mother of a 13-year-old "with several handicaps, including a cranial facial anomaly" speaks of his experience in a public school: "'Athelantis is a special, exotic kind of child—he doesn't look like other children. . . . It was very difficult for him in the mainstream. If the teachers had been calm about it, the other children would have accepted him. But the teachers were physically repulsed—they freaked—and so the children thought they could say whatever they liked'" (Dullea 1982).

Just before surgery on a 17-year-old American girl for wholly disfiguring facial tumors ("Elephant Man" disease), her doctor said, "Her face just won't allow people to react normally to her." A newspaper article reports that "people . . . somehow feel compelled to ridicule her in public," that insults "have followed her to crowded shopping centers, to the campus of her university, even to the quiet woodlands where she goes walking near her home," that "men and women, who have never seen her before and do not know anything about her, have abused her before their children." "Lisa is clearly tired of being told that the most important things are her mind and her personality. 'I don't want anybody to tell me that beauty isn't important, that just what I have inside is important,' she said. 'I know that I am not going to look like Farrah Fawcett-Majors. I don't want to look like Farrah Fawcett-Majors. But I can't take this abuse all of my life and you'll never make me believe that most people will ever accept me for what I am'" (Severo 1981). Nearly three years later, despite relatively major improvements, she does not often leave home (Rothstein 1984).

The weight of Western civilization, burden not heritage, keeps her from being accepted "for what she is." A "beautiful face" is a sign of God's Grace; on every face are the prime signs of our most marked differences from all other living creatures—verbal language and imagination. Masking these symbols, facial disfigurement blurs the line of difference, as it may also mask conventional expressions of approval or chagrin, for example, which we expect to read clearly in others' faces. Confronting such ambiguities and unsure of their meanings and of how to respond, rather than *ask* for clarification, stigma flees enigma.

Our civilization more often than not uses crudely disparaging, abusive, denigrating, and fateful strategies in responding to conceptual contradictions, consigning the signs of them to social limbo, beyond the pale of belonging. These remain subterranean and treacherous in everyday life—God's Wrath, The Devil's Work, and every other haphazard *"moralitates"* derived from them.

LOCKING OUT CHILDREN

"Anyone who hates children and dogs can't be all bad," W. C. Fields is said to have thought. Americans "seem increasingly to dislike our kids, or the *idea* of them," John Leonard once complained, speaking as a "cultural correspondent" in *The New York Times*. He recounted how badly his children had been treated by the rules and the guards at the Museum of Modern Art and at The Frick Collection; on a trip to the Bronx Zoo he found so many toilets had been removed that "when a child needs one, it's a major project" (1978). Most children, he went on, are unwelcome in New York restaurants that aren't Chinese; babies are especially resented by other passengers on airplanes—because they may be noisy. That article brought him sacks of antichildren mail. Raging, he reported that people believe children "are an anarchy to be suppressed. . . . [C]hildren are the *other*. Their hands are dirty and their mouths are wounds. They ain't got no civilization. . . . I don't want to be liked by people who don't like children" (1979).

About CHILDREN a policeman in a Minneapolis suburb said to me: "Children always have a way of irritating someone, no matter what they do. And of course, kids don't always follow all the rules. They should. They cut across neighbors' lawns, and they know the neighbor doesn't like it sometimes. They take apples off the trees, sometimes do worse things. They throw eggs at people's houses when they get irritated at them. And kids fight among themselves sometimes. We get complaints from parents who say the neighbor boy assaulted my child." One woman involved in her suburb's community relations program shook her head in despair: "All the police do is chase the teenagers from one spot to another. Well, that's no answer. There's got to be a place for those kids in society. But there doesn't seem to be any place for them here."

If not CHILDREN, then who is to belong in America? Assessing their standing in American institutions, the Carnegie Council on Children asks: "Do Americans really like children? Are we the child-centered, child-loving people we claim to be?" On just about every issue affecting children's well-being—health, poverty, intact families, day care, schooling—the decisions adults make in the public domain turn out to be as likely to work against children's interests as for them.

> The conclusion is simple: we are a rich, prosperous nation, endowed not only with material goods but with knowledge and with human talent. We pride ourselves on our devotion to children. Yet if we search for programs

that support the development of children and help meet the needs of their families, we are a backward society, an underdeveloped nation. . . . [I]s it because at some level, we secretly hate and despise our children, because our lip-service to the next generation is insincere? (Keniston 1977: 235–236)

For all the loving families, dedicated teachers, and caring civic organizations there are, a two-sided "idea" of children permeates our politics and institutions.

Only in 1967 did the Supreme Court explicitly extend to CHILDREN the same constitutional protections afforded ADULTS, when it established that juveniles are as much protected by the due process clause of the Fourteenth Amendment as adult citizens (*In re Gault*). Withal, CHILDREN continue to raise a cultural issue as little likely to go away as the unleashed dog, for W. C. Fields' epigram keeps coming into its own in residential America. The manager of several apartment buildings in the Minneapolis suburbs put it to me this way: "The tenants who like to live in a no-children, no-pet building can *smell* a child. And they can smell pets. And by gosh they let you know it. If people have pets or dogs—'scuse me, I mean pets or children—you take them last. Basically that's what this business is all about: you take children and pets when you absolutely have to keep up occupancy. And I don't mean if you're just running 1 or 2 percent vacant, but only if you're in a position where you're running 20 to 30 percent vacant, you have to take those types." If the apartment building is located along a busy highway or at a well-travelled intersection, even more likely is their welcome.

Children may be cherished at home, but finding one they are allowed to live in is getting to be increasingly difficult. About 25 percent of all rental housing and 10 percent of all cooperatives and condominiums do not now permit people below the age of 18 to live in them. Suburbs spend much money and time on studies designed to "cost out" NEWCOMERS arriving with children whose education and play spaces will add to OLD-TIMERS' tax bills. With these studies they justify zoning to keep out housing designed with enough bedrooms for children.

Not long ago the Los Angeles Superior Court required landlords to apply a balancing test between the rights of families with children and the rights of people who want to avoid children before they could put up "Adults Only" signs. Apartment leases also often include a "no pet" clause; when pets are allowed, landlords may charge additional rent. Now that so many apartments are being converted to condominiums and cooperatives, however, covert pet-owners now and then come out of the closet to insist on property owners' rights. Older people moving into public housing frequently face a battle over permission to keep their pets, and losing the battle as they often do means putting good friends out of their lives.

Subdivisions for retired people have been zoning out children entirely; they may also have elaborate rules governing grandchildren's visits, limiting their stay to a certain number of days. One apartment complex is "a childless oasis in suburbia, the nursery of the Republic. Outside the gates, [residents] see a world where babies drool and toddlers cry in restaurants, where children trample lawns and flower beds while adolescents squeal tires at midnight and hang out on street corners, up to no good. In advertisements headlined 'We Kid You Not,' the complex bills itself as a community of 'child-free' living; the word 'child' here seems to take on the pejorative connotation of a pollutant or an unwanted additive. . . . Residents . . . said they are here for the companionship of others their age, trying to buy a little peace and quiet. They said they came here seeking refuge from sticky little fingers and dirty little hands, from muddy shoes and high pitched voices that shriek in the afternoon and cry at night. Most of them were grandparents. None offered to show any pictures" (Geist 1982a).

Of the 40,000 developments sold as co-ops or condominiums in 1981, about 10 percent are governed by minimum-age restrictions, according to one estimate. Even when unforeseen situations arise where owners find themselves housing children—a divorced daughter and her child, the child of a first marriage who unexpectedly joins a parent—residents don't amend or eliminate the regulations; those people have to find another place to live. "'To remove the age restriction would be removing an amenity that attracted them there in the first place,'" said one real estate agent in Connecticut. "'They were buying peace and quiet and they want to keep it that way'" (Brooks 1981: 8).

In trying to adopt age-restrictive zoning, many localities found themselves confronting unreceptive state courts (Connecticut, New York, New Jersey). But by 1975 that trend began to be reversed in decisions that turned on the question of whether age is a constitutionally "suspect" criterion, as race is held to be. Given the "general welfare" intentions of the zoning provisions at issue, several decisions have determined that age is not. In 1977 the U.S. Supreme Court held, however, that zoning cannot "definitively restrict which family members may live with one another," a decision that, by implication, could affect age restrictions. A woman who had no choice but to have a grandchild live with her was the subject of this case (*Moore* v. *City of East Cleveland*). One interpretation of that decision is that "an age-restrictive zoning ordinance cannot constitutionally bar younger persons from living together with an older relative who is properly a resident of an age-restricted district" (Strom 1981: 255). More particularly, this case "teaches that family zoning may not attempt to limit family households to a 'nuclear family' pattern. . . . The Court rejected

East Cleveland's contention that the constitutionally protected family was the nuclear family, stating that '[t]he tradition of uncles, aunts, cousins, and especially grandparents sharing a household along with parents and children has roots equally venerable and equally deserving of constitutional recognition'" (ibid.).

In strictly legal terms, however, the *East Cleveland* case doesn't bear directly on the age-restriction issue. No directly excluded younger adults have yet brought challenge to such zoning laws, but the size of the baby-boom generation and a continuing shortage of housing could change that. To forestall such litigation and to legitimize a ban on children, some states have already amended their enabling statutes specifically to permit zoning that promotes housing for the elderly.

A national survey of 1007 people living in privately owned rental units and of 629 apartment managers found that about 25 percent of renters not having children prefer not to live near them—more than half said that children are too noisy. One in five said that they chose to live where they do exactly because there were no children, but four in five said they wouldn't move if children were allowed. More than half of the building managers, on the other hand, said that families without children are bothered by them and that children increase maintenance costs (Robey 1981: 2). (The U.S. Department of Housing and Urban Development sponsored in 1980 this first-ever study of housing policies excluding children in response to several events—the International Year of the Child, the White House Conference on Families, and the advocacy of fair-housing groups and the Children's Defense Fund.)

Managers' beliefs and profit margins are increasingly taking control. Children were excluded in 17 percent of all private rental units in 1974, and by 1980, in 25 percent of them. The exclusions increase with numbers of children per family: with one child, a family can choose from 64 percent of all units, with two, from 55 percent (only 46 percent are eligible when the two children are of opposite sex), and with three children, only 41 percent of units in the rental housing market are open. It is true, of course, that most families with children prefer not to live in apartments (even if they own them). For those unable to act on that preference, housing managers and landlords keep the gates as near to closed as they can get away with.

Demographic trends will continue to push against these gates. Between 1970 and 1978 there was no change in the proportions of one- and two-children families renting, but, reflecting the trend to smaller families generally, there was a drop from 13 to 9 percent of renting families having three children. Those one- and two-children families will become much more numerous as the baby-boom generation becomes parents. In many housing markets around the country, they will have no choice but to rent and, like it or not, given land and construction costs, interest rates, and scarce money, to remain.

Not wanting to "hear a kid anywhere" was the reason for building a wall in a Houston subdivision, a woman who lived there told me: "When the subdivision was built a major street ran through the center. On the north side they were going to sell to all families and on the south side they were going to sell to all adults. But the adult community did not sell. Finally, after building for adults on just nine sites with only 59 units, and putting in its own pool, tennis court, and clubhouse, the developers put an eight-foot wooden fence around these nine buildings because these 59 adults did not want to hear a kid anywhere around in the vicinity. Then they sold the rest of what was to have been the adult community as single-family."

Among the least favored of newcomers are those with children who will pry open the public purse and keep asking old-timers to dig into their pockets for more: the current antipathy toward children also festers partly because they can cost their neighbors money. Schools may need to be built or reopened, teachers and administrators paid, public health doctors and nurses employed, buses and vans operated on children's schedule. The work of growing up is no less an enterprise requiring capital and human resources than any other sector of the economy, but it is one dependent on public financing and, on top of that, culturally problematic in its own right. That adult citizens were once children whose education and well-being their hometown supported goes unremembered. (California has recently circumvented these public issues by requiring housing developers to pay taxes earmarked for schools, a cost that is reflected in the house price and, for the moment at least, privatized.)

Citizens' pockets may be less full than they would like, it is true—and increasingly so. Developments designated for only those of a certain "age" are likely also to house those on fixed incomes. Retired people cannot easily afford the tax bill increases that families still moving up the ladder may be able to pay for. Old-timers in settled suburbs have by now sent their own children off into the world, and they may be unable to take on the costs of the next generation. As long as property taxes finance schools, people can be expected to respond negatively to families with children.

Nevertheless, such unmistakably economic pressures are not the only ones at work. One mother talking to me in Minneapolis thought it would help to treat children within the family "more like human beings rather than inferior children": "Oftentimes you're a lot more tolerant of people outside your family. You have more patience, and you treat them with a little more respect. It's really a shame, but that's the way it is. I might not put up with as much within my own family as I would from somebody else. If my kids have an accident, spilling milk or whatever, I'd tend to jump on them more. What we have to learn is to behave the same way toward our children that we do toward others. I think that it would help to treat them more like human beings rather than inferior children. I was a teacher, so I really feel that a child's image—self-image—is important for parents to build up."

American culture has a long history of adults' failing to acknowledge children in their own right: only after cruelty to animals became fixed in public consciousness did laws extend the same humane sensibility to children. The New York Society for the Prevention of Cruelty to Animals was established in 1866, dedicated to lightening the burdens of working horses. Using the rationale of its charter, its founder Henry Bergh initiated legal proceedings to remove Mary Ellen Wilson, an 11-year-old, from an abusive fostering situation, on the grounds that she was also a member of the animal kingdom. Until that moment in 1874, there were no legal means for protecting abused children. "Mr. Bergh does not confine the humane impulses of his heart to smoothing the pathway of the brute creature toward the grave or elsewhere but he embraces within the sphere of his kindly efforts the human species also," editorialized *The New York Times* on April 10, 1874 (Bremner 1971: 8)—and not with its tongue in its cheek.

The history of opposition to the various cadres of the American "child-saving" movement—tenement-house reform, child labor laws, the establishment of a federal children's bureau—reveals begrudging when not hostile attitudes toward children. The United States Supreme Court upheld in 1977 the right of schools to apply corporal punishment, ruling that the Eighth Amendment prohibition of cruel and unusual punishment does not apply to swatting or paddling children in public schools. The fact that teachers traditionally have been allowed to use such punishment is the rationale for this decision (*Ingraham* v. *Wright*). As for the claim that the decision intrudes into the privacy of the parent-child relationship, it may be so, but the fact is that most American parents already use physical force: between 84 and 97 percent of all parents "use some form of physical punishment on their children," imperfect adults that they are (Gelles [1978] 1979: 53).

This same study of 2143 families in a national probability sample, conducted in 1976, asked both women and men to report on their acts of "physical force and violence" within the single previous year. The fact that parents were willing to report their behavior indicated to these investigators that "many of our subjects did not consider kicking, biting, punching, beating up, shooting, or stabbing their children deviant. In other words, they may have admitted to these acts because they felt they were acceptable or tolerable ways of bringing up children" (ibid.: 64). The "most dangerous period in a child's life is from three months to three years of age," many child-abuse researchers and clinicians claim (ibid.: 62). Youngest children of large families are likely to be singled out (Zigler 1980: 20). Are they the most imperfect of a perfecting group?

Trickster tales echo the ambivalence toward children. Trickster is sometimes "the invincible child," sometimes adult; half god, half animal; sometimes female and sometimes male (Babcock 1975: 159–160). Anarchy is the specialty of trickster figures of folktales and clowns of ritual performance. Inverting conventions and expectations, their outrageous behavior calls into question each and every familiar and established system of significance. Trickster is "the spirit of disorder, the enemy of boundaries" (Kerényi 1976: 185). In the folktales of the early Church that were popular for 1500 years, until the beginning of the sixteenth century, even Christ in his infancy and childhood was coupled with Satan as a trickster.

Recounted in the "Apocryphal Gospel of Thomas" are stories that "explore the paradox of one who is both human and divine, the ambivalent quality of a being who has divine omnipotence and human limitations like a bad temper. The powers which are legitimately exercised on his antagonist Satan in the official versions of the life of Christ are here indiscriminately vented upon innocent playmates. The ambivalence of the infant Christ is perfectly shown in one story which tells of his passing through the city when a child throws a stone that hits him on the shoulder. Jesus curses him and the child instantly dies. . . . He is a bundle of paradoxes: creative and destructive at the same time, wise and foolish by turns. Significantly, most of these stories were not taken up into the official canon; they are too close to pure folklore, too full of unexpurgated ambiguities. . . . It is only after the Renaissance that rationalism drowns out all other voices, and the trickster, the mythical breaker of taboos and violator of boundaries who is both a sacred and a dangerous figure, is exiled from the theological and ritual center of society" (Ashley 1982: 133, 137). Modern scholars have "patronized if not disdained" this "theory of salvation" which "offers a supreme deity who uses divine trickery to outwit his opponent trickster. . . . And it is just this trait of using the Devil's tricks that satisfies the folk instinct for justice while offending the scholar, who perceives in it a contamination of the rational idea of goodness" (ibid.: 126, 130, 132).

Children and clowns also go together. Mythologically and ritually, clowns' "violation of taboo is their *raison d'etre*—just as the trickster has no other reason to exist in myth" (Makarius 1973: 53). Real people acting out taboos, clowns personify discrepancy in a safely circumscribed, ritualized setting. Raising the level of visceral discomfort considerably despite their stylized environment, clowns like tricksters evoke the laughter of relief. In

North American Indian groups people look to the clown "for his capacity of healing, purifying, bringing happiness and luck, and at the same time recoil from him as from an unclean being, to whom every kind of impurity is assimilated and whose contact is defiling and baneful—the kernel of that apparently unfathomable mystery of what is termed the 'sacred.' . . . Eccentricity in dress and demeanour; systematic trampling over rules and norms; full license to ignore prohibitions and break them; ambivalence; magical power; ominousness, . . . asocial characteristics, insolence, buffoonery, phallicism, vulgarity, a sort of madness." Clowns represent an "amalgamation of power to do good with power to do evil" (ibid.: 54, 56, 67–68). So does the fool—rather, the inseparable duo of kings and their fools. Clowns and court jesters share a common ancestor in "the sacred or possessed man who is out of his normal wits only because he is inspired with a higher wisdom" (Welsford 1935: 198). The "wise child" is a similar association.

Literature too reflects adults' versions of children. Both serious and popular literature—Dickens and Salinger, *The Bad Seed* and *Dennis The Menace*—reveal concepts that children signify. Each work reflects its time and place and comes to add to the store of metaphor, myth, and legend reflecting and shaping public perceptions. That the child is "unknowable" is a major motif: an enigma, the child is thus an empty vessel for many signs. In fiction and poetry the child is often "an unfathomable being, a stranger with whom adults cannot communicate although they are irresistibly attracted to him. . . . His existence represents a closed system but one that exerts an extraordinary attraction on the adults who are transformed by its impact. . . . His appearance is transparent, but in its inexplicability forever opaque" (Kuhn 1982: 20).

The "fate of the enigmatic child" of literature is "often a tragic one, for his puzzling nature evokes fear in adults, especially those whose existence is assured by an armature of reason. For them the irrationality which he embodies is a threat" (ibid.: 25). "The enigmatic child has the uncanny knack of seeing life as it is, stripped of all human pretenses and conventions. Since man cannot stand too much reality, the unwavering stare of the child which reveals it in a stark and unadorned fashion is a serious threat" (ibid.: 36). Even when children's fate is not tragic, their position in fictional life is often punishing: adults make of them orphans, illegitimate, unbaptized, or nameless (e.g., Little Orphan Annie, Little Father Time in *Jude the Obscure*).

Victorian novels may have chronicled the shameful facts of children's abuse in a bleak milieu, but they also seem "intended to conceal the real hatred of adults for their progeniture. By a calculated and systematic denigration of spontaneity, they seem intent on destroying as ruthlessly as possible all vestiges of childhood and on making their offspring little adults as quickly as possible" (ibid.: 95). Emily Brontë provides Lockwood with this nightmare in *Wuthering Heights* (1847), "one of the cruelest scenes of the Gothic novel":

> "I discerned, obscurely, a child's face looking through the window—Terror made me cruel; and finding it useless to attempt shaking the creature off, I pulled its wrist on to the broken pane, and rubbed it to and fro till the blood ran down and soaked the bed-clothes: still it wailed, 'Let me in!' and maintained its tenacious gripe [*sic*], almost maddening me with fear." (Ibid.: 95)

Ambivalence toward children also refracts familiar confusions between Love and Money. Until relatively recently, even urban children were economically productive members of the family. Now they are "economically worthless and emotionally priceless" yet costly (Zelizer 1981: 1052). In debates over the probity of children's life insurance in the late nineteenth century, the family was acknowledged as an economic unit to which children made a measurable financial contribution—among working-class people, that is, for "construction of the economically worthless child was completed among the urban middle class" by the middle of that century (ibid.: 1038, 1052).

That children and adults divide the continuum of human beings we take for granted, but the sharp contrast has not always been drawn socially. In earlier times "the mingling of children and adults" was common in everyday life—in schools, in trade, in crafts, even the army: "In short, wherever people worked and also wherever they amused themselves, even in taverns of ill repute, children were mingled with adults. In this way they learnt the art of living from everyday contact" (Ariés 1962: 368). After about 1500, that demarcation from adult society of the ever-lengthening period called childhood and youth came into being. As "the western world grew ever more complex" it demanded "more skilled and trained men for commerce and the professions," divorcing childhood and youth from adults and placing the young in a "world of their own—their own music, their own morals, their own clothes, their own literature" (Plumb 1972: 165).

A turning point was the publication in 1530 of a short treatise "On Civility in Children," by Erasmus of Rotterdam. Social restraints on children had not been much greater than those imposed on adults. Gradually, over the centuries, Erasmus' book of rules for everyday conduct, from eating and eliminating to greeting and visiting, evolved into the widespread conventions we call manners and the instinctual inhibitions we call repression. Today, "children have in the space of a few years to attain the advanced level of shame and revulsion that has developed over many centuries. Their instinctual life must be rapidly subjected to the strict control and specific molding that gives our societies their stamp. . . . The history of a society is mirrored in the history of the individual within it. The individual must pass through anew, in abbreviated form, the civilizing process that society as a whole has passed through over many centuries; for he does not come 'civilized' into the world" (Elias [1939] 1978: 140, 306).

Wild until Tamed, Barbaric until Civilized, BEASTS to be trained up as ANGELS—so have we been constituting CHILDREN, whose rights to belong and to thrive are jeopardized in America. With more than an anxious slip of the tongue, we animalize children (and humanize dogs): "If people have pets or dogs—'scuse me, I mean pets or children . . ." A television program goes by the title "Kids Are People Too!" Census takers are often asked, "Should we count the babies and children?" Fueling the denials of their humanity are children, who are our chief manufacturers and wholesalers of ambiguity and novelty. Children compete against the basic industry of culture, to create and sustain reliable meanings. Their snow-white questions confuse what adults believe has been clarified, perhaps established for all time. They cast doubt on one idea after another through which adults have been playing upon life's ambiguities, for just by answering their questions, adults have to think again about the answers they give. With fresh eyes, children see an arbitrary world they have to be taught revolves around an absolute center of equilibrium. "For the children's own good" is likely to be as much for adults' "good."

The children's "noise" that adults flee is the quintessential sign of the doubt and distress they raise. Once heard as well as seen, children specialize in reminding adults that dilemmas remain. Spontaneous, curious, imaginative, thriving on exploration and discovery, children arouse the same prickly reactions we have to uncertainty and ambiguity, to innovation, novelty, and change. Tricksters too specialize in innovation: Hermes' name also translates as "the tricky"; in an early Greek poem " 'The Father called him the Clever One . . . because he excelled all the blessed gods and mortal men in gainful crafts . . . and stealthy skills . . .' " (Brown 1969: 24). So is Prometheus, the Greek's patron of handicrafts and a benefactor of mankind, also a cunning trickster and thief of fire. Tricksters' "cleverness," "stealth," and "cunning" speak to the innovations and novelties they introduce, realigning and upsetting known systems of reward and sanction.

Adults use their power over children to institutionalize discomfort; adults devise many strategies for avoiding the uncertainties children's innocence and openness introduce. One is to maintain equilibrium and comfort by elevating familiar and predictable meaning systems to the status of dogma. Another tactic is to educate children out of curiosity, spontaneity, and initiative. American education displays

> a growing emphasis upon the child as a brain; upon the cultivation of narrowly defined cognitive skills and abilities; and above all upon the creation, through our preschools and schools, of a race of children whose value and progress are judged primarily by their capacity to do well on tests of intelligence, reading readiness, or school achievement. Although children are whole people—full of fantasies, imagination, artistic capacities, physical grace, social inclinations, cooperation, initiative, industry, love, and joy—the overt and, above all, the covert structure of our system of preschooling and schooling largely ignores these other human potentials to concentrate on cultivating a narrow form of intellect. (Keniston 1977: 240)

This contemporary strategy is reinforced by its history. Beginning in the Jacksonian period "many institutions affecting the young, from the school to the church to the reformatory, were more carefully and precisely age-graded" than at any time in American history. "Traditional interpretations view this . . . as evidence of an increasing sensitivity to the various stages of childhood and youth, and another step in the rise of child welfare. But there is a darker side that should not be so completely ignored. Age-grading may have been part of an effort to lock-step the child into rigid and predetermined modes of behavior. The change looked not to his benefit, but to the rationalization of childhood so that behavior would become more predictable and manageable" (D. J. Rothman [1971] 1973: 189).

Flight into adult-only enclaves is still another tactic. Toward TEEN-AGERS, denial is the favorite: they just aren't there, so there's no need to make a place for them in the community or the economy before they arrive full-grown. Still MINORS, belonging to no part of the adult world, some adolescents are left with little choice but to make up worlds of their own, as gang members, shopping mall "rats," drug takers, drop-outs, and incipient alcoholics. Pushed out to the edge, they retreat into their province of cardom, until their isolated frenzy kills them (and some adults) on their roads to nowhere.

These little strangers are the next generation, of course, and as it matures, it laces skepticism with naiveté and comes to ask harder questions and address its own interests, not likely to be wholly congruent with its elders'. The "dramas" of each generation's youth are these very "reorientations," which endure in both memory and meaning (Mannheim [1928] 1952: 301). The flotilla of generations is as influential upon the structure of society as is the division of labor and the distribution of wealth and power, for as older generations both welcome and repel the "fresh contact" of the younger with its heritages, these encounters shape many facts of history. "Noise" intrudes on stable systems—of politics, art, business, science—and how radically it can change them is each drama's center.

> [T]he continuous emergence of new human beings in our own society acts as compensation for the restricted and partial nature of the individual consciousness. The continuous emergence of new human beings certainly results in some loss of accumulated cultural possessions; but, on the other hand, it alone makes a fresh selection possible when it becomes necessary; it facilitates re-evaluation of our inventory and teaches us both to forget that which is no longer useful and to covet that which has yet to be won. (Ibid.: 294)

But these disruptions of their "inventory" of meanings older generations do not experience tranquilly; elders also are likely to have the power to translate their distresses into banishments, punishments, and that pervasive ambivalence which does children so little good.

The powers of ambiguity personified in mythic gods and ritual clowns are like those each new generation dispenses when it comes upon forbidden thoughts and plays with established meanings. For these timeless motifs represent the scaffolding between what is known and unknown: that which can be imagined. Trafficking as it does in visions, inventions, and options, the imagination can untie meanings from their moorings. Gods and tricksters "thieve" and "rob" us of certainty (Seth is "Lord of lies; king of deceit"), and Hermes works stealthily, mostly at night, our time to dream. The most breathtaking of all human faculties, imagination lifts us across the boundary between daylight and dreaming, unweighted by stones of familiarity. Those flights are thrilling often enough, for the poetry and art we love (and, at intervals, can hear and see again and again) combine novelty with resonance; they arouse and buoy our curiosity and our growth. Yet, like mythic figures, our own specialists in imagination are, for that, feared as much as worshipped, for we prefer those flights to be short and land us safely on home ground. So we starve *and* revere poets, artists, playwrights, philosophers, scientists . . . and love and hate CHILDREN for signifying the kinds of fun, trouble, and surprises imagination creates.

REPRISE

The aversive, distancing, and denigrating vocabulary of liminal discourse is so thoroughly naturalized that it has to be counted among the most stubbornly silent of all that goes without saying. But it seriously mistakes consequence for cause, once seen in terms of the neurophysiology of fear and curiosity. Its imprecations have the wrong target: the problem, for person and society alike, is to examine what it is about that which is already-known and familiar that makes the particular unfamiliarity or difference fearsome and painful. Without that work, the most elementary level of human response prevails, and "novelty neurons" of the hippocampus register the pain of difference and its frustration and disappointment, above a certain threshold, without consciousness having consulted the content, implications, and entailments of hitherto sustaining meanings. The familiar defines the menace of the strange, yet the "strange" may only be the *un*familiar: Barthes could well despair of the Neutrality of differences—human/animal, male/female, disabled/able-bodied. . . .— locked into the vocabulary of aversion as we are. The silences of slash lines are the potential emancipators of "imprisoning" difference.

These semantic and physiological processes are revealed not only in spontaneous, untutored responses in daily life. They are also present in "scientific affairs" where "there should be no place for recoiling from novelty." In 1925 Freud wrote "The Resistances to Psycho-analysis" in response to the "particularly bad reception" it was accorded in medicine and philosophy (Freud [1925] 1939: 163, 164). He begins his discussion with these observations: "A child in his nurse's arms will turn away screaming at the sight of a strange face; a pious man will begin the new season with a prayer and he will also greet the first fruits of the year with a blessing; a peasant will refuse to buy a scythe unless it bears the trade-mark that was familiar to his parents. The distinction between these situations is obvious and would seem to justify one in looking for a different motive in each of them. . . . Nevertheless, it would be a mistake to overlook what they have in common. In each case we are dealing with unpleasure of the same kind. The child expresses it in an elementary fashion, the pious man lulls it by an artifice, while the peasant uses it as the motive for a decision. The source of this unpleasure is the demand made upon the mind by anything that is *new*, the psychical expenditure that it requires, the uncertainty, mounting up to anxious expectancy, which it brings along with it" (ibid.: 163).

The indispensable skepticism of science sometimes "shows two unexpected features: it may be sharply directed against what is new while it spares what is familiar and accepted, and it may be content to reject things before it has examined them. But in behaving thus it reveals itself as a prolongation of the primitive reaction against novelties and as a cloak for the retention of that reaction" (ibid.: 163–164). Although Freud's explanations of the "emotional sources" of the resistance to psychoanalysis turn on the substance of its theses (e.g., "a reduction in the strictness with which instincts are repressed"), he alludes to the possibility of the more general, primitive issues which this neurophysiology of fear and curiosity explores: "It would be interesting to devote a whole study to mental reactions to novelty" and to "a thirst for stimulation which flings itself upon anything that is new merely because it *is* new" (ibid.: 171, 163).

The discourse of difference expresses the primitive response through the hyperbole of death-dealing metaphors—contamination, pollution, chaos, monstrosities . . . as expressions of affects which remain unexamined vis-à-vis the differences themselves. The vocabulary of a cultural or secondary response would mark down the affect as disconcerting, surprising, controversial, provocative, refreshing, disorienting, bold, innovative. . . . None imply immediate acceptance of a difference; they are responses from the standpoint of the familiar system at issue. They do not make the difference alone the target of the affect.

An imaginative reading of the conceptual sources of eroticism's "danger" and "dirt" suggests, for example, that sexual activity disorients the "cognitive categories" of everyday reality.

> [T]he particular features of sex considered dangerous can reveal the general features of the world view they threaten. These aspects of sex must confute a category in a classification scheme if those who believe in this scheme are disgusted enough to proscribe them. . . . By analyzing each proscribed aspect of sex into its unnatural and immoral components and its natural and moral component [*sic*], we can determine the precise conjunction of actual and implied categories that produces a sickening cognitive disorientation. . . . The systematic interrelation of these primary dimensions constitutes the sanctified substructure of a cosmos. In short, the system of the sacred can be derived from the chaos of the obscene. (M. S. Davis [1983] 1985: 94–95)

"Sex is dirty to the extent that erotic reality threatens to undermine the cosmic categories that organize the rest of social life. This is the source of the fears that surround sex . . ." (ibid.: 245). The fear, I suggest, is prior; "dirt" is the name under which fear attacks.

Disorder is a major preoccupation of this discourse, in which the already-known is defined as constituting *order*. Disorder is also a more general preoccupation, especially the social disorder of both crime and deviance. The extent to which there is explicit, collective discussion yields our social responses to crime, deviance, and difference, I suggest. What is criminal a community defines through promulgated laws, arrived at through discussion and negotiation, and open to amendment through the same processes. What is deviant is less openly defined; it is prelegal, existing in the interstices of conventions and norms that go without saying until they are breached and begin to be discussed, perhaps renegotiated. Deviance accounts of course for innovation and creativity and ultimately for social change, as negative affects decay and the breaches come to be seen for their content. What is different or discrepant is more likely to be defined wholly by its silences and to be nonnegotiable.

When it comes to *difference*, what is most apparent is the poverty of concepts by which we are able to characterize it, beyond the "elementary displeasure" from which the highly charged, blinding vocabulary is constructed. "It is part of our human condition to long for hard lines and clear concepts. When we have them we have to either face the fact that some realities elude them, or else blind ourselves to the inadequacy of the concepts" (Douglas 1966: 191–192). This poverty makes of rationality the problem it is, rather than the solution it is taken for: because we do not today originate and articulate concepts adequate to account for the differences there are, we borrow from yesterday. Under the glaze of centuries of civilization are unexamined if not medieval meanings and symbols which maintain and sustain our frightened apprehension of difference.

THE CONSTITUTION OF
MEN AND WOMEN

Why are women so often the second sex, and men the first? Why are females in America and elsewhere discrepant from a male ideal, and apparently for that reason alone, vulnerable to being disvalued and denigrated (away from their hearths at least) and set out in social margins? For all that we know now about the sources of gender hierarchy and for all the improvements in women's condition, that susceptibility remains, in this culture and in most others.

Rather than looking at the line between the sexes, this essay turns outward, to consider how this species differentiates itself from every other: how humankind is constituted may have much to tell about how its two sexes are constituted. One universal distinction between ourselves and other species is entirely familiar, yet in most cultures unspeakable and absolute: the systems of meaning by which humans learn to control urination and defecation. Cleanliness training is the first rite of passage separating humans from all other animals and marking their readiness to belong in their own social world. How might the moral concepts of shame and disgust now essential to this training influence both men's and women's sense of themselves as human beings? How might speaking of this moral, symbolic, and metaphysical system of meaning increase our understandings of the legal, economic, historical, sociological, and philosophical underpinnings of gender stratification?

This essay tests Malinowski's suggestion that the "drab, minor and everyday events" of human life may hold as many keys to the mysteries of the human condition as the "sensational large-scale happenings" on which he admitted to having lavished his ethnographic "love and interest." Silences on this everyday subject run so deep, however, that there is little systematic evidence to call upon in the scientific literature of the late twentieth century, compared with studies of nutrition and the cultural significances of foods.

To construct the inner constraints by which we count ourselves members in good standing on the human side of the species line, our society, like every other, relies on its versions of Shame, Dishonor, Sin, Guilt, and

175

Justice to instill and maintain the moral orders by which humans alone live. We may be animals, but we are not, these concepts assert unambiguously, animalistic. Yet not all humans are allowed to belong on the same side of this line: women are positioned on the continuum of living beings closer to uncivilized animals, children, and other imperfect people burdened by stigma. Women's biological and social sexuality, it keeps being believed, associates them "with wildness, evil, lack of control . . . and, more generally, with an animal or primitive order of being" (Friedrich 1978: 187). That lesser humanity then justifies women's socially inferior position; women's reproductive abilities, child-care responsibilities, domestic duties, and, overarching all those, men's domination keep them closer to "nature" and apart from public and political realms in which power, recognition, and prestige are most likely to be conferred.

The demons and angels, goddesses and witches haunting the poetics of confusion are emblems of suprahuman qualities attributed to the female sex. As seen by nineteenth-century men who were novelists, scientists, and painters, women were both "angels" and "demons" with "disruptive powers" likely to "erupt in sudden magical transformations" and, in being "vehicles of incessant metamorphosis," altogether ambiguous and unpredictable (Auerbach 1982: 2, 4, 8, 26, 36). Not only is their sexuality read as a sign of social disorder: to women's body products are attributed bizarre and mysterious powers of pollution and contamination. Even today, many American men and women alike associate pollution with these products, to the extent of abstaining from sexual intercourse postpartum and during menstruation; the medical evidence for these prohibitions is weak, but the cultural advice strong (Paige 1977).

That women are the second sex and men the first remains a cultural conviction that has yet to yield to reason, to law, or to custom. Male has implied the norm to which female is anomalous; here, along the line dividing men from women, the auras of ambiguity display their ultimate social force. Today, the most adroit and sophisticated constitutional analyses of American women's status exhaust their case with a single plea: if only society valued the concept of WOMAN more highly, as the concept of MAN is valued, the many prejudicial practices of this society would be well on their way to disappearing. Where does MEN's higher valuation originate? Not from their social dominance, I suggest, but from the same source that disvalues WOMEN. MEN's value is also derivative and construed.

The proposition I explore is that the genders are each defined by the same system of meaning that marks all human beings off from all other living creatures: keeping some lines clear between ourselves and other species is "the civilizing process," and toilet training is the prime line. Through the symbolic, moral, and metaphysical system of cleanliness training, human beings know themselves to be not merely different from but superior to all other animals. Both sexes unquestionably belong to the same species: the social valuation of males depends as much on how humans construe and maintain themselves as different from and superior to animals as does the valuation of females. To be inhuman is not to belong morally to this species; to be a human animal is to belong, yet not wholly. That is the timeless ambiguity upon which all human beings play, and one from which the poetics of ambiguity draws many other images, as humans and animals incessantly transform from one into the other, mythically allegorizing this everlasting dilemma.

The socialization of the digestive system is total: public, social, and highly valued, eating together is constituted as a major sign of belonging; excreting remains the most isolated and socially unspeakable of our private acts, signalling not only the civility we prize but shame, repulsion, taboos, embarrassment, and denial as well. The substances essential to our daily cycle of staying alive and keeping fit, food and the waste we convert it to, are oppositely valued socially, even though each is biologically essential.

Our bodily, daily matters, as essential to living as food, water, and air, are construed no less than are other matters of plain fact: mastery of bowel and bladder is mastery of a fateful cosmology. Excrement could just as well be a sign of vitality and health; it could be a sign of experiences of well-being and renewal. Instead, it is associated with Hell, the death chamber of sinners. Dante's Inferno is the "Devil's domain . . . 'a vast excremental dungeon'" (Pops 1982: 53). Not only daily life but the great literature of the world calls upon and reconstitutes this same symbolic system, relying on it for both comic and tragic commentary, subtle or gross, from the Greek myths to Swift to Melville to Grass. Like the moral concepts weighting differences between the hands, the races, the species, these concepts are arbitrarily, unnaturally associated with the plain facts of the digestive system and habits of personal cleanliness.

The concepts of Disgust and Shame have been essential in the rite of passage by which humans learn to excrete in the socially appropriate place, at the right time. Successful cleanliness training depends on learning disgust toward body wastes; disgust is neither instinctive nor passively learned, but a social concept actively taught by parents: "instilling psychic dams of loathing and disgust," Freud puts it. Bodily control over elimination is achieved by learning to feel Shame, and lacking that control, in the case of feces' odor especially, to experience Ostracism; child or adult, we are unfit for society. Short of death, abandonment and social exile are the worst punishments, shame and humiliation the harshest blows to self-esteem.

Body wastes are constituted from ideas about social order as residing in the victory of Good over Evil. Evil is embodied, according to Western beliefs, in excrement; Defilement, Deviltry, Disease, and Sin shape this conceptual system. Men and women alike hope to be free from all signs of animality and from Evil, Sin, and Damnation, and to be associated with all that is Human, Good, and Pure. Disassociating themselves from the negative signs of this cosmology and attaching themselves to positive signs assures them that they are worthy human beings. Yet, partly because of constitutional differences present from birth, and partly because of their distinctive biological functions, male and female strategies for maintaining their self-esteem as fully human beings are different. These different "cosmological" strategies constitute many of the significant social differences between the genders.

Men's *modus vivendi* consists of distancing themselves from and avoiding the negative signs of this symbolic system—primarily, losing control and dealing with waste products; these strategies for maintaining self-esteem as human beings are seen as evidence of men's moral and social superiority. Women's *modus vivendi* is no less preoccupied with losing control and with distancing from the same negative signs, but in being mothers associated with incontinent children and stereotypically assigned to dealing with the body products of family members, their strategies for maintaining self-esteem are to seek social reassurance of their worth through affiliation and appeasement, seen as social submissiveness and subordination. *Both sexes are acting, not toward each other, as is conventionally believed, but in the terms of the same social and moral system by which both know themselves to be human beings.* The facts of the sexes' unequal access to valued social resources, which are signs of human beings' social worth, honor, self-esteem, and self-respect, are derived fundamentally from the terms of that system.

(I exaggerate here and throughout, of course: the sexes share these patterns, but each appears to emphasize one over the other. I try to use the terms "male" and "female" when discussing each sex unencumbered by this system of meaning, and to use "men" and "women" when they are acting within it, but that's not an easy convention to maintain, under the circumstances!)

Those ideas compose the proposition this essay elaborates. For the sake of brevity and to clarify its main lines of argument, I do not qualify this proposition, as of course it must be qualified by every other kind of factor that enters into this most complex of conundrums. This discussion is in implicit dialogue with every other perspective on gender stratification— economic, historical, sociological, legal, psychoanalytic, philosophical— for it is, in fact, already buried within these perspectives. Those discourses tend, however, either to deal with "anality" as a personal or character issue rather than as a social issue; or, more frequently, they are unaware that this belief system is lodged between their lines. This discussion aims only to make it more explicit, the better ultimately to be evaluated for how it may and may not amplify current understandings of the constitution of the genders.

Yes, cleanliness training conveys directly society's altogether sensible standards for being a socially welcome person, and it has essential hygienic functions. Most people probably feel that their body functions are personally unproblematic, and they're able to treat the social taboos around them with the earthy irony they deserve. But the practical and functional are terribly far from telling this whole story. What I am exploring is a metaphysical system by which the species knows itself, not the cleanliness standards which make our lives pleasant and healthful. These meanings, more deeply perhaps than any of the others these essays have suggested, are likely to be outside of awareness: because the issue is trivial and settled or because it's highly significant? I too can see good reason to regard the whole subject matter of factly, and for that reason the evidence I present is all on the side of significance, to help us to choose.

The moral and "religious" dimensions of this system are very old. Rituals throughout the world in centuries past used body wastes as symbols of both the sacred and the profane; these are documented in a classic work, unduplicated since its publication in 1891: *Scatologic Rites of All Nations*, with the subtitle *Dissertation upon the Employment of Excrementitious Remedial Agents in Religion, Therapeutics, Divination, Witchcraft, Love-Philsters, etc. in all Parts of the Globe*. Captain John Gregory Bourke, Third Cavalry, U.S.A., is the author; a Fellow of the American Association for the Advancement of Science, a member of the Anthropological Society of Washington, D.C., and among other affiliations, a member of the Society of American Folklore, Bourke was an established expert on American Indians—Moquis, Apache, Mohave, Cheyenne. Freud wrote the preface to the book's German edition, published in 1913.

An 1885 monograph of Bourke's recording the Urine Dance of the Zunis (in which the participants drink it) elicited from historians, anthropologists, explorers, missionaries, physicians, and philosophers many of the materials of *Scatologic Rites*, in which human, avian, and animal excrement figures in curing and religious rites, in exorcism and sacrifice, and in sorcery, witchcraft, and augury. "That these disgusting rites are distinctively religious in origin, no one, after a careful perusal of all that is to be presented upon that head, will care to deny. . . . Hebrews and Christians will discover a common ground of congratulation in the fact that believers in their systems are now absolutely free from any suggestion of this filth taint . . ."—so Bourke reassured readers of the late nineteenth century (Bourke 1891: 2, 3).

The Romans, Egyptians, and Mexicans had gods and goddesses of excrement. "The Roman goddess was called Cloacina. She was one of the first of the Roman deities, and is believed to have been named by Romulus himself. Under her charge were the various cloacae, sewers, privies, etc., of the Eternal City. . . . The Romans [according to another source] had a god of ordure named Stercutius; one for other conveniences, Crepitus; a goddess for the common sewers, Cloacina" (Bourke 1891: 129). The Mexican goddess Suchiquecal, both mother of the gods and "the mother of the human race [is] represented in a state of humiliation, eating [feces]." Another goddess was Tlacolteotl, the "goddess of ordure, or . . . the eater of ordure, because she presided over loves and carnal pleasures" (ibid.: 130–131).

During the fifteenth century, scholars agree, "the main feature of the European witchcraze was the 'witches' Sabbath,' the climax of which was a huge orgy between the devil and witches" (Ben-Yehuda 1985: 28); witches were all women, the devil and his aides, men. True to his trickster lineage, "the devil generally chose a place where four roads met . . . [and] having assumed his favorite shape of a very large he-goat, with a face in front and another in his haunches, took his seat upon a throne; and all present kissed the face behind. . . . This done, a master of ceremonies was appointed, with whom Satan made a personal examination of all the witches to see whether they were stamped with his secret mark. Those who did not have it were stamped immediately. This done, they all began dancing and singing in the most furious manner. Then they stopped, denied their salvation, kissed the devil's back, spit upon the Bible, and swore obedience to the devil in all things . . ." (ibid.: 29).

In every detail, this is a ritual of reversal, emphasizing the hegemony of Christian belief by dramatizing the demands of Satan. These stories and myths "were the exact opposite of what was supposed to be the true faith, that is, Christianity. . . . [I]n the church, people kiss the cross; at the witches Sabbath, they kiss the he-goat's posterior" (ibid.: 32). A similar rite of reversal is the Feast of Fools, celebrated all over Europe and in England, which occurred inside of churches; it featured, as did the Urine Dance of the Zuni, excrement, nudity, and males disguised as females. During high mass, according to an authoritative French description of 1825, the participants took possession of the church, their faces daubed and painted or masked as harlequins, dressed as clowns or as women, and ate upon the altar *boudin*, sausages and blood-puddings; the term also translates as excrement. "The reference to the use of pudding or sausage on the altar itself is the most persistent feature in the descriptions of the whole ceremony. But little difficulty will be experienced in showing that it was originally an excrement sausage, prepared and offered up, perhaps eaten, for a definite purpose" (Bourke 1891: 20). "Add to this the feature that these clowns, after leaving the church, took their stand in dung-carts (*tombereaux*), and threw *ordure* upon the by-standers. . . . [I]t must be admitted that there is certainly a wonderful concatenation of resemblances between these filthy and inexplicable rites on different sides of a great ocean" (ibid.: 12). Many such sacred and magical associations seem to have been secularized; we remain much under their influence.

Even the harmless microbes on human beings we lump together with obscenity, disease, and dirt, says Theodor Rosebury, a microbiologist, in his unique work *Life on Man* (1969). "Germs produce disease, and so we think of them as nasty little things in their own right. Traces remain of the puritan notion that our bodies, or parts of them, their functions and products, are ugly, dirty. Sex has been entangled in this notion. Feces, filth, dirt, soil, earth—these are all related. Now that we know that germs are active in all of them, it looks as though there may be sense in the whole idea. But microbiologically speaking—and for other good reasons as well—it just isn't so. . . . The microbes that live on us [in that balanced state we call health] are part of the 'dirt'—speaking broadly, the *excrement*—that we try hopelessly and irrationally to get rid of" (xiv, xvi).

Imploring us to change our "prejudices," Rosebury wants us to "lift the veil of obscenity" from excretory behavior. Obscenity should apply not to "sex or scatology at all, but to any offense to human decency, to human values we call moral. . . . If there is nothing ugly or reprehensible about man except what can be defined as disease and treated accordingly, we ought to separate the notion of obscenity from all healthy human acts and functions, and from the parts of our bodies concerned with them . . ." (ibid.: 188). "Obscenity" only reveals our choice of concepts by which these healthy acts take their meaning.

Despite differences between the sexes by virtue of strictly biological, constitutional differences, they are, as members of the same species, more alike than different psychologically, studies repeatedly reveal. Why then are their social and economic situations in society more different than alike? The answers are not likely to be found in the sexes, but in what society makes of them. Anatomy may nevertheless remain destiny: the gastrointestinal tract. Not women or men, nor mothers and fathers, but the conceptual and biological system of digestion is the never-never land I explore.

LEARNING TO BELONG

Learning to control the body's elimination reflexes is the rite of passage just after weaning, the first one following birth, circumcision, and christening to carry social weight. Parents teach Control of defecation and urination by teaching the consequence of losing it: their Disgust and Disapproval, to which the child's appropriate response is Shame and behaviors aimed at restoring parental Love and Approval.

Children learn disgust toward excrement at a time when they see their body products as being part of themselves. On the evidence, human infants know no revulsion toward their body wastes. Freud observed in his preface to Bourke's work that

> the human infant is obliged to recapitulate during the early part of his development the changes in the attitude of the human race towards excremental matters which probably had their start when *Homo sapiens* first raised himself off Mother Earth. In the earliest years of infancy there is as yet no trace of shame about the excretory functions or of disgust at excreta. Small children show great interest in these, just as they do in others of their bodily secretions; they like occupying themselves with them, and can derive many kinds of pleasure from doing so. Excreta, regarded as parts of a child's own body and as products of his own organism, have a share in the esteem—the narcissistic esteem, as we should call it—with which he regards everything relating to his self. Children are, indeed, proud of their own excretions and make use of them to help in asserting themselves against adults. Under the influence of its upbringing, the child's coprophilic [attraction to fecal matter] instincts and inclinations gradually succumb to repression; it learns to keep them secret, to be ashamed of them, and to feel disgust. (Freud [1913] 1939: 89–90)

The learning process is successful only when the child has internalized disgust: disgust with the odor of feces is essential to effective toilet-training in Anglo-American societies. But neither too much nor too little, according to one experiment that found a clear relationship between the intensity of the disgust reaction and encopresis (a disorder defined as inappropriate fecal soiling lasting more than about one month at four years of age or older). "The 'potting couple,' the training mother and the trainee child . . . are required to produce, within a certain period, a 'normal' reaction of disgust, strong enough to influence the behaviour of the individual for the rest of his life." Each culture has its own measure so that a "culturally normal feeling of disgust will lead ultimately to a culturally acceptable technique for the disposal of personal excreta. Where the proper disposal of excreta is faulty, the disgust reaction will be found abnormal" (Anthony 1957: 165).

Learning disgust toward excrement, children also learn to be disgusted with this part of themselves: "the first ego is a body ego" and all that happens between mother and her child's body "will inevitably be incorporated into the child's emerging sense of self-regard and will affect profoundly the child's self-esteem. . . . Virtually all maladaptive defensive patterns in childhood, adolescence, and adult life have as at least one major purpose protection from the pain associated with lowered self-esteem" (J. E. Mack 1983: 26, 37, 38; see also R. W. White 1963: 48–54). The shame children learn should they lose control is a feeling of " 'something inimical in one-self which keeps love from reaching completion and perfection,' " as Hegel defined it (in Piers and Singer 1953: 16).

Toilet training also teaches them that there is an incomplete difference between "me" and "not me," humans' second early experience of ambiguity and discrepancy; for example, "[t]o small children [seeing the BM flushed away in the toilet] is as disturbing as if they saw their arm being sucked down the toilet" (Spock and Rothenberg 1985: 314–315). Learning bladder and sphincter control seems to stand as a decisively discrepant experience in children's schema of bodily and psychic unity.

As complete a cultural and ethnographic account as I have been able to find of this American rite of passage from both child's and adult's perspectives, behavioral and conceptual, was compiled by John Dollard and Neal Miller, psychologists once specializing in child development research at Yale University.

> If the child has come safely and trustfully through the early feeding and weaning experience it may learn for the first time in its cleanliness training that the culture patterns lying in wait for it have an ugly, compulsive aspect. No child may avoid this training. The demands of the training system are absolute and do not take account of individual differences in learning ability. The child must master cleanliness training or forfeit its place in the ranks of socially acceptable persons. Freud describes the culture's task as building within the personality of the child the psychic dams of loathing and disgust . . . for urine and feces and particularly for the latter. . . .
>
> Observation of children within the home indicates that children begin with the same naive interest in their feces and urine that they have in other parts and products of their bodies. . . . The morning will arrive in every nursery when the astonished parent will observe their beloved child smearing feces over his person, his hair, and his immediate environment with gurgling abandon. This may be the first occasion for sharp, punishing exhortations, for angry dousing, for the awakening of anxiety in connection with fecal materials. On pain of losing the parents' love . . . the child must learn to attach anxiety to all the cues produced by excretory materials—to their sight, smell, and touch. It must learn to deposit the feces and urine only in a prescribed and secret place and to clean its body. It must later learn to suppress unnecessary verbal reference to these matters, so that, except for joking references this subject matter is closed out and excluded from social reference for life. . . .
>
> The child must learn to wake up in order to go to the toilet, though sleep seems good. It must learn to stop its play even when social excitement is strong. It must learn to discriminate between the different rooms of the house—all this by crude trial and error. In this case, "trial" means urinating

or defecating in an inappropriate place, and "error" means being punished for the act so that anxiety responses are attached to the cues of this place. In the trial-and-error situation this must be repeated for each inappropriate place—bed, living room, dining room, kitchen, "outside." . . . This training necessarily takes considerable time, perhaps several years in all, in which child and parent are under severe pressure. . . . Learning cleanliness is no mere behavioral routine. It arouses strong emotions—perhaps as strong as are ever evoked in the child again. Anger, defiance, stubbornness, and fear all appear in the course of such training. Fear may generalize to the toilet itself and excite avoidance responses in the very place where the child is expected to "go."

Any one of us may have been through a stormy period of this kind and yet have no recollection of it. The results may show themselves in our symptoms, our most deeply embedded "character" traits, in our dreams, in our intuitive presuppositions about life, but they will not show themselves in our verbal behavior. The record of this training will be found in no man's autobiography, and yet the fate of the man may be deeply influenced and colored by it.

The first broad strands of what Freud calls the Superego are laid down at this time. Anxiety reactions, never labeled, are attached to stimuli, also unlabeled. When these stimuli recur later the anxiety reactions automatically recur. The resulting effect Freud has called the "superego" or unconscious conscience. When unconscious guilt reactions are severe, the personality is suffused with terror. It is hard to say whether a morbid conscience is a worse enemy of life than a disease like cancer, but some comparison of this kind is required to emphasize the shock produced in the witness when he sees a psychotic person being tortured by such a conscience. Enough is known now to convince us that we should make the humble-seeming matter of cleanliness training the subject of serious research. (Dollard and Miller 1950: 136–141)

Training consists of rewarding and praising success and punishing failure with shaming, blaming, scolding, threatening, ridiculing, spanking, and other forms of verbal disapproval and varying degrees of physical assault. Typical training methods probably include most of the practices, to one degree or another, that one American specialist warns against.

1. *Do not* use harsh punishments when a child has an accident. Spanking or hitting a child tend to make the problem worse.
2. *Do not* use such negative tactics as blaming, shaming, threatening, moralizing, or name calling. These methods tend to exacerbate the problem by making the child nervous, embarrassed, resentful, and unhappy. Examples of such methods are: "For shame!" "You're going to be very sorry if you dirty your pants again." "Bad boy!" "What a baby you are!" "That's disgusting!" "If you loved me you'd stop that wetting." "You're just lazy and don't care." "What's the matter with you?" (Schaefer 1979: 110)

(Toilet training difficulties may well be a precipitating cause of adults' abuse of children; but studies which find that children are most vulnerable between three months and three years do not also speak of adults' training practices.)

A study of 24 American families, middle-class members of the same Baptist congregation in a New England town in 1954–55, found that mothers express the "ideal" that "the mother should not force the child in any way," but when their child is not easy to train, "the ideal is very distant from the real practice, and more severe measures are used."

> . . . [O]ur impressions as to the frequency of certain toilet training techniques mentioned by mothers . . . :
>
> Holding pot on lap and small baby on pot while feeding—rare
> Putting on pot at regular times after child is able to sit up—frequent
> Use of suppositories, soapsticks, or enemas at regular times—one fourth to one third of all mothers used these for bowel training
> Spanking—occasional
> Shaming—very frequent
> Rubbing nose in feces—occasional
> Praising for proper performance—very frequent
> Taking up at night—frequent
> Restriction of water after 4 or 5 P.M.—frequent
> Promise of rewards for not wetting bed—frequent with bed wetting problems
>
> (Fischer and Fischer 1966: 72)

Toilet-training ultimately enhances self-esteem, of course, in terms of these same concepts, as well as representing the acquisition of competence in a new skill. That "skill" is understanding the concept of Control. Children "first value their stools as part of themselves and then learn to value their control over the stools" (Cotton 1983: 128), yet that control itself paradoxically depends on children's also learning to feel disgusted with themselves. Children "suffer" an original "narcissistic injury . . . in attaining sphincter control" (Orbach, Bard, and Sutherland 1957: 127).

Needless to say, this injury is ameliorated to a greater or lesser degree over time, as people become competent at mastering other life tasks and challenges. By itself, it is by no means debilitating to self-esteem. Yet it needs to be acknowledged as a special kind of injury, first because it arouses "strong emotions" in both child and parents at a developmentally vulnerable time, and second, because it recurs daily throughout life, directly in bodily habits and attitudes and subliminally in the associations of disgust with evil, control with human perfection, and shame with humiliation. Cleanliness training's moral connotations implant "our intuitive presuppositions about life," as Dollard and Miller express it.

Toilet-training is the crux of the second of Erik Erikson's "eight ages of man," introducing the conflict between autonomy on the one hand and shame and doubt on the other. People draw upon these modalities throughout life. "Doubt is the brother of shame. . . . The "behind" is the small being's dark continent, an area of the body which can be magically dominated and effectively invaded by those who would attack one's power of autonomy and who would designate as evil those products of the bowels which were felt to be all right when they were being passed. . . . From a sense of self-control without loss of self-esteem comes a lasting sense of good will and pride; from a sense of loss of self-control and of foreign overcontrol comes a lasting propensity for doubt and shame" (Erikson 1963: 253–254).

The history of American toilet-training advice during the past 70 years or so reveals how unsettling this domain is even for experts, with confusing consequences for both children and adults: "A high incidence of enuresis [bedwetting], chronic constipation which can last into adulthood, and soiling or smearing with feces by four- and five-year-old children are problems that seem to be all too common in our Western cultures" (Brazelton 1978: 142–143). Experts' counsel swings so immoderately as to verify that it draws more on cultural premises than on specialist knowledge. *Infant Care*, first issued in 1914, was the best-selling *government* publication of all time by some accounts, and it recommended that bowel training should begin by the third month or even earlier. By 1921 it had moved the training up to birth! In 1929, it relented, suggesting waiting until the child was one month old. The American mother was instructed, by the famous Dr. Watson, to "spend a great deal of time holding a 'porcelain cuspidor' to her infant's rear end," according to one historical survey (A. Mack 1978: 8). She was Watsonized even if her child wasn't.

She may also have been herself a recent arrival or a first- or second-generation daughter of immigrants who followed what has been characterized as a European pattern of early training. In the 1960s, the median age for beginning regular training was 4.6 months in London, 7.8 months in Paris, and 12.4 months in Stockholm (Schaefer 1979: 23). The mother of 60 years ago was likely to be eager for relief from laundry chores, which disposable diapers and home washers and dryers have finally brought to those who can afford them; American lower-class mothers appear to begin training earlier in both sexes than do middle-class mothers. Yet, given American patterns of social-status mobility, middle-class mothers may themselves have been trained by lower-class mothers, and the nursemaids and nannies of children in upper-middle-class and upper-class families are likely to use the high-pressure tactics and methods they were raised by (Gathorne-Hardy 1972).

Dr. Benjamin Spock has been the dominant influence on American practices since 1945 when *The Common Sense Book of Baby and Child Care* was first published; over 30 million copies have been sold ("The Century's Greatest Bestseller," says the current cover blurb). The latest edition is dated 1985, now written with a co-author and "revised and updated for the 1980's." Between the 1968 and 1985 editions, Spock changed his mind about when toilet training should begin. In the 1968 edition he suggests that toilet training "before a year" may provide "early conditioning [that] may help the baby and [mother] through the later and more important stages," but in the 1976 edition he changes this to a flat "I don't recommend any training efforts in the first year" and repeats it in 1985 (1968: 250; 1976: 287; Spock and Rothenberg 1985: 314). Toward the moral system involved in bowel training, Spock has been more and less explicit over the years. In the 1961 printing of the 1957 edition, but dropped from all subsequent editions, there's this advice: "Parental angriness, if it doesn't succeed right away in small doses, only makes him feel guilty; it doesn't make him good. Excessive shaming about his messes, trying to develop in him an intense sense of disgust, usually doesn't make his training go any faster. But after he finally gives in, it may make him an overly fussy person—the kind who's afraid to enjoy himself or try anything new, the kind who is unhappy unless everything is just so" (1961: 255).

In 1968, the advice is: "I think it is sensible for you to encourage the swing of the pendulum, from possessiveness to aversion, by emphasizing the uncomfortableness of having the movement in the diaper. You can explain to the child, as you clean up, that he will feel good, and be more like grown-ups, if he will tell you beforehand next time so that you can put him on the seat. But it's better not to make the child feel intensely disgusted or ashamed; that might instill too much squeamishness into his character" (1968: 253–254, 255). In both the 1976 and 1985 editions, Spock says forthrightly, "I don't think it's wise or necessary to give a child a strong disgust reaction about his bowels or any other body function" (1976: 289; Spock and Rothenberg 1985: 316).

Since 1976, Spock approvingly quotes his pediatric colleague Dr. T. Berry Brazelton's "philosophy and method" of "readiness" training, but Spock does not also quote Brazelton's doubts about children's "preference to be clean":

> Children do see their urine and bowel movements as part of themselves—even precious parts of themselves. I have never been convinced that babies are uncomfortable instinctively when they are wet or dirty. I think that revulsion and discomfort are built in from the outside and cannot be depended on to be a force for a child's wanting to be trained. (Brazelton 1978: 135–136)

MOTHERING, FATHERING, AND DIRTY WORK

Toilet training is a prime line between family and society and a common threshold requirement for children's acceptance into nursery schools and day-care centers, and women continue to have primary responsibility for bringing children to this critical point. "The anal sphincters are present in all cultures, and it is the business of mothers everywhere to give these small circular muscles a social consciousness and responsiveness" (Anthony 1957: 154). Until about 10 years ago Spock's *Baby and Child Care* addressed only "mother" when giving toilet training instructions and other advice; now he and other advice-givers are careful to say "parents" throughout.

But it is still fair to say that American toddlers live through cleanliness training more in the company of their mothers and other women—the grandmothers, aunts, big sisters, mother's helpers, maids, nannies, who may help out mother—than in the company of their fathers. Despite their increased involvement in child care, the evidence shows that fathers continue to have less to do with children's excretory behavior than do mothers. The biological and historical facts are that women cannot avoid an intimate relationship with incontinent children. Not only can they not avoid it, the symbiotic relationship of mother and child seems to be an evolutionary requirement; the mother-child attachment or bond that forms in the first days of an infant's life appears to be a survival necessity. In being our cultural specialists in personal excrement, women are associated only more practically than men with the concepts it signals: their learned aversions are no less strong than men's.

Of a group of middle-class parents of 144 first-born children observed in 1972, only 7.6 percent of fathers shared infant-caretaking equally with their wives, and 64 percent of the mothers were "totally and solely responsible." For the care of infants 6–21 months old, 75 percent of fathers had no regular responsibilities, and 43 percent reported they had never changed their babies' diapers (Kotelchuck 1976: 338). For the number of times diapers require changing at those ages, that would suggest fathers' active avoidance. Moreover, whether the fathers who did change diapers did so when they contained a bowel movement is not reported; anecdotally, it appears to be common practice for men to refuse to deal with feces even when they will handle a wet diaper. Neither mothers nor fathers were asked about their feelings toward feces compared with urine. However, in not speaking of this unmentionable topic, such studies lump all tasks under "housework," "caretaking," or "child care," leaving us to read between their lines: cleaning bathrooms, dealing with bladder and sphincter functions, and handling soiled clothing and linens are not discussed in their own right.

Men's role in toilet training appears to be indirect; being out of a child's presence during weekdays partly accounts for their not being equally involved in the practicalities of training. But conventionally, even so, men's contact with soiled diapers, accidents, and training pants is likely to be minimal. Men's repugnance for diapering, changing soiled underwear and bedlinen, or cleaning up a fecal accident is entirely within their cultural rights. (In September 1985 the Syracuse, New York, airport opened a "gender-free fathers' and mothers' nursery" after the Fathers' Rights Association of New York State brought suit on the grounds of being "denied equal facilities" in male restrooms which are not designed, as females' are, with a "changing room" for babies. The suit also "addressed sex discrimination . . . against women who are assumed to have the total responsibility for children while traveling" [DeCrow 1986]). Not only are women assumed to have the responsibility, they are also assumed not to experience the same repugnance: women are presumed to have a greater tolerance for the same smells and mess. But the same training in disgust has been women's experience too, and mothers, despite their bonding to their newborns, have to learn a tolerance that doesn't come naturally.

Everything metaphysical about this symbolic scheme translates directly into the ways people act and airports are designed. Cleaning the bathroom is their wives' domain, 78 percent of American men believe, just as 75 percent leave the cooking to them, according to a telephone survey of 200 men in 20 cities by the advertising firm of Batten, Barton, Durstine, & Osborne. Men whose wives work outside the home fear first for their children's well-being, and fear next that the household's "cleanliness standards" will decline, according to another advertising agency study, which finds that laundry is the chore men are least likely to do. That agency, Doyle Dane Bernbach, Inc., concluded, " 'It's easier for men to accept the possibility of women as brain surgeons than to release their own wives from the drudgery of laundry and cleaning the bathroom' " (Foreman 1980: 21; Brozan 1980). Another study corroborates those reports: "Although men appear to do more around the home than ever before (take out garbage, cook, grocery shop, and wash dishes), there are still some activities that men do not perform to any degree, such as cleaning the bathroom, sorting the laundry, or cleaning the refrigerator or oven" (Lewis, Feiring, Weinraub 1981: 14). Women's "least favorite household task" by a margin of almost two to one is "washing dishes," followed by "cleaning the bathroom," according to a nationwide Gallup survey made in 1981 for *Parade Magazine*—"washing dishes" of course includes dealing directly with garbage.

Because men have been removing themselves from all they associate with losing control and diminishing their self-esteem, the life and death matter of their family's hygiene has come to foist on women a moral and practical "care" and "responsibility." Since the beginning of modern sanitarian knowledge, men have continued to appoint women guardians of their household's hygiene as an explicitly moral duty, sisters to the humiliated goddesses of other times and places. Today's soap, detergent, cleanser, and Lysol commercials only continue a tradition begun in America in 1885 when *Women, Plumbers, and Doctors*, written expressly for .women, appeared. Mrs. H. M. Plunkett, also editor of the "Sanitary Department" of a New York daily paper, surveyed the sanitarian knowledge of the day for the enlightenment of women, "whose destiny it is to remain a large share of the time at home, whose divinely appointed mission it is 'to guide the house'" (Plunkett 1885: 10). Any woman who fails to do her dirty work well enough, Plunkett warns, might find herself standing "beside the still form of some precious one, slain by some one of those preventable diseases that, in the coming sanitary millennium, will be reckoned akin to murders" (ibid.). In the chapter "Sewerage and Plumbing" an illustration carries the caption "A properly-plumbed house—Woman's 'sphere'" (ibid.: 112). Without patience for "misplaced delicacy," Plunkett writes:

> The urgent and instinctive need of absolute removal [bowel movement] is felt by every one; but the squeamishness which would regard the deliberate and thorough consideration of this subject by a faithful mother as a needless occupation of her thoughts by a repulsive and disagreeable matter, is certainly a misplaced delicacy. Neglected, it will thrust itself forward upon offended senses, and wreak its baleful power of sickness and death. Not so does the most refined mother feel, when she sees some darling first-born still in death, slain by the neglected poison. From the day when Moses issued the explicit directions contained in Deuteronomy . . . to this latest hour of the nineteenth century, it has formed one of the urgent problems of civilization. But it has remained for this age of Baconian scientific investigation to demonstrate that the origin of those mediaeval "plagues," which swept off twenty-five millions of people, was largely due to preventable unsanitary conditions as a predisposing cause, after the fatal seed had once entered a province. (Ibid.: 93)

In the preface to Plunkett's book, the male president of the British Medical Association (like Romulus, empowering women's work) pins on women the moral responsibility for life itself, declaring that "it is the women on whom full sanitary light requires to fall," finding men to be "practically of no assistance whatever" (I think he means "as a practical matter"):

> As a rule, to which there are the rarest exceptions, [the blame for contagious disease] is dependent on the character of the presiding genius of the home, or the woman who rules over that small domain. The men of the house

come and go; know little of the ins and outs of anything domestic; are guided by what they are told, and are practically of no assistance whatever. The women are conversant with every nook of the dwelling, from basement to roof, and on their knowledge, wisdom, and skill the physician rests his hopes. How important, then, how vital, that they should learn, as a part of their earliest duties, the choicest sanitary code. (Plunkett 1885: 10–11)

(Some scholars trace the American feminist movement to women's involvement during the Civil War in the United States Sanitary Commission, a medical and relief agency which, under men's aegis, offered women their first public roles, albeit as nurses and nurturers of the wounded and war-deprived.)

Domesticity, its cleaning, cooking, child care, and their associations within this cosmology, drowns women in the negative and denigrating meanings of "their proper place." Domesticity remains the lodestone of this personal domain of disvalued substances, whose daily control keeps firm the line between humans and animals. Women's work is never done, and, because we are irrevocably human animals, never can be done. As long as women stay around home within this precinct of meanings, they are no threat, but when they leave, and especially when they go out to work in man's world, they get into tricksterish trouble. Women entering man's world are more expendable and paid less; and in what they have to say, interrupted more (Maltz and Borker 1982: 198). It is not women's work that follows them out the front door, but this symbolic scheme by which everyone tenaciously asserts membership in this species.

Away from their hearths, women are wrapped up in housecoats labelled wife, mother, sister, daughter. As far as women may actually get from their "proper place," what the concept WOMAN signifies allows them little room to maneuver. They are likely to have jobs where they provide domestic, subordinate, or personal services: secretary ("office wife"), nurse, waitress, salesperson, assistant manager. . . . Their professional and managerial jobs cluster at the bottom of male hierarchies, in pay if not in rank. Hoping to rise on these ladders, young women have been costuming themselves in severely tailored suits and ties as androgenous colleagues, less to be appealing than appeasing.

Nor do women who opt out of "domestic life" by remaining unmarried, childless, and not subordinate to a man escape a place at the bottom of male hierarchies. Is that because they don't also abandon cooking for themselves and friends, because they have a room or two of their own needing to be dusted and swept, because they launder soiled clothes and bedlinens? There are always scrubbing and garbage. Men on their own also do these wholly domestic tasks, but they are not paid less at their jobs on that account. Male distancing, institutionalized as superiority, more than counterbalances any acted "domesticity," merely a witty sideline for "real" men and to be expected of male homosexuals, who are seen to partake of the concept WOMAN in any case.

Yet men by the millions go out to jobs that are boring, repetitive, isolating, dirty, demeaning, subordinate, and underpaid without affecting their cultural superiority. Men may prefer to leave the cooking to their wives, but until very recently, men have been the only renowned chefs. Men's "domesticity" they themselves acknowledge and enjoy: men are as dedicated as women to the institution of the family; men, just as much as women, want to parent the next generation. Men take many risks and take on many responsibilities in providing their mates and children with a home. The "family man" is an ideal most American men live up to. Unmistakably, men like to be married (divorced and widowed men remarry at a great rate), or they like living with a woman or a man and having all the comforts of home. Away from work, men are as much homebodies as women, "never straying from their yards at all." Men are indispensable to the American conception of home: the U.S. Census Bureau customarily defines it in terms of their absence, namely "female-headed household," as do the neighbors and friends of widows and divorcees.

But the fact remains that *only* at home is male limited to husband, father, son, brother. Shedding domestic roles at the factory gate and behind their desks, men's titles locate them in that man's world of unions, clubs, professional associations, and corporate and bureaucratic ladders. Personal services are delegated either to females or to men not initiated into the power leagues, men who are young, black or Hispanic, newcomers. Women are tethered to active domesticity even when they're on the job away from home. Based on a nationally representative sample, a 1977 study "found that husbands of employed wives spend more absolute time in child-care and household task performance than husbands whose wives are not employed outside the home." Yet employed wives "do between two and four times as much family work" as their husbands, while housewives are likely to do "six times as much" (Bloom-Feshbach 1981: 104–105). Even more to the point, another study found, for just about every household and child-care task, wives and husbands believe the primary responsibility to be the mother's.

Those figures make faint the hope that the symbolic scheme beclouding WOMAN might lose "its purely abstract characteristics." Georg Simmel, more than 60 years ago, hoped that with industrialization these "abstractions" would diminish when a woman works outside the home and is "released from this all-embracing tie which had been tantamount to her total subordination to the man. . . . The traditional identification of the concept "woman" with the special role of women in the home is extraordinarily close; it is much closer than the corresponding identification of the con-

| | Person Believed to Be Primarily Responsible | | |
Task	Mother	Father (percent)	Both[a]
Prepare the meals	77	1	22
Stay home when children are sick	72	1	26
Shop for children's clothes	66	1	32
Clean the house	65	1	33
Take children for checkups	63	1	35
Go to open school week	22	1	76
Help the children with homework	20	5	72
Speak to teachers if children are in trouble	20	8	71
Decide on children's allowances	9	20	67
Discipline the children	7	9	83
Teach the children sports and how to ride bikes	4	36	57

Percentages have been rounded.

Source: Bloom-Feshbach 1981: 105, reporting on a study conducted by the General Mills Consumer Center. Reprinted by permission from Michael E. Lamb, ed., *The Role of the Father in Child Development*, copyright © 1981 John Wiley & Sons, Inc. Reprinted by permission of John Wiley & Sons, Inc.

[a] Responses were volunteered.

cepts 'worker' or 'trader' with their special roles" (Simmel [1922] 1955: 182–184).

Men's "help around the house" is all of a piece with the worldly connections their aversive strategies lead them to: they do the shopping in supermarkets and its universe of brand names, and they take out the garbage, sending it on its way into the maw of a masculine industrial order. Although taking out the garbage may *seem* to be men's customary specialty, even that common pattern has its subtleties: 66 percent of wives in one study reported that they emptied the garbage at least half the time. That leaves "household repair" as the single male "bastion of household work contribution . . . with only 28 percent of the wives participating at the level of husbands." Those findings are from a sample of "predominantly white, upper-income families" living in suburbs (Berk 1980: 72).

Neither women nor men care much for cleaning bathrooms, or cleaning in general, but women are likely to continue to end up doing more of it. "Domesticity" implies that women will use a significant proportion of their energies in the physical care, feeding, and cleanliness of their children and partners, who will continue to use less of their energies in these activities. There's no way around it: much of women's work is dirty work, and men share least in it, even among the first of the "counterculture" generations. "Even primary caretaking fathers behave like secondary caretaking fathers rather than primary caretaking mothers in many respects": fathers are more associated with playing, mothers with caretaking (Lamb

1981: 14; see also Clarke-Stewart 1980: 146; Parke 1981: 38). During the 1970s, studies consistently found that "pregnancy and birth of a first child, in particular, are occasions for a shift toward a more traditional division of roles." Indeed, "husbands help less with housework after the arrival of a first child than they did before," and these "patterns held regardless of whether their initial role division was traditional or egalitarian," confirming the finding of an earlier study of the impact of a first child on a couple's relationship: " 'Despite the current rhetoric and ideology concerning equality of roles for men and women, it seems that couples tend to adopt traditionally defined roles during times of stressful transition such as around the birth of a first child' " (Cowan et al., quoted in Parke and Tinsley 1981: 435). Considering how many other life events are "stressful transitions"—job changes, moving house, the illness and death of a parent—it would seem that over the life course, the division of domestic labor will be very slow to shift.

People involved in dealing with waste products come out last in any social hierarchy, pretty much the world over. Michael Walzer hopes that in a utopia of equals we might come to share the "dirty work"—dealing with "dirt, waste, and garbage"—in order "to break the link between dirty work and disrespect" (Walzer 1983: 174, 175). We should all be cleaning up our own dirt, at home, at work, in school: "There would probably be less dirt to clean up if everyone knew in advance of making it that he couldn't leave the cleaning to someone else" (ibid.: 175). His concern is with occupational respect for garbage collectors, domestic workers, and hospital caretakers, "who do for strangers, day in and day out, what we can only just conceive of doing in emergencies for the people we love" (ibid.: 181). (Again, we are left to read between the lines. Why should we be able to "only just conceive" of giving what Walzer speaks of only as "the most intimate service" even within our families? [ibid.])

" 'Because they do dirty work, it does not mean they are dirty,' Norman Steisel, Commissioner of the [New York City] Sanitation Department, told a crowd of politicians, artists, union officials and sanitation workers" as they opened an art exhibit "designed to celebrate the 8,500 men and women who clean New York City's streets and to do away with the image of the derogatory nickname 'garbage man.' " A garbage truck sheathed in mirrors and labelled "The Social Mirror" dramatized the direct connection of garbage producers to garbage handlers (Brooke 1984).

American garbage collectors, especially white garbage collectors, feel the stigma so keenly that they keep their work secret from neighbors in white-collar occupations or with college degrees, partly because they and their wives judge themselves by the prestige standards of the white mainstream. Wives are reluctant even to specify their husband's occupation to interviewers: "He works for the city." But black garbage collectors, already on the American bottom (about 90 percent of the garbage collectors are black in one city where blacks make up only 7 percent of the population) see their work as providing the steady income that many of their black neighbors don't have. They see themselves as better off (Walsh 1975: 9, 14, 43–45). Yet nationally the rate of accidental injury among garbage collectors, black and white, is high compared with other occupations (M. Walzer 1983: 178). Is this a sign of their lesser self-regard?

A white sociologist, Edward Walsh worked alongside garbage collectors for about three years.

> Because my wife and I had an apartment in one of the older sections of Ann Arbor, I found myself also concerned with establishing (and, more importantly, protecting) my identity as a neighbor. I was very comfortable when working in every section of the city except along the street where I lived. It did not help when a woman a few blocks down the street (not an acquaintance) compulsively apologized to me for her little boy's hailing me with a "Hi, Mr. Garbageman!" She tactfully added, "Now there's a nice title, huh? Don't worry, though, 'cause some days that's about all I amount to around here." (Walsh 1975: 13)

She may get some days off from being a "garbageman," but not from the meanings of WOMAN.

Even when garbage collectors are entrepreneurs, the taint remains. A garbage-collection cooperative in San Francisco "made some problems of dirty work somehow more manageable," but discussions of its members' "public image" was "unsettling," a "potentially anxiety-provoking subject." One scavenger "felt that people he knew did not want to have anything to do with him because he was a garbageman. 'Maybe it is all in my head, but it seems like they go to the other side of the street if they see you coming!'" (Perry 1978: 108).

It is all inside all of our heads.

TRAINING BOYS

Boys learn bowel and bladder control later than girls, and because they are twice as likely as girls to wet their beds (Schaefer 1979: 92), boys are likely to be involved longer in the whole learning process than are girls. Boys are more likely, that is, to bear the brunt of parental frustration. Of 1170 children whose mothers kept records, on average boys "took 2.5 months longer to complete training than girls, and first children [of both sexes] were delayed 1.7 months in relation to their siblings" (Brazelton 1978: 140). At 21 months, 32 percent of boys and 20 percent of girls were regularly soiling, and 62 percent of boys and 43 percent of girls "regularly

Age at Training	Numbers Trained	
	Boys	Girls
11–12 months	2	
1–1 ½ years	2	4
2–2 ½ years	3	8
3 years	1	
4 years	1	
5 years	1	
over 5 years	2	

Source: Fischer and Fischer 1966: 73. Reprinted by permission from John L. and Ann Fischer, *The New Englanders of Orchard Town, U.S.A.*, copyright © 1966 John Wiley & Sons, Inc. Reprinted by permission of John Wiley & Sons, Inc.

wet themselves by day at 21 months" (P. Leach [1976] 1983: 342–343). Boys suffer more from encopresis than girls, 3.5 to 1, and they are also likely to be first-born sons: "This finding is in keeping with the usually higher frequency of problem behaviors and subtle neurological difficulties in boys" (Schaefer 1979: 6).

The later that toilet training is begun in both sexes, the less time it takes in all; somewhere between 18 and 24 months is the physiologically optimal time. When parents began bowel training "before the child was five months old, nearly 10 months (on average) were required for success. But when training was begun later (at 20 months or older), only about five months were required" (ibid.: 23). Among the small group of children of 24 American families studied in the 1950s, the spread of ages for boys' completion of training compared with girls' is graphic evidence of the different physiological resources they and their mothers work with.

Boys' readiness for training is later because their pace of physiological maturation is slower than girls'. Constitutional differences between the sexes reveal themselves at birth. Girls "generally display a more lawful developmental sequence. . . . [G]irls [appear to be] less variable than boys on constitutional dimensions" (Kagan 1971: 184). Physically, "males tend to be larger and heavier from the beginning, and from the second month on they have a larger caloric intake. The female is born more mature (four to six weeks ahead at birth) and will sit up, crawl, walk, and talk sooner than the male." Even "a few days after birth it becomes apparent that males and females have different types of spontaneous activity. The male's tends to be gross and vigorous, involving the whole body" (May 1980: 96, 97).

"The boy's original thrust is . . . more likely to present his parents with the challenge of both fostering and helping to direct his random muscular excursions, his propensity for outward movement . . . and as he grows the parents begin to emphasize control and to use coercion when necessary. He is encouraged to practice his strength, but always with the issue of limits in the foreground" (ibid.: 112–113). The female's spontaneous activity "is more centered in the muscles and skin of the face and shows itself in rhythmic mouthing and spontaneous smiling." In general, maleness "is associated with restlessness, irritability, and a style of physical movement that is vigorous, all-encompassing, and poorly organized. Already the focus is on large muscle systems and abrupt movement. The infant girl is more in touch, both in the sense of being more alive to physical contact and in the sense of using her mouth to be in touch with others by means of smiles and babbling. . . . She is more able to sit still and watch" (ibid.: 96, 97).

Boys learn bladder control later than they learn sphincter control; during this time they are likely to hold back on bowel movements. Parents may misinterpret this as "resistance," "opposition," or "regression," and again make of toilet habits a major issue. Boys are vulnerable to the possibility of an extended period of parental messages of displeasure, at the least, and renewed lessons in disgust, shaming, ridicule, spankings. Mothers are unhappy with the added laundry and bed-changings. Boys are more likely than girls to be the victims of child abuse (Gelles [1978] 1979: 62).

Their nocturnal, unconscious loss of control boys experience as setbacks in a major stage of growing up. "Staying dry all night is a very big step in the process of maturation, and a very important one to a child's self-image. As long as he wets himself at night, he sees himself as immature and inadequate. Helping him with these feelings is the important job—not pushing him, or punishing him if he doesn't stay dry" (Brazelton 1978: 140). Later, when bladder control is firmly established, and adolescent boys awake to nocturnal emissions of semen, these earlier anxieties of that "stormy period" may be remembered; now the anxieties are overtly attached to control over both sex and elimination.

Even in the normal course of events, given boys' higher levels of activity and slower physiological development, toilet training may be a major preoccupation for boys and their mothers, a prolonged period of alternating success and failure, of disappointment and strong feelings, on the part of both. Fathers, mess-aloof but observant, may reexperience the salience of these same issues, perhaps indirectly communicating their anxieties, if they aren't also taking an active role in both praising and shaming their children. Toilet training of boys is more likely to be a battleground than for girls, and its scars (from which girls, especially if they are first-borns, are not immune, however) are not only lifelong. For males, these experiences may turn out to be life-threatening when experiences in other realms resonate with these earliest presuppositions about the relation between shame and loss of control and the heightened self-esteem associated with overcontrol.

LOSING CONTROL

Studies of the significance to adults of losing control over elimination are rare. One reported on 48 American colostomy patients' "feelings, beliefs and unformulated assumptions about the properties of feces, uncontrolled bowel movements and the irrigation procedure" (Orbach, Bard, and Sutherland 1957: 122). Postoperatively, all patients felt some degree "of inacceptability to others or self-hatred and withdrawal from social relationships." Three kinds of adaptation to their condition suggest types that may be generally present among Americans. One group of patients had a "history of freedom from aversions, taboos and avoidances in relation to dirt and feces" and was also "more spontaneous and assertive" (ibid.: 172). A second group showed more aversion and avoidance, but these patients were able to accept that control over their bowel function "could never be foolproof" and that they could manage by preventing "spillage in public along with the consequent expectation of social rejection" (ibid.: 171). The third group suffered postoperatively with "a profound agitated depression," saying, " 'I am no longer human,' 'I have been transformed into an animal' " (ibid.: 171).

   This last group was evenly divided between the sexes. The "convictions and unformulated assumptions about feces verbalized by women . . . indicate that they were much more threatened by the filthy and potentially disease-bearing qualities of feces than the men were" (ibid.: 136). They were also more fearful of odor, using much perfume; women performed more than twice as many special procedures for "detoxification of feces or decontamination of self and the environment following evacuation. "These patients always considered feces as a degrading and animal-like activity and as filthy or poisonous. . . . The self-condemnation and body hatred were the basis for a complex projection in which it was believed that other people would condemn the noises and smell associated with defecation in the same way that the patient herself did," and evacuation was "invested with an air of secrecy" (ibid.: 141–142). From these data it appears that "excessive cleanliness often represents a fundamental technique of acceptability with the goal of controlling the reactions of others" (ibid.: 143). "Strong self-condemnation with respect to anal function was usually paralleled by revulsion about feces and handling diapers" as well as a history among these women of their coercive, early training of their own children (ibid.: 144). Those realistic fears of losing control reveal how deeply implicated cleanliness concepts are in the emotional concern with being more human than "animal."

Males' life strategies build upon their susceptibility to being over-trained in control; control is fundamental to their general orientation to the world. Control over tools, property, and people is well understood, but what is less overt, because it is symbolic, is the control males exercise over the distance they maintain from all that losing control signifies. The concept MEN claims a "superiority" derived from this cosmology which presses males and females equally to associate themselves with valued do-mains mainly by distancing themselves from those that are disvalued. For males, aversion is socially reinforced by their lack of a biological role in the nurture of incontinent infants. They are unable, however, to distance themselves from their own gastrointestinal tract. The cosmology legiti-mates the "superiority" of their aversions: it is better to be associated with good than evil, with cleanliness than dirt, with the sacred than the profane, with humans than with animals. To capture males' actual behaviors, these may be better stated as negatives: avoidance of evil, dirt, and the shame and humiliation associated with them. Men's distancing strategies (avoid-ance of cleaning bathrooms, doing laundry, and changing diapers) reveal the tendency to phobic behaviors—phobic in the sense of externalizing self-disgust and shame and displacing them on the significance of those domestic activities. Or phobic in the other direction, with the cleanliness and control preoccupations that characterize the "anal personality."

To men, "letting go" emotionally may signify "losing control," with its earlier personal associations to animality, shame, and lowered self-esteem. A study of how married men under stress find support from their spouses reports that men "at work and at home . . . seemed to want to keep con-trol of the expression of their feelings and of the feelings themselves." These conclusions are drawn from about six hours of interviews with each of 62 men living in upper-income suburbs in the Boston area.

> Men seemed especially reluctant to report feelings of insecurity or anxiety, unless the incident that gave rise to these feelings could later be shown to have ended in success. Reporting negative feelings seemed itself to produce discomfort. . . . Both at work and at home men seemed to want to keep control of the expression of their feelings and of the feelings themselves. An exception might be made for anger; some men said they permitted themselves an angry outburst if they believed it would have strategic as well as cathartic value. A professional negotiator described, with some pride, being able to lose his temper when it was good tactics to do so. This sort of controlled aggression seemed often valued. Sometimes, to be sure, the control failed and a display got out of hand. . . . There could be shame

> or chagrin afterward. Yet controlled anger (in a situation that justified it) seemed almost alone among the emotions acceptable to our respondents. . . . The man who appears to his wife to be emotionally unresponsive may in fact have many powerful, if conflicting, feelings, but he may have schooled himself to keep his more suspect emotions under control (Weiss 1985: 56–58).

For females, their easier learning experience only apparently diminishes the salience of losing control and all it signifies. Encouraged to continue to identify with mother, girls have no choice but to interiorize the animalistic associations of body wastes and their self-disgust and shame. Sex stereotyping keeps girls aware (as they change dolly's diaper) that they are destined to be specialists in handing down this conceptual system and its practices. Then, maturing, girls find themselves producing the fluids of sexual arousal as well as menstrual blood over which they have no control; the possibility of leaking or staining is an anxious preoccupation. Moreover, their fathers are also likely to avoid the subjects both of menstruation and mature sexuality; how mothers introduce daughters to menstrual hygiene and beliefs about its pollutions is likely to influence their approach to the inevitable leakages once they are themselves training toddlers; what sons learn of these matters is just as significant. Throughout their lives, that is, women live with a wider set of anxieties over losing control, for not only do they have none over these other bodily fluids, they have none over any of those produced by family members they care for as mothers and wives.

To account for men's tendency not to express their feelings, some influential feminist analyses rely on what I call passivity theory, which proposes that men avoid giving in to an immature desire for a *nurturing* relationship; they deny their needs for "attachment" by living out their masculine stereotype.

> Learning to master passion and weakness became a major task of growing up as a man. . . . In fact, men are strongly pulled both toward other people sexually and in a more total emotional sense; but they have also erected strong barriers against this pull. And here, I think, is the greatest source of fear: that the pull will reduce them to some undifferentiated mass or state ruled by weakness, emotional attachment, and/or passion and that they will thereby lose the long-sought and fought-for status of manhood. This threat, I believe, is the deeper one that equality poses, for it is perceived not as equality only but as a total stripping of the person. (J. B. Miller, 1976: 23)

For this reason, men ward off so-called feminine qualities, according to passivity theory. They "become doubly fearful because [feminine qualities] look as if they will entrap men in 'emotions,' weakness, sexuality, vulnerability, helplessness, the need for care" (ibid.: 120). Men's defenses leave them with a poorly developed ability to experience intimacy because intimacy, it is said, signifies to them the stereotypically unmasculine passivity of being fed, stroked, and cared for, with all wants anticipated, just as infants are (Chodorow 1978: 218).

Looking not at maternal or sexual relationships but at the difference between this species and all others opens up a significant alternative. I view men's rein on expressing their emotions as avoidance not of infantile "attachment" or "weakness," but of reexperiencing the specific meanings of losing control: being a child, whose incompetence makes him less than human, socially unacceptable, and vulnerable to being humiliated. That "total stripping of the person" which men are said to avoid is their avoidance of painful memories of their earliest experiences of humiliation over losing control. (Extreme fear in both humans and animals is accompanied by involuntary defecation [Gray 1982: 40].)

As part of this same distancing style, men's lesser inclination to express their feelings also keeps them from having a sufficiently sustaining network of friendships with both men and women, perhaps based on an expectation that the deep knowledge another might have of them could recapitulate that earliest, most intimate injury to self-esteem. Remembering their earliest narcissistic injury, men's lack of expressiveness may be their way of avoiding the "unbearable emotional pain associated with a devalued self-image and low self-worth" (J. E. Mack 1983: 36). Their wives, many men claim, are their "best friends," and upon their spouses' deaths, men can be socially bereft as well.

This distancing style leads men to experience, more so than women, emotional and social isolation throughout their lives, cresting in their later lives. Social isolation appears to mediate sex differences in longevity and in responses to stressful life events: married men live longer than single men. The isolation itself appears to lower men's physical resistance to stresses that women seem better able to withstand (and isolated women also have lower resistance than those who are not) (Lynch 1977). As I soon discuss, the same issue of low self-worth influences women's longevity as well: because their strategies revolve around seeking others' approval, this sociability may help them live longer.

The significance to each sex of losing control suggests alternative readings of important findings in male-female differences, which have been interpreted, however, with no reference to anal development, like all other sex-difference research. A series of studies replicated between 1966 and 1979 finds consistent differences between the sexes in the kinds of fantasies they make up about the same picture of a pair of acrobats working at the very top of a circus tent, in which the man is holding onto a trapeze with his legs bent over the bar at the knees while grasping the woman's wrists as she flies through the air. Males' fantasies consistently exhibit a greater fear of failure, females' a greater sense of optimism. Women weave fantasies that move "from pain to pleasure, from difficulty, effort, and doubt to success and reunion . . . through a time of suffering and doubt and then on to final success and happiness." Men's fantasies see "soaring strength ending in destruction," telling a story that begins "in both physical and emotional excitement, even pride, but soon collapses into failure and despair" (May 1980: 16–17).

The emotional tone of the stories people tell expresses negative feelings such as "physical need or tension, failure, injury, painful effort, falling, unpleasant feelings," and positive feelings such as "physical satisfaction, ability and success, growth or ascension, good feelings, being helped by others, insight" (ibid.: 17–18). Typically, males' stories shift from a positive to a negative tone, females' the opposite: between ages six and nine, for example, the "stories told by girls are more complex, less addicted to catastrophe, and more likely to chronicle the passage from bad to good" in contrast to stories told by boys. Girls' stories tend also to have a pattern of "anxiety overcome and danger survived," differing as well from boys' stories in including "other people as sources of help and comfort" (ibid.: 26).

Seen now in light of male-female differences in elimination mastery, are the "tensions, failures, injuries, painful efforts, falling, unpleasant feelings" signs of males' more crooked path to bladder and sphincter control? Are those who share in the pessimistic pattern first-borns of both sexes? Do they have a history of toilet-training difficulties? This series of studies did not, unfortunately, also seek such information from earliest care-givers or from the subjects themselves, children or adults.

The different pace at which male and female sphincter and bladder control is attained suggests a constitutional difference that could be no less significant than the sexes' different reproductive and endocrine systems. The maturation of elimination mastery is in any case not as culturally independent or inevitable as the maturation of the reproductive system apparently is; it is dependent on "the potting couple" of parent and child, itself a social and cultural system. These body differences together with their different toilet-training experiences may help to account for the emotional orientations associated with each sex; these are, however, likely to be significantly affected also by birth order (a variant of the sociocultural system of parents and child).

More direct evidence for these several propositions remains unavailable, however, for the research into the lifelong consequences of "the humble-seeming matter of cleanliness training" that Dollard and Miller called for more than three decades ago has not been undertaken.

MAINTAINING SELF-ESTEEM

The "narcissistic self-esteem" rightfully belonging to infancy matures into an endowment on which people draw throughout life. Its level is critical to the ability to withstand stress, even to survive.

> In the child's eyes, his sense of self-worth is *essential* to his survival. The child who does not experience his value in the eyes of his parents will fear their abandonment and its attendant dangers to his existence. The older child and adolescent may even contemplate suicide. The maintenance of positive self-esteem is so fundamental a task that all of the structures of personality contribute to its organization. (J. E. Mack 1983: 12)

Learning elimination mastery in the terms of the prevalent cosmology, each sex also has no choice but to learn how to deal with injured self-esteem.

Males concentrate on not losing control. They maintain a productive level of self-esteem by holding at bay feelings that signify to them the loss of physiological self-control, constituted as it is to be a sign of species inadequacy, social unacceptability, and self-doubt—as taught by parental, but mainly mothers', lessons of shaming and humiliation.

Females' strategy for maintaining self-esteem centers on assuring themselves of approval: females try to be pleasing to many people, they are compliant, they act responsibly for the approval it brings, and, to be attractive and reduce hostility to themselves, they keep themselves cleaner and smelling sweeter than boys do. Females constitutionally take more readily to their toilet training lessons, but their self-doubt is no less. They assuage it with both the comforts of affiliation and the avoidance of further disapproval via appeasement.

Again, male and female strategies build upon their constitutions at birth (Draper 1974). Infants "are quite capable of holding up their own end of a complex process of mutual influence" between themselves and their parents, and sex differences are apparent early:

> [T]he girl is generally more reachable, more accessible to influence, than the boy. . . . [T]he girl is more willing, and able, to be shaped by social forces. She is simply more susceptible to being civilized and much of what we know suggests that a frequent danger in female development is that this process will be *too* successful and thus lead to a stifling of initiative, autonomy, and assertion. The clash between the male child and his culture

is much harsher and the threat for him is that the civilizing process will be incomplete and inadequate. . . .

The girl stays physically closer to the mother and is more attuned to her. The male's greater restlessness and impulsive urge to move away make him often a difficult foreigner in the mother's arms. . . . [T]he society takes the female aptitude for tender contact and builds on it. The parents respond to the girl infant's sensitivity to touch, her readiness to smile and talk, her attention to human faces. These abilities are then drawn out, encouraged, and practiced. . . . Our cultural ideal expands this picture into a female role conception involving gentleness, the ability to care for others, an intense and complex involvement with human relationships and emotion, and a valuable conservatism that is willing to hold on to those people who matter in one's life. (May 1980: 112–113)

Out of these constitutional tendencies develop females' strategies for replenishing from others the self-esteem that the lessons of humiliation and the threats of abandonment diminish, as do males' distancing strategies for keeping further damage to a minimum build upon their restlessness. Males' aptitude for "moving away" comes to be socialized as phobic avoidance in practical matters and as the higher cultural value placed on rationality, objectivity, detachment. Males may also be more prone than females to externalize and project onto others as aggression and hostility the "unbearable emotional pain associated with a devalued self-image and low self-worth. . . . Through blaming others the self is relieved, at least temporarily, of the burden of self-reproach. Someone else is responsible, someone else is at fault" (J. E. Mack 1983: 36).

Women's reclamation of self-esteem works only up to a point, for self-doubt is born again in the maternal obligations to have a symbiotic, bonded, relationship with an incontinent infant, to handle disvalued substances, and to teach disgust and punish with shaming. Lacking men's practical distance from infant care, women's strategies tend more to nourish self-doubt, unable as they are to displace on their environment, as men are, the same signs that threaten self-esteem. Women have to deal routinely with their children's and spouses' body wastes of all kinds, as well as their own menstrual blood, its odors, and its meanings to others. Simply by distancing, men appear to be rejecting women, and once again women are threatened with abandonment and the self-doubt it evokes.

Women's greater susceptibility to culturally imposed self-doubt, combined with their interiorization of that same aggression and hostility as men experience in dealing with the pain of diminished self-worth, is apparent in the greater use they make than males of psychotherapy and counseling to deal with an impoverished self-image and depression (Weissman and Klerman 1982). "Self-esteem has its deepest root in the experience of efficacy. It is not constructed out of what others do or what the environment gratuitously provides. It springs rather from what one can make [other people] do by crying, by signaling, or by coordinated acts of competence" (R. W. White 1963: 192). Women are likely to find themselves frustrated in expressing their competences and efficacy in a social order that so often denies them the opportunity to do so. Their frustration at being unable to get positive responses solely because of their sex is still another seed of female depression and self-doubt.

For all the strengths women can call upon, why, asks a psychoanalyst, "do women feel so bad?" Men often treat a woman as an "object," and she responds by believing "that there must be something terribly bad and evil about her. It must be true, since others, the important and worthy others, seem to think she deserves to be treated as an object. Objectification adds a deep and thoroughgoing reason for women's readiness to accept the evil assigned to them. . . . Any stirrings of physicality and sexuality in herself would only confirm for a girl or woman her evil state" (J. B. Miller 1976: 58). Sexual relationships are but another of life's stages upon which women and men act out the implications of this cosmology.

Lacking sufficient self-esteem, all too readily complicitous with the subordination that is the residue of men's disassociating and distancing, women can convict themselves: of that 43 percent of middle-class fathers who never changed their infants' diapers, how many were asked to by the mothers is not reported. Culturally prescribed self-abnegation accompanies both female biology and the maternal role, as the meanings of the domain of body wastes are now constituted. The metaphysical line dividing humans from other animals appears in practice to legitimate the "superiority" of the concept MEN and the "inferiority" of the concept WOMEN; it is in fact doing neither much good as human beings.

Differences among people in psychological development and moral orientation appear to be based on priorities for "attachment" and for "separation," differences discovered only when female subjects were included in research testing a theory of moral development that had been derived from male subjects only (C. Gilligan 1982, 1986). In overlooking women's "morality of responsibility," women had been judged by a male-derived "morality of rights and noninterference" (C. Gilligan 1982: 164; 1986: 325). Women, Gilligan claims, have a greater awareness of being socially embedded by virtue of giving care to others, by contrast to men's priority to autonomy and abstraction. "The elusive mystery of women's development lies in its recognition of the continuing importance of attachment in the human life cycle. Woman's place in man's life cycle is to protect this recognition while the developmental litany intones the celebration of separation, autonomy, individuation, and natural rights" (C. Gilligan 1982:

23). Behaviorally and morally, women manifest the "importance of attachment" through their attitudes of "responsibility," "care," and "reluctance to hurt" others (ibid.: 149). (Despite her speaking of "care" repeatedly, Gilligan, like others using the term, leaves unspoken just what it entails.)

Why do men give priority to "autonomy" and "abstraction"? Why is it "woman's place in man's life cycle" to protect the importance of "attachment"? Again, looking to species' rather than to gender differentiation, there is room for an alternative reading. Men's tendency to be reluctant to "know" and be known and their moral concern with "abstraction" rather than with the involvements of real situations are expressions of their *modus vivendi* of overcontrol—specifically, control over the distance they maintain emotionally and socially both from all that might signal losing control and from body wastes and their meanings. Women's preoccupation with others expresses their primary strategy for reassuring themselves of their worth: evidence of women's "attachment" and "embeddedness" is evidence of women's propensity to search out from others the social approval this cosmology makes so elusive. Their "reluctance to hurt others" and their often-observed fears of worldly aggression and success also express females' hopes of pleasing by being compliant and otherwise acting to defuse expected hostility or injury—appeasement gestures all.

A "deliberate neglect of one's own needs" has been a common enough association to WOMAN—"an approach to life in which the stance of the sufferer, the sacrificer, is dominant" (May 1980: 154–155). Seen in its pathological state, the masochist shows "a willing acceptance of pain or humiliation," has "an intense and dependent attachment to another person," and denies "ordinary human aggressiveness," replacing it with "covert revenge and hidden tyranny" (ibid.: 158). In her earlier work, Gilligan alludes to the fact that with the help of feminist activism women are coming to see that it is "moral to care not only for others but for themselves" (C. Gilligan 1982: 149). Recently, she suggests that modern women are "reconsidering what is meant by care in light of their recognition that acts inspired by conventions of selfless feminine care have led to hurt, betrayal, and isolation. . . . I describe a critical ethical perspective that calls into question the traditional equation of care with self-sacrifice. . . . My studies of women locate the problem in female development not in the values of care and connection or in the relational definition of self, but in the tendency for women, in the name of virtue, to give care only to others and to consider it 'selfish' to care for themselves. The inclusion of women's experience [in studies of moral development] dispels the view of care as selfless and passive and reveals the activities that constitute care and lead to responsiveness in human relationships" (C. Gilligan 1986: 326–327, 332).

Wishing does not make it so: indeed, women's patterns of care and responsibility for others are constructive, far from passive, and enjoyable for themselves and for others. But they also have that "virtue" of being wholly masochistic as set by the terms of this overarching cosmology. That "traditional equation of care with self-sacrifice" is one this symbolic system makes: if men were to give others the same sort of personal care as women do, the cosmology would likewise make of it a sacrifice of self-esteem and social honor. In the thirteenth century, English men who were not expected to make this sacrifice received three times the going rate for cleaning out the latrines of Newgate Jail; in this century, longshoremen have demanded "shame pay" for handling shipments of new toilets (Rosebury 1969: 97).

REMEMBERING THINGS PAST

Socially aggressive attitudes include the *attribution* of disagreeable body smells; prejudice often includes beliefs that strangers and "others," for example, have an unpleasant odor. "Unpleasant or violent" smells, experiments show, "cause a rise in blood pressure," and there is "convincing evidence" that in adult male mice "aggression is released by olfactory signals alone" (Douek 1974: 202). Both smell and aggression seem to appear in the same site (the amygdala), recent brain research in humans suggests.

That smells are powerful in evoking memories long out of conscious reach we know from experience and from literature:

> Perhaps Proust used [his madeleine] incident simply as a clever introduction to a novel, but the profound role which smells can have in evoking memory cannot be denied. It may be that what is evoked is not memories in the chronological sense but an emotion. It is the state of mind of one's childhood or past which is suddenly and temporarily regenerated with all its beliefs, fears, and lack of experience. . . . [Past feelings] can be brought into consciousness by an olfactory stimulus and may well be recordable as electrical potentials. (Ibid.: 160)

Do the practicalities of daily bowel and bladder functions summon the "state of mind of one's childhood or past which is suddenly and temporarily regenerated with all its beliefs, fears, and lack of experience"? Are the odors of body wastes, feces especially, continual "regenerators" for these buried metaphysical issues, inextricably cultural and emotional? Do trace memories of those earliest associations with shaming and humiliation and the original experiences of failure and self-doubt keep alive male and female strategies? Do these daily reminders of low self-worth keep men's aggression on tap? Do their own trace memories evoke in women self-doubts which they assuage with the appeasements of care, submissiveness, and perfume from Paris? Is the entire semantic domain of body wastes a releaser for the aggression born of the pain of self-hate, turned outward by men, more inward by women? Men who use social, economic, and political power to keep women from belonging are both keeping them at a distance and being aggressive. Women who are "reluctant to hurt" others yet suffer more explicitly from depression and masochism than do men seem to be turning that aggression upon themselves.

The place of scent in human social (including sexual) behavior has been little studied, despite both the ubiquitous preoccupation with deodorizing and the fact that the behaviors and daily routines of most mammals are much determined by smell. Freud seems prematurely to have suggested that humans' assumption of the upright posture attenuated their olfactory sensibilities in favor of visual acuity: human mothers "can identify their infants by smell alone at 6 hours post partum after a single exposure to their babies. This ability persists to 48 hours post partum with no improvement with additional experience. Fathers were not able to make the same discrimination. . . . Recognition is a prerequisite to successful attachment, and failure of such attachment may explain why children removed from their mothers at birth and maintained separately for brief periods suffer much higher incidences of battering and failure to thrive after returning to their natural parents" (Russell, Mendelson, and Peeke 1983: 29). Human infants also appear to recognize the smell of their mothers' milk soon after birth (Konner 1982: 33). In psychoanalytic theory, smell has been related largely to fetishism and "has received little or no attention" (Bieber 1959: 852). Recent research is suggesting that women's sense of smell remains more acute than men's throughout life: is it more acute or do men deny the significance of odor more?

"Malodorous air pollution," one American experiment found, has stressful effects similar to noise and density (Rotton 1983). Another found that pleasant scents sometimes, but not always, "exert beneficial effects on social behavior (e.g. reduce aggression, enhance attraction)" (Baron 1981: 172). An impressionistic survey of the "sociology of odors" found it to be a "much-neglected field of sociological analysis" (e.g., the relationship among perceived odors, social labelling, spatial arrangements, odor control and manipulation) (Largey and Watson 1972). The biochemical and socialized properties of smells remain another frontier in human studies.

Nor does language compose smells into a discrete semantic domain: "in none of the world's languages does there seem to be a classification of smells comparable, for example, to colour classification" perhaps for the reason that "there is nothing for such a work to be about" (Sperber [1974] 1975: 115). In the domain of smells, cultural knowledge remains "scattered among all the categories whose referents have olfactive qualities" (ibid.: 116). Smells are known by "their causes or their effects. Their cause: the smell of incense, the smell of a rose, the smell of coffee, the smell of wet grass, a putrid smell, an animal smell, etc.; their effects: a nauseating smell, a heady perfume, an appetising smell. While in the domain of colours, similar designations end up by becoming lexicalised and losing all metonymic character ("rose," "orange," and "purple" may be used without evoking respectively the flower, fruit and dye), in the domain of smells, on the contrary, metonymy remains active and infallibly evokes cause or effect" (ibid.: 115–116). Scientific efforts at identifying and classifying smells proceed apace, and while the molecular structures of odors used in research are designated under general headings—for example, ethereal (as in ether), camphoraceous, musky, floral, minty, pungent, and putrid—warnings are essential: "cultural, educational and professional factors have . . . important significance" (Douek 1974: 86, 91).

Ignoring a semiotics of smells may lead to misinterpretations of certain social patterns (Corbin 1986). For example, in preliterate societies, the institutions of men's houses, the residential segregation of men from women, children, and animals who live together, and postpartum sexual prohibitions are conventionally read as forms of "sex segregation" that should be reconsidered to be "smell segregation." Mothers are likely to sleep with incontinent infants and children in many societies, as well as to carry them for nursing a good part of the day (Whiting 1981). Women's prolonged and physically intimate association with incontinent children, the concepts associated with feces within the particular cosmological system, women's cultural status relative to men, and patterns of male-female behaviors—all these seen as a single complex has had, however, no systematic ethnographic attention, as far as I have been able to discover.

The sulphurous stench of Luther's Devil is essential to Luther's God: "'The world is the Devil and the Devil is the world. . . . God takes him into His hand and says: "Devil, you are indeed a murderer and a wicked spirit, but I will use you for my purposes; you shall be only my pruning-knife, and the world, and all that depends on you, shall be my manure-dung for my beloved vineyard"'" (Brown 1959: 212, 226; see also Corbin 1986: 21). The human conviction of self-degradation acts as devil to the god of self-love.

DISTANCING FROM DISGUST

These vital functions of the alimentary canal are pretty much banished in this culture to the domain of taboo and scatology, repugnance and shame, a moral province rarely to be visited objectively. In his preface to the German edition of Captain Bourke's work, Freud comments on "the way in which civilized men to-day deal with the problem of their physical nature. They are evidently embarrassed by anything that reminds them too much of their animal origin. They feel like the 'more perfected angels' in the last scene of *Faust*, who complain: 'We still have a trace of the Earth, which is distressing to bear; and though it were of asbestos it is not cleanly.' Since, however, they must necessarily remain far removed from such perfection, men have chosen to evade the predicament by so far as possible denying the very existence of this inconvenient 'trace of the Earth,' by concealing it from one another, and by withholding from it the attention and care which it might claim as an integrating component of their essential being. The wiser course would undoubtedly have been to admit to and to make as much improvement in it as its nature would allow. . . . It is far from being a simple matter to survey or describe the consequences involved in this way of treating the 'distressing trace of the Earth,' of which the sexual and excretory functions may be considered the nucleus. It will be enough to mention a single one of these consequences, the one with which we are most concerned here: the fact that science is prohibited from dealing with these proscribed aspects of human life, so that anyone who studies such things is regarded as scarcely less 'improper' than someone who actually *does* improper things" (Freud [1913] 1939: 88–89).

Writing this essay has been difficult—personally, certainly, belonging in this culture as I do, but more so as a scholar, finding scant research attention or reliable evidence; for just as Captain Bourke's work is likely to have been found in a locked case in the library, this topic remains locked out of contemporary consciousness. Credible information about Americans' ideas and habits of personal hygiene didn't make an appearance until 1966 when Alexander Kira published the first systematic study of the anatomical and cultural issues involved in American notions about body waste, personal cleanliness, and privacy in *The Bathroom: Criteria for Design*, based on research he conducted at Cornell University. "The simple and inevitable body functions have largely come to be regarded as unmentionable and vulgar. At the same time, however, the sexual functions and aspects of the body are almost a staple of modern conversation" (Kira 1966: vi). In 1986, after Ronald Reagan's surgery for cancer of the colon, newspaper articles and television programs reported that doctors were grateful for the detailed publicity about a part of the anatomy whose symptoms Americans tended to ignore until too late.

Humor has been one way around the topic's difficulties, and not all of it scatologic or infantile. In *Cleanliness and Godliness*, published in 1946, Reginald Reynolds, an Englishman, modelled his text on that of Sir John Harington's *The Metamorphosis of Ajax*, and provides an exemplary historical survey of public sanitation practices the world over. The text is serious, self-aware, and charming.

> The *taboo* against dirt and against uncleanly habits belongs, as we have seen, to all time and to all portions of the globe. But there is a secondary *taboo* that would appear to be peculiarly Puritan in origin, and for this reason of a specifically Anglo-Saxon character, a *taboo* found principally in Britain and in the United States of America, not against dirt itself or filthy habits, but against any mention of things related to excretion. Thus, the writing of this book is a breach of this particular *taboo* because society conspires to pretend that the principal objects of discussion do not exist. (Reynolds [1946] 1974: 204–206)

Deep cultural resistance to acknowledging this earlier, buried stage of physical and social development may be partly responsible for the preponderance of analyses focussing on sexuality. The first volume of a projected history titled *Education of the Senses*, for example, recounts "the [Western] bourgeois experience of the nineteenth century" mainly in terms of erotic "senses," despite using an overtly Freudian framework (Gay [1984] 1985: 16). Sexuality may itself mask these prior associations, for of course it shares anatomically and ideologically some of the same issues of this domain of body wastes. "Pudenda," the term for both male and female genitals, derives from the gerund of the Latin *pudere*, to be ashamed. The socialization of anal functions is well in place before sexuality is socialized—a fact Freud acknowledges, but one often lost in interpretations of his original postulate of "anal erotism."

> [T]he feelings of disgust . . . seem originally to be a reaction to the smell (and afterwards also to the sight) of excrement. But the genitals can act as a reminder of the excretory functions; and this applies especially to the male member, for that organ performs the function of micturition as well as the sexual function. Indeed, the function of micturition is the earlier known of the two, and the *only* one known during the pre-sexual period. Thus it happens that disgust becomes one of the means of affective expression in the sphere of sexual life. The Early Christian Father's *"inter urinas et faeces nascimur"* [we are born between urine and feces] clings to sexual life and cannot be detached from it in spite of every effort at idealization (Freud [1905] 1953: 31–32).

He immediately says that although this association exists it is not inevitable that it be "called up" in "normal circumstances."

Alongside the sexuality revolution, a proliferation of enlightened advice about toilet training and about keeping healthy and fit has been evident within the past 10 or 15 years. Both legislating and complying with "scoop laws"—publicly picking up dog feces—have to be counted as a genuine cultural shift. Nevertheless, the general cultural tension about personal excrement remains undispelled, exemplified, at the least, by the scarcity in America of decent public lavatories, wide variations in euphemisms for urination and bowel movements, and by the prevalence of excretory expletives and dirty words as aggressive acts of denigration and disparagement (Dundes 1966: 93; Sagarin 1962). The rhetoric of *End Product: The First Taboo*, a book purporting to demystify the compartmentalization of matters anal from all others indexes this tension and the ambivalences it expresses (Sabbath and Hall 1977). Throughout its pastiche of folklore, reports of weird, sometimes perverse behaviors, and an unsystematic panorama of historical anecdotes, the authors favor the word "shit," and they succeed with ridicule and high-jinks humor in conveying how deeply, yet certainly not inevitably, identified with anger, denigration, and defilement this body product is. In her preface to this work, Abby Rockefeller, the manufacturer of the Clivus Multrum, a composting toilet that converts excrement and garbage into fertilizer, comments astutely on the issues of this discourse:

> *End Product* could serve as a reference anthology of excremental lore. It is a veritable catalog of the subject, exhaustively documenting the problems of our relations and attitudes to excrement and the way in which we reproduce or hide this problem with language. This is an important task right now, and the authors have done this with wit and erudition. But while I agree with their purpose, I do not agree with their tone. Their treatment of the subject represents as much as it opposes the very attitude from which we are suffering. . . . The authors may very well protest that their language is intentionally ironic and that they must invite us to see the situation from *their* angle by using what seems to be *our* language. But this contradiction raises a fundamental question: just what is the proper language to use in talking about excrement? Sabbath and Hall write "shit" as if this were the "real" word and therefore respectable, that is, respectful of excrement. This is understandable. For most of us, this is the word we really use when we are more or less at ease, and surely the use of euphemisms and circumlocutions can convey an even deeper loathing. But I suggest that the more serious the context in which we use the word "shit," the more evident is its intrinsically denigrating nature. When we use it lightly in an oath or humor, we imply more a recognition of our problem with what it stands for than an assertion of hostility. A book like this which undertakes so radical a project offering serious opposition to our attitude of loathing toward excrement must itself abandon the language of loathing.
>
> But if I take them to task on this score, I must confess that I cannot solve the question authoritatively myself. Indeed, this is a task for our whole culture. What language *can* we use when we wish to speak soberly and with no negative undertones about excrement? Even that very word "excrement"

sounds quite as boring as clinical terms like "feces." But right action is reflected in right language, and since we are not "doing right," it's hard for us to speak right. Any word other than those which express our anxieties and bad feelings will seem euphemistic. Assuming that we will one day do right in regard to excrement—sorry, but I'd rather risk sounding boring than derisive—we must try to begin to practice language appropriate to that state of mind. (Ibid.: 1–2)

Even scholars consign body wastes, inseparable from the meanings they have been constituted to carry, to a subterranean realm. Tending to be matters we would just as soon not consider, outside of the biological sciences they receive little serious attention from professional historians, psychologists, psychoanalysts, even social and biological anthropologists (Miner 1956; Konner 1982; Dundes 1984: ix). "Of toilet training I have found nary a word, but then it would be difficult to prove that eighteenth century Americans ever urinated and defecated from the existing source materials" (J. F. Walzer, 1974: 366). If brought up at all in analysis, the subject is likely to be covered merely by reference to a stereotypical "anal character"—the "*compulsive* type, who is stingy, retentive, and meticulous in matters of affection, time, and money as in the management of his bowels" (E. H. Erikson 1968: 108). Scholars who interpret social attitudes toward defecation and excrement tend to concentrate on a "money-feces" equivalence or attempt to label one or another "national character" as being susceptible to emphasizing the "anal personality" (Rancour-Laferriere 1987; Dundes 1984).

Reporting experiments designed to determine the proper treatment for children having unusual difficulties with learning bowel habits, E. J. Anthony, a British psychiatrist, comments: "When I first broadcast my research intentions, the clinic trickle was rapidly converted into an appreciable stream as referring agencies rushed to rid themselves of their most unpopular customers. Clinicians on the whole, perhaps out of disgust, prefer neither to treat [encopretic children] nor to write about them. The literature as compared with enuresis is surprisingly scanty, and what there is seems superficial, as if the children had been observed from a respectable distance" (1957: 157). We might expect that kind of aversion from lay people, but that physicians should also act on their revulsion is testimony to the density of this cultural glacier.

Not considering toilet training to be a cultural form that will affect subsequent psychological, social, and moral development, specialists in sex differences on these subjects tend to ignore it. In my discussions with male child psychiatrists, psychologists, and anthropologists specializing in developmental studies, they claimed to take toilet-training entirely for granted—an essential but wholly unremarkable step. One said that among developmental psychologists toilet-training is not regarded as a "critical" issue—indeed, he said that he and his colleagues find it "boring." Freud and Erikson, like most other commentators on the psychosocial consequences of cleanliness training, based their theories on individual patients' reports rather than on longitudinal behavioral evidence, which remains scarce (P. Leach, [1976] 1983: 247). Yet even when the cases they discuss feature children unable to learn bowel and sphincter control, psychoanalytic specialists in the development and maintenance of self-esteem do not also report on parental toilet training concepts and practices (Huizenga 1983).

Not only does denial affect the availability of data and the formulation of research problems, but by comparison to sexual perspectives, this complex of anality and morality is rarely used in interpreting social, behavioral, evolutionary, and psychological evidence. A recent collection of psychoanalytic interpretation and case studies in the "development and sustenance of self-esteem," while asserting the singular importance of the integrity of the body-self to self-esteem, has a single index entry for toilet training (Mack and Ablon 1983). A leading expert on "readiness training" says at one point, "The best thing about toilet training is that when it is done successfully, everybody can forget about it," and only pages later: "I'm sure that many adults who put themselves down at every turn can trace the early beginning of a poor self-image to their 'failures' in achieving autonomy in the area of toilet training" (Brazelton 1978: 140, 149).

Although the myths, rites, and folktales of the poetics of ambiguity often make much of feces (e.g., Radin [1956] 1972: 27–28), most commentators tend to ignore the scatology and stress the sexuality they also dramatize. The one commentator to offer a major excursus on the overlooked social significances of anality has been Norman O. Brown, in his 1959 book, *Life Against Death: The Psychoanalytical Meaning of History*. Commenting on Jonathan Swift's work and the critical literature it spawned, Brown concludes, "The history of Swiftian criticism, like the history of psychoanalysis, shows that repression weighs more heavily on anality than on genitality" (Brown 1959: 180). Reconstructing historically what "was surrendered by default to psychoanalysis," Brown discusses interpretations of the relationship between anality and money ("filthy lucre") and "the Protestant Era," especially the relationship "between the Devil and anality" and "between the Devil and Protestantism": "If we want to understand Luther . . . [we must take] Luther's Devil as seriously as we take Luther's God" (ibid.: 229, 210). Christianity's Devil "reflects the history of anality" as the "lineal descendant of the Trickster . . . through such intermediary figures as the classical Hermes" and "Culture-hero type," who are sources of "man's material culture"—the Devil of Luther, that is, seen as "the spirit of capitalism" and "usury" marked by "filth" and "stench" (ibid.: 301, 302, 220–225). "For Luther the Devil is the father of lies, of deceit, of trickery . . . a robber and thief" (ibid.: 220). (Brown also quotes Ernest Jones's commentary on the reception accorded to Freud's analysis of anal character traits, and one I fear for this essay: "'The liveliest incredulity, repugnance, and opposition . . .'" [ibid.: 177].)

A social anthropologist who is also a physician wrote not too long ago that even in his own fieldwork and medical practice among the Zulu "I missed chances of exploring further what no doubt exists, namely a close association between bowel habits and ideas about them, and wider aspects of status and morality. Nor did I consider collecting direct concrete evidence about the mundane minutiae of excretion behavior" (Loudon 1978: 173). His survey of ethnographies also turned up few reports specifically about the significance of excrement, "raw material for thought and action in all human societies" (ibid.: 162–163). Anthropologists' accounts of particular societies do reveal, however, much about the beliefs of preliterate peoples concerning the contaminating and polluting powers of menstrual blood, afterbirth, and milk, but these tend not to be compared with conceptions governing urine, feces, semen, spittle, and hair of both sexes, and the cultural logics governing the body-waste domain as a whole remain obscure (as they have until recently for such related conceptual domains as "honor and shame," "prejudice," and "the evil eye") (Herzfeld 1980a, 1980b, 1981).

We owe current understandings of American emotional and social transformations of cleanliness training more perhaps to Erikson than to any other interpreter (E. H. Erikson 1963, 1968). Yet he does not propose sex differences in these experiences. In his elaboration of Freud's views of anality, Erikson suggests that "holding on" and "letting go" are two modalities brought to many life situations; each has its appropriate place in our personal repertoires. Toilet training teaches, dealing as it does with both retention and elimination, a balance between self-determination and mother's determination, Erikson claims. "A sense of self-control without loss of self-esteem is the ontogenetic source of a sense of *free will*. From an unavoidable sense of loss of self-control and of parental overcontrol comes a lasting propensity for *doubt* and *shame*" (1968: 109–110). Too much "shaming" results in a *"precocious conscience,"* and at an institutional level, Erikson claims that the "lasting gains" of "well-balanced" toilet training are "safeguarded" by "law and order," which also provide "a sense of rightly delimited autonomy" (ibid.: 111, 113).

One work in feminist theory that obliquely deals with the lifelong reverberations of the lessons of toilet training in the sociology of the sexes is *The Mermaid and the Minotaur: Sexual Arrangements and Human Malaise,* by Dorothy Dinnerstein ([1976] 1977). Basing her analysis on Freud's theory of libidinal repression, Dinnerstein argues that because females have a "monopoly" on teaching renunciation of infantile joys in the flesh, they are targets of a "filial spite" from both sexes, from which fathers are exempt, a hostility further complicated by their differing experiences during the "oedipal" stage. "Woman" is the source of our first understandings of "defeat": "Through woman's jurisdiction over child's passionate body, through her control over what goes into it and what comes out of it, through her right to restrict its movements and invade its orifices, to withhold pleasure or inflict pain until it obeys her wishes, each human being first discovers the peculiarly angry, bittersweet experience of conscious surrender to conscious, determined outside rule" (ibid.: 166).

Maternal domination not balanced by paternal lessons in instinctual repression during infancy is Dinnerstein's theme. From the ways that she characterizes anality whenever she mentions it and from her emphases on maternal power, on nursing and weaning, and on sexual eroticism, the relationship she sees among shame, what is considered loathsome, and repression remains unclear—again, characteristic of most discussions of "caretaking," "dirty work," and feminine "evil." The mother's "domination" (here the context is not specified) includes using corporal punishment "to teach the child obedience. The rewards of submitting to the mother's will are correspondingly carnal—body warmth, food, caresses and soothing sounds, ravishing smiles and glances" (ibid.: 131–133). The child remembers "the many times that its will in the past has been subordinated to her own . . . when—after starting to take pride in using the toilet—it made an accidental puddle or an accidental mess. Female will is for each of us the will of the human presence in whose sentience our own will's earliest, most intimate, defeats have been reflected. When humiliation was new to us, and we had no defenses against its sting, our humiliations . . . were seen by female eyes, recorded in female memory. Woman, de Beauvoir says, 'knows everything about man that attacks his pride and humiliates his self-will' " (ibid.: 168). And everything about woman that attacks her pride and humiliates her.

Mothers are degraded, Dinnerstein suggests, by the negative side of sons' and daughters' ambivalence; "the dirty goddess" reminds them of what they feel ashamed about and have repressed. Carnality, as eroticism and sexuality, is her focus, as I read this: "The love of the flesh that woman stands for thus includes . . . an ashamed love for something actively loathsome" (ibid.: 147). Their father appears to sons and daughters "as a more *human* being than the mother" for having "orbited" for so long "outside the enchanted mother-infant pair," then becoming *"a sanctuary from maternal authority"*; until "male imperfection . . . becomes as culpable as female imperfection" and men are no longer a "permanent class of human . . . exempt from this role of target," there will be "no fundamental change in the situation of women" (ibid.: 175, 137, 89).

I fix responsibility not on the fact that mothers nurture children, but on the established, conventionalized scheme of biology, belief, and practice by which children learn from both parents that they are human beings and not animals of another species. It needs to be acknowledged that men are equally vulnerable not to being "imperfect" but to the authority of this same system of meaning. The equality lacking between the genders is not their lack of equal treatment by "spiteful" children, but acknowledgement of their equal vulnerability to impaired self-esteem for feeling less than human. The "more human" quality attributed to MEN is purchased at as high a price as is the "less human" quality attributed to WOMEN.

REPRISE

We have little idea, then, of our qualities free from the meanings by which this species has been clarifying its differences from other animals. In males' and females' experience of the cleanliness complex distinguishing us from animals, to be human is to experience humiliation and self-doubt. We know as little of men's potentialities beyond the reach of this system of meaning as we do of women's. Whatever we know of constitutional sex differences this cultural system blunts, stunts, distorts, perverts, by the evidence of the kinds of personal stresses and angst men and women today live with.

Not being one of our instinctual energies, disgust remains essentially untransformed. It is not sublimated, but tethered concretely and indissolubly to daily concerns with everything the odor and appearance of excrement entails: losing control, feeling ashamed of oneself, and fearing social humiliation and ostracism. The daily cycle of the body is a direct, nearly iconic reminder of the earliest lessons in anxiety, and the idiom of shame itself reappears in many kinds of social situations whenever we experience a "wound" to "self-esteem, a painful feeling or sense of degradation excited by the consciousness of having done something unworthy of one's previous idea of one's own excellence" (Lynd 1958: 24; see also E. H. Erikson 1968: 110). The conventional Freudian analysis of anal sublimination refers only to the "erotogenic significance of the anal zone," not to the "loathing and disgust" socially attached to this part of the body-self (Freud [1908] 1963: 28). Feces may be symbolized by play, gift, property, or weapon, and the lessons of cleanliness training transformed as "reaction formations" into the character traits of orderliness, parsimony, reliability, and obstinacy, as well as defiance, mastery, and the will to power (Brown 1959: 191, 192). Disgust and self-disgust remain themselves.

Do Americans learn the disgust response with a higher intensity of parental disapproval and anxiety than do people in other societies? "The Puritans of the 17th and 18th century in New England were especially afflicted with self-doubt and belief in their unworthiness. As soon as they landed in Massachusetts the Puritans were preoccupied with the notion that they were declining, falling short of their own and God's expectations. Seeking to give each child the best chance to escape damnation and to emerge as one of the elect, they instituted harsh child-rearing approaches, relying on shaming techniques which were devised to break the child's will" (J. E. Mack 1983: 3). "The Puritan's horror," writes Captain Bourke, "of heathenish rites and superstitious vestiges had for its basis something far above unreasoning fanaticism; he realized, if not through learned study, by an intuition which had all the force of genius, that every unmeaning practice, every rustic observance, which could not prove its title clear to a noble genealogy was a pagan survival, which conscience required him to tear up and destroy, root and branch. The Puritan may have made himself very much of a burden and a nuisance to his neighbors before his self-imposed task was completed, yet it is worthy of remark and of praise that his mission was a most effectual one in wiping from the face of the earth innumerable vestiges of pre-Christian idolatry" (Bourke 1891: 21). The practices may have been erased, but the "vestiges" of their meanings seem to have survived.

One analysis of child-rearing practices found American toilet training to be more severe than that of other cultures. It compared the findings of a study (made in the early 1940s) of a group of 50 white middle-class families living in Chicago with studies made of 74 other cultures. Even compared with other aspects of American child-rearing practices, such as those dealing with dependence and aggression, oral and sexual behaviors, toilet training was managed in the most severe, least indulgent way (Whiting and Child 1953: 67, 114).

Another study contradicts that finding of American severity, however; reports of 379 mothers interviewed in the mid-1950s show that while "the average age at the beginning of training was about eleven months, and at completion, about eighteen months . . . the prevailing mode of training was not very severe. The great majority of mothers used practically no punishment, though there was some scolding for accidents. Only about a fifth of the mothers reported definite punishments or emphatic, repeated scoldings" (Sears, Maccoby, and Levin 1957: 109, 120). Those that did, however, reported giving "a few little slaps on her behind," shaming a son by "bringing up the fact that his clothes and everything were all dirty," and "really" spanking; one mother "put it under her nose a little bit, and [told] her the next time she did it in her pants, she was going to get it in the face" (ibid.: 118). Without direct observations, it is safer to assume on this subject that there is very little reliable information on what parents say and do compared with what they report or think is appropriate to report.

Do other cultures have some better way to teach cleanliness habits?

> . . . [T]here are no human societies where the act of excretion and its products are not subject to public and private arrangements, to expectations involving time and space, regularity and appropriateness. . . . In all societies some demarcations seem to apply to excretion; an important considera- tion in most cases seems to be the smell of human faeces. The importance attached to it may be only relative, however. (Loudon 1978: 168–169; see also Mauss 1979: 118)

Other cultures remind us mostly of the true universal: how arbitrary and conventionalized meaning systems are. Body products carry valence everywhere, but how that meaning elaborates into the social construction of human beings and thence influences the constitution of the genders is not only particular within each cosmology. What is most striking is how unthinkable one cosmology is in the terms of any other. The single con- stant, perhaps a universal, does appear to be the actual division of domestic labor between the sexes: to what extent that division in all other social roles is traceable to beliefs surrounding the mother's bonding to a newborn and close contact with incontinent infants is a question for cross-cultural studies of sexual stratification and gender psychologies.

Examples of surface behaviors in other cultures not placed in cosmo- logical context only mislead. Among the Chagga of Tanzania the male initiation ritual is called "the stopping up of the anus." Men put it about to women and children that they never defecate, and, although everyone knows that the women and children know better, keeping up this fiction is central to the maintenance of the entire social order—to the point that "when a man emits wind, his child must take the blame and apologize!" (Raum 1940: 320). Moreover, should any one of his children suffer from enuresis, a man has grounds for divorce (ibid.: 109). Chagga cosmology relates these rites and rules, not as we would to disgust and cleanliness training, but to the significance of procreativity. Men's feces and women's menstrual blood are both signs of sterility. "The vulnerability to sterility is connected with death. . . . The man or woman who has no offspring dies, and his line dies, and that is the end of him, or her, the complete, absolute end. It is not just the end of life in this world, but the total end. . . . The capacity to procreate is also the capacity to guarantee oneself a peaceful immortality, a comfortable perpetuity as a link in the unend- ing chain of ancestors and descendants." For the Chagga believe that once initiated a "man may be as fertile as any woman. Once he can beget children, he runs the risk of becoming pregnant or of impregnating another man through anal intercourse. . . . For a man to become pregnant in this way would mean death because, being closed, he has no birth canal out of which the child can pass. . . . The initiation lesson of the plug is that from that time on the male anus is sealed for sexual purposes. To achieve fatherhood, to beget children, men must copulate with women and abjure other men" (Moore 1976: 358–359).

One more example illustrates the point that even as feces seem universally to be constituted as a disvalued substance, the source of that value is itself likely to be constituted by worldviews and belief systems which fix themselves upon body wastes. In Sri Lanka, a social constellation of disvalued feces, denigration of the self, depression, and death is unusually clear. There, the disgust reaction is taught with great intensity, yet little issue is made during training of the time and place for excreting. In Sri Lanka there is

> extreme permissiveness: time and place are not defined; the child gradually moves from the home to the backyard and, when he is old enough to look after himself, to the outhouse or bush. But this idyllic picture is soon dispelled when we focus on the maternal attitude towards feces; her reaction is one of horror if the child attempts to play with it. *Chi* is the typical Sinhala expression of revulsion, which prototypically refers to feces. In socialization, the child is soon made to feel that all dirt is feces; thus when a child plays with mud, the exclamation "chi, feces" is used. In training, the mother may even rebuke a child by saying "Chi, feces baby," which is the earliest usage of the metaphor of feces to lower someone's self-esteem. The idiom of feces and foul smells are extended to other contexts also, for example, to "shame": a person who has lost face is someone who "stank"; dirt, mud, and bad smells all appear in the idiom of shame. (Obeyesekere 1985: 146)

In "probably the most common form of meditation practiced in Sri Lanka," known as the "meditation on revulsion," this nexus of feces, shame, and lowered self-esteem reappears. Buddhist laymen temporarily become monks or novices, engaging in various religious activities including meditation, and on holy days during the four phases of the moon, they observe this "especially popular" section of a "meditation on mindfulness." Professional monks contemplate a corpse "in ten separate stages of decay" intended to "produce in the meditator a sense of disgust for sense pleasure, which will then lead him to realize the sense of the transitoriness of the body. In the lay tradition this is not the case: one does not meditate on an actual decaying corpse but one conjures in one's own mind the putrescence of the body. . . . The layman . . . has to evoke this putrescence through various metaphors of revulsion, the most conspicuous being that of feces. Feces is the one object par excellence that everyone in the society is familiar with as a revulsive object. It then becomes a metaphor for the revulsiveness of the body in the 'meditation on revulsion'" (ibid.: 141). The text of the meditation "deliberately denigrates the body in order to deny the self itself as real. The metaphor used in the denigration of the body and the self is feces. In major depression also the self is denigrated: lowering of self-esteem and self-worth is conspicuous in this state" (ibid.: 145).

An Anglo-American understanding of the relationship between feelings of low self-worth, depression, and excrement is documented in the *Oxford English Dictionary*. The first meaning of "dejection" is "a state of depression; melancholy," and it has two medical meanings as well: "evacuation of the bowels" and "excrement." Both share the Latin root *dejicere*, "to throw down, let fall," but apart from the commonsensical association with a physical "casting down" of excrement and the feeling of being "cast down," their true etymology has not, so far as I can discover, been documented. The *OED* does provide a fascinating clue to Anglo-American culture's association between depression and excrement; the first illustrative usage quoted is from 1483: "Lucifer . . . was dejecta and caste out of heven," and in 1560, from Rolland, "he . . . was deiect with schame fra all honour downcast, dispirited, dejected" (152–153). Dejection as melancholy, is, then, early associated with social shame and with the loss of honor. The second meaning of "dejection" given by the *OED* is therefore "cast down from one's position, lowered in fortunes; lowered in character, abject, abased." The medical meanings appear to come later, but aside from the gravitational facts involved, the connection remains a puzzle.

Feces *are* decaying matter; they are composed of the dead cells of the body; they are not symbols of or metaphors for putrid smells, decay, and death—they are all those things, in the midst of daily life. In being first an element of the body-self, then constituted as "bad self," feces represent the injury that becomes an integral part of the psychobiological self. The revulsion, shame, and humiliation so wholly bound up with feces and the anxieties over their control can turn into to self-hate: self-hate is the death within depression. This ego damage, occurring to one degree or another, may be a human constant, but, as I have stressed, the injury to earliest narcissism does not wholly or forever determine the quality of self-esteem; other aspects of parenting and experiences of social efficacy doubtless compensate. This "lasting propensity for *doubt* and *shame*" (in Erikson's words) may, however, be a constitutional predisposition for depression which a social environment can shape more in one direction than another.

This theory of gender stratification suggests reexamining male-female patterns of behavior and relationships as being themselves evidence of the variety of ways by which people repair constitutional self-esteem some-how damaged in learning and maintaining each society's disgust response, as evidence of the concepts designating the meaning of feces within a number of semantic systems, and as evidence of the concepts delineat-ing differences between humans and animals. In Western societies, the questions change. Is the "penis envy" women are believed to feel instead "escape envy"? Females observe males' apparently successful avoidances of the signs of the same shame, self-denigration, and social stigma imprison-ing them. The phallus as the chief sign of "nonfemaleness" is, by the lights of this cosmology, the more valuable social identity. In this sense of pro-tecting self-esteem and enhancing social honor, "femininity" is definitely "thwarted masculinity." Males' putative fear of "castration": Is castration-fear a fear of that "total stripping of the person" by which shame instills the control of elimination, given the penis' function of micturition? Is castration-fear a fear of losing control and of experiencing humiliation and wounded self-esteem? Are both female self-abnegation and the male cas-tration complex a consequence of intense cleanliness lessons that can leave children feeling overpowered, weak, and ashamed? "Patriarchy": is men's domination of women an epiphenomenon of their physical and social dis-sociation from the activities and relationships that are signs of dishonor and animalistic disgrace? "Matriarchy": is respect for women respect for their powers over the daily havoc threatening the species' superiority?

Gender stratification in many of its fundamentals is a consequence of a metaphysical and biological system that is not condemning WOMEN and blessing MEN, but is equally fateful for people of both sexes, I am proposing. Correcting misleading pictures of men's condition as being in-herently more favorable than women's seems necessary for understanding why men's behaviors can be self-destructive, and given the realities of their power, species-destructive, and for understanding why women's "power-lessness," often seen as being complicitous with their denigration, is part of their search for social approval.

Human self-esteem is least in doubt when males and females feel loved as offspring, parents, siblings, lovers, friends. Yet men are powerless to defeat the cultural convictions at war with their personal love and regard for daughters, sisters, partners, and colleagues; men helplessly watch as the wider world blights their opportunities and self-assurance. The love of a good woman for a son, brother, partner, or friend is inadequate for an authentic sense of social worthiness that he can sustain without concentrat-ing on control and self-protection. Social victory over this metaphysical scheme seems beyond reach.

The feminist program, subscribed to by men and women alike, is based on proposals such as transforming the neighborhood kindred, as I call it, into a formal, cooperative work group, increasing the availability of professional child-care services, equalizing pay, instituting child-support allowances, limiting men's work-related travel, allowing for flexible work hours and for working at home, providing paternity leave, increasing the availability of part-time jobs for both men and women—options that will surely help to improve the conditions under which people live. Women and men who share each other's perspectives will be more in touch with themselves as people. But these are goals. They do not also change the fundamental cultural premises that have made "domestic life" so problematic: "Laws, customs, and prejudices keep women down, yet even when they don't women still find equality hard to get. There are many reasons for this, but chief among them are the sexual relationships and roles that make women responsible for domestic life" (O'Neill 1976: 363). "Domesticity" is hardly restricted to home, we might now see.

The paramount question is whether cleanliness learning can be taught without this system of meaning constituting human beings' difference from other animals, considering now that it may be elaborated into our conceptions of WOMEN and MEN and into a constituent of the psychobiological self. The possibilities can be heady and mundane. Can we redefine the sources and manifestations of evil? Can humans agree on less cataclysmic ways of defining their differences from other animals? Can the surface changes advocated to reform "domestic life" help in breaking apart this glacier of moral associations? If fastidious fathers no longer stand aside from diapers and laundry and begin to wipe up urine puddles, clean up after fecal accidents, and toilet train their children with love and some "right amount" of friendly disapproval, the arbitrariness of conventional associations may become apparent to the next generation and everybody else. Younger parents could begin to tailor training expectations and routines differently for boys and girls and try to lessen their pressures on firstborns (child-rearing advice books tend not to make these obvious suggestions). But only if cleanliness training shifts to the morally neutral ground of physiological well-being and personal and social hygiene (with which grandparents can learn to concur) can these meanings also shift. Breaking apart the identification of physiological disgust with moral disgust is one challenge.

Those who are now cultural elders—grandparents, teachers, judges, senators, generals, ourselves—are generations of women and men indoctrinated without knowing why to leave the dirty work and every one of its species implications and moral evocations to women. In elders' hands the reins over our common life remain—men encased in distancing strategies, women hobbled by appeasing tactics. Real change will be slow. Nor is it any consolation to believe that only the ignorant and unsophisticated act on this system of meaning or that the disvalue of women and the distancing of men are idiosyncratic and not systematically under the control of a metaphysics. Rational men who, as this same system of meaning has it, have come to control the scientific professions can be equally helpless in its grip, at a loss to deal with women, for example, who have chosen not to appease:

> Perhaps the most disturbing trend is that the equalization of opportunities is considerably better for women with only bachelor's degrees than for those with either master's degrees or Ph.D's. Women are rewarded far less than men for the larger investment in career preparation represented by graduate degrees. . . . Even among faculty, women earn far less than men. In 1981, the salaries of women faculty in science and mathematics were only 78.2 percent of those of men, and in the social sciences, 81.5 percent. The actual dollar differences were $5300 and $4670, respectively. (Vetter 1981: 1320)

" 'Every place you look, if the wages are under control of some arbitrary factors, women are paid less. . . . Any place wages are set by any kinds of judgment, it seems to me we have discrimination,' " said a male member of a National Academy of Sciences panel on equal employment opportunity—"judgments" that are positive evidence of the workings of this system of meaning in social order. " 'Women's work' paid about $4,000 a year less than work usually performed by men," whose distancing strategies are clear occupationally as well: "Seventy percent of the nation's working men and 54 percent of the working women were concentrated in jobs done by those of their own sex" (occupational segregation was more pronounced by sex than by race) (Shribman 1981). Among ministers, "women are paid less, even though their educational level is generally higher, with 90.8 percent having seminary degrees, three years beyond college, against 72.2 percent of the men"—about $6000 less annually than the male median of $20,000 to $22,000 (*The New York Times* 1984).

The redress of women's condition that feminists of both sexes seek through our constitutional system is essential. But legal discourse does not usually use the discourse of cultural systems, and the vocabularies of briefs, judicial opinions, and constitutional amendments are worlds apart from our constellations of meanings. Legal recourse has the single virtue of keeping up hope that patent injustices will be remedied, but then, only those human injustices that manifestly afflict women: what men suffer from this same cosmology remains more latent but no less debilitating to them as human beings. As things stand, however, in the distribution of power and influence, until men are able to speak, in these terms or some others, of their own struggles to be fully human beings and can see their struggles as stemming from the same source as women's, neither sex will be liberated from culturally invented bonds.

The constitution of humankind, the teachings of parents, the role of olfaction in aggression and depression, differences in male and female physiology and psychology, and the varieties of ways that males and females maintain self-esteem are subjects for philosophers, scientists, and ourselves to keep considering. In the meantime, another "drab, minor, and everyday event" may be occurring in the backyards of our neighbors. They may reveal clear evidence of Americans' "misplaced delicacy" and the system of meaning sustaining it: if neighbors are drying their laundry outdoors, it's probably in violation of the community's zoning ordinance, another ubiquitous carrier of cosmologies constituting this social order.

Conclusion

SILENCE AS *THE OTHER*

When speaking of "community" and of "justice," Americans leave much unsaid. We use words but are often silent about meanings. Once finding their wellsprings, we might begin to see which American assumptions and beliefs are not oases but mirages we must keep travelling beyond.

Once we see American meanings at all, in North, South, East, and West, we are likely to see them differently, and that is the point: to render from many biases and biographies our accounts of meanings and the ambiguities they attempt to put to rest. In those very renditions culture becomes a collaborator in creating its own possibilities and alternatives. Unlike ethnographies of distant and exotic systems of meaning, this work has to share its "authority" in a dialogue with readers' myriad experiences, their positions toward "mainstream" American norms, and their various intellectual, political, and social orientations. Those dialogues are sources of intellectual reconstructions, cultural transformations, and hope: the ultimate saviour of this republic is its constitutional commitment to renegotiate the meanings we live by. But to do that we have first to give them voice; what goes without saying leaves truth only half spoken.

I have been seeing privacy, kinship, friendship, homeownership, neighboring, suburbs, racism, credit, dog ownership, stigma, cleanliness training, and gender stratification as each being modern complexes where ideology and practice meet to generate ambiguities and meanings, contradictions and coherencies. It is no longer possible in industrialized, literate, and plural societies to tell the kind of "whole" story that ethnographers traditionally have tried to tell (Marcus and Fischer 1986; Stein [1960] 1964: 334; Varenne 1977: 7). Nor does the research record presently allow for cross-cultural comparisons of such complexes; the comparisons here are instead internal, between ideals and practice, between the said and the unsaid.

From anthropology and history we expect to learn of other peoples' unfamiliar ways, and from that, to see our own anew. At home *the other* I seek is the universe of undiscussed presuppositions and perceptions, not marginalized, enclaved, or other territorial groups of citizens; trying to make utterly familiar assumptions strange enough to be reconsidered is the central problem of doing at home what has more often been done abroad. Such silences are the contexts through which we decipher our own discourses—the layers of tacit understandings by which we know what is going on and why. One aim of these essays is to break their silence, to stop culture from giving us answers for which there have never been questions, answers that can unwittingly deprive citizens of their very birthright of life, liberty, and the pursuit of happiness.

Silences also mute other kinds of discourses to which we look for help in understanding and interpreting the events and experiences of our common life. The social sciences speak little of social meanings; the psychological sciences speak much of personal meanings; and the bridge between our interior and our surround we must build ourselves. We are happy enough to call it culture but, under the dominance of normal science, not to let it matter all that much to other forms of "real" knowledge on which inquiry and action, it is believed, should rely. The most worrisome and the most pregnant silences are those of legal discourse; only recently is it becoming aware of those that lie between the lines of a "legalist" tradition (Unger 1986). No less compulsory, sovereign, and coercive than law are the implicit ideas constituting the hundreds of systems of meaning and conduct that are American culture. These stand as clauses in the contract that allows us to make all our others—a shadow constitution—yet many of the most coercive remain unassimilated to and unaired in legal discourse. Little wonder that formal law has only been inching us toward a more authentic sense of community and a fairer share of justice among the races and between the genders, for what progress can we make on roads that keep disappearing from beneath our feet?

Within constitutional discourse we come closest to using and changing overtly that about which we are able to speak. The text and texture of culture are most likely to be acknowledged through legislation and adjudication, yet those develop without the contributions that the situated semiotic and semantic tools of this trade might make. These tools of observation and interpretation help to make limpid the natures and principles of social relationships whose conceptual stratigraphy and structures we may previously have been able only to intuit. Like microscopes and telescopes, they can open our eyes to phenomena escaping the nets of artificial and static typologies and typifications; they can identify and articulate social meanings in accordance with the highest standards for evidence, both scientific and legal. The challenge is to allow our cultural logics their rightful place within every other kind of logic—sociologic, economic, legal, historical (Geertz 1983: 167–234). Why does so much persist despite so many attempts at improvement? In scanting culture, the meanings at stake go unacknowledged; forged on invisible anvils, plans for change can collapse under the weight of the meanings of events.

REDUCING DISTRUST

The real American Dream is the one we've lived out: that people of every belief and custom could live in harmony without defended boundaries. Yet tensions between how we bring people in and keep them out, how we trust and distrust, how we honor and disparage are never very far from the surfaces of American life. When ordinary social trust is missing, so is the foundation of democracy. "The role of social trust and cooperativeness as a component of the civic culture cannot be overemphasized. It is, in a sense, a generalized resource that keeps a democratic polity operating. . . . Social trust facilitates political cooperation . . . and without it . . . [formal] institutions may mean little (Almond and Verba 1963: 356–357). Belonging depends on trust; the less there is of any kind, the less there is of every kind.

Outside of protected learning environments people are left largely to their own devices when perceiving or experiencing threats to established meanings and the satisfactions they guarantee. In "politics" and "religion" they may find ways of dealing with the stress of alienation and their need to act. Yet ideologies and cosmologies can generate as much social strain as they relieve when they dogmatically assert singular sources of equilibrium (truth, beauty, faith) and make threats of different beliefs. In preserving its collective representations and in maintaining its accustomed conduct, each group tends to define every other beyond its pale of meaning and belonging. That is the constant paradox and tension of social orders. The specific seams of meaning—its own "logic of relatives"—fashioning such lines in each culture are keys to understanding what people see as tearing them apart, from within and without.

Discussing the social implications of fear, one biological anthropologist throws caution to the winds: "Let it suffice to remark that no reasonable analysis of human behavior can fail to grant that the situations that most seriously jeopardize human survival and human dignity, past, present, and future, owe much more to irrational fear than to irrational rage" (Konner 1982: 234). That fears are often *not* "irrational," however, is the true human dilemma: they are "biosemantic" fears having the same integrity as those we consider rational (of tornadoes, of armed bandits). Every group lives through the significances it imposes; protecting its semantic infrastructure is far from irrational. Social hostility, disparagement, avoidance, stigma, and enmity expressed in social thought and social patterns are tragic strategies for keeping intact meanings and the capacity to act that they insure. The most prevalent strategy is avoidance, and the many forms of distancing in which we are adept are perhaps the most familiar experiences we have not only of peacekeeping but also of alienation. But in estranging ourselves from others, we have only ourselves to retreat into.

What is needed are questions that address these biological and cultural issues, not exhortations that wish them away. One question is how to give voice to silent traditions that come without saying but which cannot go without putting fear in their place. Fear is dependent on familiar meanings and beliefs: how can comfort and predictability be better safeguarded in a world where much readily becomes unfamiliar and ambiguous yet where people must still be able to act confidently? The beliefs and behaviors of peoples of this country and the world do not have to become more alike for trust and peace to prevail, but the intensity of fear and threat that their differences signify or are made to signify needs to be reduced. Maximizing ideological likenesses and minimizing differences is a promising answer, but it may remain unfulfilled because it deprives politics of its polarities and the media of much of what they decide is "newsworthy." The nations of the world and the many kinds of belief systems that live under their flags may give peace a better chance by self-policing the rhetoric that exaggerates differences and plays down similarities than by policing territorial borders—not by restraining demagogic and inciteful speech, but by publicly doubting it. We will live, all of us, only if we can let live.

Education continues to be the single appealing route to greater social tolerance. But oh so slow: the history of changes in American prejudices might equally be read as the documentation of cultural persistence. As much as seems to be affected on the surface, this culture tends to keep its icebergs. For there is another barrier still: even as practice may change, symbols carrying the earlier nexus of affect and association remain evocative, because through them people are accustomed to locate the balance in their lives. Imprisoning symbols may also be deliberately refueled by those out to keep political and economic power (Sederberg 1984). Elites may be cynical and manipulative, of course, but they may also be caught up in systems of meaning so wholly taken for granted as never to be taken apart, least of all by themselves.

Nor is that the end of it. The intertextuality of symbols keeps denigration, distrust, and stigma emotionally available, for all daily signs of lesser social respect are perceptual reminders that some meanings and the people who represent them (or are made hostage to them) are constituted as being eccentric to some middle ground (Sollors 1986). The more any group is believed to be a minority to an imputed majority, the more it is regarded as being oblique to "the center," and the more it does not appear to be valued and to belong, the less chance of belonging it has. Even as "tokens" may help to diminish the degree of unfamiliarity of a group, they can also draw attention and negativism, if seen as discrepant.

A high tolerance for discrepancy, according to studies of Americans' attitudes toward "nonconformity," appears among people who are less susceptible to helplessness because they have access to a wide range of options. They have, above all, higher levels of formal education, which is the most important single dimension; they live in metropolitan areas compared with people on farms, who are least tolerant; they are male, more so than female; and they work in white-collar occupations (R. M. Williams 1977: 5). That this evidence points to a necessarily circular conclusion is, needless to say, discouraging: to assure the trust and tolerance that will contribute to a more just society requires more justice in the distribution of access to options.

As juridically and politically maddening as the gradualism of "conservatism" may be, it is biologically and culturally sane until there are social forms that are as effective in protecting people from experiencing and displaying their semantic distresses as educational institutions are in promoting the pleasures of curiosity, novelty, and difference. Tolerance for degrees of difference appears to have limits, no less than tolerance for disease and environmental stress has limits and requires remedies. A world of differences is the one we live in.

That social condemnations have biological sources is a proposition for which the terms of behavioral biology and evolutionary theory are inadequate, to say the least. Their neutral, functional constructs of "survival," "adaptation," "reproductive fitness" are irrelevant to the genocides of history and the little murders of everyday life that horrify ordinary reason and devastate simple justice. For these matters of human choice and action, the ethical, moral, and cultural perspectives of philosophic and constitutional discourse remain indispensable.

BRINGING IN BIOLOGY

This ethnography has singled out for attention social fears and anxieties arising from the stresses that accompany the disappointment or interruption of expectancies, seen as the conceptual systems through which every person and group lives. Its analyses of myth and ritual and contemporary social patterns and behaviors have been informed by such understandings of these processes as modern neurophysiology, behavioral biology, and psychology are able now to supply and as I've been capable of understanding.

Culture, ours and every other, resists both revision and interrogation;

its resilience, set at equilibrium, makes it friendly to few new concepts and inimical to doubt. But its tenacity is rationale for existential despair only from the perspective that, like an immovable mountain, culture is all immanent essence. Seeing its conventions, standards, ideals, and norms anew as representing filaments of constituted meanings and constructed metaphors allows us to come into our species' own, using intelligence, feeling, and imagination to instead view culture's "nature" (as we may also begin to see "lines"), as being artificial, arbitrary, and malleable.

Yet we must have expectations and the meanings they both nourish and supply. In addressing questions of the "Real and Practical Relations Between Psychology and Sociology" in 1924, Marcel Mauss, author of classic studies in cultural analysis, singled out as being "most urgent" the subject of "expectation." He called it "one of the phenomena on which we need [psychologists] to shed light, the study of which . . . presupposes this consideration of the totality of man: his body, his instincts, his emotions, his will and his perceptions and his intellection. . . . Expectation is one of the phenomena of sociology closest both to the psychical and the physiological, and at the same time it is one of commonest" (Mauss 1979: 29, 30).

> Particularly fruitful are the study of moral expectation and illusion, the disappointment of the expectations of individuals and collectivities, the study of their reactions. . . . A good psychological and above all physiological description will enable us the better to describe the "vague anxieties" . . . the precise images that replace them, and the violent movements and absolute inhibitions which expectation arouses in us. . . . Lastly, expectation is one of those facts in which emotion, perception and more precisely the motion and state of the body directly condition the social state and are conditioned by it. As in all the facts I have just quoted, the triple consideration of the body, the mind and the social environment must go together. (Ibid.: 30–31)

In this vein, I've been suggesting that the discourses of biology and culture unite to consider the materiality of meanings in human physiology and in the constitution of the very worlds we investigate. Doing so introduces other ways of looking at relationships among social meanings, social structure, and social process and the relationship between persistence and change. As normal as fears and anxieties are that expectations will be disappointed, the immensity of their social consequences is inadequately acknowledged: fear and anxiety are as significant in ordering human affairs as are sex and subsistence. Indeed, this synthesis of cosmology, ecology, and biology is no different from that with which we understand the universality of kinship systems and their unique manifestations in local forms and patterns. No less potent than the kinship concepts and conduct that connect and nurture is this darker side of constituting social order that can divide and harm.

Against claims and overclaims that human destructiveness is "inborn," that people "need" others against whom to define themselves, and that alienation is a given of the human condition, this collaboration of biology and culture instead suggests that human aggression and hostility are situationally and semantically specific. The context "determines" which of this species' instincts, drives, affects, perceptions . . . are mobilized, to what degree and extent, and with what consequences. It is possible now, I am suggesting, to be much clearer about which processes are involved, how people (and not "social structures") manifest them neurophysiologically, psychologically, and socially, and how these together can open the way to still more grounded and comparative accounts of social systems and the organization of social life (Averill 1980; Barchas and Mendoza 1984; Crick 1982: 296; Jones et al. 1984; Levy 1983: 133). Far from suggesting that our biological commonalities will better explain behaviors than will humankind's various cosmologies and ecologies, this work is intended to inspire more widespread curiosity about the ways in which human biology and local cultures are, case by unsettling, wayward case, implicated in one another.

The anthropological project remains the same: to answer the question "What is humankind?" by documenting variation around the core of the human constitution in order to extend understandings of that core. In my analysis of the dog-human relationship and of gender hierarchy, for example, I've placed two developmental events—the separation-individuation phase and cleanliness training—in the contexts of particular social thought and practice. Both of these events include some of the same processes as are central to the production of fear and anxiety—interruption of schemata— and each is embedded in a unique institutional complex of belief and practice, whose consequences I trace out in many domains of social life. How are these developmental events situated and construed elsewhere? Recognizing that there are biological consistencies in this species' characteristics —"consistencies" which represent a particular moment in scientific knowledge—is not to succumb to determinism or reductionism but to allow for limits. The recognition does no more than acknowledge that historical moment, the deficiencies of the knowledge, the comparative purpose of the anthropological project, and the role of cultural particularities in constructing general propositions about human nature and conduct.

This view proposes that there is nothing "superorganic" or transcendent about culture; to create interpretations of its worlds is the unique biological imperative of this species. "Culture patterns—religious, philosophical, aesthetic, scientific, ideological—are 'programs'; they provide a template or blueprint for the organization of social and psychological processes, much as genetic systems provide such a template for the organization of organic processes" (Geertz 1973: 216). Like other biological givens, culture is irrevocably implicated in the questions natural scientists ask. Acknowledging that makes ethnographies of meanings more, not less, critical to every other science of humankind. Without documentation, other scientists have little choice but to be anecdotal and superficial about contextual influences generally agreed to be crucial. The shoe is on the other foot: natural scientists require the authority of the cultural sciences. Bringing in biology makes even more important the translation of the poetry of meaning and symbolic systems into prose.

Until recently, work in cultural analysis has either relied unselfconsciously on generally understood relationships between emotions and behaviors or it has deliberately set affects aside in favor of models of ("purely") logical or perceptual thought processes (Levy 1984: 214–217; Lutz and White 1986; Piaget 1967). Despite the fact that the subjects of symbolic, semiotic, and semantic analyses are often highly charged affectively and that these evaluations are reproduced in spatial, temporal, and sociological structures, their emotional content per se has tended not to be a dimension of analysis. The study of affect in cultural analysis has recently moved toward the relationship between emotion and "self," a reintroduction of concern with the "individual" and subjectivity in psychological anthropology (although not to be confused with a return to issues of "personality and culture") (Shweder and LeVine 1984).

In finding American culture in social meanings, I've set aside the possibility of an "American character" or an "American mind," and have instead taken our notion of American *dreams* seriously: the sleeping images, symbols, ideals, ideas, myths, meanings, and beliefs by which we understand, interpret, and act in waking life. There is no question that in seeing and using these differently as we do, we are each, in our individuality, a cultural surprise. But I've chosen to emphasize the social force of affects over their personal and individual force. I find that Americans are already well supplied with ways of clarifying the relationship between their feelings and the constitution of their selves, their identities, their personalities, their egos, their characters. In understanding their social situations, perhaps the first (and often the last) kind of explanation Americans are likely to use is individualistic, subjective, and personalized. I have hoped instead to suggest the possibility of thinking about and reconstructing culture by using culture itself in doing so. Intertwined with the silences of the self are those of culture.

My choice of language also has had that possibility in mind. Throughout, I've tried to avoid using social scientific constructs in favor of images and vocabulary that remain closer to lived-in experiences. For that is the ultimate proof "positive" of my readings: whether they resonate credibly and, if they do not, to leave readers free to say how in their own terms, rather than to feel silenced by the authority of an established terminology. Throughout, I deliberately haven't used the terms "code" or "cultural code," as useful a shorthand as they may be. Among other things, "code" connotes secrecy or an intention to misrepresent or deceive. Culture is not deliberately withheld from us; our conventions and usages and their institutionalizations, fateful to be sure, are under no one's control but our own. I prefer the term "sign": we might all be able to read and follow signs, but it is given to few specialists to break codes.

IMAGINING

One source of the underdevelopment of cultural knowledge is the American hierarchy of knowledge. Believing in its superior ability to displace the ambiguities at the very center of our lives with certainty, we give priority to Science and its canons. We are led to see the world as being amenable to either Hard or Soft explanation, and those differences too are evaluated and moralized, as Best and Worst, Literal and Figurative, Cognitive and Emotional, Rational and Irrational. The Humanities are residual—all of ethnography, history, literature, art, philosophy, criticism from which we construct the insights into our human condition, which bring us to have still others. From an epistemology which divides legitimate understanding between Facts and Everything Else, we are left with a rich record that documents the artifacts of meanings without also annotating their manufacture. Too much of social science and socially germane science offers thick description with thin gloss. Yet meanings are fundamentally shaping perceptions of every dimension of society—economic, political, ecological, scientific, social.

This hierarchy of knowledge reproduces the hierarchy of the genders, for it too is generated by the eternal ambiguities human beings encounter in being also animals. In Western thought, "reasoning is the peculiar prerogative of masculine pursuits, and therefore of the male sex," but this idea "is not so much a prejudice against women as a conviction built on the notion that reason is a distinct faculty present only in those pursuits for which there are no parallels in the animal world" (McMillan 1982: 56). This philosopher points out that "the difficulty with this view of the distinction between rational, 'masculine' and intuitive, 'feminine' knowledge is not the argument that women are inhibited from using their reason but the presumption that 'masculine' activities like science and mathematics are the sole proprietors of reason. The assertion that only men reason . . . is tantamount to the assertion that it is impossible for men and women to communicate, since women are supposedly arrested at the level of instinctive, animal existence" (ibid.: 40–41). For both men and women, intuitive and experiential knowledge is no less knowledge, no less reasoned and logical (ibid.: 42). The heart has its reasons, and reasons have their hearts.

Emotion is "a master Western cultural category" which is "opposed . . . to the positively evaluated process of thought," an anthropologist finds (Lutz 1986: 289). The distinction between "emotion and thought" is one as central "in Western psychosocial theory as . . . those between mind and body, behavior and intention, the individual and the social, or the conscious and the unconscious" (ibid.: 287, 289). The unspoken assumptions constituting this category identify "emotion primarily with irrationality, subjectivity, the chaotic and other negative characteristics." Then, because women have been labelled "the emotional gender, cultural belief reinforces the ideological subordination of women" insofar as beliefs about emotion also entail beliefs about the mutually exclusive relationships between cognition and emotion, facts and value, passion and reason, feeling and thinking (ibid.: 288, 289). The emotions are associated "with all that is precultural and presocial, which is to say, with the natural in its brutish and Darwinian forms. . . . When combined with the idea that it is via the mental that we have distinguished ourselves from lower forms of life, this [is] another route by which emotion is devalued. . . . [P]ositive views about emotion and the . . . denigration of thought are not appropriate for males in this society" (ibid.: 293, 294, 296). Perhaps now we may better understand some of the cosmological sources of these beliefs.

Imagination falls victim not only to that artifice, but to ambiguity as well. The most pernicious, most ironic power of ambiguity may be its silent effect upon imagination. The quest to tie down the loose ends of experience itself disables our capacity to entertain alternatives; people get comfortable with the metaphors, models, and "templates" that have been helpful in interpreting what is inchoate and enigmatic. So then do the highest rewards go to predictability and all that falls in behind it: convention and custom, tradition and continuity. But creativity, spontaneity, and invention are no less likely than rationality and deliberation to be constructive. For the disquiet they can evoke, however, they are rewarded less and set apart from pragmatic concerns. So does imagination atrophy.

Living as social beings we in fact maintain a dialogue between spontaneity and predictability, between surprise and deliberation, between invention and custom, between feeling and thought, between imagination and convention, between fancy and practicality. They each should but do not get equal time. Not that imagination works only to serve human life; imagination makes weaponry and poetry. But when it is missing, the most vital and valuable property of any community is missing: its capacity for imagining human possibilities. Here and now, we are free to originate contemporary meanings through which more people can feel they belong in America, if only our imaginations will.

Acknowledgments

The John Simon Guggenheim Memorial Foundation made it possible to begin this work. A travel and study award from the Ford Foundation helped me to continue it, as did the hospitality of the Bunting Institute, Radcliffe College. For a month of coddled writing time I'm grateful to the Rockefeller Foundation and to Robert and Gianna Celli and the staff at the Villa Serbelloni.

For their questions, disagreements, suggestions, and encouragement, I thank Nadya Aisenberg, Phyllis Pease Chock, John-Paul Dumont, James W. Fernandez, Michael M. F. Fischer, Richard Madsen, Barbara D. Miller, Maurice Stein, Roy Wagner, and James Wilkinson. The editorial queries of Marie Cantlon, James Clifford, George Marcus, and Robin Whitaker were inspiring. To commentators on bits and pieces earlier and later, my thanks: Alan M. Beck, Jules R. Bemporad, Michael Curtis, Jarl E. Dyrud, Susanne Fischer, Fritz Fleischmann, Bruce Fogle, Morris Freilich, Edwin T. and Ruth Haefele, Robert LeVine, Frank Michelman, and Ruth Saxe. Grace Clark and Joan Dineen provided superior deciphering and typing help; Molly Sherry was adept in the library.

Cambridge, Massachusetts
January, 1988

Bibliography

The year in brackets is that of the first publication of the work in any language; the second year is that of the source used.

ABRAMS, David M., and Brian Sutton-Smith. 1977. The development of the trickster in children's narrative. *Journal of American Folklore* 90 (355, Jan.-Mar.): 29–47.

AGEE, James, and Walker Evans. [1941] 1960. *Let us now praise famous men*. Boston: Houghton Mifflin.

AINSWORTH, Mary D. Salter. 1977. Attachment theory and its utility in cross-cultural research. In *Culture and infancy: Variations in the human experience*, ed. P. H. Leiderman, S. R. Tulkin, and A. Rosenfeld, pp. 49–67. New York: Academic Press.

ALDOUS, Joan. 1977. Family interaction patterns. In *Annual review of sociology*, ed. Alex Inkeles, James Coleman, and Neil Smelser, Vol. 3, pp. 105–135. Palo Alto: Annual Reviews.

ALLAN, Graham A. 1979. *A sociology of friendship and kinship*. London: Allen and Unwin.

ALLPORT, Gordon. 1958. *The nature of prejudice*. New York: Anchor Books.

ALMOND, Gabriel, and Sidney Verba. 1963. *The civic culture: Political attitudes and democracy in five nations*. Princeton: Princeton University Press.

American Humane Association. 1974. *Proceedings of the national conference on the ecology of the surplus dog and cat problem*. May 21–23. Denver, Colorado.

American Humane Association. 1976. *Proceedings of the national conference on dog and cat control*. Feb. 3–5. Denver, Colorado.

American jurisprudence: A modern comprehensive statement of American law: State and federal. 1962. 2d ed. San Francisco: Bancroft-Whitney.

American jurisprudence proof of facts annotated. 1959. Vol. 1. San Francisco: Bancroft-Whitney.

The American Scholar. 1976. Social science: The public disenchantment—A symposium. Summer.

ANDERSON, Elin L. 1937. *We Americans: A study of cleavage in an American city*. Cambridge: Harvard University Press.

ANDERSON, Robert K., Benjamin L. Hart, Lynette A. Hart, eds. 1984. *The pet connection; Its influence on our health and quality of life*. Minneapolis: University of Minnesota, Center to Study Human-Animal Relationships and Environments.

ANDERSON, R. S., ed. 1975. *Pet animals and society*. Baltimore: Williams and Wilkins.

ANTHONY, E. J. 1957. An experimental approach to the psychopathology of child-hood: Encopresis. *British Journal of Medical Psychology* 30: 146–175.

APTE, Mahadev L. 1985. *Humor and laughter: An anthropological approach.* Ithaca: Cornell University Press.

ARCHER, John. 1979. Behavioural aspects of fear. In *Fear in animals and man*, ed. W. Sluckin, pp. 56–85. New York: Van Nostrand Reinhold.

ARIÉS, Philippe. 1962. *Centuries of childhood: A social history of family life.* New York: Vintage Books.

ARKOW, Philip S., and Shelby Dow, 1984. The ties that do not bind: A study of the human-animal bonds that fail. In *The pet connection: Its influence on our health and quality of life*, ed. Robert K. Anderson, Benjamin L. Hart, and Lynette A. Hart, pp. 348–354. Minneapolis: University of Minnesota, Center to Study Human-Animal Relationships and Environments.

ASHLEY, Kathleen M. 1982. The guiler beguiled: Christ and Satan as theological tricksters in medieval religious literature. *Criticism: A Quarterly for Literature and the Arts* 14 (2, Spring): 126–137.

AUERBACH, Nina. 1982. *Woman and the demon: The life of a Victorian myth.* Cambridge: Harvard University Press.

AVERILL, James R. 1980. A constructivist view of emotion. In *Theories of emotion*, ed. R. Plutchik and H. Kellerman, pp. 305–339. New York: Academic Press.

BABCOCK, Barbara A., ed. 1979. *The reversible world: Symbolic inversion in art and society.* Ithaca: Cornell University Press.

BABCOCK, Barbara A. 1975. "A tolerated margin of mess": Trickster and his tales reconsidered. *Journal of the Folklore Institute* 11 (3, Mar.): 147–186.

BAKER, Russell. 1981. The unwelcome wagon. *The New York Times*, May 6, p. A31.

BARCHAS, Patricia R., ed. 1984. *Social hierarchies: Essays toward a sociophysiological perspective.* Westport, Conn.: Greenwood Press.

BARCHAS, Patricia R., and Sally P. Mendoza, eds. 1984. *Social cohesion: Essays toward a sociophysiological perspective.* Westport, Conn.: Greenwood Press.

BARON, Robert A. 1980. Olfaction and human social behavior: Effects of pleasant scents on physical aggression. *Basic and Applied Social Psychology* 1 (2): 163–172.

BARON, Robert A. 1981. Olfaction and human social behavior: Effects of a pleasant scent on attraction and social perception. *Personality and Social Psychology Bulletin* 7, 4 (Dec.): 611–616.

BARTH, Fredrik. 1969. *Ethnic groups and boundaries: The social organization of cultural difference.* Boston: Little, Brown.

BARTHES, Roland. [1951] 1972. *Mythologies.* New York: Hill and Wang.

BARTHES, Roland. [1967] 1983. *The fashion system.* New York: Hill and Wang.

BARTHES, Roland. 1968. *Writing degree zero* [1953] and *Elements of semiology* [1964] (published in one book). Boston: Beacon Press.

BARTHES, Roland. 1979. *The Eiffel Tower and other mythologies.* New York: Hill and Wang.

BATTEAU, Allen. 1982. Mosbys and broomsedge: The semantics of class in an Appalachian kinship system. *American Ethnologist* 9 (3, Aug.): 445–466.

BAUN, Mara M., Nancy Bergstrom, Nancy F. Langston, and Linda Thoma. 1984. Physiological effects of petting dogs: Influences of attachment. In *The pet connection: Its influence on our health and quality of life*, ed. Robert K. Anderson, Benjamin L. Hart, and Lynette A. Hart, pp. 162–170. Minneapolis: University of Minnesota, Center to Study Human-Animal Relationships and Environments.

BEAGLEHOLE, Ernst. 1931. *Property: A study in social psychology*. London: Allen and Unwin.

BEAN, Susan S. 1978. *Symbolic and pragmatic semantics*. Chicago: University of Chicago Press.

BECK, Alan M. 1974a. The dog: America's sacred cow? *Nation's Cities*, 12 (2, Feb.): 29–35.

BECK, Alan M. 1974b. The experience of U. S. cities. In *Pets and society: An emerging municipal issue*, pp. 57–59. Canadian Federation of Humane Societies, First Canadian Symposium, Toronto.

BECK, Alan M., and Aaron H. Katcher. 1983. *Between pets and people: The importance of animal companionship*. New York: G. P. Putnam

BECK, Alan M., and Aaron H. Katcher. 1984. A new look at pet-facilitated therapy. *Journal of the American Veterinary Medical Association* 184 (4, Feb.): 414–421.

BECK, Alan M., and N. Marshall Meyers. 1984. The pet owner experience. Paper presented at meeting "Allergies to animals in the home and workplace." National Institute of Allergy and Infectious Diseases, Washington, D.C. Mimeo.

BECKER, Howard. 1963. *Outsiders*. New York: Free Press of Glencoe.

BEER, William Reed. 1982. *Househusbands: Men and housework in American families*. South Hadley, Mass.: Bergin.

BEIDELMAN, Thomas O. 1978. Review, *The reversible world*, edited by Barbara A. Babcock, *Anthropos* 73: 934–936.

BEIDELMAN, Thomas O. 1980. The moral imagination of the Kaguru: Some thoughts on tricksters, translation and comparative analysis. *American Ethnologist* 7 (1): 27–42.

BEMPORAD, Jules R., Richard A. Kresch, Russell Asnes, Arnold Wilson. 1978. Chronic neurotic encopresis as a paradigm of a multifactorial psychiatric disorder. *The Journal of Nervous and Mental Disease* 166 (7): 472–479.

BENEDICT, Ruth. 1946. *The chrysanthemum and the sword: Patterns of Japanese culture*. Boston: Houghton Mifflin.

BENNING, Lee E. 1976. *The pet profiteers: The exploitation of pet owners—and pets—in America*. New York: Quadrangle.

BEN-YEHUDA, Nachman. 1985. *Deviance and moral boundaries: Witchcraft, the occult, science fiction, deviant sciences and scientists*. Chicago: University of Chicago Press.

BERG, Ivar, Marcia Freedman, and Michael Freeman. 1978. *Managers and work reform: A limited engagement*. New York: The Free Press.

BERGER, Bennett. 1960. *Working class suburb*. Berkeley: University of California Press.

BERGER, Bennett. 1971. *Looking for America: Essays on youth, suburbia, and other American obsessions*. Englewood Cliffs, N.J.: Prentice-Hall.

BERGER, Bennett. 1981. *The survival of a counterculture: Ideological work and everyday life among rural communards*. Berkeley: University of California Press.

BERGER, Peter, and Thomas Luckmann. [1966] 1967. *The social construction of reality*. New York: Doubleday.

BERK, Sarah Fenstermaker. 1980. The household as workplace: Wives, husbands, and children. In *New space for women*, ed. Gerda R. Wekerle, Rebecca Peterson, and David Morley, pp. 65–82, Boulder: Westview Press.

BERLYNE, Daniel E. 1960. *Conflict, arousal, and curiosity*. New York: McGraw-Hill.

BERNHEIMER, Richard. 1952. *Wild men in the middle ages*. Cambridge: Harvard University Press.

BERSCHEID, Ellen, and William Graziano. 1979. The initiation of social relations and interpersonal attraction. In *Social exchange in developing relationships*, ed. Robert L. Burgess and Ted L. Huston, pp. 31–60, New York: Academic Press.

BERSCHEID, Ellen, K. Dion, E. Walster, and G. W. Walster. 1971. Physical attractiveness and dating choice: A test on the matching hypothesis. *Journal of Experimental Social Psychology* 7: 173–189.

BERSCHEID, Ellen, and E. Walster. 1984. Physical attractiveness. *Advances in Experimental Social Psychology* 7: 158–216.

BESHERS, James. 1962. *Urban social structure*. Glencoe, Ill.: The Free Press.

BIEBER, Irving. 1959. Olfaction in sexual development and adult sexual organization. *American Journal of Psychotherapy* 12 (4, Oct.): 851–859.

BIERCE, Ambrose. 1958. *The devil's dictionary: A selection of the bitter definitions of Ambrose Bierce*. Mt. Vernon, N.Y.: Peter Pauper Press.

BIERCE, Ambrose. 1967. *The enlarged devil's dictionary*, ed. Ernest Jones Hopkins. Garden City, N.Y.: Doubleday.

BLAKELY, Mary Kay. 1981. Do we hate children? The new intolerance for the next (noisy) generation and their mothers. *Vogue* 171 (Dec.): 176, 180.

BLOOM-FESHBACH, Jonathan. 1981. Historical perspectives on the father's role. In *The role of the father in child development*, ed. Michael E. Lamb, pp. 71–112, 2d ed. New York: John Wiley.

BOORSTIN, Daniel. 1973. *The Americans: The democratic experience*. New York: Random House.

BORCHELT, Peter, Randall Lockwood, Alan M. Beck, Victoria L. Voith. 1983. Attacks by packs of dogs involving predation on human beings. *Public Health Reports* 98 (1, Jan.-Feb.): 57–66.

BOSSARD, J. H. S. 1944. The mental hygiene of owning a dog. *Mental Hygiene* 28: 408–413.

BOSSARD, J. H. S. 1950. I wrote about dogs: A mental hygiene note. *Mental Hygiene* 34: 385–390.

The Boston Globe. 1981. Lead editorial: Handicapped neighbors. Oct. 21, p. 14.

BOTT, Elizabeth J. 1957. *Family and social network*. London: Tavistock.

BOUISSAC, Paul. 1976. *Circus and culture: A semiotic approach*. Bloomington: Indiana University Press.

BOURDIEU, Pierre. 1966. The sentiment of honour in Kabyle society. In *Honour and shame: The values of Mediterranean society*, ed. J. G. Peristiany, pp. 193–241. Chicago: University of Chicago Press.

BOURDIEU, Pierre. [1972] 1977. *Outline of a theory of practice*. Cambridge: Cambridge University Press.

BOURKE, John G. 1891. *Scatologic rites of all nations*. Washington, D.C.: W. H. Lowdermilk.

BOWLBY, John. 1969. *Attachment and loss*. Vol. 1, *Attachment*. New York: Basic Books.

BOWLBY, John. 1973. *Attachment and loss*. Vol. 2, *Separation—Anxiety and anger*. New York: Basic Books.

BOWLBY, John. 1982. *Attachment and loss*. Vol. 3, *Loss and depression*. New York: Basic Books.

BRACEY, Howard. 1964. *Neighbours: On new estates and subdivisions in England and USA*. Baton Rouge: Louisiana State University Press.

BRAIN, Robert. 1977. *Friends and lovers*. St. Albans, Hertfordshire: Paladin.

BRAZELTON, T. Berry. 1978. *Doctor and child*. New York: Delta.

BREHM, Jack W., and Arthur R. Cohen. 1962. *Explorations in cognitive dissonance*. New York: John Wiley.

BREMNER, Robert H., ed. 1971. *Children and youth in America: A documentary history*. Vol. 2. Cambridge: Harvard University Press.

BRODY, Jane E. 1981a. Removing barriers in relationships with the disabled. *The New York Times*, Dec. 2, p. C13.

BRODY, Jane E. 1981b. Effects of beauty found to run surprisingly deep. *The New York Times*, Sept. 1, p. C1.

BRODY, Jane E. 1982. Biological role of emotional tears emerges through recent studies. *The New York Times*, Aug. 31, p. C1.

BRONSON, G. W. 1972. Infants' reactions to unfamiliar persons and novel objects. *Monographs of the Society for Research in Child Development* 37 (3).

BROOKE, James. 1984. Sanitation art showings brighten workers' image. *The New York Times*, Sept. 10, p. B4.

BROOKS, Andree. 1981. Adults-only enclaves find wider market. *The New York Times*, Oct. 25, Section 8, pp. 1 and 8.

BROWN, L. T., T. G. Shaw, and K. D. Kirkland. 1972. Affection for people as a function of affection for dogs. *Psychological Reports* 31: 957–958.

BROWN, Norman O. 1959. *Life against death: The psychoanalytical meaning of history*. New York: Vintage.

BROWN, Norman O. 1969. *Hermes the thief: The evolution of a myth*. New York: Random House.

BROZAN, Nadine. 1980. Men and housework: Do they or don't they? *The New York Times*, Nov. 1, p. 52.

BRUNER, Edward. 1972. Kin and non-kin. In *Urban anthropology*, ed. Aiden Southall, pp. 373–392. New York: Oxford University Press.

BRUNER, Jerome S. 1957. Going beyond the information given. In *Contemporary approaches to cognition: A symposium held at the University of Colorado*, ed. Jerome S. Bruner, pp. 41–69. Cambridge: Harvard University Press.

BRUNER, Jerome S., J. Goodnow, and G. A. Austin. 1956. *A study of thinking*. New York: John Wiley.

BUCHLER, Justus, ed. [1940] 1955. *Philosophical writings of Peirce*. New York: Dover Publications.

BUCKE, W. F. 1903. Cyno-psychoses: Children's thoughts, reactions, and feelings toward pet dogs. *Pedagogical Seminar* [continued by *Journal of Genetic Psychology*]. 10: 459–513.

BURNHAM, David. 1984. U.S. agencies to get direct link to credit records. *The New York Times*, Apr. 8, p. 23.

BURNS, Susan. 1978. Paws on the pavement: A look at city pets. *Animals* 3 (Feb.): 26–31.

CAILLOIS, Roger. 1961. *Man, play, and games*. Glencoe, Ill.: The Free Press.

CAINE, Lynn. 1974. *Widow*. New York: Bantam Books.

CAMPBELL, John K. 1964. *Honour, family, and patronage: A study of institutions and moral values in a Greek mountain community*. Oxford: Clarendon Press.

CAPLOVITZ, David. 1974. *Consumers in trouble: A study of debtors in default*. New York: The Free Press.

CAPLOVITZ, David. 1977. Testimony for *Hearings on the Fair Debt Collection Practices Act*, pp. 237–245. U.S. Congress. Senate. Subcommittee on Consumer Affairs of the Committee on Banking, Housing, and Urban Affairs. 95th Cong., 1st sess.

CAPLOW, Theodore, Howard M. Bahr, Bruce A. Chadwick, Reuben Hill, Margaret Holmes Williamson. 1982. *Middletown families: Fifty years of change and continuity*. Minneapolis: University of Minnesota Press.

CASSON, Ronald W. 1983. Schemata in cognitive anthropology. *Annual Review of Anthropology*, ed. Bernard J. Siegel, Alan R. Beals, Stephen J. Tyler, Vol. 12, pp. 429–462. Palo Alto: Annual Reviews.

CHAMBERLAIN, Tony. 1981. Of a fence, a Yankee and a long-lost family feud. *The Boston Globe*, Aug. 16, pp. 29 and 33.

CHARLESWORTH, William R. 1974. General issues in the study of fear. In *The origins of fear*, ed. Michael Lewis and Leonard A. Rosenblum, pp. 262–268. New York: John Wiley.

CHARSLEY, S. R. 1974. The formation of ethnic groups. In *Urban ethnicity*, ed. Abner Cohen, pp. 337–368. London: Tavistock.

CHODOROW, Nancy. 1978. *The reproduction of mothering: Psychoanalysis and the sociology of gender*. Berkeley: University of California Press.

CLARKE-STEWART, K. Alison. 1980. The father's contribution to children's cognitive and social development in early childhood. In *The father-infant relationship: Observational studies in the family setting*, ed. Frank A. Pederson, pp. 116–146. New York: Praeger.

COLBY, Benjamin N., James W. Fernandez, David B. Kronenfeld. 1981. Toward a convergence of cognitive and symbolic anthropology. *American Ethnologist* 8 (3, Aug.): 422–450.

COLLINS, Glenn. 1986. Insensitivity to the disabled. *The New York Times*, Aug. 11, p. A17.

CORBIN, Alain. 1986. *The foul and the fragrant: Odor and the French social imagination*. Cambridge: Harvard University Press.

COTTON, Nancy S. 1983. The development of self-esteem and self-esteem regulation. In *The development and sustenance of self-esteem in childhood*, ed. John E. Mack and Steven L. Ablon, pp. 122–150. New York: International Universities Press.

COX, Harvey. 1969. *The feast of fools: A theological essay on festival and fantasy*. Cambridge: Harvard University Press.

CRICK, Malcolm. 1976. *Explorations in language and meaning: Towards a semantic anthropology*. New York: John Wiley.

CRICK, Malcolm. 1982. Anthropology of knowledge. In *Annual Review of Anthropology*, ed. Bernard J. Siegel, Alan R. Beals, Stephen A. Tyler, Vol. 11, pp. 287–313. Palo Alto: Annual Reviews.

CULLEN, J. M. S. 1966. Reduction of ambiguity through ritualization. In *A discussion of the ritualizations of behaviour in animals and man*, pp. 363–372. Philosophical Transactions of the Royal Society of London, Series B, Biological Sciences, Vol. 25, No. 772. London.

CULLER, Jonathan. 1975. *Structuralist poetics: Structuralism, linguistics and the study of literature*. Ithaca: Cornell University Press.

CULLER, Jonathan. 1981. *The pursuit of signs: Semiotics, literature, deconstruction*. Ithaca: Cornell University Press.

DARNEAL, Thomas L. 1976. Problems in enforcement and prosecution. In *Proceedings of the national conference on dog and cat control*, pp. 194–198. Feb. 3–5. Denver, Colorado.

DAVIS, Murray S. [1983] 1985. *Smut: Erotic reality/obscene ideology*. Chicago: University of Chicago Press.

DAVIS, Nanette J. 1978. Review, *Implicit meanings: Essays in anthropology* by Mary Douglas. *The Sociological Quarterly* 19: 362–364.

DEAUX, Kay. 1985. Sex and gender. In *Annual Review of Psychology*, ed. Mark R. Rosenzweig and Lyman W. Porter, Vol. 36, pp. 49–81. Palo Alto: Annual Reviews.

DEAUX, Kay, and L. L. Lewis. 1984. The structure of gender stereotypes: Interrelationships among components and gender label. *Journal of Personality and Social Psychology* 46: 991–1004.

DECROW, Karen. 1986. Letter. *The New York Times*, Dec. 29, p. A20.

DEVEREUX, George. 1967. *From anxiety to method in the behavioral sciences*. The Hague: Mouton.

DILLMAN, Don A., Kenneth R. Tremblay, Jr., and Joye J. Dillman. 1979. Influence of housing norms and personal characteristics on stated housing preferences. *Housing and Society* 6 (1): 2–19.

DIMAGGIO, Paul. 1979. Review essay: On Pierre Bourdieu. *American Journal of Sociology* 84 (6): 1460–1474.

DINNERSTEIN, Dorothy. [1976] 1977. *The mermaid and the minotaur: Sexual arrangements and human malaise*. New York: Harper Colophon Books.

DOBRINER, William M. 1963. *Class in suburbia*. Englewood Cliffs, N.J.: Prentice-Hall.

DOLENSEK, Emil P., and Barbara Burn. [1976] 1978. *The Penguin book of pets: A practical guide to animal-keeping*. New York: Penguin Books.

DOLLARD, John, and Neal E. Miller. 1950. *Personality and psychotherapy: An analysis in terms of learning, thinking, and culture.* New York: McGraw-Hill.

DOMÍNGUEZ, Virginia R. 1977. Social classification in Creole Louisiana. *American Ethnologist* 4: 589–602.

DOUEK, Ellis. 1974. *The sense of smell and its abnormalities.* London: Churchill Livingstone.

DOUGLAS, Mary. 1966. *Purity and danger: An analysis of concepts of pollution and taboo.* London: Penguin.

DOUGLAS, Mary. [1966] 1970. *Natural symbols: Explorations in cosmology.* New York: Pantheon.

DOUGLAS, Mary. 1968. Pollution. In *International Encyclopedia of the Social Sciences,* pp. 336–342. New York: Macmillan and The Free Press.

DOUGLAS, Mary. 1973. *Rules and meanings: The anthropology of everyday knowledge.* Hammondsworth: Penguin Books.

DOUGLAS, Mary. 1980. Purity and danger revisited. *Times Literary Supplement,* Sept. 19, pp. 1045–1046.

DOWNS, James. 1960. Domestication: An examination of the changing relationships between man and animals. *Kroeber Anthropological Society Papers* 22: 23–60.

DRAPER, Patricia. 1974. Comparative studies of socialization. In *Annual Review of Anthropology,* Vol. 3, ed. Bernard J. Siegel, Alan R. Beals, and Stephen A. Tyler, pp. 263–278. Palo Alto: Annual Reviews.

DRUMMOND, Lee. 1978. The Transatlantic nanny: Notes on a comparative semiotics of the family in English-speaking societies. *American Ethnologist* 5 (1, Feb.): 30–43.

DRUMMOND, Lee. 1980. The cultural continuum: A theory of intersystems. *Man,* n.s. 15: 352–374.

DULLEA, Georgia. 1982. Handicapped pupils join the mainstream. *The New York Times,* Sept. 13, p. B8.

DUMANOSKI, Dianne. 1982. It's more than puppy love. *The Boston Globe Magazine,* Jan. 17, pp. 12–13, 36–45.

DUMONT, Louis. [1966] 1970. *Homo hierarchicus: The caste system and its implications.* Chicago: University of Chicago Press.

DUNDES, Alan. 1966. Here I sit—a study of American latrinalia. *Kroeber Anthropological Society Papers* 28 (34): 91–105.

DUNDES, Alan. 1984. *Life is like a chicken coop ladder: A portrait of German culture through folklore.* New York: Columbia University Press.

DURHAM, William H. 1978. The coevolution of human biology and culture. In *Human behaviour and adaptation,* ed. N. Blurton Jones and V. Reynolds, pp. 11–32. London: Taylor and Francis.

DURKHEIM, Emile. [1915] 1965. *The elementary forms of the religious life.* New York: The Free Press.

ECO, Umberto. 1976. *A theory of semiotics.* Bloomington: Indiana University Press.

EICKLEMAN, Dale. 1979. The political economy of meaning: Review article. *American Ethnologist* 6 (2): 386–393.

ELIAS, Norbert. [1939] 1978. *The civilizing process: The history of manners.* Trans. Edmund Jephcott. New York: Urizen Books.

ELIAS, Norbert, and J. L. Scotson. 1965. *The established and the outsiders: A sociological enquiry into community problems*. London: Frank Cass.

ELLEN, Roy F. 1979. Introductory essay. In *Classifications in their social context*, ed. Roy F. Ellen and David Reason, pp. 1–31. New York: Academic Press.

ELLMAN, Tara. 1976. Fiscal impact studies in a metropolitan context. In *Economic issues in metropolitan growth*, ed. Paul Portney. pp. 8–47. Baltimore: The Johns Hopkins University Press for Resources for the Future.

ELSHTAIN, Jean Bethke. 1981. *Public man, private woman: Women in social and political thought*. Princeton: Princeton University Press.

EL-ZEIN, Abdul Hamid. 1977. Beyond ideology and theology: The search for the anthropology of Islam. In *Annual Review of Anthropology*, ed. Bernard J. Siegel, Alan R. Beals, and Stephen A. Tyler, Vol. 6, pp. 227–254. Palo Alto: Annual Reviews.

ERIKSON, Erik H. 1963. *Childhood and society*. 2d ed. New York: W. W. Norton.

ERIKSON, Erik H. 1968. *Identity: Youth and crisis*. New York: W. W. Norton.

ERIKSON, Kai T. 1966. *Wayward Puritans: A study in the sociology of deviance*. New York: John Wiley.

FABIAN, Johannes. 1983. *Time and the other: How anthropology makes its object*. New York: Columbia University Press.

FABREGA, Horacio, Jr. 1977. Culture, behavior, and the nervous system. In *Annual Review of Anthropology*, ed. Bernard J. Siegel, Alan R. Beals, and Stephen A. Tyler, Vol. 6, pp. 419–455. Palo Alto: Annual Reviews.

FAITHORN, E. 1975. The concept of pollution among the Kafe of the Papua New Guinea highlands. In *Toward an anthropology of women*, ed. R. R. Reiter, pp. 127–140. New York: Monthly Review Press.

FARRELL, Michael P., and Stanley D. Rosenberg. 1981. *Men at midlife*. Boston: Auburn House Publishing.

FEDERAL Trade Commission. 1979. Compliance with the Fair Credit Reporting Act. Division of Credit Practices, Bureau of Consumer Protection, Washington, D.C. 2d ed., March.

FEDERAL Trade Commission. 1980. Final Order Docket No. 8954, in the matter of Equifax, Inc., a corporation (formerly Retail Credit Company, a corporation). Washington, D.C.

FEDERAL Trade Commission. n.d. Know your rights under the Fair Credit Reporting Act: A checklist for consumers. Consumer Bulletin No. 7. Washington, D.C.

FEELEY-HARNIK, Gillian. 1981. *The Lord's table: Eucharist and Passover in early Christianity*. Philadelphia: University of Pennsylvania Press.

FELDMANN, Bruce Max, and Tony H. Carding. 1973. Free-roaming urban pets. *Health Services Reports* 88 (Dec.): 956–962.

FERNANDEZ, James W. 1974. The mission of metaphor in expressive culture. *Current Anthropology* 15 (2): 119–145.

FERNANDEZ, James W. 1979. Strategic nexi: Seventeen (plus or minus two) types of ambiguity in understanding and explaining human behavior. Mimeo. 15 pp.

FESTINGER, Leon. 1957. *The theory of cognitive dissonance*. Palo Alto: Stanford University Press.

FIEDLER, Leslie A. 1978. *Freaks: Myths and images of the secret self.* New York: Simon and Schuster.

FIELD, Tiffany. 1983. Child abuse in monkeys and humans: A comparative perspective. In *Child abuse: The nonhuman primate data,* ed. Martin Reite and Nancy Caine, pp. 151–174. New York: A.R. Liss.

FIRTH, Raymond, Jane Hubert, and Anthony Forge. 1970. *Families and their relatives: Kinship in a middle-class sector of London.* New York: Humanities Press.

FISCHER, Claude S. 1975. The study of urban community and personality. In *Annual Review of Sociology,* ed. Alex Inkeles, James Coleman, and Neil Smelser, Vol. 1, pp. 67–89. Palo Alto: Annual Reviews.

FISCHER, Claude S. 1982. *To dwell among friends: Personal networks in town and city.* Chicago: University of Chicago Press.

FISCHER, John L., and Ann Fischer. 1966. *The New Englanders of Orchard Town, U.S.A.* Six Cultures Series, ed. Beatrice B. Whiting, Vol. 5. New York: John Wiley.

FLETCHER, Susan K. 1981. Holding court for canines. *American Way* (Aug.): 44–48.

FOGLE, Bruce, ed. 1981. *Interrelations between people and pets.* Symposium on the Human-Companion Animal Bond. British Small Animal Veterinary Association. Springfield, Ill.: Charles Thomas.

FONER, Anne. 1979. Ascribed and achieved bases of stratification. In *Annual Review of Sociology,* ed. Alex Inkeles, James Coleman, and Ralph H. Turner, Vol. 5, pp. 219–242. Palo Alto: Annual Reviews.

FOOTE, Nelson N. 1956. A neglected member of the family. *Marriage and Family Living* 18: 213–218.

FOREMAN, Judy. 1980. Men are resisting sweeping changes. *The Boston Globe,* Dec. 23, pp. 19 and 21.

FORER, Lucille K. (with Henry Still). 1976. *The birth order factor: How your personality is influenced by your place in the family.* New York: MacKay.

FOUCAULT, Michel. 1972. *The archeology of knowledge.* London: Tavistock.

FOWLER, Harry. 1965. *Curiosity and exploratory behavior.* New York: Macmillan.

FRANTI, C. E., J. F. Kraus, and N. O. Borhani. 1974. Pet ownership in a suburban-rural area of California: 1970. *Public Health Reports* 89: 473–484.

FREEMAN, Susan Tax. 1970. *Neighbors: The social contract in a Castilian hamlet.* Chicago: University of Chicago Press.

FREUD, Sigmund. [1905] 1953. Fragment of an analysis of a case of hysteria. In *The Standard Edition of the Complete Psychological Works of Sigmund Freud,* V. VII, ed. James Strachey in collaboration with Anna Freud, pp. 3–122. London: Hogarth Press and the Institute of Psychoanalysis.

FREUD, Sigmund. [1908] 1963. Character and anal erotism. In *Character and culture,* ed. Philip Rieff, pp. 27–33. New York: Collier Books.

FREUD, Sigmund. [1913] 1939. The excretory functions in psycho-analysis and folklore. In *Collected papers,* Vol. 5, ed. James Strachey in collaboration with Anna Freud, pp. 88–91. London: Hogarth Press and the Institute of Psychoanalysis.

FREUD, Sigmund. [1917] 1963. On the transformation of instincts with special reference to anal erotism. In *Character and culture,* ed. Philip Rieff, pp. 202–209. New York: Collier Books.

FREUD, Sigmund. [1925] 1939. The resistances to psycho-analysis. In *Collected papers*, Vol. 5, ed. James Strachey in collaboration with Anna Freud, pp. 163–174. London: Hogarth Press and the Institute of Psychoanalysis.

FRIEDL, Ernestine. 1975. *Women and men: An anthropologist's view.* New York: Holt, Rinehart, and Winston.

FRIEDMAN, John Block. 1981. *The monstrous races in medieval art and thought.* Cambridge: Harvard University Press.

FRIEDMANN, Erika, Aaron Katcher, Muzza Eaton, and Bonnie Berger. 1984. Pet ownership and psychological status. In *The pet connection: Its influence on our health and quality of life*, ed. Robert K. Anderson, Benjamin L. Hart, and Lynette A. Hart, pp. 300–308. Minneapolis: University of Minnesota, Center to Study Human-Animal Relationships and Environments.

FRIEDRICH, Paul. 1978. *The meaning of Aphrodite.* Chicago: University of Chicago Press.

FROST, Robert. [1914] 1969. Mending wall. In *The poetry of Robert Frost*, ed. Edward Connery Lathem. New York: Holt, Rinehart, and Winston.

FURTENBERG, Frank. 1966. Industrialization and the American family: A look backward. *American Sociological Review* 31 (June): 325–338.

GALATY, John. 1979. Pollution and pastoral antipraxis: The issue of Maasai inequality. *American Ethnologist* 6: 803–816.

The Gallup Organization. 1981. Survey of women concerning their least favorite household task, conducted for *Parade Magazine*. Aug. 12 pp. Mimeo.

GANS, Herbert J. 1967. *The Levittowners: Ways of life and politics in a new suburban community.* New York: Vintage Books.

GANS, Herbert J., Nathan Glazer, Joseph R. Gusfield, Christopher Jencks, eds. 1979. *On the making of Americans: Essays in honor of David Riesman.* Philadelphia: University of Pennsylvania Press.

GATHORNE-HARDY, Jonathan. 1972. *The rise and fall of the British nanny.* London: Hodder and Stoughton.

GAY, Peter. [1984] 1985. *The bourgeois experience: Victoria to Freud.* Vol. 1, *Education of the senses.* New York: Oxford University Press.

GAYLIN, Willard. 1979. *Feelings: Our vital signs.* New York: Ballantine.

GEERTZ, Clifford. 1973. *The interpretation of cultures: Selected essays.* New York: Basic Books.

GEERTZ, Clifford. 1983. *Local knowledge: Further essays in interpretive anthropology.* New York: Basic Books.

GEERTZ, Clifford. 1984. Anti anti-relativism. *American Anthropologist* 86 (2, June): 263–278.

GEIST, William E. 1981. A suburban tempest: Neighbors riled by in-house apartments. *The New York Times*, Dec. 8, p. B2.

GEIST, William E. 1982a. Child-free living: Cries and screams set aside, deliberately. *The New York Times*, Apr. 13, p. B2.

GEIST, William E. 1982b. Housing a home: Neighbors balk at residence for retarded. *The New York Times*, Feb. 2, p. B2.

GELLES, Richard J. [1978] 1979. Violence toward children in the United States. In *Critical perspectives on child abuse*, ed. Richard Bourne and Eli H. Newberger, pp. 53–66. Lexington, Mass.: Lexington Books.

GELLES, Richard J., and Murray A. Straus. 1979. Violence in the American family. *Journal of Social Issues* 35 (2): 15–39.

GILLIGAN, Carol. 1982. *In a different voice: Psychological theory and women's development*. Cambridge: Harvard University Press.

GILLIGAN, Carol. 1986. Reply. *Signs: Journal of Women in Culture and Society* 11 (2, Winter): 324–333.

GILLIGAN, James. 1976. Psychoanalytic reflections on shame, guilt, and love. In *Moral development and behavior: Theory, research, and social issues*, ed. T. Lickona, pp. 144–158. New York: Holt, Rinehart and Winston.

GOFFMAN, Erving. 1963. *Stigma: Notes on the management of spoiled identity*. Baltimore: Penguin Books.

GOLDFARB, Lewis H. 1979. Privacy, the insurance industry, and the consumer: The FTC's view. In *Privacy and the insurance industry*, ed. Harold D. Skipper, Jr., and Steven N. Weisbart, pp. 151–168. Research Monograph No. 83, College of Business Administration, Georgia State University, Atlanta.

GOODE, William J. 1978. *The celebration of heroes: Prestige as a control system*. Berkeley: University of California Press.

GOODMAN, Jack, ed. 1943. *The fireside book of dog stories*. New York: Simon and Schuster.

GOULD, Stephen Jay. 1981. *The mismeasure of man*. New York: W. W. Norton.

GRAY, Jeffrey A. 1971. *The psychology of fear and stress*. New York: McGraw-Hill.

GRAY, Jeffrey A. 1982. *The neuropsychology of anxiety: An inquiry into the functions of the septo-hippocampal system*. New York: Oxford University Press.

GROSS, Beatrice, and Ronald Gross, eds. 1977. *The children's rights movement*. Garden City: Anchor/Doubleday.

GRUBER, Howard E., and J. Jacques Vonéche, eds. 1977. *The essential Piaget*. New York: Basic Books.

GULLESTAD, Marianne. 1986. Symbolic "fences" in urban Norwegian neighbourhoods. *Ethnos* 51 (I–II): 52–70.

HAMBURG, David A. 1963. Emotions in the perspective of human evolution. In *Expression of the emotions in man*, ed. Peter H. Knapp, pp. 300–317. New York: International Universities Press.

HAMILTON, David L., ed. 1981. *Cognitive processes in stereotyping and intergroup behavior*. Hillsdale, N.J.: Erlbaum.

HAMILTON, Vernon. 1983. Cognition and stress: An information processing model. In *Handbook of stress: Theoretical and clinical aspects*, ed. Leo Goldberger and Shlomo Breznitz, pp. 105–120. New York: The Free Press.

HANDWERKER, W. Penn, and Paul V. Crosbie. 1982. Sex and dominance. *American Anthropologist* 84 (1, Mar.): 97–104.

HARRIS, Louis, and Associates, Inc. 1984. *The road after 1984: The impact of technology on society*. New Haven: Southern New England Telephone.

HARRIS, Louis, and Associates, Inc., and Alan F. Westin. 1980. The dimensions of privacy: A national opinion research survey of attitudes toward privacy. In *Hearings on the Fair Financial Information Practices Act: S. 1928*, Part I–Insurance, Title V, pp. 480–567. U.S. Congress. Senate. Subcommittee on Consumer Affairs of the Committee on Banking, Housing, and Urban Affairs. 96th Cong., 2d sess.

HAUSER, Arnold. [1974] 1982. *The sociology of art.* Trans. Kenneth J. Northcott. Chicago: University of Chicago Press.

HAVILAND, John B. 1977. *Gossip, reputation, and knowledge in Zinacantan.* Chicago: University of Chicago Press.

HAWKES, Terence. 1977. *Structuralism and semiotics.* Berkeley: University of California Press.

HAYDEN, Dolores. 1981. *The grand domestic revolution: A history of feminist designs for American homes, neighborhoods, and cities.* Cambridge: The MIT Press.

HEBB, Donald O. 1946. On the nature of fear. *Psychology Reviews* 53: 259–276.

HEBB, Donald O. 1949. *Organization of behavior.* New York: John Wiley.

HEBB, Donald O. 1955. Drives and the C.N.S. (Conceptual Nervous System). *Psychological Reviews* 62 (4): 243–254.

HERZFELD, Michael. 1980a. Honour and shame: Problems in the comparative analysis of moral systems. *Man,* n.s. 15: 339–351.

HERZFELD, Michael. 1980b. On the ethnography of "prejudice" in an exclusive community. *Ethnic Groups* 2: 283–305.

HERZFELD, Michael. 1981. Meaning and morality: A semiotic approach to evil eye accusations in a Greek village. *American Ethnologist* 8 (3, Aug.): 560–574.

HERZFELD, Michael. 1983. Signs in the field: Prospects and issues for semiotic ethnography. *Semiotica* 46: 99–106.

HIGHAM, John. 1963. Strangers in the land: Patterns of American nativism 1860–1925. Rev. ed. New York: Atheneum.

HIGHAM, John. 1975. *Send these to me: Jews and other immigrants in urban America.* New York: Atheneum.

HILL, Frederick, and William Michelson. 1981. Towards a geography of urban children and youth. In *Geography and the urban environment,* ed. D. T. Herbert and R. J. Johnston, pp. 193–228. New York: John Wiley.

HINDS, Michael deCourcy. 1980. Unwelcome guests: Infants in public places. *The New York Times,* Nov. 29, p. 48.

HOCART, A. M. [1936] 1970. *Kings and councillors: An essay in the comparative anatomy of human society.* Chicago: University of Chicago Press.

HODGE, Guy. 1976. The reign of dogs and cats; or, contemporary concepts of animal control. International City Managers Association, Management Information Report, Vol. 8, No. 10, Oct., pp. 1–20.

HOLMES, John. 1975. *The family dog: Its choice and training; a practical guide for every dog owner.* 7th ed. New York: Arco Publishing.

HUIZENGA, Judith N. 1983. The relationship of self-esteem and narcissism. In *The development and sustenance of self-esteem in childhood,* ed. John E. Mack and Steven L. Ablon, pp. 151–162. New York: International Universities Press.

HULL, Raymond. 1972. *Man's best fiend.* New York: Hippocrene Books.

ISHIGE, Naomichi. 1977. Roasting dog (or a substitute) in an earth over: An unusual method of preparation from Ponape. In *The anthropologists' cookbook,* ed. Jessica Kuper, pp. 203–205. New York: Universe Books.

JABLOW, Alta. 1979. The many faces of trickster. *Anthropology* 3 (1 and 2, May–Dec.): 59–71.

JANEWAY, Elizabeth. 1980. *Powers of the weak.* New York: Alfred A. Knopf.

JONES, Barbara A. 1981. *The psychology of the human/companion animal bond: An annotated bibliography.* Center for the Interaction of Animals and Society, School of Veterinary Medicine, University of Pennsylvania.

JONES, Barbara A., and Alan M. Beck. 1984. Unreported dog bite and attitudes toward dogs. In *The pet connection: Its influence on our health and quality of life*, ed. Robert K. Anderson, Benjamin L. Hart, and Lynette A. Hart, pp. 355–364. Minneapolis: University of Minnesota, Center to Study Human-Animal Relationships and Environments.

JONES, Edward E., Amerigo Farina, Albert H. Hastorf, Hazel Markus, Dale T. Miller, Robert A. Scott, and Rita de S. French. 1984. *Social stigma: The psychology of marked relationships.* New York: W. H. Freeman.

JORDAN, James William. 1975. An ambivalent relationship: Dog and human in the folk culture of the rural South. *Appalachian Journal* 2 (3, Spring): 238–248.

JOSEPH, R. 1956. *A letter to the man who killed my dog.* New York: Frederick Fell.

KAGAN, Jerome. 1971. *Change and continuity in infancy.* New York: John Wiley.

KAGAN, Jerome. 1974. Discrepancy, temperament, and infant distress. In *The origins of fear*, ed. Michael Lewis and Leonard A. Rosenblum, pp. 229–248. New York: John Wiley.

KAGAN, Jerome. 1981. Universals in human development. In *Handbook of cross-cultural human development*, ed. Ruth H. Monroe, Robert L. Monroe, Beatrice B. Whiting, pp. 53–62. New York: Garland STPM Press.

KAGAN, Jerome, and Steven R. Tulkin. 1971. Social class differences in child rearing during the first year. In *The origins of human social relations*, ed. H. R. Schaffer, pp. 165–186. New York: Academic Press.

KANTER, Rosabeth Moss. 1972. *Commitment and community: Communes and utopias in sociological perspective.* Cambridge: Harvard University Press.

KATZ, Irwin. 1981. *Stigma: A social psychological analysis.* Hillsdale, N.J.: Erlbaum.

KATZNELSON, Ira. 1981. *City trenches: Urban politics and the patterning of class in the United States.* New York: Pantheon.

KEATS, John. 1956. *The crack in the picture window.* Boston: Houghton Mifflin.

KEESING, Roger M. 1974. Theories of culture. In *Annual Review of Anthropology*, Vol. 3. ed. Bernard J. Siegel, Alan R. Beals, and Stephen A. Tyler, pp. 73–98. Palo Alto: Annual Reviews.

KELLERT, Stephen R. 1980. American attitudes toward and knowledge of animals: An update. *International Journal of Studies of Animal Problems* 1 (2): 87–119.

KELLERT, Stephen R., and Joyce K. Berry. 1980. *American attitudes, knowledge and behaviors toward wildlife and natural habitats, Phase III: Knowledge, affection and basic attitudes toward animals in American society.* Yale University, School of Forestry and Environmental Studies.

KEMP, Evan J., Jr. 1981. Aiding the disabled: No pity, please. *The New York Times*, Sept. 3, p. A19.

KENISTON, Kenneth. 1977. Do Americans *really* like children? In *Environmental issues: Family impact*, ed. Evelyn Eldridge and Nancy Meredith, pp. 235–249. Minneapolis: Burgess.

KERÉNYI, Karl. 1976. *Hermes, guide of souls.* Trans. Murray Stein. Zurich: Spring Publications.

KERMODE, Frank. 1979. *The genesis of secrecy*. Cambridge: Harvard University Press.

KINNEY, James R. 1966. *How to raise a dog in the city and in the suburbs*. 3d ed. New York: Simon and Schuster.

KIRA, Alexander. 1966. *The bathroom: Criteria for design*. New York: Bantam Books for Cornell University.

KLAPP, Orrin E. 1962. *Heroes, villains, and fools: The changing American character*. Englewood Cliffs, N.J.: Prentice-Hall.

KLAPP, Orrin E. 1971. *Social types: Process, structure and ethos*. San Diego: Aegis Publishing.

KLINEBERG, Otto. 1968. Prejudice. I. The concept. In *International Encyclopedia of the Social Sciences*, Vol. 12, pp. 439–448. New York: Macmillan and The Free Press.

KONNER, Melvin. 1981. Evolution of human behavior development. In *Handbook of cross-cultural human development*, ed. Ruth H. Monroe, Robert L. Monroe, Beatrice B. Whiting, pp. 3–51. New York: Garland STPM Press.

KONNER, Melvin. 1982. *The tangled wing: Biological constraints on the human spirit*. New York: Holt, Rinehart, and Winston.

KOTELCHUCK, Milton. 1976. The infant's relationship to the father: Experimental evidence. In *The role of the father in child development*, ed. Michael E. Lamb, pp. 329–394. New York: John Wiley.

KRAUSE, Harry D. 1977. *Family law in a nutshell*. St. Paul: West Publishing.

KUHN, Reinhard. 1982. *Corruption in paradise: The child in Western literature*. Hanover, N.H.: University Press of New England for Brown University Press.

LAKOFF, George, and Mark Johnson. 1980. *Metaphors we live by*. Chicago: University of Chicago Press.

LAMB, Michael E. 1981. Fathers and child development: An integrative overview. In *The role of the father in child development*, ed. Michael E. Lamb, pp. 1–70. 2d ed. New York: John Wiley.

LAMB, Michael E., and Abraham Sagi, ed. 1983. *Fatherhood and family policy*. Hillsdale, N.J.: Erlbaum.

LAMENDELLA, John T. 1980. Neurofunctional foundations of symbolic communication. In *Symbol as sense: New approaches to the analysis of meaning*, ed. Mary L. Foster and Stanley H. Brandes, pp. 147–174. New York: Academic Press.

LANDERS, Ann. 1983. Leash laws. *The Boston Globe*, Mar. 20, p. B25.

LANGNESS, L. L. 1976. Discussion. In *Man and woman in the New Guinea Highlands*, ed. Paula Brown and Georgeda Buchbinder, pp. 96–106. Special Publication 8. Washington, D.C.: American Anthropological Association.

LARGEY, Gale Peter, and David R. Watson. 1972. The sociology of odors. *American Journal of Sociology* 77 (6): 1021–1034.

LASLETT, Barbara. 1973. The family as a public and private institution: An historical perspective. *Journal of Marriage and the Family* 35 (3, Aug.): 480–492.

LASLETT, Peter. [1972] 1974. Introduction: The history of the family. In *Household and family in past time*, ed. Peter Laslett with the assistance of Richard Wall, pp. 1–73. Cambridge: Cambridge University Press.

LAUMANN, Edward O. 1973. *Bonds of pluralism: The form and substance of urban social networks*. New York: John Wiley.

LAWICK-GOODALL, Jane van. 1971. Some aspects of mother-infant relationships in a group of wild chimpanzees. In *The origins of human social relations*, ed. H. R. Schaffer, pp. 115–128. New York: Academic Press.

LEACH, Edmund. [1964] 1972. Anthropological aspects of language: Animal categories and verbal abuse. In *Mythology*. ed. Pierre Maranda, pp. 39–67. Baltimore: Penguin Books.

LEACH, Edmund. 1976. *Culture and communication: The logic by which symbols are connected*. Cambridge: Cambridge University Press.

LEACH, Penelope. [1976] 1983. *Babyhood*. 2d ed. New York: Alfred A. Knopf.

LEACH, Penelope. [1978] 1982. *Your baby and child: From birth to age five*. New York: Alfred A. Knopf.

LEHMAN, F. K. 1967. Ethnic categories in Burma and the theory of social systems. In *Southeast Asian tribes, minorities, and nations*, ed. Peter Kunstadter, pp. 93–124. Princeton: Princeton University Press.

LEMERT, Charles C. 1972. Invisible religion: An empirical appraisal. Ph.D. diss. Harvard University.

LEONARD, John. 1978. Private lives. *The New York Times*, Dec. 20, p. C10.

LEONARD, John. 1979. Private lives. *The New York Times*, Jan. 17, p. C14.

LERNER, Max. 1957. *America as a civilization*. New York: Simon and Schuster.

LEVINE, Donald N. 1979. Simmel at a distance: On the history and systematics of the sociology of the stranger. In *Strangers in African societies*, ed. William A. Shack and Elliott P. Skinner, pp. 21–36. Berkeley: University of California Press.

LEVINE, Donald N. 1985. *The flight from ambiguity: Essays in social and cultural theory*. Chicago: University of Chicago Press.

LEVINE, Robert A., and Donald T. Campbell. 1972. *Ethnocentrism: Theories of conflict, ethnic attitudes, and group behavior*. New York: John Wiley.

LÉVI-STRAUSS, Claude. 1962. *The savage mind*. Chicago: University of Chicago Press.

LÉVI-STRAUSS, Claude. 1963. *Structural anthropology*. New York: Basic Books.

LEVY, Robert I. 1983. Introduction: Self and emotion. *Ethos* 11 (3): 128–134.

LEVY, Robert I. 1984. Emotions, knowing, and culture. In *Culture theory: Essays on mind, self, and emotion*, ed. Richard A. Shweder and Robert A. LeVine, pp. 214–237. Cambridge: Cambridge University Press.

LEWIS, Michael, Candice Feiring, and Marsha Weinraub. 1981. The father as a member of the child's social network. In *The role of the father in child development*, ed. Michael E. Lamb, pp. 259–294. 2d ed. New York: John Wiley.

LICHTMAN, Allan J., and Joan R. Challinor, eds. 1979. *Kin and communities: Families in America*. Washington, D.C.: Smithsonian Institution Press.

LINDENFELD, F., and J. Rothschild-Whitt. 1979. *Workplace democracy and social change*. Boston: Porter Sargent.

LINDSEY, Robert. 1978. "Adults only" housing policies appear to be spreading. *The New York Times*, May 4, p. A20.

LINOWES, David F. 1980. Testimony and report, "A research survey of privacy and big business." In *Hearings on the Fair Financial Information Practices Act*:

S. 1928, Part II–Credit, Titles I and II, pp. 156–216. U.S. Congress. Senate. Subcommittee on Consumer Affairs of the Committee on Banking, Housing, and Urban Affairs, 96th Cong., 2d sess.

LITTLEJOHN, James. 1973. Temne right and left: An essay on the choreography of everyday life. In *Right and left: Essays on dual symbolic classification*, ed. Rodney Needham, pp. 288–298. Chicago: University of Chicago Press.

LITWAK, Eugene, and I. Szelenyi. 1971. Kinship and other primary groups. In *Sociology of the family*, ed. Michael Anderson, pp. 149–163. London: Penguin.

LLOYD, Geoffrey. 1973. Right and left in Greek philosophy. In *Right and left: Essays on dual symbolic classification*, ed. Rodney Needham, pp. 167–186. Chicago: University of Chicago Press.

LOEW, Frank M., and A. F. Fraser. 1977. The anti-social behavior of urban dogs. *Applied Animal Ethology* 3: 101–104.

LOFLAND, Lynn. 1973. *A world of strangers*. New York: Basic Books.

LOPATA, Helena Znaniecki. 1971. *Occupation: Housewife*. New York: Oxford University Press.

LOPATA, Helena Znaniecki. 1973. *Widowhood in an American city*. Cambridge, Mass.: Schenkman Publishing.

LOPATA, Helena Znaniecki. 1979. *Women as widows: Support systems*. New York: Elsevier.

LORENZ, Konrad. 1954. *Man meets dog*. London: Methuen.

LOUDON, J. B. 1978. On body products. In *The anthropology of the body*, ed. John Blocking, pp. 161–178. New York: Academic Press.

LUTZ, Catherine. 1986. Emotion, thought, and estrangement: Emotion as a cultural category. *Cultural Anthropology* 1 (3, Aug.): 287–309.

LUTZ, Catherine and Geoffrey M. White. 1986. Anthropology of emotions. In *Annual Review of Anthropology*, 15, eds. Bernard J. Siegel, Alan R. Beals, and Stephen A. Tyler, pp. 405–436.

LYNCH, James G. 1977. *The broken heart: The medical consequences of loneliness*. New York: Basic Books.

LYNCH, James G. 1985. *Language of the heart: The body's response to human dialogue*. New York: Basic Books.

LYND, Helen M. 1958. *On shame and the search for identity*. New York: Harcourt Brace.

LYND, Robert S., and Helen Merrell Lynd. 1929. *Middletown*. New York: Harcourt, Brace, and World.

LYND, Robert S., and Helen Merrell Lynd. 1937. *Middletown in transition: A study in cultural conflicts*. New York: Harcourt, Brace, and World.

LYONS, John. 1973. Structuralism and linguistics. In *Structuralism: An introduction —Wolfson College lectures 1972*, ed. David Robey, pp. 5–19. Oxford: Clarendon Press.

McCLELLAND, David C., Carol A. Constantian, David A. Pilon, and Carolyn Stone. 1982. Effects of child-rearing practices on adult maturity. In *The development of social maturity*, ed. David C. McClelland, pp. 209–249. New York: Irvington Publishers.

MacDonald, John D. 1977. *Condominium.* New York: Fawcett Crest.

Mack, Alison. 1978. *Toilet learning: The picture book technique for children and parents.* Boston: Little, Brown.

Mack, John E. 1983. Self-esteem and its development: An overview. In *The development and sustenance of self-esteem in childhood,* ed. John E. Mack and Steven L. Ablon, pp. 1–42. New York: International Universities Press.

Mack, John E., and Steven L. Ablon, eds. 1983. *The development and sustenance of self-esteem in childhood.* New York: International Universities Press.

McLaughlin, Marsha Morrow, and Suzanne Vaupel. 1975. Constitutional right of privacy and investigative consumer reports: Little Brother is watching you. *Hastings Constitutional Law Quarterly* 2 (Summer): 773–828.

McLaughlin, Terence. 1971. *Dirt: A social history as seen through the uses and abuses of dirt.* New York: Stein and Day.

McMillan, Carol. 1982. *Women, reason and nature.* Princeton: Princeton University Press.

McShane, William P., Paul Menaker, Roger P. Roess, John C. Falcocchio. 1980. *Transit ridership in an intense travel environment: Some observations.* Transportation Research Board, Commission on Sociotechnical Systems. National Academy of Sciences, Washington, D.C.

Mahler, Margaret S. 1963. Thoughts about development and individuation. In *Psychoanalytic study of the child,* Vol. 18, pp. 307–324. New York: International Universities Press.

Mahler, Margaret S. 1965. On the significance of the normal separation-individuation phase. In *Drives, affects, behavior: Essays in memory of Marie Bonaparte,* ed. Max Schur, pp. 161–169. New York: International Universities Press.

Mahler, Margaret S. 1972. On the first three subphases of the separation-individuation process. *International Journal of Psycho-Analysis* 53: 333–338.

Makarius, Laura. 1970. Ritual clowns and symbolical behaviour. *Diogenes* (69): 44–73.

Makarius, Laura. 1973. The crime of Manabozo. *American Anthropologist* 75 (2): 663–675.

Maltz, Daniel N., and Ruth A. Borker. 1982. A cultural approach to male-female miscommunication. In *Language and social identity,* ed. John J. Gumperz, pp. 195–216. Cambridge: Cambridge University Press.

Mandler, George. 1975. *Mind and emotion.* New York: John Wiley.

Mandler, George. 1983. Stress and thought processes. In *Handbook of stress: Theoretical and clinical aspects,* ed. Leo Goldberger and Shlomo Breznitz, pp. 88–104. New York: The Free Press.

Mannheim, Karl. [1928] 1952. The problem of generations. In *Essays in the sociology of knowledge,* ed. Paul Kecskemeti, pp. 276–313. London: Routledge and Kegan Paul.

Marcus, George E. and Michael M. J. Fischer. 1986. *Anthropology as cultural critique: An experimental moment in the human sciences.* Chicago: University of Chicago Press.

Marriott, McKim. 1976. Hindu transactions: Diversity without dualism. In *Transaction and meaning: Directions in the anthropology of exchange and symbolic behavior*, ed. Bruce Kapferer, pp. 109–142. Philadelphia: Institute for the Study of Human Issues.

MARRIOTT, McKim, and Ronald B. Inden. 1974. Caste systems. *Encyclopaedia Britannica*, 15th Ed., Vol. 3, pp. 982–991.

MARRIS, Peter. 1975. *Loss and change*. Garden City: Anchor Books.

MAUSS, Marcel. 1979. *Sociology and psychology: Essays*. London: Routledge and Kegan Paul.

MAY, Robert. 1980. *Sex and fantasy: Patterns of male and female development*. New York: W. W. Norton.

MAYER, Adrian C. 1966. The significance of quasi-groups in the study of complex societies. In *The social anthropology of complex societies*, ed. Michael Banton, pp. 97–122. London: Tavistock.

MAYES, Andrew. 1979. The physiology of fear and anxiety. In *Fear in animals and man*, ed. W. Sluckin, pp. 24–55. New York: Van Nostrand Reinhold.

MAYO, James M., Jr. 1979. Suburban neighboring and the cul-de-sac street. *Journal of Architectural Research* 7 (1, Mar.): 22–27.

MEAD, Margaret. 1942. *And keep your powder dry: An anthropologist looks at America*. New York: William Morrow.

MEAD, Margaret. 1977. The heritage of our children. In *The children's rights movement*, ed. Beatrice Gross and Ronald Gross, pp. 150–158. Garden City: Anchor/Doubleday.

MEAD, Margaret, and Martha Wolfenstein, eds. 1955. *Childhood in contemporary cultures*. Chicago: University of Chicago Press.

MENNINGER, Karl A. 1951. Totemic aspects of contemporary attitudes toward animals. In *Psychoanalysis and culture: Essays in honor of Géza Róheim*, ed. George B. Wilbur and Warner Muensterberger, pp. 42–74. New York: International Universities Press.

MEPHAM, John. 1973. The structuralist sciences and philosophy. In *Structuralism: An introduction—Wolfson College lectures 1972*, ed. David Robey, pp. 104–137. Oxford: Clarendon Press.

MERELMAN, Richard M. 1984. *Making something of ourselves: On culture and politics in the United States*. Berkeley: University of California Press.

MESSENT, Peter, and James Serpell. 1981. A historical and biological view of the pet-owner bond. In *Interrelations between people and pets*, ed. Bruce Fogle, pp. 5–22. Springfield, Ill.: Charles C. Thomas.

MEYER, Leonard B. 1956. *Emotion and meaning in music*. Chicago: University of Chicago Press.

MILLER, Frank. 1972. *Wonderful world of dogs*. San Francisco: Chronicle Books.

MILLER, George A., Eugene Galanter, Karl H. Pribram. 1960. *Plans and the structure of behavior*. New York: Holt, Rinehart, and Winston.

MILLER, Jean Baker. 1976. *Toward a new psychology of women*. Boston: Beacon Press.

MILLS, C. Wright. 1946. The middle classes in middle-sized cities. *American Sociological Review* 11: 520–529.

MINER, Horace. 1956. Body ritual among the Nacirema. *American Anthropologist* 58: 503–507.

MITCHELL, Solace, and Michael Rosen, eds. 1983. *The need for interpretation: Contemporary conceptions of the philosopher's task*. London: The Athlone Press.

MODELL, John, and Tamara K. Hareven. 1973. Urbanization and the malleable household: An examination of boarding and lodging in American families. *Journal of Marriage and the Family* 35 (Aug.): 467–479.

MOORE, Sally Falk. 1976. The secret of the men: A fiction of Chagga initiation and its relation to the logic of Chagga symbolism. *Africa* 46: 357–370.

MORRIS, Desmond. 1977. *Manwatching: A field guide to human behavior.* New York: Harry N. Abrams.

MORSE, Stephen J. 1979. Family law in transition: From traditional families to individual liberty. In *Changing images of the family,* ed. Virginia Tufte and Barbara Myerhoff, pp. 319–360. New Haven: Yale University Press.

MULLER, Peter O. 1981. *Contemporary suburban America.* Englewood Cliffs, N.J.: Prentice-Hall.

NEEDHAM, Rodney. 1972. *Belief, language, and experience.* Chicago: University of Chicago Press.

NEEDHAM, Rodney. 1978a. *Primordial characters.* Charlottesville: University of Virginia Press.

NEEDHAM, Rodney. 1978b. *Symbolic classification.* Santa Monica: Goodyear Publishing.

NEEDHAM, Rodney, ed. 1973. *Right and left: Essays on dual symbolic classification.* Chicago: University of Chicago Press.

The New York Times. 1983a. Dog is adjudged a "child" in custody case on Coast. Sept. 9, p. 7.

The New York Times. 1983b. Woman loses custody fight with her parents over dog. Dec. 18, p. 91.

The New York Times. 1984. Women in clergy called low-paid. Mar. 29, p. A22.

NOBLE, Kenneth B. 1983. Private credit bureaus to receive U.S. data on delinquent debtors. *The New York Times,* Sept. 24, p. 7.

NOWELL, Iris. 1978. *The dog crisis.* New York: St. Martin's Press.

OBEYESEKERE, Gananath. 1985. Depression, Buddhism, and the work of culture in Sri Lanka. In *Culture and depression: Studies in the anthropology and cross-cultural psychiatry of affect and disorder,* ed. Arthur Kleinman and Byron Good, pp. 134–152. Berkeley: University of California Press.

O'KEEFE, John, and Lynn Nadel. 1978. *The hippocampus as a cognitive map.* Oxford: Clarendon Press.

OKIN, Susan Moller. 1979. *Women in Western political thought.* Princeton: Princeton University Press.

O'NEILL, William L. 1976. *Everyone was brave: A history of feminism in America.* New York: Quadrangle/The New York Times Book Co.

ORBACH, Charles E., Morton Bard, and Arthur M. Sutherland. 1957. Fears and defensive adaptations to the loss of anal sphincter control. *The Psychoanalytic Review* 44 (2, Apr.): 121–175.

ORTNER, Sherry B., and Harriet Whitehead. 1981. *Sexual meanings: The cultural construction of gender and sexuality.* Cambridge: Cambridge University Press.

OSGOOD, Charles E. 1964. Semantic differential technique in the comparative study of cultures. *American Anthropologist* 66: 171–200.

Osgood, Charles E. 1979. *Focus on meaning: Explorations in semantic space.* Vol. 1. The Hague: Mouton.

Osgood, Charles E., G. H. Suci, and P. H. Tannenbaum. 1957. *The measurement of meaning.* Urbana: University of Illinois Press.

Packard, Vance. 1951. *Animal IQ: The human side of animals.* New York: Dial Press.

Packard, Vance. [1972] 1974. *A nation of strangers.* New York: Pocket Books.

Packard, Vance. 1983. *Our endangered children: Growing up in a changing world.* Boston: Little, Brown.

Paige, Karen Ericksen. 1977. Sexual pollution: Reproductive sex taboos in American society. *Journal of Social Issues* 33 (2): 144–165.

Papashvily, Helen, and George Papashvily. 1954. *Dogs and people.* Philadelphia: Lippincott.

Paré, Ambroise. [1573] 1982. *On monsters and marvels.* Trans. Janis L. Pallister. Chicago: University of Chicago Press.

Parke, Ross D. 1981. *Fathers.* Cambridge: Harvard University Press.

Parke, Ross D., and Barbara R. Tinsley. 1981. The father's role in infancy: Determinants of involvement in caregiving and play. In *The role of the father in child development,* ed. Michael E. Lamb, pp. 429–458. 2d ed. New York: John Wiley.

Parkin, David, ed. 1983. *Semantic anthropology.* New York: Academic Press.

Parkin, David, ed. 1985. *The anthropology of evil.* New York: Basil Blackwell.

Parsons, Talcott. 1973. Culture and social system revisited. In *The idea of culture in the social sciences,* ed. Louis Schneider and Charles Bonjean, pp. 33–46. Cambridge: Cambridge University Press.

Peckham, Morse. 1965. *Man's rage for chaos: Biology, behavior, and the arts.* New York: Schocken Books.

Pelton, Leroy H. 1981. Child abuse and neglect: The myth of classlessness. In *The social context of child abuse and neglect,* ed. Leroy H. Pelton, pp. 23–38. New York: Human Sciences Press.

Pelton, Robert D. 1980. *The trickster in West Africa: A study of mythic irony and sacred delight.* Berkeley: University of California Press.

Pennock, Roland, and John W. Chapman, eds. 1971. *Privacy, Nomos XIII.* New York: Atherton Press.

Perin, Constance. 1977. *Everything in its place: Social order and land use in America.* Princeton: Princeton University Press.

Perin, Constance. 1982. Thinking in categories, acting on meanings: Reinterpreting liminality. Paper presented at the meetings of the American Anthropological Association, "Symbolism in Texts, Objects, and Self." Dec. Washington, D.C. Mimeo.

Perin, Constance. 1986. Speaking of tradition and modernity: A review essay on *Habits of the Heart* and other recent works on American culture. *Cultural Anthropology* 4: 425–446.

Perry, Stewart E. 1978. *San Francisco scavengers: Dirty work and the pride of ownership.* Berkeley: University of California Press.

Pet Food Institute. 1984. Fact sheet. Washington, D.C.

PETTIGREW, Thomas F. 1982. Prejudice. In *Prejudice*, ed. Thomas F. Pettigrew, George M. Fredrickson, Dale T. Knobel, Nathan Glazer, and Reed Ueda, pp. 1–29. Cambridge: Harvard University Press.

PHINEAS, Charles. 1974. Household pets and urban alienation. *Journal of Social History* 7 (3): 338–343.

PIAGET, Jean. 1967. *Six psychological studies*. New York: Random House.

PIERS, Gerhart, and Milton B. Singer. 1953. *Shame and guilt: A psychoanalytic and cultural study*. Springfield, Ill.: Charles C. Thomas.

PINE, Fred. 1971. On the separation process: Universal trends and individual differences. In *Separation-Individuation: Essays in honor of Margaret S. Mahler*, ed. John B. McDevitt and Calvin F. Settlage, pp. 113–130. New York: International Universities Press.

PINES, Maya. 1982. Down's Syndrome masked by surgery. *The New York Times*, Aug. 31, p. C2.

PITT-RIVERS, Julian. 1973. The kith and the kin. In *The character of kinship*, ed. Jack Goody, pp. 89–106. Cambridge: Cambridge University Press.

PLUMB, J. H. 1972. *In the light of history*. London: Allen Lane.

PLUNKETT, H. M. 1885. *Women, plumbers and doctors; or household sanitation*. New York: D. Appleton.

POCOCK, David. 1985. Unruly evil. In *The anthropology of evil*, ed. David Parkin, pp. 42–56. New York: Basil Blackwell.

POPS, Martin. 1982. The metamorphosis of shit. *Salmagundi* (56, Spring): 26–61.

POUND, Roscoe. 1896. Dogs and the law. *The Green Bag* 8: 172–174.

PRYOR, Edward T., Jr. 1972. Rhode Island family structure: 1875 and 1960. In *Household and family in past time*, ed. Peter Laslett and Richard Wall, pp. 571–589. Cambridge: Cambridge University Press.

QUINN, Naomi. 1977. Anthropological studies on women's status. In *Annual Review of Anthropology*, ed. Bernard J. Siegel, Alan R. Beals, and Stephen A. Tyler, Vol. 6, pp. 181–225. Palo Alto: Annual Reviews.

RABKIN, Eric S., and Eugene M. Silverman. 1979. Passing gas. *Human Nature* 2 (1): 50–54.

RADIN, Paul. [1956] 1972. *The trickster: A study in American Indian mythology*. New York: Schocken Books.

RANCOUR-LAFERRIERE, Daniel. 1987. Signs of anality: Review article. *Semiotica*, V. 63, N. 3/4, pp. 371–382.

RAUM, O. F. 1940. *Chaga childhood: A description of indigenous education in an East African tribe*. London: Oxford University Press.

RAWLS, John. 1971. *A theory of justice*. Cambridge: Harvard University Press.

REITER, Reyna R. 1957. Men and women in the south of France: Public and private domains. In *Toward an anthropology of women*, ed. Reyna R. Reiter, pp. 252–282. New York: Monthly Review Press.

REYNOLDS, Reginald. [1946] 1974. *Cleanliness and Godliness*. New York: Harcourt Brace Jovanovich.

REYNOLDS, Vernon. 1980. *The biology of human action*. 2d ed. San Francisco: W. H. Freeman.

RIESMAN, David. [1954] 1966. *Individualism reconsidered and other essays*. New York: The Free Press.

RIESMAN, David. 1958. The suburban sadness. In *The suburban community*, ed. William Dobriner, pp. 375–408. New York: Putnam.

RIESMAN, David. 1967. Some questions about the study of American character in the twentieth century. *Annals of the American Academy of Political and Social Science*, 370: 36–47.

RIESMAN, David, with Reuel Denney and Nathan Glazer. 1950. *The lonely crowd: A study of the changing American character*. New Haven: Yale University Press.

RILEY, Matilda W., M. Johnson, and A. Foner. 1973. *Aging and society*, Vol. 3, *A sociology of age stratification*. New York: Russell Sage.

ROBERTSON, Audrei K., and John O. Iverson. 1979. Why do dogs bite? An epidemiological approach. *Proceedings, second Canadian symposium on pets and society (Vancouver)*, pp. 73–79. Toronto: Standard Brands Food Company.

ROBEY, Bryant. 1981. No children need apply. *American Demographics* 3 (2): 2.

RÓHEIM, Géza. [1943] 1971. *The origin and function of cultures*. New York: Anchor Books.

RORTY, Richard. 1979. *Philosophy and the mirror of nature*. Princeton: Princeton University Press.

ROSALDO, Michelle Z. 1984. Toward an anthropology of self and feeling. In *Culture Theory: Essays on mind, self, and emotion*, ed. Richard Shweder and Robert A. LeVine, pp. 137–157. Cambridge: Cambridge University Press.

ROSCH, Eleanor. 1977. Human categorization. In *Advances in cross-cultural psychology*, ed. N. Warren, pp. 1–49. London: Academic Press.

ROSCH, Eleanor. 1978. Principles of categorization. In *Cognition and categorization*, ed. B. Lloyd and E. Rosch, pp. 3–40. Hillsdale, N.J.: Erlbaum.

ROSEBURY, Theodor. 1969. *Life on man*. New York: Viking Press.

ROSEN, Lawrence. 1984. *Bargaining for reality: The construction of social relations in a Muslim community*. Chicago: University of Chicago Press.

ROSENBLUM, Leonard A. 1971. Infant attachment in monkeys. In *The origins of human social relations*, ed. H. R. Schaffer, pp. 85–114. New York: Academic Press.

ROSS, Eric B. 1980. *Beyond the myths of culture: Essays in cultural materialism*. New York: Academic Press.

ROSS, Lloyd H. 1985. Human demographics, animal demographics, human-animal interaction and the animal control program of Baltimore City. In *Animal management and population control: What progress have we made?*, ed. Alexandra K. Wilson and Andrew N. Rowan, pp. 75–81. Boston: Center for Animals, Tufts University School of Veterinary Medicine.

ROSSI, Alice S. 1964. Equality between the sexes: An immodest proposal. *Daedalus* 93 (2): 607–652.

ROTHMAN, David J. [1971] 1973. Documents in search of a historian: Toward a history of childhood and youth in America. In *The family in history: Interdisciplinary essays*, ed. Theodore K. Rabb and Robert I. Rothberg, pp. 179–190. New York: Harper Torchbooks.

ROTHMAN, Sheila. 1978. *Woman's proper place*. New York: Basic Books.

ROTHSTEIN, Mervyn. 1984. Follow-up on the news: Lisa H. *The New York Times*, June 10, p. 49.

ROTTON, James. 1983. Affective and cognitive consequences of malodorous pollution. *Basic and Applied Social Psychology* 4 (2): 171–191.

ROWAN, Andrew N. 1984. Animal control, animal welfare, and proposals for an effective program. In *Proceedings of the first New England conference on animals and society*, pp. 37–45. Boston: Center for Animals, Tufts University School of Veterinary Medicine.

ROY, M. Aaron, ed. 1980. *Species identity and attachment: A phylogenetic evaluation*. New York: Garland STPM Press.

RUSSELL, Michael J., Terrie Mendelson, and Harmon V. S. Peeke. 1983. Mothers' identifications of their infants' odors. *Ethology and Sociobiology* 4: 29–31.

RUSSELL, P. A. 1979. Fear-evoking stimuli. In *Fear in animals and man*, ed. W. Sluckin, pp. 86–124. New York: Van Nostrand Reinhold.

RUSSO, David J. 1977. *Families and communities: A new view of American history*. Nashville: American Association for State and Local History.

RYNEARSON, E. K. 1978. Humans and pets and attachment. *British Journal of Psychiatry* 133: 550–555.

SABBATH, Dan, and Mandell Hall. 1977. *End Product: The First Taboo*. New York: Urizen Books.

SAEGERT, Susan. 1980. Masculine cities and feminine suburbs: Polarized ideas, contradictory realities. *Signs: Journal of Women in Culture and Society* 5 (3, Spring), Supplement, "Women and the American City": S96–S111.

SAFIRE, William. 1974. Three brothers. *The New York Times*, Jan. 10, p. 37, col. 5.

SAGARIN, Edward. 1962. *The anatomy of dirty words*. New York: Paperback Library.

SAGARIN, Edward. 1975. *Deviants and deviance: An introduction to the study of disvalued people and behavior*. New York: Praeger.

SAHLINS, Marshall. 1965. On the sociology of primitive exchange. In *The relevance of models for social anthropology*, ed. Michael Banton, pp. 139–236. London: Tavistock.

SAHLINS, Marshall. 1976. *Culture and practical reason*. Chicago: University of Chicago Press.

SAUNDER, Conrad. 1981. *Social stigma of occupations: The lower grade worker in service organisations*. Westmead, England: Gower.

SCHAEFER, Charles E. 1979. *Childhood encopresis and enuresis: Causes and therapy*. New York: Van Nostrand Reinhold.

SCHAFFER, H. R. 1971. Cognitive structure and early social behaviour. In *The origins of human social relations*, ed. H. R. Schaffer, pp. 247–268. New York: Academic Press.

SCHLEGEL, Alice, ed. 1977. *Sexual stratification: A cross-cultural view*. New York: Columbia University Press.

SCHMALENBACH, H. 1961. The sociological category of communion. In *Theories of society: Foundations of modern sociological theory*, ed. Talcott Parsons, Edward Shils, Kaspar D. Naegle, and Jesse R. Pitts, pp. 331–347. New York: The Free Press of Glencoe.

SCHNEIDER, David M. 1972. What is kinship all about? In *Kinship studies in the Morgan Centennial Year*, ed. Priscilla Reining, pp. 32–63. Washington, D.C.: The Anthropological Society of Washington.

SCHNEIDER, David M. 1976. Notes toward a theory of culture. In *Meaning in anthropology*, ed. Keith H. Basso and Henry A. Selby, pp. 197–220. Albuquerque: University of New Mexico.

SCHNEIDER, David M. 1979. Kinship, community, and locality in American culture. In *Kin and communities: Families in America*, ed. A. J. Lichtman and J. R. Challinor, pp. 155–174. Washington, D.C.: Smithsonian Institution Press.

SCHNEIDER, David M. 1980. *American kinship: A cultural account.* 2d ed. Englewood Cliffs, N.J.: Prentice-Hall.

SCHNEIDER R. 1975. Observations on overpopulation of dogs and cats. *Journal of American Veterinary Medicine Association* 167 (Aug. 15): 281–291.

SCHOLES, Robert. 1982. *Semiotics and interpretation.* New Haven: Yale University Press.

SCHUTZ, Alfred. 1944. The stranger: An essay in social psychology. *American Journal of Sociology* 49 (6): 499–507.

SCHUTZ, Alfred. 1945. The homecomer. *American Journal of Sociology* 50 (5): 369–376.

SCOTT, John Paul. 1971. Attachment and separation in dog and man: Theoretical propositions. In *The origins of human social relations*, ed. H. R. Schaffer, pp. 227–246. New York: Academic Press.

SCOTT, John Paul, and J. L. Fuller. 1965. *Genetics and the social behavior of the dog.* Chicago: University of Chicago Press.

SCOTT, John Paul, and C. C. Senay, ed. 1973. *Separation and depression: Clinical and research aspects.* Washington, D.C.: American Association for the Advancement of Science.

SCRUTON, David L. 1986. *Sociophobics: The anthropology of fear.* Boulder, Colorado: Westview Press.

SEARS, Robert R., Eleanor E. Maccoby, and Harry Levin. 1957. *Patterns of child rearing.* Evanston, Ill.: Row, Peterson.

SEDERBERG, Peter. 1984. *The politics of meaning: Power and explanation in the construction of social reality.* Tucson: University of Arizona Press.

SEVERO, Richard. 1981. Woman with elephant man's disease chooses bold surgery. *The New York Times*, Dec. 8, p. C1.

SHALER, N. S. 1904. *The neighbor.* Boston: Houghton Mifflin.

SHAPIRO, Judith. 1979. Cross-cultural perspectives on sexual differentiation. In *Human sexuality: A comparative and developmental perspective*, ed. Herant A. Katchadourian, pp. 269–308. Berkeley: University of California Press.

SHELL, Marc. 1986. The family pet. *Representations* 15: 121–153.

SHRIBMAN, David. 1981. Study finds women are systematically underpaid. *The New York Times*, Sept. 2, p. A15.

SHWEDER, Richard A. 1984. Preview: A colloquy of culture theorists. In *Culture theory: Essays on mind, self, and emotion*, ed. Richard A. Shweder and Robert A. LeVine, pp. 1–26. Cambridge: Cambridge University Press.

SHWEDER, Richard A., and Robert A. LeVine, eds. 1984. *Culture theory: Essays on mind, self, and emotion.* Cambridge: Cambridge University Press.

SILVERSTEIN, Michael. 1981. Reinventing the will: A philosophy of the elements of the human mind. Review of Tyler, The said and the unsaid. *Reviews in Anthropology* 8 (3, Summer): 311–334.

SIMMEL, Georg. [1922] 1955. *Conflict and the web of group affiliations.* New York: The Free Press.

SIMMEL, Georg. 1971. *On individuality and social forms.* ed. Donald N. Levine. Chicago: University of Chicago Press.

SIMON, Leonard J. 1984. The pet trap: Negative effects of pet ownership on families and individuals. In *The pet connection: Its influences on our health and quality of life*, ed. Robert K. Anderson, Benjamin L. Hart, and Lynette A. Hart, pp. 226–240. Minneapolis: University of Minnesota, Center to Study Human-Animal Relationships and Environments.

SINGER, Merrill. 1978. Pygmies and their dogs: A note on culturally constituted defense mechanism. *Ethos* 6 (4): 270–277.

SINGER, Milton. 1977. On the symbolic and historic structure of an American identity. *Ethos* 5 (4): 431–451.

SINGER, Milton. 1978. For a semiotic anthropology. In *Sight, sound, and sense*, ed. Thomas Sebeok, pp. 202–231. Bloomington: Indiana University Press.

SINGER, Milton. 1984. *Man's glassy essence: Explorations in semiotic anthropology.* Bloomington: Indiana University Press.

SKIPPER, Harold D., Jr., and Steven N. Weisbart, eds. 1979. *Privacy and the insurance industry.* Research Monograph No. 83. College of Business Administration, Georgia State University, Atlanta.

SKOLNICK, Arlene. 1979. Public images, private realities: The American family in popular culture and social science. In *Changing images of the family*, ed. Virginia Tufte and Barbara Myerhoff, pp. 297–315. New Haven: Yale University Press.

SMITH, Page. 1966. *As a city upon a hill: The town in American history.* New York: Alfred A. Knopf.

SMITH, Peter K. 1979. The ontogeny of fear in children. In *Fear in animals and man*, ed. W. Sluckin, pp. 164–198. New York: Van Nostrand Reinhold.

SMITH, Raymond T. 1978. The family and the modern world system: Some observations from the Caribbean. *Journal of Family History* 3: 337–360.

SMITH, Robert Ellis. 1979. Privacy, the insurance industry, and the consumer: A critical view. In *Privacy and the insurance industry*, ed. Harold D. Skipper, Jr., and Steven N. Weisbart, pp. 69–78. Research Monograph No. 83, College of Business Administration, Georgia State University, Atlanta, Georgia.

SMITH, Robert Ellis. 1980. *Privacy: How to protect what's left of it.* New York: Anchor Books.

SOLLORS, Werner. 1986. *Beyond ethnicity: Consent and descent in American culture.* New York: Oxford University Press.

SOLOMON, Barbara Miller. 1956. *Ancestors and immigrants: A changing New England tradition.* Cambridge: Harvard University Press.

SONTAG, Susan. 1978. *Illness as metaphor.* New York: Farrar, Straus and Giroux.

SPERBER, Dan. [1974] 1975. *Rethinking symbolism.* Cambridge: Cambridge University Press.

SPOCK, Benjamin. 1961, 1968, 1976. *Baby and child care.* New York: Pocket Books.

SPOCK, Benjamin, and Michael B. Rothenberg. 1985. *Dr. Spock's Baby and child care.* New York: Pocket Books.

SPRADLEY, James, and M. Rynkiewich, eds. 1975. *The Nacirema: Readings on American culture.* Boston: Little, Brown.

STANNARD, David E. 1979. Changes in the American family: Fiction and reality. In *Changing images of the family,* ed. Virginia Tufte and Barbara Myerhoff, pp. 83–96. New Haven: Yale University Press.

STEIN, Maurice. [1960] 1964. *The eclipse of community.* New York: Harper and Row.

STENT, Gunther S., ed. 1981. *Morality as a biological phenomenon.* Berkeley: University of California Press.

STEWART, George R. 1954. *American ways of life.* New York: Simon and Schuster.

STRAUSS, Anselm L. 1961. *Images of the American city.* New York: The Free Press.

STROM, Frederic A., ed. 1981. *1981 zoning and planning law handbook.* New York: Clark Boardman.

STURROCK, John. 1979. Roland Barthes. In *Structuralism and since: From Lévi-Strauss to Derrida,* ed. John Sturrock, pp. 52–80. New York: Oxford University Press.

SUTTLES, Gerald. 1972. *The social construction of communities.* Chicago: University of Chicago Press.

SWARTZ, Marc J. 1982. Cultural sharing and cultural theory: Some findings of a five-society study. *American Anthropologist* 84 (2): 314–338.

SZASZ, K. 1969. *Petishism.* New York: Holt, Reinhart, and Winston.

TAJFEL, Henri. 1969. Cognitive aspects of prejudice. *Journal of Biosocial Science,* Supplement 1: 173–191.

TAJFEL, Henri. 1981. *Human groups and social categories: Studies in social psychology.* Cambridge: Cambridge University Press.

TAMBIAH, Stanley J. [1969] 1973. Classification of animals in Thailand. In *Rules and meanings: The anthropology of everyday knowledge,* ed. Mary Douglas, pp. 127–166. Hammondsworth: Penguin Books.

TANNENBAUM, Jerrold. 1984. The legal status of animals. In *Proceedings of the First New England Conference on Animals and Society,* pp. 17–26. Boston: Center for Animals, Tufts University School of Veterinary Medicine.

TAYLOR, Charles. [1971] 1979. Interpretation and the sciences of man. In *Interpretive social science: A reader,* ed. Paul Rabinow and William M. Sullivan, pp. 25–71. Berkeley: University of California Press.

TAYLOR, Gabriele. 1985. *Pride, shame, and guilt: Emotions of self-assessment.* Oxford: Clarendon Press.

TE VELDE, Herman. 1967. *Seth: God of confusion, A study of his role in Egyptian mythology and religion.* Leiden, The Netherlands: E. J. Brill.

THOMPSON, Michael. 1979. *Rubbish theory.* New York: Oxford University Press.

THURBER, James. 1955. *Thurber's dogs.* New York: Simon and Schuster.

TISCHLER, Joyce S. 1977. Rights for nonhuman animals: A guardianship model for dogs and cats. *San Diego Law Review* 14: 484–506.

Tocqueville, Alexis de. [1840] 1945. *Democracy in America.* Vol. 2 (2d part). New York: Vintage Books.

Tolchin, Martin. 1986. U.S. hires private concerns to check job seekers. *The New York Times,* Feb. 1, p. 54.

Traub, James. 1979. The privacy snatchers: Are information gatherers violating your rights? *The Saturday Review,* July 21, pp. 16–20.

Tuan, Yi-Fu. 1985. *Dominance and affection: The making of pets.* New Haven: Yale University Press.

Tulin, Steven Jay. 1978. Residents' use of common areas in condominium developments. M.S. thesis, Cornell University.

Tumin, Melvin M. 1967. *Social stratification: The forms and functions of inequality.* Englewood Cliffs, N.J.: Prentice-Hall.

Turner, James. 1980. *Reckoning with the beast: Animals, pain, and humanity in the Victorian mind.* Baltimore: Johns Hopkins University Press.

Turner, Victor. 1968. Myth and symbol. In *International Encyclopedia of the Social Sciences,* Vol. 12, pp. 576–581. New York: Macmillan and The Free Press.

Turner, Victor. 1969. *The ritual process: Structure and anti-structure.* Chicago: Aldine.

Turner, Victor. 1978. Variations on a theme of liminality. In *Secular ritual,* ed. Sally F. Moore and Barbara G. Myerhoff, pp. 36–52. Assen, The Netherlands: van Gorcum.

Tyler, Stephen A. 1978. *The said and the unsaid: Mind, meaning, and culture.* New York: Academic Press.

Unger, Roberto Mangabeira. 1986. *The critical legal studies movement.* Cambridge: Harvard University Press.

U.S. Bureau of the Census. 1986. Household and family characteristics: March 1985. *Current population reports,* Series P-20, No. 411. Washington, D.C.: U.S. Government Printing Office.

U.S. Congress. House. Committee on Banking and Currency. 1970. *Fair Credit Reporting Act: Hearings on H.R. 16340.* 86th Cong., 2d sess.

U.S. Congress. Senate. Committee on Governmental Affairs. 1981. *Hearings on the Debt Collection Act of 1981.* 97th Cong., 1st sess.

U.S. Congress. Senate. Subcommittee on Consumer Affairs of the Committee on Banking, Housing, and Urban Affairs. 1975. *Hearings on the fair credit reporting amendments: S. 1840.* 94th Cong., 1st sess.

U.S. Congress. Senate. Subcommittee on Consumer Affairs of the Committee on Banking, Housing, and Urban Affairs. 1980a. *Hearings on the Fair Financial Information Practices Act: S. 1928,* Part I–Insurance, Title V. 96th Cong., 2d sess.

U.S. Congress. Senate. Subcommittee on Consumer Affairs of the Committee on Banking, Housing, and Urban Affairs. 1980b. *Hearings on the Fair Financial Information Practices Act: S. 1928,* Part II–Credit, Titles I and II. 96th Cong., 2d sess.

U.S. Congress. Senate. Subcommittee on Financial Institutions of the Committee on Banking and Currency. 1969. *Hearings on fair credit reporting: S. 823.* 91st Cong., 1st sess.

U.S. Federal Trade Commission. See Federal Trade Commission.

U.S. Privacy Protection Study Commission. 1977. *Personal privacy in an information society*. Washington, D.C.: Government Printing Office.

U.S. Supreme Court. 1974. Transcript of oral argument, *Village of Belle Terre* v. *Boraas*, Feb. 19 and 20, No. 73–191.

USEEM, Ruth Hill, John Useem, and Duane L. Gibson. [1960] 1974. The function of neighboring for the middle-class male. In *Anthropology and American life*, ed. Joseph G. Jorgensen and Marcello Truzzi, pp. 158–178. Englewood Cliffs, N.J.: Prentice-Hall.

VAN GENNEP, Arnold. [1908] 1960. *The rites of passage*. Chicago: University of Chicago Press.

VARENNE, Hervé. 1977. *Americans together: Structured diversity in a midwestern town*. New York: Teachers College Press.

VARENNE, Hervé. 1984. Collective representations in American anthropological conversations: Individual and culture. *Current Anthropology* 25 (3, June): 281–299.

VEBLEN, Thorstein. [1899] 1953. *The theory of the leisure class: An economic study of institutions*. New York: Mentor.

VENDLER, Helen. 1986. The medley is the message. *The New York Review of Books*, May 8, pp. 44–50.

VETTER, Betty M. 1981. Women scientists and engineers: Trends in participation. *Science* 214 (Dec.): 1313–1321.

Village of Belle Terre v. Borass. 1975. 416 U.S. 1.

VOGT, Evon Z. 1976. Rituals of reversal as a means of rewiring social structure. In *The realm of the extra-human: Ideas and actions*, ed. A. Gharati, pp. 201–211. The Hague: Mouton.

Vogue. 1969. *Vogue's book of etiquette and good manners*. New York: Simon and Schuster.

VOITH, Victoria. 1981. Attachment between people and their pets: Behavior problems of pets that arise from the relationship between pets and people. In *Interrelations between people and pets*, ed. Bruce Fogle, pp. 271–294. Springfield, Ill.: Charles C Thomas.

WAGNER, Roy. 1981. *The invention of culture*. 2d ed. Englewood Cliffs, N.J.: Prentice-Hall.

WALLACE, Anthony F. C. 1970. *Culture and personality*. 2d ed. New York: Random House.

WALSH, Edward J. 1975. *Dirty work, race, and self-esteem*. Ann Arbor: Institute of Labor and Industrial Relations, the University of Michigan–Wayne State University. Policy Papers in Human Resources and Industrial Relations 23.

WALZER, John F. 1974. A period of ambivalence: Eighteenth-century American childhood. In *The history of childhood*, ed. L. deMause, pp. 351–382. New York: Psychohistory Press.

WALZER, Michael. 1983. *Spheres of justice: A defense of pluralism and equality*. New York: Basic Books.

WARNER, W. Lloyd. 1953. *American life: Dream and reality*. Chicago: University of Chicago Press.

WARNER, W. Lloyd. 1959. *The living and the dead: A study of the symbolic life of Americans*. New Haven: Yale University Press.

WARNER, W. Lloyd. [1961] 1975. *The family of God: A symbolic study of Christian life in America*. Westport, Conn.: Greenwood Press.

WEBSTER, Murray, Jr., and James E. Driskell, Jr. 1983. Beauty as status. *American Journal of Sociology* 81 (1): 140–165.

WEISS, Robert S. 1985. Men and the family. *Family Process* 24 (Mar.): 49–58.

WEISS, Robert S. 1987. Men and their wives' work. In *Spouse, Parent, Worker: On Gender and Multiple Roles*, ed. Faye Crosby, pp. 109–121. New Haven: Yale University Press.

WEISSMAN, Myrna M., and Gerald L. Klerman. 1982. Depression in women: Epidemiology, explanations, and impact on the family. In *The woman patient*, vol. 3, *Aggression, adaptations, and psychotherapy*, ed. Malkah T. Notman and Carol Nadelson, pp. 189–200. New York: Plenum Press.

WELSFORD, Enid. 1935. *The fool: His social and literary history*. London: Faber and Faber.

WERNER, Oswald, and Joann Fenton. 1973. Method and theory in ethnoscience or ethnoepistemology. In *A handbook of method in cultural anthropology*, ed. Raoul Naroll and Ronald Cohen, pp. 537–578. New York: Columbia University Press.

WEST, James [Carl Withers, pseud.]. 1945. *Plainville, U.S.A.* New York: Columbia University Press.

WESTIN, Alan F. 1968. *Privacy and freedom*. New York: Atheneum.

WESTIN, Alan F., and Michael A. Baker, eds. 1972. *Databanks in a free society: Computers, record-keeping and privacy*. New York: Quadrangle. Report of the Project on Computer Databanks of the Computer Science and Engineering Board, National Academy of Science.

WHEELER, Stanton, ed. 1969. *On record: Files and dossiers in American life*. New York: Russell Sage Foundation.

WHITE, Hayden. 1972. The forms of wildness: Archeology of an idea. In *The wild man within: An image in Western thought from the Renaissance to Romanticism*, ed. Edward Dudley and Maximillian E. Novak, pp. 3–38. Pittsburgh: University of Pittsburgh Press.

WHITE, Robert W. 1963. *Ego and reality in psychoanalytic theory: A proposal regarding independent ego energies*. Psychological Issues, Vol. 3, No. 3, Monograph 11.

WHITESIDE, Thomas. 1975. Credit bureaus. *The New Yorker*, Apr. 21, pp. 45–101.

WHITING, John W. M. 1981. Environmental constraints on infant care practices. In *Handbook of cross-cultural human development*, ed. Ruth H. Monroe, Robert L. Monroe, and Beatrice B. Whiting, pp. 155–179. New York: Garland STPM Press.

WHITING, John W. M., and Irvin L. Child. 1953. *Child training and personality: A cross-cultural study*. New Haven: Yale University Press.

WILBUR, Robert H. 1976. Pets, pet ownership and animal control: Social and psychological attitudes. In *Proceedings of the national conference on dog and cat control*, pp. 21–34. Feb. 3–5, Denver, Colorado.

WILLEFORD, William. 1969. *The fool and his scepter: A study of clowns and jesters and their audience*. Evanston, Ill.: Northwestern University Press.

WILLIAMS, J., and H. Giles. 1978. The changing status of women in society: An intergroup perspective. In *Differentiation between social groups: Studies in the social psychology of intergroup relations*, ed. Henri Tajfel, pp. 431–447. New York: Academic Press.

WILLIAMS, Raymond. 1973. *The country and the city.* London: Chatto and Windus.

WILLIAMS, Robin M. 1964. *Strangers next door: Ethnic relations in American communities.* Englewood Cliffs, N.J.: Prentice Hall.

WILLIAMS, Robin M. 1977. *Mutual accommodation.* Minneapolis: University of Minnesota Press.

WILLIS, Roy. 1974. *Man and beast.* New York: Basic Books.

WILSON, Christopher P. 1979. *Jokes: Form, content, use and function.* New York: Academic Press.

WILSON, Peter J. 1973. *Crab antics: The social anthropology of English-speaking Negro societies of the Caribbean.* New Haven: Yale University Press.

WINKLER, William G. 1977. Human deaths induced by dog bites, United States, 1974–75. *Public Health Reports* 92 (Sept.–Oct.): 425–429.

WINNICOTT, D. W. 1965. *The maturational processes and the facilitating environment.* London: The Hogarth Press and the Institute of Psychoanalysis.

WITKOWSKI, Stanley R., and Cecil H. Brown. 1978. Lexical universals. In *Annual Review of Anthropology*, ed. Bernard J. Siegel, Alan R. Beals, and Stephen A. Tyler, Vol. 7, pp. 427–451. Palo Alto: Annual Reviews.

WOLF, Eric R. 1966. Kinship, friendship, and patron-client relations in complex societies. In *The social anthropology of complex societies*, ed. Michael Banton, pp. 1–22. London: Tavistock.

WOOD, Margaret Mary. 1934. *The stranger: A study in social relationships.* New York: Columbia University Press.

WRIGHT, Gwendolyn. 1980. *Moralism and the model home.* Chicago: University of Chicago Press.

WRIGHT, Gwendolyn. 1981. *Building the dream: A social history of housing in America.* Chicago: University of Chicago Press.

YAMAGUCHI, Masao. 1977. Kingship, theatricality, and marginal reality in Japan. In *Text and context: The social anthropology of tradition*, ed. Ravindra K. Jain, pp. 151–179. Philadelphia: Institute for the Study of Human Issues.

YOSHIDA, Teigo. 1981. The stranger as god: The place of the outsider in Japanese folk religion. *Ethnology* 20 (2): 87–98.

YUAN, Ying-Ying. 1975. Affectivity and instrumentality in friendship patterns among American women. In *Being female: Reproduction, power, and change*, ed. Dana Raphael, pp. 87–98. The Hague: Mouton.

ZELIZER, Viviana A. Rotman. 1979. *Morals and markets: The development of life insurance in the United States.* New York: Columbia University Press.

ZELIZER, Viviana A. Rotman. 1981. The price and value of children: The case of children's insurance. *American Journal of Sociology* 86 (5, Mar.): 1036–1056.

ZIGLER, Edward. [1976] 1979. Controlling child abuse in America: An effort doomed to failure? In *Critical perspectives on child abuse*, ed. Richard Bourne and Eli H. Newberger, pp. 171–213. Lexington, Massachusetts: Lexington Books.

Index

Books by Constance Perin

With Man in Mind: An Interdisciplinary Prospectus for Environmental Design (The MIT Press, 1970)

Everything in Its Place: Social Order and Land Use in America (Princeton University Press, 1977)

DESIGNED BY BRUCE GORE
COMPOSED BY TSENG INFORMATION SYSTEMS, INC.
DURHAM, NORTH CAROLINA
MANUFACTURED BY CUSHING MALLOY, INC.
ANN ARBOR, MICHIGAN
TEXT AND DISPLAY LINES ARE SET IN JANSON

Library of Congress Cataloging-in-Publication Data
Perin, Constance.
Belonging in America.
(New directions in anthropological writing)
Bibliography: pp. 243–273.
Includes index.
1. Suburban life—United States. 2. Ethnology—
United States. 3. Neighborhood—United States.
4. Values—United States. 5. Social Values.
6. United States—Social life and customs—1971–
I. Title. II. Series.
HT351.P47 1988 305.5'5'0973 87-40371
ISBN 0-299-11580-1